CITIES AND AFFORDABLE HOUSING

This book provides a comparative perspective on housing and planning policies affecting the future of cities, focusing on people- and place-based outcomes using the nexus of planning, design and policy. A rich mosaic of case studies features good practices of city-led strategies for affordable housing provision, as well as individual projects capitalising on partnerships to build mixed-income housing and revitalise neighbourhoods. Twenty chapters provide unique perspectives on diversity of approaches in eight countries and 12 cities in Europe, Canada and the USA. Combining academic rigour with knowledge from critical practice, the book uses robust empirical analysis and evidence-based case study research to illustrate the potential of affordable housing partnerships for mixed-income, socially inclusive neighbourhoods as a model to rebuild cities.

Cities and Affordable Housing is an essential interdisciplinary collection on planning and design that will be of great interest to scholars, urban professionals, architects, planners and policy-makers interested in housing, urban planning and city building.

Sasha Tsenkova is Professor of Planning at the School of Architecture, Planning & Landscape, University of Calgary, Canada. She has published extensively on housing and urban issues and has worked for international organisations on projects in Europe, North America and Central Asia.

CITIES AND AFFORDABLE HOUSING

Planning, Design and Policy Nexus

Edited by Sasha Tsenkova

Routledge
Taylor & Francis Group
NEW YORK AND LONDON

First published 2022
by Routledge
605 Third Avenue, New York, NY 10158

and by Routledge
2 Park Square, Milton Park, Abingdon, Oxon OX14 4RN

Routledge is an imprint of the Taylor & Francis Group, an informa business

British Library Cataloguing-in-Publication Data
A catalogue record for this book is available from the British Library

Library of Congress Cataloging-in-Publication Data
Names: Tsenkova, S., editor.
Title: Cities and affordable housing : planning, design and policy nexus / edited by Sasha Tsenkova.
Description: Milton Park, Abingdon, Oxon; New York, NY: Routledge, 2022. | Includes bibliographical references and index.
Identifiers: LCCN 2021011192 (print) | LCCN 2021011193 (ebook) | ISBN 9781032001463 (paperback) | ISBN 9781032001487 (hardback) | ISBN 9781003172949 (ebook)
Subjects: LCSH: Low-income housing. | Housing policy. | City planning.
Classification: LCC HD7287.95 .C58 2022 (print) | LCC HD7287.95 (ebook) | DDC 363.5—dc23
LC record available at https://lccn.loc.gov/2021011192
LC ebook record available at https://lccn.loc.gov/2021011193

ISBN: 978-1-032-00148-7 (hbk)
ISBN: 978-1-032-00146-3 (pbk)
ISBN: 978-1-003-17294-9 (ebk)

DOI: 10.4324/9781003172949

Typeset in Bembo
by codeMantra

CONTENTS

PART V
Perspectives on Policy Design for Affordable Housing   **245**

ILLUSTRATIONS

Tables

Figures

Boxes

CONTRIBUTORS

Jalene Anderson-Baron

Policy and Research Analyst, Capital Region Housing, Edmonton, Canada

Jalene completed her MA in human geography at the University of Alberta in 2016, where her research explored the impacts of affordable housing shortages on Housing First programmes in Alberta. Jalene's published research has looked at both policy and practice pertaining to homelessness, Housing First, harm reduction and service provision for socially marginalised populations. Her current research interests focus on policy and innovation in the Canadian social housing sector.

Jeroen Atteveld

Partner, heren 5 architecten, Amsterdam, The Netherlands

Jeroen Atteveld of heren 5 architecten is a committed architect who builds his designs around a strong idea. The basis of his work is anchored in design research on urban user groups. With his open and inquisitive attitude, he searches for new opportunities in his projects that contribute to a sustainable, inclusive and innovative living environment. Jeroen has over 15 years of experience in designing social housing complexes for housing associations in the Netherlands and is always looking for that bit of extra that adds value to the social housing project. Architects from heren 5 architecten have extensive experience with the design of living environments that people identify with; the team is driven by a mission to make neighbourhoods more beautiful, better and healthier. Their award-winning projects address issues related to mobility, inclusiveness, energy saving and climate change making complexity manageable in a design with the human dimension as a reference point.

Christelle Avenier

Partner, Avenier Cornejo Architects, Paris, France

Christelle Avenier is a partner in Avenier Cornejo Architects in Paris, France, and a graduate of the École Supérieure d'Architecture de Paris. The firm has achieved many accomplishments in the field of social housing since 2007. It was awarded the 2014 "Europe 40 under 40" prize, the French prize "Équerre d'Argent" and the Mies van der Rohe prize. Their very diverse architecture has been featured in many publications and exhibitions, notably the Annuel Optimiste d'architecture, the Pavillon de l'Arsenal in Paris, the Architectural Review and Wallpaper magazine that named Avenier Cornejo among its top 20 young architectural talents of 2013.

Abigail Bond

Managing Director, Homelessness Services & Affordable Housing Programs, City of Vancouver, Canada

Abigail Bond is the Managing Director of Homelessness Services & Affordable Housing Programs at the City of Vancouver since 2011. She has worked in affordable housing for 20 years, starting out in the not-for-profit housing sector in the UK, working for Manchester City Council to regenerate housing and communities in east Manchester. She moved to Canada in 2007 and worked on affordable housing policy and delivery at the City of Calgary. Since 2011, she has been working for the City of Vancouver and is responsible for leading a team of experts delivering affordable housing in partnerships with a wide range of non-profit and private sector agencies.

Stéphane Dauphin

Director General, Paris Habitat, Paris, France

Stéphane Dauphin has a BA degree in history and postgraduate degree in urbanism and city planning, both from the University of Paris-Sorbonne. He worked as an urban planner for local authorities in Paris, and in 2002 he joined the President of the Nantes Metropolitan area as chief of staff. For five years, from 2011 to 2016, he was Deputy-CEO then CEO of Nantes Habitat, the public social housing company. Following his appointment as a CEO of Paris Habitat in 2016, Mr Dauphin leads the largest public utility social housing company in Paris that manages 125,000 social flats and has 3,000 employees and a turnover of €1 billion per year. He is also actively involved in regional social housing activities as vice-president of AORIF, the umbrella regional organisation for social housing companies, and as chair of GPIS, an organisation maintaining security within the Parisian social housing real estate.

Avi Friedman

Professor of Architecture, McGill University School of Architecture, Montréal, Canada

Dr. Avi Friedman received his master's degree from McGill University, and his doctorate from the University of Montréal. In 1988, he co-founded the Affordable Homes Program at the McGill School of Architecture. He also holds an Honorary Professor position at Lancaster University in the UK. He is known for his housing innovation and for the Grow Home and Next Home designs. Dr. Friedman is the author of 18 books, the principal of Avi Friedman Consultants Inc. and the recipient of numerous awards, including the Manning Innovation Award, the World Habitat Award and the Lifetime Achievement Award from Sustainable Buildings Canada.

Sean Gadon

Director, Affordable Housing Office, Toronto, Canada

Sean Gadon is a recognised leader in urban and housing affairs in Canada. For more than 30 years he has been committed to the cause of providing decent and affordable housing to Canadians. He is currently director of the City of Toronto's Affordable Housing Office, previously serving as president of Raising the Roof for ten years. Sean oversees the delivery of federal, provincial and municipal funding for a range of housing initiatives, including affordable housing construction and renovation programmes. In 2017, he led the delivery of Mayor Tory's new Open-Door Initiative aimed at scaling up efforts to create affordable housing.

Teresa Goldstein

Manager of Affordable Housing, City of Calgary, Calgary, Canada

Teresa Goldstein is the manager of Affordable Housing at the City of Calgary. She is a professional urban planner with more than 15 years of experience in planning. Teresa leads a team in the development of new capital affordable housing projects and the implementation of Calgary's Corporate Affordable Housing Strategy Foundations for Home. She oversees the development of the City's policies and programmes to create and improve affordable housing opportunities. She is a member of Calgary's Community Housing Affordability Collective, a board member for Silvera For Seniors and a member of the Canadian Institute of Planners and the Alberta Professional Planning Institute.

Marietta E.A. Haffner

European Comparative Studies researcher, Delft University of Technology, Faculty of Architecture and the Built Environment, Delft, The Netherlands

Dr. Marietta Haffner is a housing economist with more than 25 years of experience in conducting European comparative studies at Delft University of Technology, with the Faculty of Architecture and the Built Environment. Dr Haffner's research interests include financial and economic aspects of housing, housing policy and housing tenures in different countries. She holds honorary research appointments at Cambridge University (UK) and RMIT (Melbourne, Australia). In addition to an extensive publication record in housing studies, she is a member of the Management Board of Housing Studies and office coordinator of the European Network for Housing Research.

Joni Hirsch

Policy Analyst, Center for the Study of Social Policy, Cleveland, Ohio, USA

Joni Hirsch works at Case Western Reserve University, where she focuses on mixed-income housing policy and community development. She has a master's degree in City Planning from UC Berkeley.

J. David Hulchanski

Professor, Factor-Inwentash Faculty of Social Work, University of Toronto, Canada

Dr David Hulchanski is a professor of housing and community development at the University of Toronto's Factor-Inwentash Faculty of Social Work, where he holds the Chow Yei Ching Chair in Housing. His PhD is in urban planning. His research and teaching focus on housing, neighbourhoods and community development. He has published extensively on these issues. He is the principal investigator of the SSHRC-funded Neighbourhood Change Research Partnership, focused on neighbourhoods and socio-spatial change in Canadian cities with international comparisons. See: www.NeighbourhoodChange.ca

Mark L. Joseph

Associate Professor of Community Development, Case Western University, Cleveland, Ohio, USA

Mark L. Joseph is the Leona Bevis and Marguerite Haynam Associate Professor of Community Development at the Jack, Joseph, and Morton Mandel School of Applied Social Sciences at

Case Western Reserve University. He is also the founding director of the National Initiative on Mixed-Income Communities. His current research focuses on mixed-income development as an anti-poverty strategy, with attention to transforming public housing developments. He is the co-author of *Integrating the Inner City: The Promise and Perils of Mixed-Income Public Housing Transformation.* Dr Joseph received his PhD in public policy from the University of Chicago and his undergraduate degree from Harvard University.

Paul Karakusevic

Partner, Karakusevic-Carson, London, UK

Partner Paul Karakusevic founded the practice with the sole intent to raise standards in housing design and public buildings in the UK after 40 years of neglect. The design firm has extensive experience in mixed-income, mixed-use redevelopment in London by successfully navigating planning, policy and national design standards to create exemplary housing that reflects a unique sense of place and responds to local character and heritage. The projects have won numerous RIBA, Housing Design, New London Architecture and Civic Trust Awards, and the practice has been named "Housing Architect of the Year" in 2012 and 2014. Paul is the lead author of *Social Housing: Definitions and Design Exemplars* and has taught extensively, but professional practice has been a paramount focus of his creative work. He maintains a hands-on role and is actively involved in all projects.

Amy T. Khare

Research Director, National Initiative on Mixed-Income Communities at the Jack, Joseph and Morton Mandel School of Applied Social Sciences, Case Western University in Cleveland

Amy T. Khare is leading grant-funded research projects, as well as consulting for city governments and public housing authorities in several cities. Her research is published in peer-reviewed journals such as *Urban Affairs Review* and *Journal of Urban Affairs*. She earned her doctorate from The University of Chicago and received her Bachelors and Masters of Social Work from the University of Kansas.

Christel Kjenner

Director, Housing and Homelessness, City of Edmonton, Canada

Christel Kjenner has over a decade of experience working in the public sector, including roles on both the administrative and political sides of government. She currently serves as director, Housing and Homelessness, at the City of Edmonton. In addition to her current role, Christel has held numerous roles at the City of Edmonton, including in the Office of the City Manager and the Real Estate Branch. Prior to her current role, Christel worked as a senior consultant at Berlin Communications, where she led public policy, research, public affairs and strategic communication projects, and she also served as chief of staff to the Minister of Health at the Government of Alberta. Christel began her career at the University of Alberta's Department of Facilities and Operations, where she developed and implemented strategies for greening the university's operations.

Suzanne LaFerrière

Senior Advisor, Residential Policies and Strategies Housing Department, Montréal, Canada

With a background in sociology and a 30-year experience in the municipal realm, Ms La Ferrière acts as senior advisor to the director of the City of Montréal's Housing Department. She has worked as policy analyst and has assisted in designing and implementing city interventions on a diversity of intersectoral issues, such as homelessness, neighbourhood redevelopment and the implementation of social and affordable housing programmes. Ms La Ferrière has been involved in the making of many municipal policy statements, most recently in the process that led to the transfer of powers and housing budgets from the provincial level to the City of Montréal level.

Bas Liesker
Partner, heren 5 architecten, Amsterdam, The Netherlands

Bas Liesker is founding partner of heren 5 architecten and a graduate of the Faculty of Architecture of the Technical University in Delft. With people as starting point, Bas builds a strong narrative in the design assignments he is working on, a story that everyone understands and that results in buildings that are rooted in their location and embraced by the people living in and surrounding it.

Claire Noble
Business Analyst, Calgary Housing Company, Calgary, Canada

Claire Noble works as a strategic business analyst at Calgary Housing Company. She has a master's degree in planning from the University of Calgary. Previously, she worked for over ten years as a research analyst in the City of Calgary's affordable housing team.

Kath Scanlon
Deputy Director, London School of Economics, London, UK

Kath Scanlon is deputy director of LSE London, a research centre at the London School of Economics. She specialises in housing, with an interest in international comparative studies. She has written about housing systems and the financing of private and social housing in the UK and Europe, and was lead editor of the authoritative Social Housing in Europe. Since 2015, she has focused on ways of accelerating housing production in London and the challenge of producing affordable housing in a city with high land costs. She is a member of the co-ordination committee of the European Network for Housing Research.

Alex F. Schwartz
Professor, Milano School of Policy, Management, and Environment; Graduate Program in Public and Urban Policy, The New School, New York, USA

Alex F. Schwartz is a professor of Public and Urban Policy at the New School. He holds a Phd in urban planning and policy development from Rutgers University. He is the author of *Housing Policy in the United States*: 3rd Edition (Routledge, 2014). He is also co-author of the forthcoming *Policy Analysis as Problem Solving: A Flexible and Evidence-Based Framework* (Routledge 2019). His research has appeared in journals such as *Cityscape, Economic Development Quarterly, Housing Policy Debate, Housing Studies, International Journal of Urban and Regional Research, Journal of the American Planning Association* and *Journal of Urban Affairs*. In addition, he is the managing editor for North America for the international journal *Housing Studies*.

Hélène Schwoerer
Deputy Chief Executive Officer, Paris Habitat, Paris, France

Hélène Schwoerer is deputy-CEO of Paris Habitat and is in charge of new construction, refurbishment and development. Architect and town planer, she worked for two French architect agencies, prior to joining the local government in Paris. Her decade-long experience there was in leadership positions as staff director of the Deputy-Mayor of Paris in charge of housing and as advisor for housing policy to the Mayor of Paris.

Meryn Severson

Policy & Research Analyst, Capital Region Housing, Edmonton, Canada

Meryn Severson joined Capital Region Housing in July 2017 after graduating from the University of Alberta from where she completed a double major in sociology and human geography. She completed her undergraduate thesis on housing affordability and life course transitions for young adults, which she presented at the Congress of the Humanities and Social Sciences. She recently published a co-authored chapter on well-being in the *Routledge Handbook of Health Geography*. Esther and Meryn presented some of this work on social sustainability at the World Congress of Sociology in July 2018.

Shomon Shamsuddin

Assistant Professor, Tufts University, Massachusetts, USA

Dr Shomon Shamsuddin is an assistant professor of Social Policy and Community Development at Tufts. He studies how institutions define social problems and develop policies to address urban poverty and inequality. His research examines the effects of local and federal housing policy on socioeconomic mobility for low-income families. Prior to joining Tufts, Shomon was a National Poverty Fellow at the University of Wisconsin-Madison and the U.S. Department of Health and Human Services. He holds a PhD in urban policy and planning from MIT, MArch from Yale University and ScB in neuroscience from Brown University.

Vincent Tong

Chief Development Officer, Toronto Community Housing Corporation, Toronto, Canada

Vincent Tong is chief development officer at Toronto Community Housing Corporation, the largest social housing provider in Canada, overseeing the real estate development and commercial assets portfolio, currently valued at $10 billion, spread across 2,200 buildings in 350 communities across Toronto. Vincent is currently overseeing a $650 million revitalisation programme that is transforming the 1960s era of social housing developments into mixed-use, mixed-tenure developments that are re-integrating large parts of the city with the surrounding neighbourhoods. Prior to joining Toronto Community Housing Corporation, Vincent was a planning and urban design consultant working on a broad spectrum of projects in Ontario, Alberta, Saskatchewan, Nova Scotia and New Brunswick.

Sasha Tsenkova

Professor of Planning & International Development, School of Architecture, Planning & Landscape, University of Calgary, Canada

Dr. Sasha Tsenkova holds a PhD in architecture (Technical University, Prague) and a PhD in geography (University of Toronto). She is a fellow of the Canadian Institute of Planners and specialises in urban planning, housing policy and comparative urban development. Her research and professional activities in these areas for the World Bank, Council of Europe and the United Nations include a range of housing and urban projects in more than 20 countries in Central and Eastern Europe, Latin America and Central Asia. She is the author of 25 books and research monographs and over 50 articles on urban policy, regeneration, urban sustainability and housing policy. Her scholarship is internationally recognised by a number of prestigious awards.

Esther de Vos

Director of Policy, Research and Education at Capital Region Housing, Edmonton, Canada

Esther brings to CRH her experience in programme oversight, including developing and monitoring performance measures, as well as improving service delivery. Esther is passionate about policy development, research and analysis, and using a systems thinking approach to address and resolve complex issues and identify process improvements. Prior to joining CRH, Esther worked for the Ministry of Justice and Solicitor General, the Maintenance Enforcement Program and Legal Aid Alberta. Esther has a master of public administration from the University of Victoria and a bachelor of laws and bachelor of arts from the University of Alberta. She obtained her Certified Housing Practitioner from the Chartered Institute of Housing (CIH) Canada in 2016. Esther is currently working towards her doctorate of social sciences at Royal Roads University, with a research focus on well-being and social housing.

Sarah Woodgate

Director, Calgary Housing and President of Calgary Housing Company, Calgary, Canada

Sarah Woodgate has over 20 years of experience in affordable housing, urban planning, real estate, land development and community development. Sarah was appointed the president of Calgary Housing Company (CHC) and director of Calgary Housing for the City of Calgary in March 2015. Sarah has led the development of strategic plans for both organisations. She holds a Masters Certificate in Municipal Leadership, is a Chartered Institute of Housing Chartered Member, a member of the Institute of Corporate Directors and is a Professional Accredited Member of the Canadian Institute of Planners.

1

AFFORDABLE HOUSING AND THE FUTURE OF CITIES

Sasha Tsenkova

Context and Rationale for the Book

The shortage of affordable housing in cities is one of the most significant global challenges. It affects 1.6 billion people (one-third of urban population) and is a key priority for policy change identified by the United Nations in the *New Urban Agenda* (Tsenkova, 2016). Globally, cities and central governments have championed housing strategies and action plans, with a strong emphasis on effective partnerships to ensure housing efficiency in an effort to make cities livable and sustainable. In the context of the COVID-19 public health crisis, access to affordable and adequate housing has become extremely important, providing a refuge in the midst of rapid urban transformation and collapsing urban economies. The need for a resilient housing system, capable of responding to external shocks with the inherent ability to bounce back, will indeed define the success of cities in the future. Problems of housing affordability and accessibility have become more pressing during the pandemic. Cities during lockdowns have delivered a rapid response through rent freezes, tenant protection, provision of emergency shelters, conversion of underutilised hotels and offices into affordable housing and the building of more permanent solution using modular and prefabricated technologies. In many places, the crisis has triggered political commitments and action to address the supply challenge, providing a sustainable range of affordable housing solutions. In the wake of post-pandemic recovery, the unprecedented challenges to public health in cities have demonstrated the need to consider affordable housing as a critical part of social infrastructure that requires sustained investment and support to establish a resilient ecosystem of housing providers (Tsenkova, 2021).

This stands in sharp contrast to the long-term decline in social and affordable housing investment in many contexts since the late 1970s (Angel, 2000). While there is no common definition of social housing, the book recognises the contextual differences in the structure, policies and trajectories in different countries (van Bortel et al., 2019). We use the term 'social housing' to recognise these differences and important nuances in interpretation to as housing systems are path-dependent. In European countries with a large share of social housing, the sector operates like a 'social market' in direct competition with private renting. The institutional arrangements favour ownership by not-for-profit or private landlords, rents are based on cost recovery principles and allocation extends access to a more diverse income group. Europe, the Netherlands, Sweden, Denmark, Germany and Austria exemplify the characteristics of such unitary systems

DOI: 10.4324/9781003172949-1

(Kemeny, Kersloot and Thalmann, 2005). The United Kingdom and France have a strong legacy of public/council housing, which despite some residualisation, has seen a growing commitment to provision of social housing through mixed-income, mixed-tenure projects in the last decade (Bailey et al., 2006; Kearns et al., 2013). At the other end of the spectrum, in most countries, social housing has a residual role, and the small sector—less than 5%—operates as a safety net. Access is reserved for low-income households, allocation is rationed, rents are heavily subsidised and management is carried out by public institutions. The terminology in housing policy discourse refers to public housing as the dominant form of social housing, while more recent programmes will target affordable housing, usually in some form of mixed income. All post-socialist countries, after a dramatic privatisation of public housing in the 1990s, fall in this category, as well as Canada and the United States (Tsenkova, 2021).

Notwithstanding these path-dependent characteristics of social and affordable housing systems in different countries, housing policy reforms since the 1990s have moved away from bricks and mortar to demand-based subsidies and towards more market-oriented provision models (Sousa & Quarter, 2003; Stephens, Burns & Mackay, 2002). The growing dependence on private housing finance and the opening up of a previously sheltered systems of social housing provision have created a more entrepreneurial model with considerable changes regarding the role of social housing in cities, the way it is provided and for whom. While historically public housing played a significant role in shaping urban communities, in the era of neoliberal reforms, its future was challenged by declining investment, ageing infrastructure and design that was less conducive to social integration (Bacher, 1993; Oxley, 2000). Over time, the compositions of actors and agencies involved shifted drastically from public provision towards multi-actor/agency collaboration (Berry, 2014). Socially owned housing managed by non-profit, private and community-based organisations in 'hybrid' forms replaced public housing to address the needs of targeted groups (i.e., the homeless, seniors, vulnerable households), but its growth remained limited despite the increasing affordability gap in many cities (Dalton, 2009; Fraser & Kick, 2007).

In the aftermath of the 2008 global financial crisis, the cracks in the models of affordable housing delivery highlighted the vulnerability of the system. The crisis also provided an opportunity to reconsider the policy support and alignment of financial, fiscal and regulatory instruments to build resilience (Tsenkova, 2014). Given the devolution of government involvement in affordable housing, consensus emerged that an effective response requires a multi-sectoral approach, including all levels of government, the private for-profit and non-profit sectors, as well as local communities. This is perceived as the most effective way of producing affordable housing to meet growing local needs within limited resources and capacity (Scanlon, Whitehead & Arrigoitia, 2014; van Bortel et al., 2019). The last decade has seen large cities across Europe and North America join their efforts with non-profit and private organisations to provide affordable rental housing in mixed-income, mixed-tenure projects. In some cases, the model had a strong legacy, and it was 'business as usual' in countries with unitary social housing systems. In other places, the shift triggered a range of experimental strategies to redevelop large-scale public housing complexes or to reinvent brownfield sites in cities into inclusive neighbourhoods emphasising social mix and integration (Tsenkova, 2019). Such solutions to the affordable housing challenge in cities demonstrated a viable alternative to address vulnerabilities in the housing market as well as make cities more inclusive and competitive.

This book focuses on these solutions and provides comparative perspectives on partnerships for mixed-income affordable housing as a model of neighbourhood revitalisation and city building. Focusing on the nexus of planning, design and policy, it explores good practices in 15 cities in Europe, Canada and USA using a strong conceptual approach and multidisciplinary methods of analysis. This richly illustrated collection of case studies includes contributions from 25 world-class scholars, architects, city leaders, planners and housing experts committed to innovative approaches to socially inclusive cities.

Conceptual Approach

The future of affordable housing requires a different approach to socially inclusive cities based on partnerships, people-centred design and innovative planning. The mixed-income model is globally recognised as the best practice in many cities in the UK, France, the Netherlands, Austria, Germany and the USA, where the provision of mixed-income housing in different forms is a normative requirement (Scanlon, Whitehead, & Arrigoitia, 2014). The overall goal of mixed-income housing is to establish better quality of life and adequate living conditions for all residents. There is ample research conducted on the efforts, rationale and importance of mixed-income housing (Bailey et al., 2006; Livingston, Kearns, & Bailey, 2013). However, the theoretical framework, conceptual clarity and empirical justification are underexamined. We have adopted a conceptual approach that focuses on place-based and people-based outcomes of mixed-income affordable housing delivered through partnerships (Tsenkova, 2014). The framework is applied to explore a variety of city-led strategies in seven European countries, USA and Canada by using original, multidisciplinary research methods of analysis. The nexus of housing policy, planning and design is a critical lens for these multi-scalar explorations at the level of cities, neighbourhoods and specific projects. The conceptual approach in the book brings a sustainability perspective to the exploration of partnership models by emphasising the need for equity and social inclusion through social mix and environmental sustainability of the built forms through design.

Efficiency through Partnerships for Affordable Housing

Recent housing reforms respond to the 'market failure' in affordable housing defined by Berry (2014) as lack of stable and consistent policies, absence of planning mechanisms that regulate affordable housing and a failure in governance to coordinate and strategise. On the policy side, a renewed commitment of governments, complemented with city-based strategies and municipal programmes, demonstrates a transformative change in the supply of affordable, adequate and secure rental housing (Kemeny, Kersloot, & Thalmann, 2005; Tsenkova, 2019). National and city-led housing strategies provide municipalities with a significant opportunity to realign resources, land and infrastructure investments, as well as leverage the capacity of the housing industry and the not-for-profit providers to support partnerships in mixed-income, mixed-tenure projects (Moore & Skaburski, 2004; Smith, 2002). This is the most efficient way of producing affordable housing to meet growing local needs, particularly in the context of inner-city neighbourhood rebuilding.

The theoretical framework for housing partnerships is based on collaborative planning, consensus-based decision-making, non-hierarchical structures and processes, synergistic interactions among partners and shared accountability for outcomes and results (see Bovaird, 2004; Brinkerhoff & Brinkerhoff, 2011). Recent research profiles a model of public, private and nonprofit (PPNP) partnership that has evolved to deliver affordable rental housing, capitalising on the strengths of each sector. The public sector (federal, provincial, municipal) is effective in the mobilisation of much-needed resources, while the private sector (designers, developers, housing industry, construction companies) is efficient in managing the construction process by maximising economies of scale and tapping into technological innovation and marketing strategies.

Not-for-profit housing institutions are more efficient in managing and operating affordable rental housing due to the extensive knowledge of the people they service (Tsenkova, 2019). In large-scale developments, such synergies are important in the provision process (design, build, finance, operate) as insights from neighbourhoods in Montréal, London, Paris, Amsterdam, Vienna and New York demonstrate.

PPNP partnerships maximise such synergies through collaborative processes of jointly determined goals, decision-making, non-hierarchical institutional structures of the housing development process and shared accountability for outcomes and results. Public authorities employ various policy instruments to implement partnership projects through a wide range of innovations in public/private funding and planning instruments with varying capacities to address the affordability gap (Black, 2012). Municipalities often take a strategic leadership role, defining the share of affordable rental housing in mixed-income neighbourhoods, leveraging the value of public land and infrastructure investment, increasing densities and incorporating planning and design strategies to facilitate social mix and integration of projects in communities.

A variety of partnerships can be delineated on a continuum, depicting the transfer of liability and risk from the public to the private and non-profit sectors in key phases of the development process—plan, finance, design, build, operate, own/lease. The institutional landscape is quite diverse, and every stage represents a mix of private, public and non-profit agencies, depending on the scale of the development and specific local housing markets (Tsenkova, 2019). While there is no set of prescribed guidelines in different cities, some of the small-scale partnership projects will typically fall in the category 'design-build', where the private sector has a limited responsibility, often referred to public-private partnerships that build on efficiencies of scale and expertise. In the case of larger, block-size mixed-income developments, a more ambitious PPNP model of 'design-build-operate' evolves, where a full range of publicly financed housing agencies (private and not-for-profit) delivers affordable rental housing, often over a period of 25–50 years. These models sketched in broad strokes capture a complex reality with very fluid institutional arrangements. The PPNP partnerships have a strong involvement and leadership of non-profit organisations acting as socially responsible developers, mobilising public sector financial and fiscal support to ensure financial viability. Public sector involvement is typically limited to financing, transfer of land and the definition of key planning outcomes (housing typology, rent levels, access to neighbourhood amenities).

Municipal governments have a critical role in the provision of affordable rental housing (Carmona, Carmona & Gallent, 2003; Whitehead, 2007). Some of the incentives and planning strategies to stimulate mixed-income, mixed-tenure housing projects include waiving development charges, selling municipal land at discounted rates, lowering property taxes, inclusionary zoning or start-up grants/loans. In addition, municipalities expedite the planning approval process and encourage private developers to join partnerships with city-owned or non-profit housing providers to build developments with varying degrees of affordable housing.

Equity through Social Mix in Affordable Housing

'Social mix' refers to the integration of people of different social standing or identity. The term is used in relation to affordable housing and sustainable neighbourhoods to describe an environment where housing offers diverse opportunities in terms of types, tenure, costs and design to respond to a diversity of needs (Galster, 2013). In many European countries, social mix through the planning process is a normative requirement, specifying targets of 20–25% affordable rental housing as a desirable tenure mix to bring a mix of people together by offering housing for a range of income levels in a single development or in neighbourhood (Scanlon,

Whitehead & Arrigoitia, 2014). The social mix approach aims at combating economic, social and ethnic segregation. It is justified on grounds of both economic efficiency—making society as a whole better-off by enhancing solidarity, labour productivity and community sustainability—and equity—improving the life-chances and social inclusion of disadvantaged groups (Bolt & van Kempen, 2010).

Social mix in North America became prominent in the 1970s as a response to growing social inequalities and stigma attached to large subsidised housing developments (Kearns et al., 2013). This resulted in the revitalisation of public housing projects and their replacement with mixed-income developments to promote social mix. Neighbourhood planning initiatives include urban regeneration, with an emphasis on housing mix, inclusion of rental housing through zoning and density bonusing policies, provision of public land for affordable rental housing, encouragement of public/private partnerships and rent supplements to allow local residents to stay-in-place (Galster, 2013; Smith, 2002). The pursuit of social mix is innovative in many contexts where the share of social and affordable housing is small. Inclusionary zoning in Canadian and US cities is used to a limited extent to guide the planning and development of inclusive and equitable neighbourhoods. Due to the dynamic nature of social mix, there are multiple ways it can be implemented at various scales, but the practice can be challenging (Arthurson, 2010; Thurber, Bohmann & Heflinger, 2018). Social mix can take place in a building, on a street, in a block or in a neighbourhood. Some of the best practices include making the difference between low-income and market housing non-existent, using common spaces to promote interaction between residents, and minimising the impacts of displacement during changes within existing communities.

Environmental Sustainability through Design

Affordable housing partnerships through PPNP collaboration in cities are used as a social planning strategy to address the shortage of affordable rental housing, foster social mix and regenerate brownfield sites (Katz, 2004). Notwithstanding the complexities of these collaborations, they provide critical opportunities to improve the built environment through coordinated investment in infrastructure, development of a variety of housing types, ownership opportunities (social and modest market rental housing and affordable homeownership) and investment in neighbourhood amenities, transit and retail (Ramzanpour & Noutaghani, 2019). Such large-scale redevelopment projects bring brownfield city sites back to life, creating new attractive neighbourhoods inspired by sustainability plans, but present significant challenges (Bond, Sautkina & Kearns, 2011). While residential intensification and planning strategies enhance the quality of built form and encourage higher-density mixed-use developments, the provision of quality affordable housing is essential to maintain diversity of residents and social mix (Karakusevic & Batchelor, 2018). The creation of mixed-income, mixed-tenure neighbourhoods depends on the plans, but also on the successful PPNP partnerships for plan implementation.

In many contexts, different systems promote energy-efficient design, smart communities and the use of strategies to enhance environmental sustainability. Partnership projects for mixed-income integrated housing development often comply with, or even lead in terms of performance related to smart location and access, street pattern and design, and the use of green technology and building techniques. The green stamp of approval, while rigorous in terms of smart, green and well-designed neighbourhoods, does not really emphasise housing affordability, so these examples are pushing the envelope in terms of social integration by design (Tsenkova, 2014). The overall goal of mixed-income housing is to establish better quality of life and adequate living conditions for all residents (Bailey et al., 2006). To understand successful mixed-income affordable housing, we have adopted a conceptual framework that focuses on place-based and people-based outcomes. The success of building such strong communities involves synergies of physical, social and environmental measures.

The built environment has an important impact on place-based outcomes, defining neighbourhood qualities, types of housing, density of urban form, amenities and access to common spaces and services (parks, schools, transit). While such qualities of the built environment have been a significant focus of housing policies, the evidence of how design impacts mixed-income housing to achieve good people-based outcomes is less conclusive (Bond, Soutkina & Kearns, 2011). Within the planning and design profession, place-based outcomes are often easier to influence, but the social impact on residents remains limited. Research recognises that people-related outcomes are about access to adequate housing, but also about social development, well-being and opportunities for civic participation (Joseph, Chaskin & Webber, 2007). The case studies in this book deliver a strong message that excellence by design is critical for the quality of affordable housing and the well-being of its residents.

Planning-Design-Policy Nexus

A final concept in the book is related to the planning-design-policy nexus (Legacy, Davidson & Liu, 2016). Nexus thinking transcends traditional policy and decision-making silos and develops approaches that build synergies across these sectors (Sharmina et al., 2016). Partnerships for affordable housing in cities are indeed very diverse multi-sectoral collaborations that leverage real estate market pressures to promote affordability goals and social mix. Cities often take the lead in managing the planning-design-policy nexus as neighbourhood rebuilding takes decades and shifting the responsibility to private developers might not work, particularly in the context of gentrification and displacement of lower-income residents. Partnerships need robust and sustained financial support, alignment of planning policies and institutional commitment to increase the supply of affordable rental housing. Such complexity by design makes statements on 'what works' and 'what does not' challenging and illustrates the interdependent nature of resilience at the nexus, raising the fundamental questions how policy might enable systemic resilience. Each city will need to develop its own successful model, based on resilience of the planning-design-policy nexus for affordable housing to respond to growing affordability pressures while emphasising diversity and social mix.

Main Themes in the Book

Building on the success of a three-year collaborative research project, the *Cities and Affordable Housing* book brings forward evidence-based research on what works and what does not work and how to move forward. Established scholars, planners and housing experts have collaborated to explore planning, policy and design innovation in Calgary, Edmonton, Vancouver, Toronto, Montréal, New York, Boston, Washington DC, Cleveland, Seattle, Paris, London, Amsterdam, Copenhagen and Vienna. The narratives are multidisciplinary, unique and richly illustrated. The chapters are organised around five themes explored through case studies, comparative research, critical reflections on innovative models and practices and evidence-based design work. The following sections highlight important issues addressed in each thematic cluster.

1. **Cities and Affordable Housing**. How to implement new planning and design strategies for mixed-income affordable housing in cities? How to mobilise the network of public, private and non-profit organisations, as well as the local communities, to support reforms for affordable housing partnerships? The development of partnerships requires funding, expertise, capacity and effective management of the interdependence between organisations

to deliver affordable homes (Tsenkova, 2019) and adapt to risks (Gilbert, 2016). The contributions in this section include best practices of city-led strategies that impact place-based outcomes—the mix of housing types, access to land and integration in the neighbourhood (Thurber, Bohmann & Heflinger, 2018).

La Ferrière explores the implementation of different initiatives to grow social and community housing in Montréal, and the success of an inclusionary strategy to support mixed-income neighbourhoods. Bond reviews planning tools to foster mixed-income communities and to provide a range of new affordable homes that meet the needs of those who live and work in Vancouver. Woodgate, Goldstein and Noble explore the affordable housing transformation in Calgary, with a strong emphasis on partnerships and collaboration to deliver tangible results. Anderson-Baron and Kjenner emphasise the role of the City of Edmonton as an enabler of affordable housing for over six decades, leveraging the capacity of diverse partners, using proactive policy development, planning tools and a unique regulatory approach to increase access to adequate and affordable housing choices. Gadon's contribution, featuring the experience of Toronto, focuses on leveraging public land for affordable housing development through a range of public/private/non-profit housing partnerships.

2. **Mixed-Income Housing and Community Building**. City-led strategies for mixed-income housing employ various policy instruments to implement transformation (Ramzanpour & Nourtaghani, 2019). Evidence documents that mixed-income development counteracts the negative effects of social isolation and concentration of inner-city poverty and promotes increased mobility among low-income residents (Joseph, Chaskin & Webber, 2007). Building on the political economy of place argument, the chapters address the successes and failures of policy instruments—regulation, resources, institutional capacity and network building—to ensure more efficient and effective implementation of mixed-income housing models (Arthurson, 2010; Atkinson & Kintrea, 2001).

Shomon Shamsuddin presents a conceptual framework for understanding mixed-income housing and illustrates how variations manifest in neighbourhoods. Hirsch, Joseph and Khare explore mixed-income public housing transformation in San Francisco and Washington DC. They examine the tensions and trade-offs of transforming public housing in these city-led initiatives and identify key implications for success in future equity-oriented mixed-income efforts. Dauphin and Schwoerer from Paris Habitat—the largest social housing provider in Paris—present an award-winning design of a new mixed-income, mixed-tenure neighbourhood. The model capitalises on a robust system of support in the French social housing system while illustrating opportunities for sustainable adaptive reuse of heritage resources. Vincent Tong discusses challenges and opportunities in the redevelopment of Regent Park—the largest public housing in Toronto—set to deliver 4,805 rental replacement units on 87 hectares of land. After 12 years of revitalisation through mixed-income opportunities, the results illustrate important lessons for cities developing inclusive social housing communities.

3. **Affordable Housing Partnerships in Practice**. How to implement new partnership models for affordable housing to increase its supply? What are the models of these collaborations? What is the strategic role of municipalities? While there is a common mandate to provide housing that is affordable, the definitions and criteria for allocation and eligibility, governance and management policies, and typologies of housing forms vary widely (Joseph & Khare, 2020). Socially owned housing managed by non-profit, private and community-based organisations in 'hybrid' forms in cities is a viable model of

mixed-income affordable housing, but is not necessarily resilient in times of fiscal austerity (Scanlon, Whitehead & Arrigoitia, 2014). The contributions in this section highlight patterns of diversity in cities and offer practical insights into the nexus of policy, planning and design affecting mixed-income housing.

Schwartz and Tsenkova review the mixed-income housing supported through a variety of housing plans in New York City. Such interventions build upon a strong political commitment to affordable rental housing since the 1980s, supportive policy environment and robust institutional partnerships with non-profits and private sector providers. Kath Scanlon explores how London deals with its growing affordable housing challenge through partnerships. New affordable housing is supplied by housing associations or by for-profit developers, who are required to build affordable homes as a condition of planning permission. Tsenkova's chapter documents patterns of resilience of social housing systems in Vienna, Amsterdam and Copenhagen. The research indicates that resilience is attributed to the robustness and resourcefulness of social housing institutions, but also to sustained and more coherent policy intervention that supports partnerships and neighbourhood rebuilding through social mix.

4. **Design Innovation for Affordable Housing**. How to support social mix and community building through better planning and design of affordable housing projects? The built form and spatial patterns of affordable housing use planning and design strategies to facilitate social mix and integration in communities (Ramzanpour & Nourtaghani, 2019). What design strategies ensure that affordable is well integrated in terms of design, built form and public spaces? The contributions focus on design innovation to support people-based outcomes—healthy and sustainable housing—but also on opportunities for community integration, diversity and social inclusion.

    Friedman advances the concept of flexible design in affordable housing, its design principles and application in the marketplace. Good-quality design in affordable and social housing is a critical component for a successful development. Avenier and Tsenkova illustrate innovative design strategies to improve the quality, functionality, asset value and acceptance of affordable housing using award-winning projects from Paris. In Europe, a new generation of architectural practices is transforming social housing across cities. Karakusevic explores how design changes the housing estates in Rotterdam and contributes to social mixing of generations, languages and cultures in Vienna. The case studies in London explore the integration of high-quality council housing in city's communities. Atteveld and Liesker illustrate how social housing projects in Amsterdam and Haarlem respond to the needs of residents through a variety of design strategies.

5. **Policy Design for Affordable Housing**. How to design policy to develop partnerships for affordable rental housing: rethinking the role of regulation, finance and resources to deliver results? Public authorities employ various policy instruments (fiscal, financial, regulatory) to implement urban transformation (Gilbert, 2016; Tsenkova, 2021). In an era of fiscal austerity, public investment in social housing has declined. In its place has come a wide range of innovations in public/private approaches to funding private rental and non-profit housing, complemented with planning instruments with varying capacities to address the affordability gap (van Bortel et al., 2019). What are the shifts in the availability of demand- and supply-support for affordable housing and what experiences can be effectively transferred to other institutional environments? What is the critical role of private rental housing for socially inclusive cities and neighbourhoods?

Haffner explores the pathways of Dutch and German housing policies that have resulted in different models of affordable rental housing. While the Netherlands has the largest social rental sector in the Western world, Germany has produced one of the largest private rental sectors in Europe where some suppliers are temporarily subsidised. Even though the systems of social renting are different, both countries have moved to locally controlled housing policy. David Hulchanski reviews the private rental housing in Montreal, Toronto, Calgary and Vancouver and its prospects to provide adequate and affordable housing. The arguments illustrate the importance of path-dependent housing policies and their potential contribution to a more inclusive and responsive housing system. Severson and Vos focus on an important policy lens for social and affordable housing that centres on social sustainability. They develop a framework linked to equity, inclusion, security and resiliency and operationalise it for housing providers so that they can manage the process in a coherent way.

Concluding Comments

The contributions in *Cities and Affordable Housing* address issues of fundamental importance to the future of cities. They provide a synthesis of academic knowledge and innovative planning and design practice on the themes of affordable housing partnerships for mixed-income, socially inclusive neighbourhoods as a model to rebuild cities. The book is the result of a three-year collaborative research project at the University of Calgary. Launched in 2018, the *Affordable Housing Research Initiative* aims to broker new knowledge, foster partnerships with industry and communities and advocate for action. It has resulted in two international conferences, public events and design exhibitions that explore strategies to create mixed-income affordable housing in compact, connected urban development. Global in scope, it has delivered rigorous research results available through a knowledge hub as a resource for students, planners, architects, developers, community activists and politicians, widely available to everyone (https://sapl.ucalgary.ca/labs/cities/housing-futures). This first action-based network received Canada Mortgage and Housing Corporation President's Award for Best Housing Research in 2019, recognising its innovative approach and the leadership of Dr Tsenkova (Figure 1.1).

Access to affordable housing in cities is of paramount importance in the context of COVID-19 pandemic, underscoring its significance for public health and urban resilience. The thematic emphasis on housing policy, urban planning and design contributes to multidisciplinary, systematic comparative perspective on the future of affordable housing that will benefit academics and practitioners. The results presented in this edited volume go a long way in disseminating evidence-based work of housing researchers, designers and policy-makers of fundamental importance for the social and economic well-being of urban residents. The book empowers practitioners, planners and community leaders through compelling narratives, critical reflections on good practices, design strategies and evidence-based approaches to affordable housing. Such call for action builds capacity for change and mobilises support for more equitable, inclusive and competitive cities.

Acknowledgements

The financial support from the Social Sciences and Humanities Research Foundation of Canada for this research is acknowledged.

FIGURE 1.1 Contributors to the Affordable Housing Research Initiative.

Source: Sasha Tsenkova.

References

Angel, S. (2000). *Housing Policy Matters – A Global Analysis*. New York: Oxford University Press.

Arthurson, K. (2010). Questioning the Rhetoric of Social Mix as a Tool for Planning Social Inclusion. *Urban Policy and Research*, 28(2), 225–231.

Atkinson, R., & Kintrea, K. (2001). Disentangling Area Effects: Evidence from Deprived and Non-deprived Neighbourhoods. *Urban Studies*, 38(12), 2277–2298.

Bacher, J. C. (1993). *Keeping to the Marketplace: The Evolution of Canadian Housing Policy*. Montréal: McGill-Queen's University Press.

Bailey, N., Haworth, A., Manzi, T., Paranagamage, P., & Roberts, M. (2006). *Creating and Sustaining Mixed Income Communities: A Good Practice Guide*. Coventry: Chartered Institute of Housing and Joseph Rowntree Foundation. Retrieved March 6, 2019, from www.jrf.org.uk/sites/default/files/jrf/migrated/files/9781905018314.pdf

Berry, M. (2014). Neoliberalism and the City: Or the Failure of Market Fundamentalism. *Housing, Theory and Society*, 31(1), 1–18.

Black, J. (2012). *The Financing & Economics of Affordable Housing Development: Incentives and Disincentives to Private-Sector Participation*. Toronto: Cities Centre, University of Toronto.

Bolt, G., Phillips, D., & Van Kempen, R. (2010). Housing Policy, (De)segregation and Social Mixing: An International Perspective. *Housing Studies*, 25(2), 129–135.

Bond, L., Sautkina, E., & Kearns, A. (2011). Mixed Messages about Mixed-Tenure: Do Reviews Tell the Real Story? *Housing Studies*, 26(1), 69–94.

Bovaird, T. (2004). Public-Private Partnerships: From Contested Concepts to Prevalent Practice. *International Review of Administrative Sciences*, 70(2), 199–215.

Brinkerhoff, D., & Brinkerhoff, J. (2011). Public-Private Partnerships: Perspectives on Purposes, Publicness, and Good Governance. *Public Administration and Development*, 31(1), 2–14.

Carmona, M., Carmona, S., & Gallent, N. (2003). *Delivering New Homes: Processes, Planners, and Providers*. London: Routledge.

Dalton, T. (2009). Housing Policy Retrenchment: Australia and Canada Compared. *Urban Studies*, 46(1), 63–91.

Fraser, J. C., & Kick, E. L. (2007). The Role of Public, Private, Non-Profit and Community Sectors in Shaping Mixed-Income Housing Outcomes. *Urban Studies*, 44, 2357–2377.

Galster, G. C. (2013). Neighborhood Social Mix: Theory, Evidence, and Implications for Policy and Planning. In Carmon, N., & Fainstein, S. S. (eds), *Policy, Planning, and People: Promoting Justice in Urban Development*. Philadelphia: University of Pennsylvania Press, 308–336.

Gilbert, A. (2016). Rental Housing: The International Experience. *Habitat International*, 54(3), 173–181.

Joseph, M., Chaskin, R., & Webber, H. (2007). The Theoretical Basis for Addressing Poverty through Mixed-Income Development. *Urban Affairs Review*, 42(3), 369–409.

Joseph, M., & Khare, E. (eds). (2020). *What Works to Promote Inclusive, Equitable Mixed-Income Communities*. Cleveland: National Institute for Mixed Income Communities.

Karakusevic, P., & Batchelor, A. (2018). *Social Housing: Definitions and Design Exemplars*. London: RIBA Publishing.

Katz, B. (2004). *Neighborhoods of Choice and Connection: The Evolution of American Neighborhood Policy and What It Means for the United Kingdom*. The Brookings Institution. Retrieved March 8, 2019, from www.brookings.edu/wp-content/uploads/2016/06/20040713_katz.pdf

Kearns, A., McKee, M., Sautkina, E., Weeks, G., & Bond, L. (2013). Mixed-Tenure Orthodoxy: Practitioner Reflections on Policy Effects. *Cityscape*, 15(2), 47–67.

Kemeny, J., Kersloot, J., & Thalmann, P. (2005). Non-profit Housing Influencing, Leading, and Dominating the Unitary Rental Market: Three Case Studies. *Housing Studies*, 20(6), 855–872.

Legacy, C., Davison, G., & Liu, E. (2016). Delivering Social Housing: Examining the Nexus between Social Housing and Democratic Planning. *Housing, Theory and Society*, 33(3), 324–341.

Livingston, M., Kearns, A., & Bailey, N. (2013). Delivering Mixed Communities: The Relationship between Housing Tenure Mix and Social Mix in England's Neighbourhoods. *Housing Studies*, 28(7), 1056–1080.

Moore, E., & Skaburski, A. (2004). Canada's Increasing Housing Affordability Burdens. *Housing Studies*, 19(3), 395–413.

Oxley, M. (2000). *The Future of Social Housing Learning from Europe*. London: Institution for Public Policy Research.

Ramzanpour, M., & Nourtaghani, A. (2019). Impact of Four Physical Design Factors on Mixed-Income Housing. *Journal of Architectural Engineering*, 25(1), 1–8.

Scanlon, K., Whitehead, C., & Arrigoitia, M. (eds). (2014). *Social Housing in Europe*. Oxford: Wiley-Blackwell.

Sharmina, M., Hoolohan, C., Bows-Larkin, A., Burgess, P., Colwill, J., Gilbert, P., Howard, D., Knox, J., & Anderson, K. (2016). A Nexus Perspective on Competing Land Demands: Wider Lessons from a UK Policy Case Study. *Environmental Science & Policy*, 59, 74–84.

Smith, A. (2002). *Mixed-Income Housing Developments: Promise and Reality*. Cambridge, MA: Joint Center for Housing Studies of Harvard University and Neighborhood Reinvestment Corporation.

Sousa, J., & Quarter, J. (2003). The Convergence of Nonequity Housing Models in Canada: Changes to Housing Policy Since 1990. *Housing Policy Debate*, 14(4), 591–620.

Stephens, M., Burns, N., & Mackay, L. (2002). *Social Market or Safety Net? British Social Rented Housing in a European Context*. Bristol: The Policy Press & The Joseph Rowntree Foundation.

Thurber, A., Bohmann, C., & Heflinger, C. (2018). Spatially Integrated and Socially Segregated: The Effects of Mixed-Income Neighbourhoods on Social Well-Being. *Urban Studies*, 55(9), 1859–1874.

Tsenkova, S. (2014). A Tale of Two Cities: Resilience of Social Housing in Vienna and Amsterdam. In Amann, W., Pernsteiner, H., and Struber, Ch. (eds)., *Wohnbau in Österreich in Europäischer Perspective*. Vienna: Manz Verlag and Universitatsbuchhandlung, 95–105.

Tsenkova, S. (2016). Sustainable Housing & Livable Cities: The New Urban Agenda. *Urban Research & Practice*, 9(3), 322–326.

Tsenkova, S. (2019). Partnerships: Creating Affordable Housing Opportunities in Canada. In Forster, W., & Menking, W. (eds)., *The Vienna Model 2: Housing for the City of the 21st century*. Berlin: Jovis, 120–137.

Tsenkova, S. (ed.) (2021). *Transforming Social Housing: International Perspectives*. Abingdon: Routledge.

van Bortel, G., Gruis, V., Nieuwenhuijzen, J., & Pluijmers, B. (eds). (2019). *Affordable Housing Governance and Finance: Innovations, Partnerships and Comparative Perspectives*. Abingdon: Routledge.

Whitehead, C. (2007). Planning Policies and Affordable Housing: England as a Successful Case Study? *Housing Studies*, 22(1), 25–44.

PART I
Cities and Affordable Housing

2

MONTRÉAL

Building an Inclusive City

Suzanne LaFerrière

Introduction

Montréal has earned an enviable reputation as a convivial urban environment. Along with densely built and lively central neighbourhoods, a thriving cultural scene and a rich historical heritage, affordable housing has been a major component of the Montréal quality of life. Steadfast efforts by the City and its partners have contributed strongly to this by supporting the development and preservation of a diversified and affordable housing stock. Some figures are revealing: since 2002,[1] the City's financial assistance programmes have led to the creation of close to 20,000 social and community housing units, the renovation of more than 35,000 private affordable housing units and the negotiation of inclusionary agreements with real estate developers calling for the construction of thousands of affordable residential units.

The City did not act alone. The production of affordable housing in Montréal stems from a true ecosystem, where City action, tangible government support and private and community partners that play a key role in the development of projects are held together by a resilient social consensus. The word "ecosystem" is used deliberately, as all these elements interact closely. Affordable housing targets have been embedded in Montréal's urban planning schemes for more than two decades. This chapter outlines the strategies put forth to turn these ambitions into reality.

Three Major Issues

Sustainable and Balanced Growth

Key metrics defining demographics, housing typologies and availability of social housing in Montréal and its agglomeration are presented in Box 2.1. Like many other large cities, Montréal has seen its population share diminish within the region under the effect of urban sprawl. While the phenomenon raises major environmental issues, it also poses the risk of demographic imbalance by drawing cohorts of young families outside of the City. Each year, Montréal sees about 20,000 people – essentially from young middle-class households – move to outlying suburban municipalities (international immigration and natural growth currently compensate for these losses). This constitutes a lifestyle choice for some families, but for many others the decisive

DOI: 10.4324/9781003172949-2

BOX 2.1: KEY STATISTICS ON POPULATION AND HOUSING IN MONTRÉAL*

Population
- 1.74 million / 779,800 households

Economic and social profile
- Single-person households: 41%
- Households with children: 33% (with children under 18: 23%)
- 29.5% of households below the low-income cutoff

Urban profile
- One in five dwelling units built before 1945
- Medium- to high-density neighbourhoods
- 39% of dwelling units in "plexes", prevalent in central neighbourhoods
- Mix of multi-unit rental buildings and single-family properties in peripheral sectors

Housing stock
- 63% occupied by tenants (493,400 households)
- Social housing (all types): 12% of the rental stock (7% of total stock).

Social housing stock**

Total: 61,100 units
- 21,600 HLM units (public, rent-geared-to-income)
- 6,900 below-market rent units owned by para-municipal corporations
- 32,600 units owned by non-profit organizations (NPOs) and cooperatives

*City of Montréal territory
**Montréal Agglomeration: includes Montréal (1.7 million population) and 15 other municipalities (0.3 million).

Source: Statistics Canada, 2016 Census; Direction de l'habitation, Ville de Montréal, 2017.

---

factor remains the 30–60% price gap between homes in Montréal and homes off the island. Moreover, new production of residential units on the City's territory is largely geared towards small units, which do not meet all the needs and expectations of families.

A Significant Rental Stock

The second issue concerns the maintenance of the rental stock – a major factor in a city where two out of three households are tenants. Montréal's diversified rental stock includes a vast offer of "plexes" – which are coveted in neighbourhoods undergoing gentrification – as well as a small but growing number of residential towers. There is also an important pool of multi-unit residential buildings constructed at the height of the demographic boom, from the 1950s to the 1970s, which today house a significant proportion of the new immigrant households. Even though Montréal's rental stock, in general, is of good quality, there is cause for concern in some areas, faced with the combined challenges of growing poverty, deteriorating or even unsanitary buildings and underinvestment by property owners. In addition, observers note an erosion of the rental stock in central neighbourhoods, reflecting the trend towards conversion to co-ownership and the increasing presence of tourist rentals.

Social Needs

The third issue concerns clients for whom the market offers no adequate options. In spite of its reputation for affordability, Montréal has close to 100,000 tenant households that earmark 50% or more of their income to rent, most of them living on very low income. The waiting list for HLMs (public rent-geared-to-income housing) steadily remains around 23,000–25,000 households. Against this background, some populations encounter specific difficulties. Such is the case for large families confronted with a chronic shortage of suitable affordable rentals. Montréal also faces significant homelessness issues: in addition to the "visible" homelessness observed on the streets and in shelters, a growing number of neighbourhoods are home to a pool of vulnerable people having to cope with social isolation and persistent residential instability.[2]

Affordable Housing Development Strategies

The City has a number of housing tools at its disposal to respond to these demographic, economic and social challenges. Two in particular have had structuring impacts on affordable housing delivery. For one, the City has steadily invested in financial assistance programmes to stimulate and steer development, an approach that gives community partners clear and predictable signals. Second, the City has developed an incentive strategy – non-regulatory at the outset – to promote the introduction of affordable housing (both social and private) in real estate projects.

Financial Assistance Programmes

When the federal government stopped funding social housing development in the 1990s, the City joined forces with various civil society actors who were calling on the Québec government to take action. The City's proposal ("Résolution Montréal", adopted by city council in 1994) paved the way for shared-cost programmes and served as a starting point for the Société d'habitation du Québec (SHQ – the provincial housing corporation) to develop a new generation of social housing. The current *AccèsLogis* programme was created in 1996.

AccèsLogis is open to both the non-profit sector (cooperatives and non-profit housing corporations) and municipal housing corporations. It incorporates a form of social mix by providing residential units with rents slightly below-market rates, with added rent supplements for low-income households. Projects for families or seniors may offer from 20% to 50% of their units with rent supplements. The programme also includes a component adapted to projects for vulnerable individuals, under which 100% of residential units can receive rent assistance. The programme's funding structure, as established by the SHQ, is based on contributions respecting the capacity and jurisdiction of funding sources. The SHQ, which is part of Québec's social and redistributive policies, therefore provides three-quarters of *AccèsLogis* programme subsidies, while the "community" (generally the municipalities) provides the rest.[3]

The creation of the *AccèsLogis* programme in 1996 coincided with a round of talks between Montréal and the Québec governments, focusing on neighbourhoods particularly hard hit by deindustrialization, where the built environment had deteriorated to alarming levels. Working with community partners in the Hochelaga-Maisonneuve district and with City experts, the SHQ designed a new financing framework intended to revitalize neighbourhoods, which gave Montréal and other urban centres in Québec the ability to develop local housing programmes within broad provincial guidelines. Now known as the *Programme Rénovation Québec (PRQ)*, this framework has made it possible for Montréal to identify and target key areas in need of assistance, whether through renovation grants for private projects, subsidies for residential demolition or reconstruction work, homeowner assistance or other initiatives. Programme costs are split evenly between Montréal and the SHQ, in line with the programme's impacts on multiple municipal issues (sanitation, maintenance of property values, revitalization, etc.).

With the creation of those two major programmes – *AccèsLogis* for social and community housing and the *PRQ* for the private housing stock – the SHQ delegated powers to the City, which became responsible for managing the bulk of provincial housing programmes on the Montréal territory.

A Regional Cost-Sharing Mechanism for Social Housing

HLM units (public rent-geared-to-income housing), which stem from tripartite (Canada-Québec-cities) agreements, and *AccèsLogis* projects financed by the SHQ and cities, were, and to this day remain, unequally distributed across the metropolitan region. The financial impact exerted by social housing on municipal budgets thus varies considerably from one municipality to another.

In 2001, as part of wide-ranging municipal reforms, the Québec government sought to correct this situation, which was weighing on cities, particularly Montréal where the concentration of social and community housing was highest. As the Communauté métropolitaine de Montréal (CMM), a regional planning body, was created, it was mandated to manage a municipal cost-sharing mechanism for social housing.[4] The 82 municipalities (Figure 2.1) that make up the CMM remit an annual contribution in proportion to their respective fiscal capacity, regardless of whether or not they have social housing within their municipal limits. In exchange, the funds collected are earmarked for the reimbursement of the share paid by the cities to social housing programmes set out under law (Communauté métropolitaine de Montréal, 2015). Thus, Montréal provides about half of the contributions made to the CMM,[5] but receives, depending on the year, between 70% and 80% of the reimbursements meted out. In 2017, for example, the City contributed a share of about $24 million to the CMM, but in exchange received reimbursements totalling $39 million for expenses incurred under the *AccèsLogis* and rent supplement programmes, and for the HLM housing stock.

By creating this mechanism, the legislator sought to help Montréal as well as encourage suburban municipalities with little or no social housing to welcome projects and contribute to a greater geographical distribution thereof (Communauté métropolitaine de Montréal, 2015). This effect is currently observed for the most part in municipalities bordering Montréal, where social housing stock already exists, but other cities are showing growing interest as well.

Delivering Social and Community Housing

While it is up to the cities to determine land use development guidelines, municipal services, conversely, seldom have the agility required to operate effectively and in a timely fashion on the real estate market, notably because the announcement of a municipal intention can have a hardening effect on prices and sales conditions.

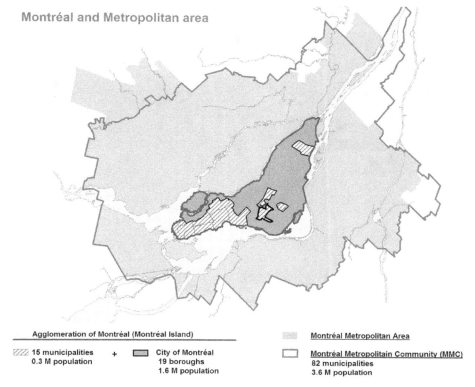

FIGURE 2.1 Montréal and Metropolitan Area.
Source: City of Montréal.

In Montréal and elsewhere in Québec, the development of social and community housing projects is thus overseen by social economy organizations specializing in housing called *Groupes de ressources techniques* (GRT). Four such technical resource groups are accredited across Montréal. Their creation dates back to the 1970s, when the SHQ supported their development to ensure that federal funds then available could be used by cooperative projects and non-profit housing corporations in Québec.[6] GRTs identify opportunities on the market, negotiate purchase offers and establish ties with organizations or citizen groups interested in developing housing projects. GRTs also coordinate the multiple inputs needed for projects (i.e. the work of architects, engineers, soil analysis, etc.) and can streamline projects to meet the requirements of financial assistance programmes. The increasing complexity of urban projects has brought the City to require that all projects submitted under social and community housing programmes involve a GRT. Figure 2.2 illustrates three examples: Coopérative Station 1 (74 family units in former electric station, Rosemont-Petite-Patrie borough), Centre Yee-Kang (84 units for seniors. Ville-Marie borough) and Coopérative Radar (47 units, Ville-Marie borough).

Upstream of GRTs, several networks of community organizations are also mobilized. These include some 30 neighbourhood roundtables and multiple other stakeholders that provide assistance to a wide gamut of clienteles. These community partners help identify issues, work with boroughs to set out local development targets and priorities and play a role in consolidating a social consensus on the importance of affordable housing. Far from being peripheral actors, community organizations are an intrinsic part of the affordable housing ecosystem.

FIGURE 2.2 Social and Community Housing Projects in Central Neighbourhoods.
Note: Coopérative Station 1 (74 family units in former electric station, Rosemont-Petite-Patrie borough); Centre Yee-Kang (84 units for seniors, Ville-Marie borough); Coopérative Radar (47 units, Ville-Marie borough).
Source: Ville de Montréal.

Urban Planning and the Inclusionary Strategy

From 1990 to 1992, in the wake of a sweeping modernization process within the municipal administration, Montréal adopted major urban planning tools, including a public consultation policy, a housing policy and the first *Master Plan* (*plan d'urbanisme*) of the city and boroughs. Today, the City's objectives and targets pertaining to housing are enshrined in the agglomeration's *Schéma d'aménagement et de développement* and in the *Master Plan*. Two key ideas have been consistently put forth in the *Master Plan* from the outset: the notion of preserving or creating "complete" and lively neighbourhoods that ensure the presence of green spaces as well as public and commercial services integrated into residential areas, and the objective of ensuring a diversified residential offer that includes an affordable housing component.

In response to a serious shortage of rental housing and the unprecedented social crisis that ensued,[7] the *2004 Master Plan* set out an objective whereby affordable products would account for 30% of residential housing starts. The following year, to lend substance to this objective, the City launched its *Strategy for the inclusion of affordable housing in new residential projects*. The Strategy includes two elements. First, it establishes overall targets for housing starts to include 15% social housing and 15% private affordable units; these general guidelines are meant to inform the work of boroughs and developers. Second, it outlines a discussion mechanism for use with real estate developers, aimed at ensuring that their projects feature an affordable component (City of Montréal, 2005).

It is important to note that under Québec's pre-2017 legal framework, cities did not have the power to require that developers integrate specific types of housing or clients. From the outset, therefore, *Montréal's Inclusion Strategy* was incentive-based and geared specifically to private residential projects in the following situations:

- projects developed on municipal lots or surplus government lands ceded for development;
- projects calling for 200 units or more (this threshold was later reduced to 100 units), which require major exemptions to urban planning or zoning regulations.

In the case of large-scale urban projects, the *Strategy* is implemented by the central municipal administration, while boroughs are involved in other projects (urban planning powers are in large part devolved to the boroughs). In practice, the social or private affordable housing ratios vary, depending on a project's characteristics, but the general trend, from the outset, has been to apply the 15/15 formula as proposed. While a few boroughs have not implemented the *Strategy*, others have put it in practice vigorously, with some demanding a ratio of 20% of social housing, together with an equal proportion of private affordable housing units (City of Montréal, 2020). Figure 2.3 illustrates projects on the site du Nouveau-Havre with private housing (left) and a social housing component (right). Coopérative des Bassins is a development with 182 units. The Les Tanneries project in Le Sud-Ouest, presented in Figure 2.4, was developed by two para-municipal corporations. Office municipal d'habitation de Montréal provided 67 social housing units and Société de développement et d'habitation de Montréal provided 143 affordable condominiums.

When it put forward its *Inclusion Strategy*, the municipal administration commissioned studies to identify the optimal conditions for the creation of mixed-income developments. Specifically, these studies concerned profitability thresholds for projects, as well as costs associated with the introduction of affordable components. Residential market studies made it possible to establish guidelines based on geographical sectors, defining what constitutes an affordable housing unit (co-ownership or rental). Focus groups were also held with developers.

At the City's request, researchers also studied issues of cohabitation in various mixed-income development projects. Their observations of projects, completed in Québec, North America and Europe, played a key part in guiding development choices.[8] Without being introduced in

FIGURE 2.3 Inclusionary Agreement Projects with Social and Private Units.
Note: Site du Nouveau-Havre: private projects and a social component Coopérative des Bassins, 182 units.
Source: Ville de Montréal.

FIGURE 2.4 Mixed-Income Project with Two Para-municipal Corporations.
Note: Les Tanneries (Borough: Le Sud-Ouest) was developed by Office municipal d'habitation de Montréal (67 social housing units) and Société de développement et d'habitation de Montréal (143 affordable condominiums).
Source: Office municipal d'habitation de Montréal.

the form of regulations, three general principles were retained in the negotiation of inclusionary projects:

1. projects should create a social continuum; situations presenting extreme income disparities should be avoided;
2. the clear definition of public and private spaces should be encouraged as it fosters optimal and harmonious use of outdoor spaces;
3. forced sociability (i.e. the integration of social housing in a private building) does not guarantee community-building; it is preferable to allow side-by-side cohabitation, in separate buildings, which gives occupants control over their environment (i.e. social and community housing as empowerment tools) and minimizes conflicts stemming from different lifestyles.

In addition, economic modelling showed that integrating social housing into a co-ownership complex could entail the risk of major financial pressures on the social housing component, thereby compromising its affordability and long-term financial viability. Since co-ownership contracts do not truly protect the social housing component against these risks, efforts have been made to avoid or limit co-ownership situations.

BOX 2.2: INCLUSIONARY AGREEMENTS, 2006–2018

- More than 70 inclusionary agreements signed
- Development potential of 45,000 residential units, including more than 6,500 social and community housing units, and close to 6,000 affordable co-ownership units and private rental units
- More than $22,000,000 has flowed through the inclusionary contribution fund.

Source: City of Montréal, 2020.

Concerning the creation of social housing within inclusionary agreements, three options are thus encouraged among developers: the on-site construction of a social housing building (which may take the form of a land sale with construction by a third party); the sale of off-site lands, with or without construction by the developer, in the same sector; and, in cases where inclusion is not possible or desirable, the payment of a financial contribution to the City.[9] All sums collected are administered through an inclusionary contribution fund managed by the City; the amounts are earmarked to complete the financing of new projects in the borough where they were collected. The management of the contribution fund is subject to a detailed annual report tabled before City council (City of Montréal, 2018).

Drawing parallels with some European countries, some researchers have viewed this strategy as a "population redistribution policy" intended to channel and control the presence of low-income populations. In fact, the Montréal initiative was designed exactly for opposite reasons. *The Inclusion Strategy* aims to open up new possibilities for the development of social and community housing across its territory, including central areas, in the context of a highly active real estate market where few land opportunities are available to non-profit developers. For the City of Montréal, the *Strategy* is part of an overall approach that recognizes the importance of city-wide affordable housing and guarantees a true social mix and an inclusive social climate.

Home Ownership Programmes

Montréal also introduced measures to assist households looking to buy property. In 2003, an initial home ownership financial assistance programme was developed as part of efforts to revitalize older industrial neighbourhoods. Historically, owners would occupy the ground floor of "plexes" in central areas, but as some sectors' economy waned, absentee landlords became commonplace. The City therefore began offering financial assistance to homeowners seeking to move into targeted areas, as part of a global strategy intended to instil a sense of belonging and repair a fraying social fabric.

This temporary programme has since been replaced by successive home ownership programmes, now expanded to include both first-time buyers and households that already own property. A perennial feature of the financial assistance programmes is that families with children benefit from increased financial aid. Surveys and studies show that the programmes frequently influence and accelerate the decision to purchase property in Montréal. More than 20,000 households have taken advantage of the home ownership programmes since they were first created.

Montréal has also taken steps to directly support the construction of affordable co-ownerships in response to market conditions. During the housing shortage of the 2000s, assistance was provided in the form of direct subsidies. Over a ten-year period, developers of more than 7,500 affordable co-ownership units received funding from the *PRQ* shared-cost programme. As market conditions evolved, this assistance was stopped, but new measures are presently under study in relation with the new inclusionary by-law set to take effect in 2021.

Furthermore, the Société d'habitation et de développement de Montréal (SHDM), a para-municipal corporation, has developed its own co-ownership construction programme in conjunction with City initiatives. Based on Toronto's *Access to Homes* model, the *Accès Condos* programme oversees the development of private projects and offers purchase credits, making units accessible for a modest down payment. More than 4,000 units have been built as a result of this initiative since 2005. This programme does not benefit from direct municipal funding, but buyers of *Accès Condos* units are by and large eligible to receive municipal home ownership subsidies.

Existing Housing Stock

Finally, the municipality also leads interventions on the existing housing stock. As this text is primarily focused on development issues, this role will be discussed only briefly:

- residential adaptation assistance programmes for individuals with physical limitations have made it possible to adapt nearly 5,000 residential units since 2002; these are provincial programmes managed by a specialized team from the City's housing department;
- over time, the City has developed a wide range of tools to enforce by-laws concerning sanitation and safety in residential building. In addition to conducting building inspections, the City has the power to carry out work on unsanitary buildings on behalf of neglectful landlords and to include a notice on land titles as a warning to prospective buyers.

New Powers, New Issues and New Solutions

Power Gains and Transfers

In 2016, Montréal and the Québec governments signed the *"Réflexe Montréal"* agreement, which recognizes the City's special status of metropolis. This resulted in the transfer of housing responsibilities and budgets from the SHQ to the City in March 2018. The renewable five-year agreement provides for the annual transfer of an overall budget allowance from three programmes: *AccèsLogis* (social and community housing), *Rénovation Québec* (housing improvement programme) and the residential adaptation assistance programme for individuals living with functional limitations. Montréal initially received 36% of the total Québec budget allotted to these programmes; the agreement calls for this share to increase each year until it reaches 40%. In 2018 and 2019, Montréal received $94 million and $103 million, respectively. The housing agreement also enables Montréal to restructure and develop programmes to better reflect the local priorities and specific conditions in the Montréal area.

Recent years had been marked by a widening gap between Québec programme standards and Montréal's actual project costs. As a result, social and community housing development had slowed considerably in Montréal and even threatened to come to a complete halt. After the agreement was signed, the City implemented the *"AccèsLogis Montréal"* programme, an improved version of the *AccèsLogis* Québec funding model. Work has started on a second version to meet several challenges, including faster project delivery and improved follow-up of completed projects. Similarly, the City has overhauled renovation assistance programmes and the residential adaptation assistance programme for individuals with functional limitations, to better adapt them to the unique situation of Montréal's rental stock.

In addition to the transfer agreement, Montréal was also granted new urban planning and housing powers. For example, the City now has the right of pre-emption, making it possible to designate, through by-laws, territories where any building or site being sold must be offered to the City first. Widely used in some European countries, this mechanism gives the City greater control over land development in sectors experiencing development or redevelopment challenges, while avoiding the complications and costs of expropriation.

A major gain was made when Montréal – along with other cities in Québec – also obtained the power to adopt legislation mandating the inclusion of social, affordable or family housing. To make this effective, the City submitted a by-law project for public consultation in 2019, after economic impact studies were conducted to assess the effects of various scenarios. *The Diverse Metropolis By-law*, which introduces territorial modulations and new rules for contributions, came into effect on April 1, 2021 (City of Montréal, 2021).

Challenges

Elected in November 2017, the Montréal administration has committed to develop 12,000 social, affordable and family housing units in the 2018–2021 period.[10] The plan is intended to meet a wide array of needs, including those from families, seniors, students, individuals experiencing homelessness or at risk of homelessness, indigenous and Inuit communities and many others. This ambitious initiative calls upon the entire range of the City's housing programmes and tools, including social and community housing development programmes, the purchase and transfer of municipal land, funding for infrastructure costs, renovation assistance programmes (to preserve older social housing stock and affordable segments of private rental stock), home ownership programmes, as well as the contributions of para-municipal housing corporations to strategic projects (City of Montréal, 2021).

One challenging aspect of the plan involves seeking new funding models for affordable housing. Work is needed to design a framework for affordable projects in a context where the future of the *Québec AccesLogis* social housing programme appears uncertain. As a first step, the City has set up a fund, with flexible guidelines designed to host and monitor pilot projects, an approach that allows to gather highly useful first-hand information. Pursuing the work will eventually require a stable financial framework as well as fixed guidelines to ensure that objectives are being met. As initial projects have already shown, one obvious challenge will be to ensure long-term affordability.

The City of Montréal can rightly be seen as a municipality that is actively engaged in improving the quality of life and housing conditions of its residents. Nevertheless, the substantial investments required to do so and the urgency of housing needs demand concerted action by the federal, provincial and municipal levels. Montréal thus continues to engage in active dialogue with Canada and Québec, making its voice heard as federal-provincial negotiations shape the funding background for the next decade.

Notes

1 The year 2002 is used to define the onset of two municipal reforms (2002–2006) that led to the current division of territory on the island. Important housing programmes and mechanisms were put in place during this period.

2 The last city-wide Homelessness Census in 2018 accounted for 3,150 homeless persons. Close to 22% of them were sleeping rough. This figure is for visible homelessness only and does not include "invisible" homelessness situations (couch surfing or other forms of residential precariousness).

3 The total subsidies (from the SHQ and the City) account for 60% of eligible project costs. The City contributes 15% of eligible costs (or one quarter of the subsidies). The developer must take out a mortgage guaranteed by the SHQ to cover residual costs.

4 The CMM (Montréal Metropolitan Community) also has specific coordination mandates in the field of public transportation, waste management and for the production of a regional planning scheme.

5 The other cities within the agglomeration (island) of Montréal provide 12% of regional contributions.

6 GRTs are currently financed through fees billed to projects, according to standards set out in programmes.

7 From 2001, Montréal experienced a series of what came to be called "July 1 crises". Due to an acute rental shortage, hundreds of low-income households were unable to find housing at the end of their leases (generally June 30), and literally found themselves out on the street. In addition to emergency measures used to put up these households, the City established permanent support services for vulnerable households. At the same time, the City and the Government of Québec made massive investments to accelerate the production of social and community housing. Along with a small private rental production, these efforts helped restore a more balanced rental market starting around 2010. The issue surfaced again in 2019 and, more severely, in 2020, in a context of rising rental prices and rental shortage.

8 Dansereau, F., et al. (2002) *La mixité sociale en habitation* – Rapport de recherche réalisé pour le Service de l'habitation de la Ville de Montréal. The City also drew from the works of Annick Germain et al., 2017 (INRS-Culture et société), and Hélène Bélanger and Richard Morin (Université du Québec à Montréal).

9 Concerning affordable private residential units, the developer is asked to provide a letter of guarantee from the bank when signing the inclusionary agreement. In the event that the project does not deliver the units to which the developer has committed, the sum is paid to the City.

10 As of November 2020, over 80% of the target had been reached.

References

City of Montréal (2005) Strategy for the inclusion of affordable housing in new residential projects. http://servicesenligne.ville.montreal.qc.ca/sel/publications/PorteAccesTelechargement?lng=Fr&systemName=7757558&client=Serv_corp, accessed January 4, 2021.

City of Montréal (2018) (In French) Review of results 2005–2018 – Montreal strategy for the inclusion of affordable housing in new residential projects. https://ocpm.qc.ca/sites/ocpm.qc.ca/files/pdf/P104/4-1-4_inclusion_bilanstrategie2005-2018_sept2019.pdf, accessed January 4, 2021.

City of Montréal (2020) An overview of the diverse metropolis bylaw (inclusionary bylaw). https://montreal.ca/en/articles/diverse-metropolis-overview-law-7816, accessed January 4, 2021.

City of Montréal (2021) Housing programs and initiatives. http://ville.montreal.qc.ca/portal/page?_pageid=9437,116487573&_dad=portal&_schema=PORTAL, accessed January 4, 2021.

Communauté métropolitaine de Montréal (2015) (In French) Five-year regional plan for social and affordable housing. https://cmm.qc.ca/wp-content/uploads/2019/04/20150618_pamlsa-2015-2020.pdf, accessed January 4, 2021.

Dansereau, F., Charbonneau, S., Morin, R., Révillard, A., Rose, D., & Séguin, A.-M. (2002) *La mixité sociale en habitation – Rapport de recherche réalisé pour le Service de l'habitation de la Ville de Montréal*. Montréal: INRS – Centre Urbanisation Culture Société.

Germain, A., Leloup, X., Rose, D., Torres, J., Préfontaine, C., et al. (2017) *La qualité de vie dans les projets résidentiels de grande densité incluant du logement abordable – Quelques leçons*. Montréal: INRS – Centre Urbanisation Culture Société.

3

AFFORDABLE HOUSING AND DIVERSITY IN VANCOUVER

Abigail Bond

How Vancouver's Housing Affordability Crisis Impacts Its Diversity

Responding to Vancouver's housing crisis and maintaining its unique and vibrant diversity are the most significant challenges facing the City today. Vancouver's housing affordability crisis is being mirrored in many cities around the world and is in part the result of pressure on the housing market created by the global flow of money, people and jobs. Responding to this crisis is the most significant challenge facing the City today – with Vancouver residents facing among the highest rents and housing purchase prices, but lowest median incomes among Canadian cities (CMHC, 2016a). This is a crisis situation experienced by many households across a broad range of incomes, but impacting low-income, vulnerable, and marginalized households most significantly. Affordable homes are foundational for a growing City, and are essential if diverse households, made up of people from all incomes and backgrounds, are able to form or arrive, and stay to make a future in Vancouver. The crisis is resulting in many people making the difficult choice to leave the City in order to find an adequate, suitable, and affordable home where they can thrive.

Like other global cities, Vancouver's middle-income households are also now experiencing challenges with securing and keeping an affordable home in the City, often having to make difficult choices about what to spend their income on. The high cost of renting in relation to income and very limited availability of rental housing, with a vacancy rate of below 1%, limits the housing choices and increases competition for both low- and middle-income households. Housing affordability is a general measure defined by Canada Mortgage and Housing Corporation as a share of household gross income of 30% on rental shelter costs, and no more than 32% of gross household income on homeownership. Using this measure, cities such as Toronto and Vancouver have over one-third of their households facing affordability problems, while in Calgary and Edmonton the share is one-fifth (Figure 3.1). The situation for renters, most of them in the private non-regulated market, is much more stressful. Paying any more than 30% of your income on rent, your other spending choices are compromised; paying more than 50%, you are in danger of losing your home and experiencing homelessness. In Vancouver, the share of renter households paying more than 30% of their income in shelter costs has increased steadily in the last 15 years as the data in Figure 3.2 demonstrate. Close to 46,000 Vancouver renters are paying more than 30% of their income on rent, and of these 15,000 renter households are paying more than 50% of their income on rent (Statistics Canada, 2017a).

DOI: 10.4324/9781003172949-3

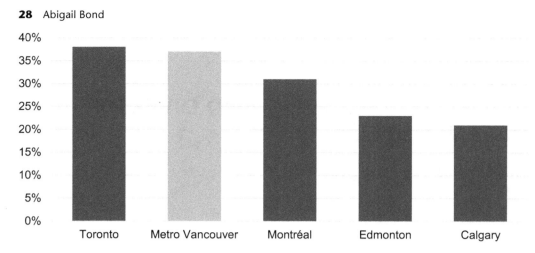

FIGURE 3.1 Share of Households Spending 30% or More on Shelter Costs, 2016.
Source: Statistics Canada, 2017b.

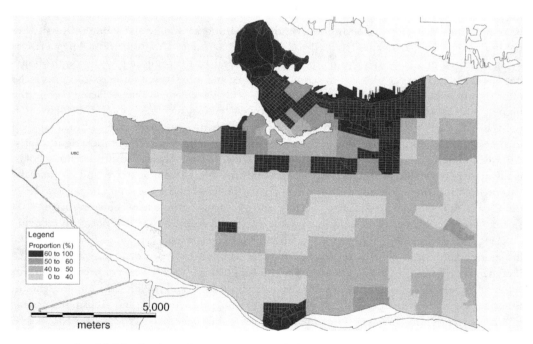

FIGURE 3.2 Spatial Distribution of Vancouver Households Spending 30% or More on Shelter.
Source: City of Vancouver, based on Statistics Canada, Census of the Population, 2017a.

The increase in numbers of those paying too much of their income has expanded the housing crisis to middle-income households, and now puts a much larger range of households at risk of not being able to afford to stay in Vancouver, including workers, immigrants, families, artists, young people, and students (CMHC, 2016b). Young households and families aged between 20 and 40 are struggling to find a way to stay, despite it being an initially attractive place to study and start their careers. Generation Squeeze is an advocacy and research group. It has shown how it takes 29 years of full-time work for a typical young person to save a 20% down payment on an average-priced home – 23 more years than when today's ageing population started out as young people (Generation Squeeze, 2019). Thus, the same age group now has far less opportunity to live in a secure, affordable home and accumulate wealth. Many are forced to live with parents, rent for longer, or even leave.

The high cost and limited availability of renting and the growing inaccessibility of home-ownership, combined with childcare costs, make it difficult for these households to stay in the City for a long-term. The last census showed that number of children aged 0–four years had declined by 1% since 2011 (Statistics Canada, 2017a). This puts our healthy and growing economy and communities at risk, as many mid-career workers see little options but to leave Vancouver. This impacts companies who lose key workers critical to their business, and communities lose families and children as a result.

The Intersection of Housing Unaffordability with Characteristics of Diverse Households

There are multiple and often intersecting characteristics of household diversity, including income, family make-up, and race to name a few. Diverse households make Vancouver both vibrant and unique, but this diversity is being placed at risk by the current housing crisis and the long-standing and systemic inequities that exist in our City. The intersection between housing affordability challenges and marginalization, including gender and sexual identity, race, poverty, family status, and mental and physical health, has become a powerful force limiting inclusion, diversity and mixed communities in our City. The lack of housing affordability affects many people in our City, but it is more likely to affect you, if you are also a member of a marginalized group. In *Shaping Futures Changing the Housing Story*, Chisholm and Hulchanski state that we need to reframe our understanding of the important role housing plays in our economy, in reducing carbon, in social inclusion, and in inequality (Chisholm and Hulchanski, 2019) (Figure 3.3).

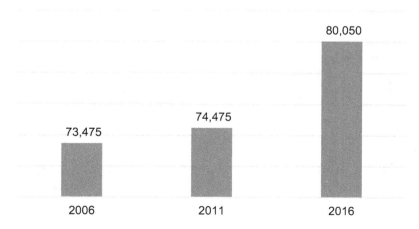

FIGURE 3.3 Renter Households Spending 30% or More on Shelter, 2006–2016.
Source: Statistics Canada, Census 2006, 2016, and National Household Survey 2011.

One example is the intersection between the lack of housing affordability and gender, as 35% of lone-parent families are considered to be low-income compared to 15% of households with two parents, and 81% of lone-parent families are led by women (Statistics Canada, 2014). Low-income women-led families are more likely to be living in poverty and will find it harder to find a home they can afford.

Homelessness has continued to rise in the City and region. Low-income seniors, Indigenous households, single-parent households, people with disabilities or mental health, addiction challenges, and youth struggling with the housing crisis are at a greater disproportionate risk of homelessness. *The 2019 City of Vancouver Homeless Count* found 2,223 sheltered and unsheltered individuals experiencing homelessness, with Indigenous residents still disproportionately represented in comparison to their overall share in the population – 39% compared with 2% (City of Vancouver, 2019d).

Vancouver's Indigenous residents are facing deeper inequities than elsewhere in the region, and so will experience the housing crisis more deeply than other resident groups. The average household income for Indigenous households in the City of Vancouver (2010) was approximately 20% lower than the Metro Vancouver Indigenous income average ($55,500 vs. $69,223) and 31% lower than the average non-Indigenous income in Vancouver (Statistics Canada, 2013).

Responding to the Challenge: *Housing Vancouver* (2018–2027)

Housing Vancouver is the City's ten-year housing strategy that was launched in 2017 as a response to the ongoing and intensive nature of Vancouver's housing crisis. It includes new approaches, tools and partnerships to ensure that Vancouver continues to support a diversity of incomes and households. *Housing Vancouver* was developed through discussions with key stakeholders and partners, with local and global housing leaders, and by talking to over 10,000 local residents. The strategy prioritizes the creation of new affordable homes and also measures to affect the housing market, so it works for a broader range of people who live and work in the City (City of Vancouver, 2019b). It is guided by the following key values:

- *Diversity* – Housing should respond to the diversity of people and households who call Vancouver home.
- *Security* – Housing is about 'homes first' and security of tenure, and is an important foundation to a sense of belonging in the City.
- *Affordability* – All residents should have access to housing options within their means that meet their needs.
- *Connection* – The right mix of homes supports resilient communities, with strong connections between people, places, and communities.
- *Equity* – Housing should promote equitable access to jobs, education, and other opportunities for economic prosperity for people of all ages, incomes, and backgrounds.

Building on these values, *Housing Vancouver* also identifies several key objectives:

- *Shift towards the Right Supply:* Make a significant shift towards rental, social, co-op, and supportive housing, as well as greater diversity of forms in Vancouver's ground-oriented housing stock. New homes must be accessible to the diversity of households who need housing.
- *Action to Address Speculation and Support Equity:* Address the impact of speculative demand on land and housing prices. Working together, partners and all levels of government to promote measures that advance equitable distribution of wealth gains from housing, learning

lessons from around the world about addressing housing market pressures due to global flows of money, people, and jobs.

- *Protect and Support Diversity:* Take actions to protect and promote diversity of incomes, backgrounds, and household types across the City.
- *Protect Our Existing Affordable Housing for the Future:* Retain and preserve the affordability of the existing rental, co-op, and non-market homes, while balancing the need to renew and expand these buildings.
- *Renew Our Commitment to Partnerships for Affordable Housing:* New commitments by the City to new directions on affordable housing delivery, supporting and aligning with partners across all sectors, particularly non-profit, co-op, and Indigenous housing partners, and building partnerships with new stakeholders.
- *Increase Supports and Protections for Renters and People who experience Homelessness:* Address affordability, security of tenure, and the determinants of poverty and housing instability.
- *Align City Processes with Housing Targets:* Align policies, processes, and tools.

Vancouver Is a City of Reconciliation

Vancouver is located on the unceded territories of the Musqueam, Squamish, and Tsleil-Waututh Nations. Vancouver is strengthened by Indigenous culture and values, lived and practised by both on- and off-reserve Indigenous residents. The City has intensified its commitment to strengthening relationships with both on- and off-reserve Indigenous partners through its City of Reconciliation initiatives, recognizing the need for important shifts in how we work together moving forward. As a City of Reconciliation, Vancouver's key priority will be to address the disproportionate effect of intergenerational cycles of poverty, often including trauma and homelessness, within urban Indigenous communities.

The principles of reconciliation determine that urban Indigenous community should be involved at all stages of the housing design, delivery, development, and evaluation process, to ensure each step is respectful of the diverse needs of the urban Indigenous community. Indigenous culture, the importance of elders, and Indigenous healing can further support dynamic housing options that foster healing and wellness, through the provision of services which are integrated into the built form and design of the project. For example, space to accommodate childcare, resident elders, Indigenous healing programmes, and social programmes for tenants links to meaningful employment and tenant counselling services.

The Right Supply Can Create More Housing Choices for Diverse Households

A key response to housing affordability needs a focus on increasing housing supply. This is an obvious and critical part of any response to big city urban housing affordability challenges, but the key shift in *Housing Vancouver* from the previous housing strategy was that this new supply had to be the right supply and affordable to people who live and work in the City – new homes with a connection to local incomes, like market rental, co-op, and social housing, as well as a new supply that provided a more varied type of home, like low- and mid-rise apartments, townhouses, coach, and laneway homes. Core goals include retaining the diversity of incomes in the City, by shifting current housing production towards rental housing in order to respond to household need. Further, targets were set for new homes across a broad spectrum of households, including those with very low income.

The strategy identifies a target of 72,000 new homes, with 65% to be new rental homes. Almost half will be for households earning less than $80,000 per year and 40% will be for families. *Housing Vancouver* quadrupled the previous target of purpose-built market rental, and it now stands at 20,000 homes, with 35% for families. At least 20% will be privately owned rental homes, with below-market rents secured on some homes for the long-term. In addition, there is target of 4,000 rental laneway homes, with 50% being suitable for families.

A significant amount of new homes will be below-market rental homes for individual households earning less than $50,000 and for families earning less than $80,000. Indeed, 12,000 new rental homes will be non-profit managed homes, including 2,000 new co-op homes and 4,100 homes with support, in order to meet the needs of lower-income households. This is a 50% increase from the previous strategy. The new social and supportive housing target will include homes for homeless individuals and vulnerable single-room occupancy (SRO) tenants currently living in inadequate housing and requiring supports.

Location, Tenure, and Built Form of the Right Supply

The location of new homes is critical, and they should be built near transit, jobs, key services, and amenities, such as community centres, schools, parks, and childcare. Higher growth corridors in the City are experiencing a growth in population, while lower density areas are seeing a decline in households, especially with families. The built form including height, density, and design has a direct impact on affordability of housing, who can live there, and how the building fits into existing neighbourhoods. A greater variety of built forms will be needed to accommodate diverse households, especially in lower density areas. The tenure of new homes is a strong determinant of who can afford to live there. Homes are needed across a broad continuum of income affordability and types, including social and co-op housing, below-market rental, market rental, and a diversity of ownership options. More recently, there has been proliferation of tenure options including rent-to-own models and co-housing.

Maintaining Diversity by Achieving the *Housing Vancouver* Targets

The City will make progress towards maintaining a diverse mix of households as a result of delivering on the ambitious *Housing Vancouver* targets, but none of this will happen without significant collaboration with private for-profit, non-profit, and government partners. An indication of the spread of affordability and new home types currently being delivered is depicted in Table 3.1. Social and supportive units did increase dramatically in 2017–2018. In terms of typology, the last five years have seen a steady increase in 1- and 3-bedroom units. For a full report on the latest progress on *Housing Vancouver*, refer to the Progress Report Dashboard 2019 (City of Vancouver, 2019a).

The City has key roles in creating the right supply, as an advocate, a regulator, and an investor, with the latter two being most significant. Some of the key strategies that optimize these roles and yield the right kind of supply are outlined below.

City as a Regulator of New Diverse, Affordable Homes

The City of Vancouver has a role in regulating land-use, which is critical when creating the right planning policy to increase the supply of rental homes (market, below-market, social, and co-op housing) along key transit corridors, which will improve access to jobs, schools, and community amenities for renters earning low and moderate incomes. The new *Broadway Plan* as and recently launched *City-Plan* are great opportunities for the City to identify areas around current and future transit hubs and corridors, as areas for growth and new rental homes,

TABLE 3.1 Social and Supportive Housing Approvals in Vancouver, 2015–2019

Year	Total Units	Shelter Rate Units (%)	HILs Units (%)[a]	LEM Units (%)[b]	Studio Units (%)	1-Bedroom Units (%)	2-Bedroom Units (%)	3-Bedroom Units (%)
2015	71	13	20	68	51	20	30	0
2016	518	16	34	47	42	23	30	13
2017	1,702	26	31	56	37	26	24	12
2018	1,938	38	18	48	47	19	20	11
2019	529	15	48	42	34	35	30	16

Source: BC Housing, 2019; City of Vancouver, 2019a, 2019c; and Government of British Columbia, 2019.

a Housing Income Limits (HIL) refers to BC Housing's maximum gross household income limits, established annually by the Canada Mortgage and Housing Corporation. For Metro Vancouver Housing, these income limits represent the maximum annual household income threshold, before taxes, for Rent-Geared-to-Income tenants.

b Low-End-of-Market (LEM) refers to a type of subsidized housing where rent is calculated based on rental market conditions. For Metro Vancouver Housing, LEM rates are generally set between 10% and 20% below true market rental rates for comparable buildings (e.g. similar area, building age, and amenities). LEM units are intended for moderate income households who exceed the income thresholds for rent-geared-to-income housing but do not exceed the asset limit or income limit for LEM housing.

including both market and below-market options. In a paper on "Strengthening Economic Cases for Housing Policies", the researchers lay out clear benefits to the creation and subsidy of new homes in key locations in urban areas, including productivity and human capital gains, effective labour supply, and productive travel time savings, which justify government investment in new homes (Maclennan et al., 2019). Sites at and near current and future transit hubs and amenity-rich areas will be prioritized for new secured rental and social housing, including housing developed under new programmes that secure affordability in new market rental. Data on approval of new housing units in 2017–2018 indicate compliance with targets (over 107%), with particularly strong performance in the category of housing for owners earning over $150,000/year (158% of the two-year target) as well as in the renter/owner category of households earning $80,000–$150,000 per year (125% of the two-year target). Most of the new housings in these two categories include higher density apartments and purpose-built rental (Table 3.2). Complementary City policies pertaining to intensification of residential areas through laneway housing have provided a boost to the affordable housing supply. The solutions for low-income renters are mostly through social housing, which is dependent on capital subsidies from senior levels of government and is relatively close to targets.

The Rental 100 Program, which has incentivized thousands of new market rental homes, is currently under review, and therefore presents an opportunity for further alignment with *Housing Vancouver's* objectives and targets. *Vancouver's Moderate Income Rental Pilot* is a new programme, wherein developments led by private for-profit developers secure a number of permanently affordable rental homes, targeted to households with annual incomes between $30,000 and $80,000. There are other *Housing Vancouver* goals that could lead to the transformation of low-density neighbourhoods by increasing the diverse supply of homes through a variety of housing types and affordable tenure options.

Housing Vancouver identifies the opportunity to include the right supply of homes into current and future planning policies, plans, and processes, including a review of *Vancouver's Sustainable Large Sites Policy.* Staff can consider moderate adjustments to height and density to enable more affordable homes to assist with affordability. The effective use of inclusionary housing policies has created a significant pipeline of new homes where the requirement was set out in a planning

TABLE 3.2 Housing Units Approved, 2017–2018

Building Type	Housing Type	Renter	Renter	Renter	Renter	Renter & Owner	Owner	Total Units
Income		**< $15K/yr**	**$15–30K/yr**	**$30–50K/yr**	**$50–80K/yr**	**$80–150K/yr**	**>$150K/yr**	
Apartment	Supportive and social	962	85	776	1,206	611		**3,640**
Apartment	Purpose-built rental			0	957	896		**1,853**
Apartment	Condos				765	4,290	3,282	**8,338**
Infill	Laneways				608	692		**1,300**
Infill	Coach houses					0	0	**0**
Townhouses	Townhouses					89	186	**275**
Units	**Total (2017–2018)**	**962**	**85**	**776**	**3,536**	**6,578**	**3,469**	**15,406**
	Two-year target	1,040	320	900	4,700	5,240	2,200	**14,400**
	Percentage of two-year target	93	27	86	75	126	158	**107**

Source: City of Vancouver, 2019c.

policy or district schedule, and the City secured new homes and/or an air-space parcel through a rezoning or development permit process. These homes are then leased long-term to non-profit or co-op housing providers, who offer a range of affordable rent to diverse households. Currently, around 2,500 homes towards the 12,000 new social and supportive *Housing Vancouver* target are being delivered through this stream.

It is not just the number and affordability of homes that is important when considering mix and diversity. Design principles that build homes that meet the needs of Vancouver's diverse households and populations are vital, including incorporating design principles for family-oriented, co-housing, seniors, and accessible housing, and emerging Indigenous housing design principles. Ideally, new rental homes should be accompanied by key services and supports for people and households with intersecting housing, childcare, health, and economic needs and challenges. *Housing Vancouver* also recognizes that simplifying city regulations and reducing approval times is a clear contribution that the City makes to the delivery of affordable rental housing.

City as an Investor in Diversity

The purchase and provision of City land has been a successful and long-standing approach to create new affordable homes and leverage investments from both non-profit and government partners. The City set up the Vancouver Affordable Housing Agency (VAHA) to oversee the acquisition and development of new affordable homes on its land. VAHA currently has around 2,500 homes in various stages of development and construction, and is also now in the process of creating the *Vancouver Affordable Housing Endowment Fund* (VAHEF), which will bring together all the City's affordable housing and land assets together in one portfolio to streamline the management and improve housing outcomes. Many of the new homes in development have brought in equity and financing from the provincial and federal governments, and they are being developed in partnership with the community housing sector.

In addition to the use of City land for new affordable housing supply, the City is also a director/investor of capital grants into the community housing sector, where they are developing new affordable homes on their own land. The City of Vancouver has been offering capital grants between $10,000 and $30,000 per home, but due to the rising costs of construction, the need to address equity imbalances, and greater affordability being targeted in *Housing Vancouver*, this grant programme is currently under review.

Preserving Existing Homes

A backdrop to the current drive to maintain diversity is through existing rental homes, including social and co-op housing, sometimes on City land, where it will be important to balance the need to prioritize reinvestment and affordability with opportunities to expand the number of affordable homes. The City has a critical role in these opportunities. It remains essential to engage with the federal government on key housing issues relating to supporting critical repairs, reinvestment, and renewal of housing subsidies for existing affordable housing through *Canada's Housing Strategy*. This includes the implementation of programmes that dedicate funding to urgent repairs in social and co-op housing.

Supportive Housing Is a Positive Contribution to Diverse Communities

A home is a primary factor for individuals experiencing homelessness in supporting the move forward towards balance and healing. The delivery of *Housing First* supportive housing is the practice of offering independent, permanent housing to those individuals experiencing homelessness, and then providing support. Supportive housing options across all communities in Vancouver provide access to those experiencing homelessness, along with mental, physical, and addiction challenges, so that they become housed in the communities they are living in or have a strong connection to. In 2019, the City of Vancouver, in partnership with BC Housing, completed phase one of a *Rapid Response to Homelessness* programme, including 600 new temporary modular supportive homes in 13 buildings across ten different sites in Vancouver, with supports provided by experienced non-profit housing providers. One of these buildings prioritizes black and Indigenous residents, two of them are managed in partnership with an Indigenous housing provider, and another two projects prioritize women with experience of homelessness. The partners are currently working together on phase two.

Conclusion

The threat of Vancouver's housing crisis on diversity has required the City to take significant actions in its housing strategy. The intersection between housing affordability challenges and marginalization, including gender and sexual identity, race, poverty, family status, and mental and physical health, has become a powerful force limiting the future of inclusion, diversity, and mixed communities in Vancouver. While mixed-income communities have long been a policy focus, *Housing Vancouver* has a broader focus on diversity and looks to provide a fuller range of new affordable homes that can better meet the needs of those who live and work in Vancouver. There is more work to be done to implement this strategy with partners like the community housing sector, more support needed from provincial and federal governments, and more bold steps by the City, if we are to keep Vancouver's diversity and enable it to be home to individuals and families from different incomes and backgrounds.

Acknowledgements

This chapter is based on the City of Vancouver's latest housing strategy, *Housing Vancouver (-2018–2027)*, and so it is important to acknowledge all the City of Vancouver's councilors, staff, partners, stakeholders, and public who contributed during the year-long process of convening and testing new ideas and approaches to addressing housing affordability in Vancouver. https://council.vancouver.ca/20171128/documents/rr1appendixa.pdf

Special thanks to Dr Tsenkova for the organization of the international symposium on partnerships for affordable housing and for her assistance with the chapter presenting Vancouver's experience.

References

BC Housing (2019). "BC Housing 2019 Housing Income Limits (HILs)". Website accessed October 2019, www.bchousing.org/publications/2019-Housing-Income-Limits-HILs.pdf

Canada Mortgage and Housing Corporation (CMHC) (2016a). "Rental Market Report – British Columbia Highlights". Website accessed October 2019, https://eppdscrmssa01.blob.core.windows.net/cmhcprodcontainer/sf/project/cmhc/pubsandreports/esub/_all_esub_pdfs/64487_2016_a01.pdf?sv=2018-03-28&ss=b&srt=sco&sp=r&se=2021-05-07T03:55:04Z&st=2019-05-06T19:55:04Z&spr=https,http&sig=bFocHM6noLjK8rlhy11dy%2BkQJUBX%2BCDKzkjLHfhUIU0%3D

CHMC (2016b). "Rental Market Report – Vancouver CMA". Website accessed October 2019, https://eppdscrmssa01.blob.core.windows.net/cmhcprodcontainer/sf/project/cmhc/pubsandreports/esub/_all_esub_pdfs/64467_2016_a01.pdf?sv=2018-03-28&ss=b&srt=sco&sp=r&se=2021-05-07T03:55:04Z&st=2019-05-06T19:55:04Z&spr=https,http&sig=bFocHM6noLjK8rlhy11dy%2BkQ-JUBX%2BCDKzkjLHfhUIU0%3D

Chisholm, S., and Hulchanski, D. (2019). "Canada's Housing Story", in D. Maclennan, H. Pawson, K. Gibb, S. Chisholm and D. Hulchanski (eds)., *Shaping Futures Changing the Housing Story Final Report*. Glasgow: Policy Scotland, University of Glasgow, p. 27.

City of Vancouver (2019a). "City of Vancouver Progress Report Dashboard 2019 – Q3 Update". Website accessed October 2019, https://vancouver.ca/files/cov/2019-housing-vancouver-dashboard.pdf

City of Vancouver (2019b). "Housing Vancouver Strategy". Website accessed October 2019, https://council.vancouver.ca/20171128/documents/rr1appendixa.pdf

City of Vancouver (2019c). "Housing Vancouver Strategy: Annual Progress Report and Data Book 2019". Website accessed October 2019, https://vancouver.ca/files/cov/2019-housing-vancouver-annual-progress-report-and-data-book.pdf

City of Vancouver (2019d). "Vancouver Homeless Count 2019". Website accessed October 2019, https://vancouver.ca/files/cov/vancouver-homeless-count-2019-final-report.pdf

Generation Squeeze (2019). "Straddling the Gap: A Troubling Portrait of Home Prices, Earnings and Affordability for Younger Canadians". Website accessed October 2019, https://d3n8a8pro7vhmx.cloudfront.net/gensqueeze/pages/5293/attachments/original/1560279096/Straddling-the-Gap-2019_final.pdf?1560279096

Government of British Columbia (2019). "Shelter Component of Income Assistance – Income Assistance Rate Table". Website accessed October 2019, www2.gov.bc.ca/gov/content/governments/policies-for-government/bcea-policy-and-procedure-manual/bc-employment-and-assistance-rate-tables/income-assistance-rate-table

Maclennan, D. with: Randolph, B., Crommelin, L., Witte, E., Klestov, P., Scealy, B., and Brown, S. (2019). *Strengthening Economic Cases for Housing Policies.* Sydney: City Future Research Centre UNSW Built Environment, UNSW Sydney, pp. 24–25.

Statistics Canada (2013). *Vancouver, CY, British Columbia (Code 5915022) (Table). National Household Survey (NHS) Profile.* 2011 National Household Survey. Statistics Canada Catalogue no. 99-004-XWE. Ottawa. Website accessed October 4, 2019, www.12.statcan.gc.ca/nhs-enm/2011/dp-pd/prof/index.cfm?Lang=E

Statistics Canada (2014*). Lone-parent Families.* Ottawa: Statistics Canada. Website accessed April 16, 2021, www150.statcan.gc.ca/n1/pub/75-006-x/2015001/article/14202/parent-eng.htm

Statistics Canada (2017a). *Vancouver, CY [Census subdivision], British Columbia and Greater Vancouver, RD [Census Division], British Columbia (Table). Census Profile.* 2016 Census. Statistics Canada Catalogue no. 98-316-X2016001. Ottawa. Website accessed October 4, 2019, www12.statcan.gc.ca/census-recensement/2016/dp-pd/prof/index.cfm?Lang=E

Statistics Canada (2017b). *Vancouver [Census Metropolitan Area], British Columbia and Greater Vancouver, RD [Census Division], British Columbia (Table). Census Profile.* 2016 Census. Statistics Canada Catalogue no. 98-316-X2016001. Ottawa. Website accessed October 4, 2019, www12.statcan.gc.ca/census-recensement/2016/dp-pd/prof/index.cfm?Lang=E

4

AFFORDABLE HOUSING TRANSITION IN CALGARY

Sarah Woodgate, Teresa Goldstein, and Claire Noble

Introduction

The past 20 years have seen a period of change in the Calgary affordable housing sector. Rising housing costs and a rapidly increasing homeless population in the early to mid-2000s drew attention to Calgary's affordable housing issue. In 2008, *Calgary's 10 Year Plan to End Homelessness* was adopted, with a Housing First approach. In 2013, Calgary's poverty reduction strategy, *Enough for All*, was adopted, followed by *Foundations for Home*, Calgary's Corporate Affordable Housing Strategy 2016–2025. The emphasis on partnerships and collaboration saw the formation of Calgary's Community Housing Affordability Collective (CHAC), the collective engine for improving housing affordability through cross-sector collaboration, specific initiatives and project delivery, as well as coordinated sector-wide community-based advocacy for housing affordability-related matters. The affordable housing sector in Calgary has made great strides towards a more collaborative system, has developed many new partnerships, and is now reaping the rewards with improved coordination of service delivery for Calgarians seeking affordable housing programmes and services. Plans are underway to expand this collaboration further, starting with an alignment between CHAC and the Alberta Seniors and Community Housing Association (ASCHA) announced in December 2020.

Public awareness and support for affordable housing remains high. In the Fall 2020 Quality of Life and Citizen Satisfaction Survey, more than half of the residents urged the City to invest more in affordable housing. Almost 95% of Calgarians indicated that affordable housing for low-income families and individuals is important. Affordable housing has been an ongoing top citizen priority. Furthermore, there is renewed national interest and support by the Government of Canada. Current conditions present an excellent opportunity to advance affordable housing solutions.

This chapter explores the City's strategic directions for affordable housing policy through three primary focus areas:

- *Preservation of existing supply:* maintain the existing affordable housing currently available through investment, renovation and repair, and programme modernization of existing affordable housing;

DOI: 10.4324/9781003172949-4

- *Scaling-up the non-profit housing sector:* moving all municipal levers available to increase the overall housing supply to at minimum achieve the average supply of non-market housing compared with Canada's big cities; and
- *Improving the housing system:* a people-centric service approach through partnerships to facilitate individual and community well-being for those served.

The Calgary Context

Housing Supply

In 2018, The City of Calgary released its report, *Housing in Canada's Big Cities,* comparing Calgary's housing supply and affordability to Canada's seven largest cities. The key findings from that report were that Calgary's housing supply differs substantially from other Canadian cities. Among the major cities in Canada, Calgary has the highest rate of homeownership and single-family housing, and the lowest supply of purpose-built rental, subsidized housing and co-operative housing. These differences appear to have been influenced by:

- Timing of development: The bulk of housing in Calgary was built during economic 'booms', when demand and incomes were high. Historic market response has been to build an expensive, homogenous supply;
- Income inequality: Calgary has the highest income inequality among the big cities. The proportion of households earning higher incomes is very large, as is the income gap. This has influenced market response, as well as public policy;
- Incentive: There has been a lack of incentive to build some types of housing. This is a result of market demand, but also government funding and policy. Calgary was a relatively small city when government incentives encouraged a wider variety of housing types, and so the City benefitted less from these investments.

The results are a well-served higher-income population and an underserved lower-income population, and while this lower-income population is small, compared to the rest of Calgary, their housing options are limited (The City of Calgary, 2018a).

Overall, the private sector meets the housing needs of over 78% of Calgary's households. Only 4% of households earning over $80,000/year spend more than 30% of their income on shelter (The City of Calgary, 2018a). In terms of policy, the City is focused on maintaining housing affordability with intentional policy effort to support low- and moderate-income households. Calgary has a number of strengths to support affordable housing strategies such as private housing industry talent, a culture of partnership and a philanthropic mindset.

Calgary's non-market housing is provided by 51 organizations operating 12,448 non-market housing units. Overall, only three organizations operate over 500 units, while most organizations (36 of 51) operate fewer than 100 units (The City of Calgary, 2016a). While optimal portfolio size is in the range of 2,000–5,000 homes, however, this is highly dependent on context, geography, and operating models. Few Calgary affordable housing operators approach these numbers. This is why it is important to explore opportunities to scale-up non-market housing to create a more robust and resilient non-profit housing sector. Calgary Housing Company (CHC), a wholly owned subsidiary of The City of Calgary and the largest landlord, provides over 9,000 housing options to approximately 25,000 Calgarians (Calgary Housing Company, 2020). This includes the provision of over half of the non-market units available in Calgary

(6,811 units) (The City of Calgary, 2016a). The successful and effective management of housing programmes and housing assets is critical to the success of affordable housing.

Housing Need

In the fall of 2018, The City of Calgary released its *2018 Housing Needs Assessment*. The assessment shows that over 80,000 (or roughly one in five) households are in need of affordable housing.[1] The incidence of need is especially high for the following populations: singles, lone-parents, youth, Aboriginals, recent immigrants, and people with disabilities (The City of Calgary, 2018b). The study predicts that over 100,000 Calgary households will be in housing need by 2025, including over 65,000 renter households. This is due to overall population increase and a relatively constant proportion of households (18%) experiencing affordability constraints during the last 25 years. The need for affordable housing is growing much faster than the supply, by over 2,000 renter households per year, compared to a supply growth of approximately 300 units per year. Furthermore, Calgary has one of the lowest shares of rental housing stock in urban Canada, as well as the most expensive entry-level housing (The City of Calgary, 2018a). Rents in the lowest quintile (one-fifth of rental units) are among the highest of all Canadian cities (CMHC, 2015).

In Alberta, housing, transportation, and food make up nearly half of the average spending in the household budget. Average annual transportation costs vary greatly throughout Calgary and tend to be lowest in more central areas and those well-served by public transit. This is why it is important to implement policies to protect overall affordability in Calgary, as well as to locate affordable housing in areas that are well-served by transit. Furthermore, an estimated 11% of Calgary households experience food insecurity, which has been linked to negative health impacts. By providing affordable housing, a household is able to free up more money for nutritious food and other basic necessities. Affordable housing services are developed with consideration to affordable living and community well-being principles to achieve broader objectives including economic prosperity for citizens (The City of Calgary, 2018a).

Research on housing need shows a shortage of affordable housing units in Calgary, as well as a growing shortage forecast over the next ten years. This is why Calgary's strategies place such a high emphasis on protecting and increasing the supply of affordable housing by leveraging all tools available locally to ensure Calgary's readiness for national and provincial housing programmes. Overall affordable housing is seen as a key aspect of Calgary's competitiveness as a foundation for individuals and families to grow.

Foundations for Home: Calgary's Corporate Affordable Housing Strategy

How the City Focused on a Systems Approach to Help Maintain and Increase Supply, Leverage, Partner, and Improve the Housing System

Foundations for Home has a vision to increase the supply of affordable housing to the national average of non-market supply of 6%, and to enable the development of a transformed housing system where collaboration between stakeholders drives better outcomes for individuals and community through safe, affordable housing solutions.

In 2016, The City of Calgary adopted *Foundations for Home*, Calgary's Corporate Affordable Housing Strategy 2016–2025. The strategy includes six strategic objectives, each hinged on bringing partnerships together, refocusing on increasing and preserving Calgary's affordable housing supply, providing expedited planning approvals or leveraging City land. Furthermore, two of the objectives focus on improving the housing system (The City of Calgary, 2016b). The strategy is accompanied by an implementation plan that defines initiatives and actions for each objective (The City of Calgary, 2016c). Together, the six objectives address every City lever to meaningfully advance affordable housing in Calgary.

Strategic Direction #1 – Get the Calgary Community Building

The City knows that it cannot meet the need for affordable housing alone, which is why the first strategic objective is to get the Calgary community building non-market housing, thereby reducing the proportion of housing offered directly by government over time. The City focused on supporting the scaling-up of non-profit providers in several ways based on feedback on gaps in the housing system. This resulted in a number of initiatives that emerged in the early 2000s including momentum created through the *10 Year Plan to End Homelessness (2008–2018)* and an ambitious $120 million affordable housing fundraising campaign, which involved the private and non-profit sectors' philanthropic mobilization. Nine large housing developments materialized enhancing the competencies of non-profit agencies to act as developers and asset managers of affordable housing on a large scale. Two key gaps where the City could play a role were the cost and time expended to process development approval applications by non-profit providers intending to build affordable housing. To increase the non-market housing supply provided by non-profit providers, the City has created a new Affordable Housing Coordinator role within the Planning & Development department, tasked to understand the housing pipeline, to ensure priority service to affordable housing development applications, and to champion these applications through the approval process. The City of Calgary also launched Calgary's *Housing Incentive Program* (HIP) in 2016 to support non-profit affordable housing developers with pre-development grants of up to $50,000 and City fee rebates that typically range from $100,000 to $400,000 per project. The programme has supported over 2,000 new affordable housing units to date. The non-profit sector has expressed a high level of satisfaction with these programmes, resulting in an average of 177 days for processing of development permits from submission to approval.

The Affordable Housing Tracker was introduced to help track progress towards addressing Calgary's shortfall of affordable housing. The toolset includes series of reports on affordable housing development in Calgary since January 2016. It captures new construction supported by the City, including active and completed developments, and includes preliminary inquiries and pre-applications. Since 2016, 1,171 City-supported new affordable housing units have been completed. There are an additional 1,806 units currently under development (The City of Calgary, 2020). This represents a progress of 20% against the 15,000 non-market units targeted in the Affordable Housing Strategy. Even with additional funding, as outlined in the *COVID-19 Community Affordable Housing Advocacy Plan*, we anticipate reaching a maximum of 6,651 units by 2025, or 44% of the 15,000 unit goal. The large majority (78%) of units that were completed or under development came from the non-profit sector.

December 2020 marked another milestone in scaling-up the non-profit housing sector in Calgary. The Government of Canada announced $24.6 million in *Rapid Housing Initiative* funding for 176 new units of affordable housing in Calgary through a new innovative municipal bilateral stream. The new units will be delivered through three projects: a hotel conversion into a seniors' resident (by Silvera for Seniors), new modular homes for women and children fleeing domestic violence (by Horizon Housing), and new homes for Indigenous people as part of a rehabilitation of an old building (by HomeSpace Society). There is additional funding available under the *Rapid Housing Initiative* in 2021 that could help further add affordable housing supply in Calgary for citizens experiencing or at-risk of homelessness. With the Government of

Canada announcement in 2020 to eliminate chronic homelessness, there is potential for future significant additional investment to support the scaling-up of non-profit housing (The Government of Canada, 2020). While there is much work that needs to be done to close the supply gap for affordable housing in Calgary, the newly established programmes offered by the City in partnerships with housing providers positively position the City to benefit from federal affordable housing programmes. One limitation to increase the affordable housing supply is the gap of available operating dollars for supportive housing and rent supplement programmes to expand housing options for the lowest-income households.

Strategic Direction #2 – Leverage City Land

In 2015, non-profit housing providers identified access to land at discounted value as a key barrier towards increasing affordable housing supply. Another challenge for non-profits was navigating timing and criteria for federal, provincial, and municipal housing programmes. To address these barriers, the second strategic direction leverages City land to support and scale-up non-market housing providers, allowing them to build their assets, scale-up their housing portfolios, and increase their financial sustainability while also accessing federal and provincial housing programmes. The initial target approved by City Council was to sell ten parcels of City-owned land below the market value for affordable housing by 2018 through a pilot programme. Successful applicants automatically qualified for grant funding through the City's HIP and Canada Mortgage and Housing Corporation's (CMHC) SEED Funding programme. The pilot resulted in the sale of six development sites, generating up to 165 new affordable homes constructed and occupied in about two years. The City invested $6.4 million in land value, which brought in more than $30 million in federal, philanthropic, and private sectors funding for the projects. This initiative provided a variety of new affordable housing choices meeting gaps in housing supply, including home ownership for families through Habitat for Humanity, tiny modular housing for veterans by Homes for Heroes in partnership with Atco, and permanent supportive housing for singles provided by Home Space in partnership with private sector builders.

The success of the pilot project resulted in a Council-approved Non-Market Housing Land Disposition Policy and ongoing City land programme committing to release up to ten parcels of developable land every two years (The City of Calgary, 2019). Subsequently, five City-owned development sites were offered to non-profits at below-market value in January 2020. New to the programme in 2020, successful applicants were eligible to receive additional funding under CMHC's *National Housing Co-Investment Fund* through an expanded City/federal programme coordination pilot.

Land sale is currently the preferred method over land leases to scale-up the non-profit financial capacity and asset-building opportunities and provide the non-profit with greater accountability over the condition of the building and the land asset to achieve strategic housing objectives. To ensure that the public benefit is met over a long term, the City is entering into housing agreements with the successful non-profits, a new provision under the *Alberta Municipal Government Act*. This programme will support affordable housing providers to develop institutional capacity of the sector as well as result in increased supply.

Strategic Direction #3 – Design and Build New City Units

The third strategic direction is the design and build of new City-owned affordable housing units. The City's short-term target to open 270 units in 2017 and 2018 represents a near-doubling of the number built in previous years and accounted for all of the remaining capital dollars in

FIGURE 4.1 Affordable Housing in Wildwood and Rosedale.
Source: © Sasha Tsenkova.

the City's affordable housing budget. This strategic direction is critical given Calgary's shortage of affordable housing, and complements the new affordable housing built by the non-profit sector. Wildwood is an example of a recently completed City-initiated development (see Figure 4.1).

The City's previous affordable housing developments were often done on large rectangular lots. Recent solutions utilize other types of lots, such as remnant parcels, transit-oriented development sites, and restoration and reuse of heritage properties. The City piloted 16 narrow units on eight sites in Calgary created through a City-wide redevelopment initiative along Highway 1. These Rosedale homes shown in Figure 4.1 are now complete and occupied.

The City is also developing 62 units in Bridlewood community. The energy-efficient performance of these homes is 41% better than standard in the 2015 National Energy Code for Buildings. Water efficiency meets LEED V4 requirements. Five units have photovoltaic solar cells linked to the individual electrical metre system to support the tenants in their bills. One of the seven town homes is built to higher energy efficiency standards allowing for the comparison of simple return on investment through lower operating costs in relation to the increased construction costs. In addition, the City is developing 145 units in the Rundle community and completing the concept design of 200 units in Southview community along International Avenue.

The City is also looking for opportunities to both retain existing units and incorporate new units along the future green line of the light rail transit (LRT) system and to integrate affordable housing with other civic uses, such as fire halls, libraries, and recreation centres. The combination of mixed used facilities optimizes City land holdings and creates opportunities for vibrant, dynamic, and successful living environments for the future residents with access to quality programmes, services, and volunteer opportunities. Furthermore, the City is moving towards creating 1-, 2-, and 3-bedroom accessible units to accommodate both individuals and families with accessibility needs.

Strategic Direction #4 – Regenerate City-owned Properties

The strategic direction is intended to protect the existing affordable housing supply, which is important given Calgary's large supply shortage. The average age of affordable housing provided by CHC is over 30 years and in need of major repairs. Since 2017, hundreds of existing homes have undergone critical major repair and condition assessment. The majority of existing City- and CHC-owned affordable housing properties can be fully retrofitted at a fraction of the cost of investing in new units. In the case of a redevelopment in Bankview, the investment prolonged the building's life by 25 years, while improving and updating the building to meet the current demographics and building condition standards. The full repair and renovation of Bankview affordable housing was $50,000/unit. The project also transitioned units from full market rental housing (rent-geared-to-income) to mixed-income rental housing offering an increased supply of homes to low- and moderate-income households without the requirement for government subsidy.

Undertaking strategic redevelopments has allowed the City to stretch capital funding even further to optimize land and real estate options. In 2021, a rental housing property with 75 units in the community of Rundle is being closed due to the site conditions. Plans are underway for a new mixed market development to proceed on the site, with up to 145 new homes further expanding housing options. The decision to close a property is significant and impacts residents. CHC has been actively supporting tenants to transition to alternate housing. These supports include linking tenants to other available housing providers and offering discounted rents for 18 months and partnering with a non-profit provider who is helping residents save up to $7,000 to support their housing transition. Five households are participating in an affordable homeownership programme for acquiring their own home. The current residents are also involved in the redesign process for the new development.

Strategic Direction #5 – Strengthen Intergovernmental Partnerships

This strategic direction reflects the philosophy that affordable housing is a shared responsibility of all orders of government, as well as the value that the City places on collaboration. The City's *Non-Profit Land Transfer Program* is an example of where collaboration has occurred between the City and the federal government. Successful recipients of the programme also receive funding from the City's HIP and a dedicated addition from the CMHC's SEED funding programme, marking a meaningful collaboration between two levels of government. CMHC reviewed the applications concurrently to analyse them for SEED Funding eligibility. This is the first-of-its kind collaboration between The City of Calgary and the federal government to expedite the release of land and funding for affordable housing development through a streamlined application process for non-profit providers. This collaboration allowed for a stacking of programmes between governments to respond to local need, have one application point for non-profit providers, and reduce the application review time. The coordination of government programmes results in more streamlined process for government officials administering the programme and has supported efficient housing delivery timelines for housing providers. By leveraging the unique roles of each government through coordinated programme delivery, there is significant opportunity to more rapidly deliver affordable housing solutions and to align the different levels of government. This approach for coordinated affordable housing application review between local, provincial, and federal governments can be a model for future intergovernmental partnerships (Box 4.1).

The City is also working closely with the Provincial Government through the City's participation in the *Big City Housing* collaborative to improve the quality of life of Albertans in need of affordable housing. In July 2020, the City and the Province of Alberta signed a four-year, $34-million operating funding agreement governing the delivery of the City's Community

BOX 4.1: HOMESPACE-36 STREET SE

HomeSpace Society was selected as the successful organization to purchase a parcel of land in the City's Southeast through the City's non-profit land transfer programme. The programme offered City land at below-book value to eligible non-market housing providers with the goal of helping to scale-up the housing sector and increase the supply of non-market units in the City. HomeSpace's proposed project will provide 38 studio units of permanent supported living in the southeast community of Forest Lawn. The units range in size from 250 to 300 square feet, and the building also includes common spaces such as a communal kitchen to serve as a gathering area for the residents.

The City supported the project by placing all related development applications on prioritized accelerated timelines. The complete approval timeline from submission of the land-use re-designation application to the approval of the development permit application was 105 days. The project also received support from the City's HIP including a $50,000 grant to cover pre-development expenses and an estimated additional $92,000 to cover City development application fees and offsite levy costs. CMHC partnered with the City to provide dedicated funding towards supporting the feasibility and start-up costs associated with the project, helping it as it proceeds forward through development.

Housing Portfolio (CHP) of 1,048 units. This new agreement, to maintain the supply of existing housing through a mixed-rent model, comes into effect in 2021. This agreement is a joint affordable housing commitment and partnership between the City and the Province that helps ensure that affordable housing in Calgary is adequately funded and maintained to meet health and safety standards and to provide opportunities to low-income Calgarians.

The signing of this progressive funding agreement with the Province will enable the transition of all City-owned housing to a mixed-rent model. Mixed-rent housing allows households of mixed financial means to live as neighbours. The renewed operating agreement, which will be implemented through a gradual transition towards mixed-rent housing, will enable more operating flexibility with simplified regulation, serve a diversity of households that fall under the income thresholds, and reduce government subsidy over time. This initiative, combined with additional federal and provincial investment in new affordable housing units, will support a more sustainable affordable housing supply in the long term that requires less government subsidy over time.

Strategic Direction #6 – Improve the Housing System

The final strategic direction is to improve the housing system through research, programmes, and partnership to create better outcomes for people. This reflects the values of becoming people-centred as well as evidence-based. It also reflects the recognition of the complexity of the housing system, and that collaboration is necessary for the most effective delivery of services to people. *The Foundation for Home Community Development Plan*, One Window Project, and the City's participation in CHAC fall under this strategic direction.

In 2016, the City launched *The Foundation for Home Community Development Program ("The Home Program")*. This micro grant programme includes a number of projects aimed at meeting two key outcomes for people living in affordable housing: to improve resident self-sufficiency and enhance community well-being. RentSmart is an adult education programme developed by Ready to Rent BC. It aims at empowering renters, who understand their rights and responsibilities with a focus on stable and successful tenancies. The curriculum covers a number of topics including the understanding the *Residential Tenancies Act*, managing finances, and taking care of the home. So far, *The Home Program* has supported over eight cohorts of CHC tenants, more than 68 tenants in total, to graduate from RentSmart. It has also supported over 12 non-profit organization to attend a trainer course to deliver RentSmart to their own tenants looking to move from supportive care and shelters into independent living.

The One Window Project is another example of efforts to improve the housing system. It aims at creating a coordinated intake process across 60 independent organizations that operate non-market housing in Calgary. The goal is to improve the application experience from a client perspective, so that more people can be efficiently and successfully housed. CHAC has expressed the desire to extend the One Window solution for Province-wide application. In December 2020, The Government of Alberta accepted the *Alberta Affordable Housing Review Panel* recommendation #14 to "Work with housing operators to develop a centralized housing portal to manage waiting lists, including vacancies, and develop standardized application forms for the community housing and seniors lodge programs" (SHS Consulting, 2020).

Affordable Housing Service Delivery by Calgary Housing Company and The City of Calgary

How the City's Housing Policy Has Refocused on Maintaining Existing Affordable Housing through Investment, Renovation, and Programme Modernization of Existing Social Housing Projects

In 2015, Calgary City Council identified a need to reorganize how housing services were delivered. The change included bringing the City-owned not-for-profit corporation – CHC – and the City affordable housing functions together as two legal entities under one service called Calgary

---

BOX 4.2: PARTNERSHIP WITH LEFTOVERSYYC

The City's partnership with LeftoversYYC is an example of an activity to increase affordable housing residents' access to well-being services and activities (Leftovers Calgary Foundation, 2018). The Community Mobile Food Market is a community-driven grocery store on wheels that increases the availability of healthy and affordable foods in underserved neighbourhoods of Calgary. The goals of the Community Mobile Food Market are to:

- Build upon existing community assets to strengthen community;
- Highlight other organizations in the community as opportunities to strength partnerships/ leverage existing services;
- Increase access to affordable, healthy products.

The market is open to all regardless of financial income with a goal to bring healthy food to the door at a reduced cost, and, as a result, reduce potential barriers individuals may face. The work of community organizations to leverage partnerships and pilot innovative programmes such as LeftoversYYC has worked to increase access to residents' well-being services, creating stronger ties within between neighbourhoods and increasing in volunteerism.

Housing. The idea behind the reorganization was to maintain the existing affordable housing supply, work collectively with both the creation and operation of new and regenerated affordable housing, as well as modernize existing programs and services. Calgary Housing is embedded within the Community Service department, which includes fire, parks, recreation, emergency management, neighbourhoods, and community standard (911) services. This change has enabled the frontline housing services staff to coordinate service needs with other municipal functions, thereby streamlining processes and focusing on citizen-centred service delivery. Many of the initiatives described below target CHC's top challenges: insufficient and uncertain funding, management of third-party assets, and incomplete operating agreements with government partners.

Asset Management

Calgary Housing Company's Strategic Asset Management Program supports long-term planning of its assets. CHC is now providing asset management service to the City for housing that is in their ownership and has begun investing in the upgrading of City-owned social housing units including the upgrading of units in community housing to a new base standard. There is a cultural shift from an emphasis on modest standard to an emphasis on competitive rental products to shift to a mixed market portfolio approach. A focus on asset management is critical given that the condition of third-party assets and the inadequate reserve funds are among CHC's top challenges. The *Municipal Stimulus Program* (MSP) will fund $9.3 million in major repairs in 2021.

Sustainability

CHC's *Sustainability Program* uses operational data and financial forecasting to identify recommendations and innovations to address the impact of the expiry of federal and provincial operating agreements to CHC. This programme is informed by best practices to ensure financial sustainability and viability for CHC. The programme includes the optimization of assets as well as the provision of data and information to inform advocacy and future decision-making.

The sustainability programme also supports deeper analysis of the viability of mixed market portfolios offering a mix of near-market rent and deep subsidy without operating subsidies. To date, applying a mixed market portfolio has provided over $25 million in returns to the City in ten years, which is reinvestment in new housing and City programmes. The CHC also has programmes in place for temporary relief of rent for near-market tenants who may need additional social supports and who face financial challenges, which is a unique role compared to a traditional landlord.

Mixed Market Model

CHC is transitioning to a mixed market rental model as it adds new buildings to its portfolio. This type of portfolio offers several benefits in that it is more financially sustainable, socially integrates low-income households throughout the portfolio, and has the potential to support and accommodate households as their circumstances and needs change. It is both sustainable and people-focused.

Portfolio Management Approach

To leverage the implementation of sound asset management, sustainability, and mixed market principles, a portfolio management approach has been implemented which involves cross-corporate integration of information on property condition, operation, and tenancy to optimize the provision of safe affordable housing into the future. Portfolio management introduces the alignment of capital investments, maintenance, and tenancy with the intention of delivering housing that is financially sustainable, supports defined programme requirements, and remains operationally viable. The intent of portfolio management is to monitor property performance, strategically invest in existing properties when appropriate, and make the recommendation to discontinue property operation when it can no longer viably sustain required operational and financial requirements. An example of the implementation of this portfolio management approach is the assessment and decision to redevelop the Rundle property described above. An assessment of the current property based on property condition, forecasted investment requirements, potential for increased unit intensity, and property location was conducted. This resulted in a decision that the current infrastructure on the property was no longer viable, but the land provided excellent proximity to amenities for families and allowed an increase in the number of units. A recommendation was made to demolish the current property, reallocate tenants, and commission a preliminary design to determine the need for new funding.

A People-Focused Approach

CHC has transitioned from a focus on primarily bricks and mortar to a more people-focused approach. This reflects a gradual philosophical shift that is related to the Housing First concept. CHC believes that tenant perspectives should play a significant role in shaping priorities for tenant service. In 2017, the tenant advisory group (TAG) was formed, and the first Tenant Satisfaction Survey was administered. Tenant engagement has also been utilized as a tool to inform the future state for Calgary Housing's Transformation. It will be important to ensure that such engagement continues and informs decision-making and continuous improvement for all facets of service delivery. Together the goal is to provide services that support tenants to achieve individual and community well-being towards their highest potential, including opportunities for civic engagement.

Partnerships and coordinated services between providers is key to delivering this people-focused approach. An example is CHC's *Opportunities for Homeownership Program* which brings five local agencies together to educate tenants on their options for home ownership. As well, CHC has partnered with Habitat for Humanity to identify new homes specifically for tenants and has seen over 100 households per year transition to affordable home ownership since 2016. Another example is *Bridging the Gap*, a CHC programme aimed at supporting people in their transitions from supportive housing to independent housing. This transition programme has freed up homes for new Housing First clients with successful transitions for the graduates into independent living.

Conclusion

Over the past 20 years, Calgary has seen a period of significant change in the affordable housing sector. Research on housing need highlights the continued pressing need to increase the affordable housing supply and to scale-up non-profit affordable housing providers. The change to bring CHC and the City affordable housing functions together has created a number of opportunities for increased collaboration and aligned service delivery. This, combined with philosophical shifts and market challenges, has led to the advancement of a number of initiatives around asset management, sustainability, and a more people-focused approach. In the future, CHC will emphasize programmes that are flexible, tied to the person, and empowering. The

City is on track to meet the targets and commitments laid out in *Foundations for Home: Calgary's Corporate Affordable Housing Strategy*. Through the creation of strong partnerships across the sector and within CHAC, and plans to expand this collaboration further, Calgary is well underway to realize its vision for affordable housing.

Across all activities within the Calgary affordable housing sector, the key to success has been collaboration: within The City of Calgary itself, with other orders of government, with housing providers, with community organizations, and with affordable housing residents. It takes a coordinated effort from everyone to deliver safe, appropriate, inclusive housing options for the entire community. A strong and healthy housing system is one that is flexible to respond to market and political changes, and it is dependent on long-term political support. Working together, the capacity exists to establish programmes and policies that will create success into the future, remove barriers, generate creative solutions, and drive systemic change to improve the lives of low- and moderate-income Calgarians.

Acknowledgements

The authors acknowledge the contribution of the following experts: Cheryl Selinger, Leanne Hall, Medhat Hanna, Raja Brahmakshatriya, Tim Ward, Meaghan Bell, Kendra Ramdanny, Katherine Plotnick, Susan Sanderson, Katie Gusa, Nina Nagy – The City of Calgary; Community Housing Affordability Collective Steering Committee members 2018; Calgary Housing Corporate Management Team – Aminda Galappaththi, Maureen Swanson, Greg Wilkes, Meaghan Bell, John Veenstra, Bruce Sinclair, Bo Jiang, Brandi Kapell, Jana Tchinkova; Calgary Housing Company Board of Directors

Note

1   The City of Calgary defines a household as in need of affordable housing if they are currently spending more than 30% of income on shelter and they earn no more than 65% of the Calgary median income.

References

Calgary Housing Company. (2020). Calgary Housing Company Annual Report 2019. http://calgary housingcompany.org/wp-content/uploads/2018-Annual-Report_Final_opt.pdf, accessed December 18, 2020

Canada Mortgage and Housing Corporation. (2016). Purpose-Built Rental Apartments with Rents in the Lowest Rent Quintile. http://publications.gc.ca/collections/collection_2017/schl-cmhc/nh12-268/NH12-268-2016-2-eng.pdf, accessed December 18, 2020

Leftovers Calgary Foundation. (2018). https://yyc.rescuefood.ca/cmm-project, accessed August 31, 2018

SHS Consulting. (2020). Final Report of the Alberta Affordable Housing Review Panel. https://open.alberta.ca/publications/final-report-of-alberta-affordable-housing-review-panel, accessed January 4, 2021

The City of Calgary. (2016a). Housing in Calgary: An Inventory of Housing Supply, 2015/2016. www.calgary.ca/content/dam/www/cs/olsh/documents/affordable-housing/housing-in-calgary-inventory-housing-supply.pdf, accessed December 18, 2020

The City of Calgary. (2016b). Foundations for Home: Calgary's Corporate Affordable Housing Strategy 2016–2015. www.calgary.ca/cs/olsh/affordable-housing/affordable-housing.html, accessed December 18, 2020

The City of Calgary (2016c). Foundations for Home: Calgary's Corporate Affordable Housing Strategy Implementation Plan. www.calgary.ca/cs/olsh/affordable-housing/affordable-housing.html, accessed December 18, 2020

The City of Calgary. (2018a). Housing in Canada's Big Cities. www.calgary.ca/CS/OLSH/Documents/Affordable-housing/Housing-in-Canadas-Big-Cities.pdf, accessed December 18, 2020

The City of Calgary. (2018b). Housing Needs Assessment 2018. www.calgary.ca/content/dam/www/cs/olsh/documents/affordable-housing/affordable-housing-needs-assessment.pdf, accessed December 18, 2020

The City of Calgary. (2019). Non-Market Housing Land Disposition Policy. www.calgary.ca/content/dam/www/ca/city-clerks/documents/council-policy-library/non-market-housing-land-disposition-policy-2019.pdf, accessed January 5, 2021

The City of Calgary. (2020). Calgary Needs More Affordable Housing. www.calgary.ca/cs/olsh/-affordable-housing/community-affordable-housing-advocacy-plan-community-plan.html?redirect=/communityplan, accessed January 4, 2021

The Government of Canada. (2020). A Stronger and More Resilient Canada: A Speech from the Throne to Open the Second Session of the Forty-Third Parliament of Canada. www.canada.ca/content/dam/-pco-bcp/documents/pm/SFT_2020_EN_WEB.pdf, accessed January 5, 2021

5

AFFORDABLE HOUSING CHALLENGES

The Experience of the City of Edmonton

Jalene Anderson-Baron and Christel Kjenner

Introduction

The development of affordable housing[1] in Canada can be characterized as a patchwork of responses, cobbled together over the decades as support has fluctuated with prevailing political winds, shifting economic conditions, and changes in public support. For communities across Canada, partnerships have been necessary to leverage the resources of diverse partners working towards a common goal: the adequate provision of affordable rental housing. The City of Edmonton has fully embraced this collaborative approach. In recognizing that housing need is best understood at the local level, while explicitly acknowledging their fiscal limitations, the City has taken on the unique role of lead coordinator and facilitator, working to mobilize networks through a shifting approach over the decades. As political, economic, and social environments have changed, the City of Edmonton has adapted its response accordingly, variously working to set priorities and a guiding vision; advocate, develop, and deliver programmes and housing projects; facilitate partnerships; create and implement policy, regulations, and zoning; provide land or funding; and offer administrative leadership, depending on the era and context.

This chapter describes the City of Edmonton's experience in mobilizing networks in support of affordable rental housing. It reviews the context for affordable housing provision in Edmonton, from the early post-war years until today, describing key partnerships and the role the City has held in them. It then turns to the future of affordable housing in Edmonton, covering the City's plans for moving forward, and conditions the City hopes to generate to promote affordable housing development. Following this, it details the unique circumstances that have helped facilitate collaboration, providing two case studies that characterize the City's approach. This chapter concludes by reflecting on what has worked well over the past several decades.

History of City of Edmonton Involvement in Affordable Housing

Post-War Years: Early Collaboration and Unwilling Partners

Federal housing policy throughout the 1940s and 1950s focused on enabling market housing production, targeting Canada's broad middle class (Suttor, 2016). Social housing for low-income earners was a minor consideration of the National Housing Act (NHA), with two funding and

DOI: 10.4324/9781003172949-5

delivery models operating from 1949 to 1964: public housing units and charitable or municipal limited dividend (LD) units (Suttor, 2016). The former required direct provincial involvement, while the latter did not. Despite these opportunities, the Alberta government remained largely passive during this time, diverting responsibility for affordable housing to municipalities (City of Edmonton [COE], 2018a) who were ill-equipped to handle the financial burden. Direct federal relationships with municipalities were common, and most of the (minimal) affordable housing developed prior to 1964 was done so at the municipal level or through charitable organizations (Suttor, 2016). Some of the first examples of targeted affordable housing production in Edmonton occurred through the Greater Edmonton Foundation, established in 1959 to create lodges for low-income seniors (Greater Edmonton Foundation, 2018). The City provided land, the Province constructed the buildings, and entities were established to operate buildings. These lodges were constructed until 1984, and many remain operational today.

1960s–1970s: Patchwork of Partnerships in Search of Funding Opportunities

Amendments to the NHA in 1964 included provisions to empower provincial housing corporations in addition to increased federal funding (Suttor, 2016a). The *Alberta Housing Act* passed in 1965, and the Alberta Housing Corporation formed shortly thereafter. Additional amendments in 1967 were intended to clarify municipal and provincial roles and set the stage for a new era in affordable housing development, characterized by increased provincial involvement in housing matters (Suttor, 2016b). However, provincial programmes were slow to start. Throughout the 1960s, Edmonton's population grew rapidly, rising from just under 270,000 to well over 400,000 (COE, 2018b). The 1967 Alberta oil boom contributed to extraordinary growth in the City (COE, 2018a). Housing affordability was at the forefront of public concern, and in 1968, the City Council recognized the mounting need for social housing. In response, they authorized administration to expedite the provision of public housing units (COE, 2002). The Edmonton Community Housing Organization (ECHO) was established, representing the City's first foray into the direct provision of social housing as developer and owner of land and buildings. From then until 1974, 1,030 units were created in 14 Community Housing projects under this initiative (COE Real Estate and Housing, 1980). Today, these projects still represent a large proportion of the City's affordable housing stock.

In line with the growing public support (and demand) for affordable housing in the 1970s, the City's involvement in housing grew, along with increased advocacy to other levels of government. An oil and housing boom coincided as the baby boomer generation moved into home ownership. However, the City's strong economic position and substantial federal funding meant that conditions for a housing crisis could largely be responded to at this point (COE, 2018a). This decade is characterized by a whirlwind of developments in housing policy, funding agreements, and policy initiatives at all three levels of government, contributing to a complicated patchwork of housing development. The City's integral role in affordable housing began to take shape through the direct provision of land, subsidies, development sponsorship, and advocacy (COE Real Estate and Housing, 1980). More direct policy statements regarding affordable housing began to appear, marking a shift in the City's approach and setting the stage for future involvement. The *1971 City of Edmonton General Plan* contends,

> A primary goal of government is the responsibility of ensuring that every citizen is afforded the opportunity to have a decent place in which to live (…) public housing is necessary to provide safe decent accommodation at reasonable rent levels.
>
> *(COE Planning Department, 1971, p. 7)*

In an early example of the City recognizing their limited funding capacity and in an effort to advocate to other levels of government, this qualifying statement followed,

> It should be recognized, however, that it is the responsibility of the senior levels of government to provide the financial backing for this program as it is beyond the City's present financial capacity to implement the program with its own limited resources.
>
> *(COE Planning Department, 1971, p. 7)*

In 1973, changes were made again to provincial policy. The Alberta Housing Corporation outlined a new framework for social housing development (COE Real Estate and Housing, 1980). Under this agreement, the Province developed, owned, and operated Community Housing projects on land leased from the City for 60 years. Around 1,200 units were developed under this agreement (COE Real Estate and Housing, 1980). Prior to this, cooperation between the municipality and other partners remained limited. However, growing provincial interest in housing and ongoing federal funding provided many opportunities for collaboration, often in response to particular funding opportunities. Rapid developments continued throughout this decade, including the creation of the Edmonton Housing Authority (later called Capital Region Housing Corporation) as property manager of public housing developments in 1970; the establishment of an interdepartmental Housing Task Group on behalf of the City of Edmonton and subsequent release of the first housing-specific policy document, *Housing in Edmonton: Directions for the Future* in 1975; the resulting formation of a new City department, the Real Estate and Housing Department, and its council approved 1979 document, *A Housing Strategy for the City of Edmonton* (COE, 2018; COE Real Estate and Housing, 1980). The 1979 *Housing Strategy* solidified the City's commitment to affordable housing provision and was the first policy to explicitly describe the City's role in housing, as well as outlining expectations of the private sector, non-profit organizations, and other levels of government. This *Housing Strategy* marked the start of an increasingly proactive and direct City role. The document described the municipal role in housing at the time as including, "provision of land for social housing, research and policy formulation regarding social housing programmes, initiation and delegation of innovative housing solutions, limited housing production, support of private sector activities, and promotion and conservation of existing housing stock where possible" (as cited by COE Real Estate and Housing, 1980, p. 79). These considerations are remarkably similar to present-day policy directives, demonstrating the forward-thinking nature of administration in addressing affordable housing concerns.

Federal housing policy trends and funding model adjustments significantly impacted the direction of affordable housing production in Edmonton from the early 1970s to mid-1980s. Suttor describes this era as the "first non-profit decade" (Suttor, 2016, p. 103). The first half was characterized by large social housing production on behalf of provincial housing corporations, with a growing non-profit and co-op housing sector. After 1978, public housing production halted in favour of a complete pivot towards non-profit and co-op housing, with municipal non-profit housing corporations (like HomeEd) filling the void for public housing. Nationally during this time, co-op housing accounted for about one quarter of production, while provincial and municipal agencies accounted for about one third. The remaining (and largest) share was developed by community-based non-profit groups including social agencies and ethnic associations (Suttor, 2016). During these years, affordable housing development took place amidst a complicated interplay of government and non-profit involvement. As of February 1980, 2,769 Community Housing units had been created on 65 sites provided by the City, through various methods of partnership (COE Real Estate and Housing, 1980).

1980s–Early 1990s: Foundations of the Partnership Era amidst Growing Housing Challenges

In contrast to the previous decade, the 1980s were a tumultuous time for housing and economic conditions in Edmonton. Two oil crashes, a real estate crash, massive job loss, and provincial cuts to services left many Edmontonians struggling. By April 1987, Edmonton was home to more people out of work than all of Alberta had been in 1980 (Goyette & Jakeway Roemmich, 2004, p. 331). Nationally, rising interest rates and pressures on the rental market kept public concern over housing affordability high, supporting an active government role in housing (Suttor, 2016a). Homelessness emerged as a growing concern in Edmonton, permanently shifting the way in which housing affordability concerns were framed by the public and in policy responses. This trend was echoed at the federal level. There was a move away from a comprehensive policy response supporting mixed-income and mixed-tenure projects, towards a targeted response for "special" populations like those experiencing homelessness (Suttor, 2016a, p. 10). Despite relatively sustained funding levels throughout the 1980s, responsibility for social housing was being incrementally devolved to the provinces, setting the stage for the end of active federal housing policy.

At the initiative of the City, representatives from local community-based groups met to discuss the growing challenge of homelessness in 1986 (Edmonton Joint Planning Committee on Housing, 1991). The Edmonton Coalition on Homelessness (ECOH) was formed as a result, with a mandate to identify the scope of homelessness, identify solutions, and develop an implementation plan (Edmonton Task Force on Homelessness, 1999). The coalition grew in membership from 30 founding member agencies to over 100, becoming a catalyst for collaboration and an important mechanism for community representation in housing and homelessness concerns. The formation of ECOH represents an important turning point in the City's approach to action. Amidst a growing housing crisis, the City recognized it could not tackle the problem alone, turning instead to the expertise of diverse community partners. The following year, ECOH released its major report: *No Place Like Home – Homelessness in Edmonton*. This endorsed 43 recommendations to address homelessness, support services, and housing affordability concerns (Edmonton Joint Planning Committee on Housing, 1991). A major recommendation encouraged the Government of Alberta to formally partner with community groups to identify problems and coordinate adequate resources. As a result, a committee was struck in 1988 with representation from Alberta Municipal Affairs, Alberta Mortgage and Housing Corporation, the City of Edmonton, and ECOH. The committee commissioned a study, Edmonton's first focused assessment of affordable housing need and demand (Edmonton Joint Planning Committee on Housing, 1991).

In response to an identified need in this assessment, the Edmonton Joint Planning Committee on Housing (EJPCOH) was established in 1990 as an inter-jurisdictional group, bringing together representatives of the three levels of government with partners in the private and non-profit sectors, including four members appointed through ECOH (Community Plan Committee, Nichols Applied Management Inc., & Soles and Company, 2011; Edmonton Task Force on Homelessness, 1999). The City held membership on the EJPCOH and contributed financial and administrative support. The initial mission of the EJPCOH focused on six goals. In addition to addressing and preventing homelessness, these included coordinating and integrating the many relevant stakeholders, policies, programmes, and budget processes related to housing and homelessness, and ensuring input and involvement of the community and private sectors in plan development and implementation (Edmonton Task Force on Homelessness, 1999).

1990s–Early 2000s: Creative Collaboration to Fill the Federal Void

Between 1993 and 1995, the productive years of Canadian social housing came crashing to an end. The federal government devolved responsibility for programme management to the provinces, new funding for social housing ceased, and social housing was removed as a key feature of federal policy (Suttor, 2016b). By the late 1990s, Edmonton housing advocates recognized that funding was too unstable and tied to the political whims of the provincial and federal governments to adequately address housing concerns. In 1997, ECOH applied for and was granted funding as part of the CMHC Homegrown Solutions programme to investigate the creation of a housing trust fund (Edmonton Task Force on Homelessness, 1999). This resulted in establishment of the Edmonton Housing Trust Fund (EHTF) by ECOH in 1999 to financially resource housing solutions. A steering committee oversaw the fund, including members from the City, Alberta Municipal Affairs, and Capital Region Housing Corporation (Edmonton Task Force on Homelessness, 1999). The original intention was to create a dedicated, sustained housing funding stream – out of the political realm – although proposed funding models were not immediately successfully.

During this same time frame, Edmonton Mayor Bill Smith and several provincial partners agreed to review the ongoing issue of homelessness through the creation of the jointly chaired Edmonton Homelessness Task Force. As part of their mandate to involve broad community partners in developing solutions to homelessness, the Task Force prepared and released a report in 1999, *Homelessness in Edmonton: A Call to Action* (Edmonton Task Force on Homelessness, 1999). This was intended to guide future action in housing and homelessness, building on the broad base of work already underway within the City. This report recommended that the EJPCOH lead implementation of its recommendations and the EHTF be responsible for funding concerns.

A serendipitous series of policy events unfolded over the next several years, setting the stage for Edmonton's present-day approach. In 1999, the *Federal National Homelessness Initiative (NHI)* was announced with $753 million "designed to foster partnerships and investment that contribute to the alleviation of homelessness" (Organisation for Economic Co-Operation and Development, 2002, p. 144). The three-year, $305 million *Supporting Communities Partnership Initiative (SCPI)* was a cornerstone of this federal funding project. The SCPI was intended to increase community capacity to plan, set priorities, and implement initiatives (Organisation for Economic Co-Operation and Development, 2002). Most of this funding (80%) went to Canada's ten largest cities, Edmonton included. Communities could choose between two programme delivery models, "community entity" or "shared decision making".

Communities with a baseline capacity were encouraged to adopt the "community entity" model to make the most of funding commitments (Organisation for Economic Co-Operation and Development, 2002). In many Canadian cities, the requirement that a community entity be formed to administer SCPI was a catalyst for new cooperative relationships. In Edmonton, this requirement merely formalized a series of networks decades in the making, with the added benefit of a new federal funding source.

In response to the NHI funding announcement, the EJPCOH hosted a planning charette on homelessness to kick-start the development of Edmonton's first community plan. Through a broad consultative process, the EJPCOH undertook writing this three-year plan, designating the EJPCOH and EHTF as the "community entity" (Edmonton Joint Planning Committee on Housing, 2002) (in 2008, these would amalgamate to form the organization presently known as Homeward Trust). Published in 2000, the *Edmonton Community Plan on Homelessness* (Edmonton

Joint Planning Committee on Housing, 2000) was recognized by all three levels of government, and City staff were actively represented on its associated steering committee.

Despite active involvement with and support of the EJPCOH and the EHTF, the City had not explicitly defined its role in this new era of action until 2002 when *Building Together: The City of Edmonton Low Income and Special Needs Housing Strategy 2001–2011* was published and approved by City Council. This document provided the cornerstone around which all detailed strategies and actions would be built over the next decade, laying the foundation for future housing policy and programmes. The strategy aptly summarized the City's role in the fast-paced transition period characterizing the early 2000s;

> The City of Edmonton has been actively involved, contributing its experience and knowledge of its local communities. Growing housing and homeless needs, along with governments' commitment to do things differently and better, have highlighted the need for the City to clearly define its role in this area over the next decade.
>
> *(COE, 2002, p. 1)*

This role is clearly defined as "lead coordinator and facilitator" and characterizes the City's involvement to the present day.

2000s: Stalling Progress Despite Unprecedented Cooperation

In the early 2000s, unprecedented cooperation was taking place in Edmonton towards efforts to alleviate homelessness and address ongoing housing concerns. Partly in response to federal funding background report arrangements, and partly due to an emerging crisis tied to yet another one of Alberta's economic booms, housing and homelessness became increasingly linked in formal policy and political rhetoric. Despite focused efforts on behalf of countless community partners, prevailing social and economic conditions stalled major progress, and they would continue to drastically impact the response well into the late 2000s. In April 2002, the EJPCOH published a review and update of Edmonton's original community plan. This document described the ongoing challenges as follows:

> Although significant progress has been made toward addressing the gaps identified in the Community Plan, the recent economic boom has accelerated the homelessness and affordable housing crisis in the City. The economic climate in Edmonton has changed dramatically (…) Net in-migration has reached levels of over 10%, there has been a significant increase in cost of living (utilities, rent, food), vacancy rates have dropped dramatically and real estate prices in all market segments have risen significantly (…) The extreme lack of affordable rental housing is creating pressure on the continuum of facilities providing emergency, transitional and long-term supportive housing. As a result, existing emergency and transitional facilities are housing people for increasingly longer periods due to the lack of housing further along the continuum.
>
> *(Edmonton Joint Planning Committee on Housing, 2002, p. 7)*

The underlying message of this review was that more than ever, local partners (including the City) did not have the capacity to address these issues alone. The plan included several new recommendations for advocacy to other levels of government and emphasized financial resources as a key limiting factor.

During the same period, the Edmonton Task Force on Affordable Housing was established by resolution of City Council with the primary goal of creating a sustainable framework to encourage new affordable rental production. A background report was published in 2003, detailing recommendations for the market and non-profit sectors to "build modest quality units at moderate rent (…) distinct from housing in which subsidies are required to bridge the gap between market housing and the amount that households can afford to pay at 30% of income" (COE, Pomeroy, Focus Consulting Inc., & Lampert, 2003, p. i). The focus on housing that operates without the need for subsidies is indicative of this era, when federal funding for new social housing had essentially ceased. The shortcomings in support from the provincial and federal governments, including a recently announced federal-provincial capital programme – the *Affordable Housing Partnership Initiative* – were explicitly noted. Here it was described as "limited in scope and scale" (COE et al., 2003, p. 32). This background report laid the groundwork for a new direction in the City's response, endorsing a novel set of proactive land-use planning tools, including an affordable housing density bonus and zoning changes to encourage the development of secondary apartments.

The next several years were characterized by a relentless housing crunch as the City's population boomed again. The EJPCOH and EHTF continued to support policy directives outlined in the *Call to Action* report and the *Edmonton Community Plan*. Following the 2004 civic election, Mayor Mandel made affordable housing a key priority, proposing a new and improved affordable housing initiative. In part, this was spurred by the recognition that many municipal regulations were cumbersome and limited affordable housing development. The resulting outcome was *Cornerstones Plan – Edmonton's Plan for Affordable Housing* (Cornerstones: Edmonton's Plan for Affordable Housing, 2006–2011, 2006). Endorsed by City Council in 2005, Cornerstones outlined a series of 15 bold directions the City would take towards its goal of providing 2,500 units of long-term housing over the proceeding five years. These included the creation of a substantial new funding pool to leverage resources from other levels of government, the establishment of an affordable land bank, and an incentive fund to promote secondary suites (Cornerstones: Edmonton's Plan for Affordable Housing, 2006–2011, 2006). The City's role in this response was clearly defined as leader, facilitator, and active advocate (COE, 2012). The plan emphasized collaboration, inviting "all levels of government, the non-profit and private sector and individuals to join the City as partners in working towards this outcome" (Cornerstones: Edmonton's Plan for Affordable Housing, 2006–2011, 2006, p. 1). To this end, the City cultivated partnerships with other levels of government, the general public, and private and community-based housing providers, exceeding City Council's initial housing targets (COE, 2012). Between 2006 and 2011, Cornerstones helped create or upgrade 553 secondary suites and over 3,300 safe and affordable homes (COE, 2018d).

The City continued to explore land-use planning as an innovative tool for creating and maintaining affordable housing. The previously discussed Mayor's Task Force Report on Affordable Housing (2003) spurred the City to initiate a study on the relationship between land-use planning and affordable housing. *Key Connections: Affordable Housing and Land-Use Planning* was the outcome. It concluded that through targeted planning measures, the City's Planning and Development Department could play an important role in facilitating affordable housing provision. It determined that administration lacked an adequate policy framework for affordable housing and was particularly critical of the existing Municipal Development Plan (1998) in this regard (COE, 1998; City Spaces Consulting, 2006).

Late 2000s: Established Partnerships Respond to the Homelessness Crisis

Concern over rising rates of homelessness in Edmonton peaked in the late 2000s, and the response shifted – this time to addressing urgent crisis conditions. Between 2004 and 2006, there was a 19% increase in those counted as homeless; the vacancy rate dropped to 1.2%, from over 5% two years prior, and the average price of a single-detached home increased by 52% in 2006 (COE, 2007). Across the housing spectrum, Edmontonians were feeling the housing crunch. A series of major policy initiatives directed at homelessness was soon underway on behalf of the provincial and municipal governments, many of which remain in place today. Despite the clear link between homelessness and housing, the City of Edmonton's homelessness plan explicitly stated it was not intended to address broad affordable housing concerns, but would cooperate with relevant initiatives (Edmonton Committee to End Homelessness, 2009, p. 2). As part of a provincial consultative process during this time, the City prepared and presented a series of specific municipal-provincial partnership opportunities that could generate affordable housing units. Some of these recommendations were very forward thinking, including a proposed real estate transfer fee (up to 1% of real estate value) to generate municipal capital for affordable housing and amendments to provincial legislation that would enable inclusionary zoning (COE, 2007, p. 8).

The mandate of established City housing policies carried on well into the late 2010s, with housing and homelessness remaining distinctively separate policy concerns. The City continued to support implementation of Edmonton's homelessness plan and Cornerstones, and the work of Homeward Trust. Edmonton's plan for affordable housing was updated in 2012 through the endorsement of *Cornerstones II (2012–2016)* (COE, 2018f). This updated policy outlined similar actions with renewed funding commitments, remaining active until the end of 2016. In 2014, federal social housing policy returned to the forefront of concern. Operating agreements set up during the productive years of social housing were set to expire over the next several years, affecting up to 11,367 units of social housing in Edmonton (Social Housing Regeneration Advisory Group [SHRAG], 2015). In response, in April 2014, Edmonton Mayor Don Iveson hosted a roundtable discussion on emerging housing issues in support of the Federation of Canadian Municipalities national advocacy campaign. The conversation focused on expiring federal-provincial operating agreements and regenerating the ageing social housing stock. Edmontonians from the non-profit and private housing sectors were invited to the table alongside representatives from provincial and municipal government (COE, 2018e). The Social Housing Regeneration Advisory Group (SHRAG) was formed to keep the conversation going. Co-chaired by Iveson, members of the group included social housing providers, community agencies, City representatives, private developers, and representatives from First Nations organizations. The group released a summary report in 2015, setting direction for ongoing collaboration. They identified a necessity to step away from the current operating model and find a new way to deliver housing for households in need (SHRAG, 2015, p. 8). Key to this was reconceptualizing social housing "as a contributor to diverse, inclusive communities with the potential to act as a catalyst for community development" (SHRAG, 2015, p. 8).

Bringing It All Together: In Support of Complete Communities in the City of Edmonton

The notion of affordable housing as part of diverse, inclusive communities set a new direction for the City, laying the foundation for present-day policy efforts that conceptualize housing need more broadly than in the past. This echoes other recent updates to City policy including *The Way We Live: Edmonton's People Plan* (2010), and a bold new collective impact movement spearheaded by the City: *EndPoverty Edmonton*. This began as a Task Force appointed by City Council in 2014 with over 200 members, including people impacted by poverty. The Task Force worked to identify priority actions towards the goal of ending poverty in one generation, communicated through a 2015 strategy document (EndPoverty Edmonton, 2015). As part of this initiative, housing is inextricably linked to poverty. The City's current role in this initiative is one of champion, advocate, partner, and investor.

Another driving force behind the current City action is the recent shift in federal and provincial support for housing. Both governments released housing strategies in 2017, and Edmonton is actively working to take advantage of significant funding opportunities. Towards this end, and as part of the expanding vision on affordable housing, the City is working to address considerations for the context in which affordable housing is situated, seeking to cultivate an environment in which opportunities for affordable housing flourish.

Cultivating Environments in Support of Affordable Housing

The *City of Edmonton Affordable Housing Strategy* is the most recent major policy development. Released in 2015, it establishes a bold new direction to guide City action until 2025. It formalizes the City's role as leader, coordinator, and advocate, uniquely positioned to leverage a tool box of municipal resources including funding, land, regulations, and policies.

The City is working to enable supportive environments in several ways, building off momentum of the *Affordable Housing Strategy*. One such approach is to engage community partners around the importance of affordable housing by means of a compelling and consistent narrative (COE Communications and Engagement, 2018). In August 2018, the City announced a five-year marketing and communications initiative: The *Affordable Housing Public Information Campaign*. The goal for this strategy is "to shift negative attitudes and behaviours related to affordable housing by bridging existing values with the facts and particularly the benefits of affordable housing" (COE Communications and Engagement, 2018). Collaboration is a key feature of this plan, as housing partners must be actively engaged in joint communication efforts, working together to change the community conversation on affordable housing. The campaign aims to build community buy-in for affordable housing in support of Edmonton's long-term, City-wide neighbourhood affordable housing target of 16% (COE, 2018c).

Mobilizing Partnerships in the City of Edmonton: Conditions for Success

Over the past six decades, Edmonton's approach to developing affordable rental housing can be characterized as adaptive, proactive, and collaborative. Every decade brought with it a new set of local and national challenges. Responses have been tailored to make the most of funding opportunities and align with prevailing public and political rhetoric. When federal support for social housing was strong, policy was designed to acquire and effectively distribute available resources. With federal devolution for housing responsibility and growing concerns around homelessness in the 1980s, the need for collaboration became increasingly apparent to maximize scarce resources and rally broad community support behind initiatives. In the present context of renewed provincial and federal support, the City's response is once again underscored by the need to position itself to attract funding dollars.

Throughout every era, the mobilization of diverse partners has been key in expanding access to affordable rental housing in Edmonton. A series of unique factors has contributed to the City's success in this regard.

Strong Policy Framework to Guide Housing Action

Since the late 1970s, the City has maintained a strong housing policy framework to clearly delineate roles and expectations, set priorities, and guide collective action. This has had the dual benefit of keeping housing at the forefront of political concern for over three decades, despite shifting economic conditions and wavering public concern for affordability issues, as well as providing an overarching framework under which partnerships could be developed in support of specific outcomes.

Direction on housing has not been limited to a single stream of policy documents; it is multifaceted, reflecting the diverse ways in which housing impacts the Edmonton community. This policy framework includes focused housing policy documents, as well as those which pertain more broadly to homelessness, poverty reduction, and municipal development. Some have been authored directly by the City, while others have been community-led with City contribution. The framework is characterized by a strong commitment to community-based priority development, including clear processes for inclusion and participation in policy formation. In part, this reflects an early recognition on behalf of the City that bureaucrats did not have all the answers. However, this process also serves to build community buy-in and increase the likelihood that policy directives will live beyond political cycles. Also evident in the policy framework is a concerted effort on behalf of the City to clearly define its role and responsibilities, and that of its partners, within each response.

The first housing-specific strategy was prepared by the City Planning Department in 1978. Its stated purpose was to ensure continuity in municipal housing programmes. Notably, it was developed in response to recommendations of the Interdepartmental Housing Task Group with considerable public participation. This document included an extensive overview of the role of the City, private sector, and "third sector" in addressing housing challenges. A series of annually released reports followed, providing ongoing and updated direction. This cycle of policy development has been consistently employed in the Edmonton housing context. A problem is recognized; a task group, coalition, or committee is formed to obtain input from diverse partners; a policy is developed, implemented, and revised to ensure ongoing relevance. Often, an entity is tasked with championing the plan. The first *Edmonton Community Plan on Homelessness* is another key example. Prepared by the EJPCOH in 2000, this plan was developed in consultation with partners from the private, non-profit, and public sectors, and people with lived experience of homelessness. It was created in response to an identified need by the Edmonton Task Force on Homelessness. Although the City was not a direct author, it was a key partner in the strategy's development, which was intended to guide a coordinated response to housing and homelessness throughout the City. As with earlier policy documents, roles and responsibilities were clearly defined.

This consistent framework has served as an important catalyst for collaboration in Edmonton. Through various policy development processes, partners have been brought together and cooperative relationships formed. In a context where end-goals are clearly outlined, partnerships could be selectively and deliberately developed in support of these objectives. The clear delineation of roles and responsibilities has also ensured that resources are maximized and efforts not replicated.

City as Lead Coordinator and Facilitator, Supported by Strong Policy Frameworks

The City has taken on various roles in promoting the development of affordable rental housing over the past several decades. These have included direct developer of housing, provider of land, policy maker, regulator, administrator, and advocate. A role they have consistently maintained is that of lead coordinator and facilitator. Edmonton's strong housing policy framework has supported this role immensely, providing a road map upon on which collaborative relationships could be deliberately built, as the City worked to leverage the capacity of other partners. Many policy objectives were met through the combined efforts of various partners.

The following examples (Boxes 5.1 and 5.2) illustrate distinct approaches the City has taken to mobilizing networks. Each was successful, resulting in the development of affordable rental units, albeit in very different ways. These cases are underscored by the same fundamental approach – the City worked in a supportive role to leverage the capacity of other partners towards stated policy objectives.

Key Housing Champions Build Relationships and Foster Trust

The influence of key people in Edmonton's housing circle over the past several decades cannot be overstated. They have been integral to building lasting relationships in the sector, fostering trust, and pushing for bold housing initiatives. A core group of City staff were closely involved in policy formation and implementation and were active members of established working groups, with close working relationships with many community partners. This allowed for an open line of communication between the City and housing management bodies, advocacy groups, community organizations, and the public, and provided a wealth of institutional knowledge.

BOX 5.1: CITY AS ENABLER OF PUBLIC ROLE IN INCREASING HOUSING SUPPLY

Cornerstones I is considered one of Edmonton's most successful initiatives for increasing affordable rental housing. Through a variety of means including new construction, regeneration of existing spaces, and rental supplements, 3,000 affordable housing units were created between 2006 and 2011 (COE, 2018d). Although partnerships were integral to the strategy's overall success, the Secondary Suites Grant Program endorsed a particularly novel and interesting approach to collaboration between the City, home builders, and the people of Edmonton.

Funding for Secondary Suites Grant Program predates the Cornerstones programme. Following the 2003 affordable housing study, the City recognized they could not adequately address the demand for affordable housing alone, so they willed the public. City staff sat down with home builders to develop an initial framework, first running the programme as a limited pilot project. Edmonton provided funds, but also made significant changes to land-use regulation and municipal processes to allow the programme to operate effectively. A great deal of collaboration occurred within the City to iron out details, and in June 2008, the Secondary Suites Grant Program was formally announced to the public.

The Secondary Suites Grant Program encouraged upgrading and creating new secondary suites in compliance with health and safety standards through a financial incentive for homeowners under specified terms. These terms included an agreement to rent units to approved low-income households for five years. This approach was very popular, contributing to widespread support for secondary suites in Edmonton and exponentially increasing the number of safe, legal suites available. The grant was so successful in raising awareness of the benefits of legal secondary suites, that up to half of new suites were created voluntarily by homeowners without financial incentive (COE, 2012). The programme had the dual benefit of increasing the number of safe, affordable rental units, while also providing mortgage assistance to participating homeowners. Through this initiative, the City took steps to create an enabling environment for affordable housing development, leveraging the capacity of everyday Edmontonians to be part of the solution.

BOX 5.2: CITY AS PROVIDER OF LAND AND ADMINISTRATIVE SUPPORT

In 2014, a key recommendation of the SHRAG encouraged the City to "partner with social housing providers operating on City-owned land to develop pilot regeneration projects" (SHRAG, 2015, p. 10). This recommendation was the catalyst for a partnership between the City of Edmonton and Capital Region Housing Corporation (CRHC), Edmonton's largest provider of social and affordable housing. The result of this partnership was the first social housing regeneration project in Edmonton – featuring an innovative new model for affordable housing provision and a regenerated building that tripled the number of affordable housing units from 80 to 240.

The City of Edmonton was the beneficial owner of the Londonderry Housing Complex, built in 1971. It was City-owned, on City land, operated by CRHC. Once it was determined that redevelopment was the most viable option for the site, the City acted to bolster the capacity of CRHC in their role as project lead. They introduced CRHC to the community league, supported facilitation, and provided staff and resources. CRHC employed a new method to public engagement – approaching the surrounding community with no pre-existing notions of design other than the intended number of units. Public engagement began in January 2015 and went very well, with no public opposition to the rezoning application despite a tripling in density. In this partnership, the City leveraged all available resources to support CRHC in its Londonderry regeneration endeavour. Once complete (estimated 2018), this mixed-income project will allow families to stay in place even as their incomes change. This partnership has set the course for future engagement and redevelopment on City-owned sites, marking the start of a new era in innovative social housing development in Edmonton.

The impact of these personalities on the collaborative nature of Edmonton's housing field is immense.

Edmonton has also been home to a succession of mayors and city councillors who have been incredibly supportive of affordable housing development. Several key initiatives were spearheaded by elected officials, including the Social Housing Regeneration Advisory Committee, the Cornerstones Plan, and the Edmonton Committee to End Homelessness. Many successful programmes and initiatives would have never taken off without these bold champions leading the way.

Opportunities for Collaboration through Formalized Channels

The creation of ECOH in 1986 and EJPCOH in 1990 was formative in establishing Edmonton's partnership era, providing long-term, formalized outlets for collaboration and communication between diverse partners. In the case of ECOH, the City initiated a conversation on homelessness, recognizing they did not have the expertise or capacity to tackle the issue alone. ECOH was the result of that conversation and came to have representation from over 100 agencies. ECOH was closely involved in municipal policy-making, ensuring housing advocates had a seat at decision-making tables. It was also the driving force behind the innovative EHTF, which now operates as the City's homelessness systems planner – Homeward Trust. To this day,

ECOH (now ECOHH) remains an important advocate, providing a unified voice in policy conversations.

The EJPCOH was also established with a primary goal of bringing together government, private, and community partners, in part to determine priority needs and set policy direction. The City was an active member and supporter, providing funding and administrative assistance. In addition to developing key housing strategies, including Edmonton's first community plan, the EJPCOH was tasked with overseeing City progress in other policy initiatives. This group eventually amalgamated with the EHTF to form Homeward Trust. In addition to providing formalized, ongoing opportunities for collaboration and playing an important role in policy development and implementation, the early formation of ECOH and the EJPCOH was key in establishing a lasting culture of cooperation in Edmonton. Many later initiatives endorsed the formation of working groups, task forces, and committees to encourage partnerships, provide a forum for discussion, and influence policy direction.

Taking Stock: Lessons Learnt from Six Decades of Support for Affordable Housing

The City of Edmonton has not always been successful in its efforts to develop affordable rental housing. Over the past several decades, many initiatives failed to take off as planned, projects were scrapped, and annual targets went unmet. After an initial explosion of social housing development in the 1960s–1980s, decades are characterized by lulls in affordable rental production, until a modest return to development in the mid-2000s. The Londonderry development represents the first increase in targeted social housing units in Edmonton in nearly 30 years.

Despite progress in recent years, the challenge remains to meet the needs of roughly 70,000 renter households in Edmonton living in unaffordable housing (COE, 2015). In a context of economic boom and bust cycles, limited funding terms, and growing housing affordability challenges, there is no silver bullet. As the City works to develop new and innovative solutions to meet housing demand, it is imperative to analyse and learn from failed initiatives. However, it is equally importantly to understand what has worked well for Edmonton and why. In reviewing the City's most successful initiatives to date, partnerships are the common denominator.

The purpose of this chapter was to review the City's involvement in affordable housing development since the 1960s, shedding light on key partnerships in every era and the City's shifting role. It has focused on the positive, drawing attention to the circumstances that supported successful outcomes, ultimately contributing to affordable housing creation. In an effort to provide other jurisdictions with some tangible takeaways, this chapter concludes with lessons learnt from experiences of what worked well.

Lessons learnt:

- Know when to lead and when to follow
- Deliberately create opportunities for collaboration
- Engage the public as a key partner
- Do not underestimate the power of people.

Know When to Lead and When to Follow

Although the City of Edmonton often defers to lead coordinator and facilitator, some of the most successful housing outcomes have been the result of initiatives in which the City took on a supporting role. As a municipality, they are uniquely positioned to impact policy levers, like zoning and regulations, that other partners cannot. Other contributions, like administrative support or research capacity, are also inherent strengths of a government body. It is important to identify these distinct capacities and leverage them, while doing the same for other partners.

There is no shortage of innovation and resolve in Edmonton, particularly in the non-profit and housing advocacy sectors. In recognizing this, the City has sought to take stock of what each partner brings to the table in every collaborative relationship. At times, this has involved acting as a connector of other organizations who might be a better fit for a project or passing on a funding opportunity to an agency with more specialized knowledge. Ultimately, in prioritizing the end goal over who gets the credit, better housing outcomes can be achieved.

Deliberately Create Opportunities for Collaboration

Sometimes partnerships are formed organically, through proximity, joint advocacy efforts, or existing relationships. Although these types of cooperative relationships are productive, they often develop and operate within distinctive silos. In cultivating and supporting opportunities for collaboration with diverse partners, like formalized working groups, committees, and coalitions such as the EJPCOH, stakeholders who otherwise might not interact are brought together, lines of communication are opened, trust is built, and policy direction better reflects community priorities.

Engage the Public as a Key Partner

Members of the public are often viewed as impediments to affordable housing production, rather than potential partners. As the success of the City's Secondary Suites Grant Program shows, engaging the public can be an effective strategy for increasing affordable housing supply. There are many opportunities for innovative community involvement in housing issues if appropriate conditions are enabled. Whether this be zoning changes, incentives, or education, the broader community should not be overlooked in efforts to mobilize networks.

Do Not Underestimate the Power of People

The individual people involved in Edmonton's housing sector have been integral to the success of many initiatives over the past several decades. It is imperative to recognize these stakeholders – their established relationships, their reputations with partner organizations, and their vast institutional knowledge – and take efforts to ensure these unique assets are not lost as people retire or otherwise leave the sector. As a new generation of housing professionals, advocates and City staff move into key roles; care should be taken to foster opportunities for mentorship, network building, and the transfer of institutional knowledge.

Acknowledgements

Thank you Jay Freeman and Kent Fletcher for your helpful contributions on the history of affordable housing development in Edmonton.

Note

1 In this chapter, **affordable housing** broadly refers to any type of rental housing with rents below average market cost, targeted to mid- to low-income earning households. It may include (but is not limited to) social housing, as well as units developed through City initiatives like the Secondary Suites Grant. Affordable home-ownership programmes are not in the scope of this chapter.

    Social housing refers specifically to units with rent geared to income, developed as part of a formal initiative such as the federally funded Community Housing programme during the 1960s–1980s. The term is interchangeable with public housing.

References

City of Edmonton. (1998). *Plan Edmonton – Edmonton's Municipal Development Plan*. Edmonton: City of Edmonton Planning Department. Retrieved May 6, 2021 from www.edmonton.ca/city_government/documents/PDF/MDP_Bylaw_15100.pdf

City of Edmonton. (2002). *Building Together: The City of Edmonton Low-Income and Special Needs Housing Strategy 2001–2011*. Edmonton: City of Edmonton Planning Department.

City of Edmonton (2006) *Cornerstones: Edmonton's Plan for Affordable Housing*, 2006–2011. Edmonton: City of Edmonton Planning Department.

City of Edmonton. (2007). Building the Capital Partnership – Growing Housing Needs and Effective Edmonton Solutions. Retrieved May 6, 2021 from http://webdocs.edmonton.ca/InfraPlan/Current Projects/cityedm_housing_initiative.pdf

City of Edmonton. (2012). *Cornerstones: Building Success*. Retrieved October 5, 2019 from www.edmonton.ca/programs_services/documents/PDF/Cornerstones_Building_Succes s_web.pdf

City of Edmonton. (2015). *City of Edmonton Affordable Housing Strategy (2016–2025)*. Retrieved May 6, 2021 from www.edmonton.ca/programs_services/documents/PDF/CityOfEdmontonAffordableHo usingStrategy2016-2025.pdf

City of Edmonton. (2018, July 13). *City Involvement in Affordable Housing*. Retrieved July 13, 2018, from www.edmonton.ca/programs_services/housing/city-involvement-in-affordablehousing.aspx

City of Edmonton. (2018a). *Edmonton's Urban Neighborhood Evolution: Evolving Infill*. Retrieved October 5, 2019 from www.cityofedmontoninfill.ca/public/download/documents/46666

City of Edmonton. (2018b). *Population History*. Retrieved August 25, 2018, from www.edmonton.ca/city_government/facts_figures/population-history.aspx

City of Edmonton. (2018c, August). *City Policy – City-Wide Affordable Housing Framework*. Retrieved May 6, 2021 from www.edmonton.ca/programs_services/documents/PDF/C601AffordabeHousing-Framework.pdf

City of Edmonton. (2018d, August 23). *Cornerstones: Edmonton's Plan for Affordable Housing*. Retrieved August 23, 2018, from www.edmonton.ca/programs_services/housing/cornerstones.aspx

City of Edmonton. (2018e, August 23). *Moving on Housing*. Retrieved August 23, 2018, from www.edmonton.ca/city_government/initiatives_innovation/moving-on-housing.aspx

City of Edmonton. (2018f, August 23). *Secondary Suite and Garden Suite Grants*. Retrieved August 23, 2018, from www.edmonton.ca/programs_services/funding_grants/cornerstonesgrant-secondary-suite.aspx

City of Edmonton Communications and Engagement. (2018, August). *Affordable Housing Public Information Campaign Proposal*. Edmonton: City of Edmonton Planning Department.

City of Edmonton Planning Department. (1971). *Appendix No. 11. Amendments to the City of Edmonton General Plan*. Retrieved October 5, 2019 from https://issuu.com/aesdl/docs/edmonton__alta.___1971_-_amendment

City of Edmonton, Pomeroy, S., Lampert, G. (2003). *Improving Opportunities for Affordable Housing in Edmonton: Background Report of the Edmonton Task Force on Affordable Housing*. Edmonton: City of Edmonton Affordable Housing Department. Retrieved May 6, 2021 from www.edmonton.ca/programs_services/documents/PDF/Improving_Opportunities_for_Affordable_Housing_in_Edmonton.pdf

City of Edmonton Real Estate and Housing. (1980). *1980 Annual Housing Report*. Retrieved October 5, 2019 from https://issuu.com/aesdl/docs/edmonton__alta.__-_1980-1981_-_annu

City Spaces Consulting. (2006). *Key Connections: Affordable Housing and Land Use Planning*. Vancouver: CitySpaces.

Community Plan Committee, Nichols Applied Management Inc., & Soles and Company. (2011). *Edmonton and Area Community Plan on Housing and Supports 2011–2015*. Retrieved October 5, 2019 from www.edmonton.ca/programs_services/documents/PDF/Edmonton_and_Area_Community_Plan_on_Housing_and_Supports_2011-2015.pdf

Edmonton Committee to End Homelessness. (2009). *A Place to Call Home: Edmonton's 10-Year Plan to End Homelessness*. Retrieved May 6, 2021 from http://homewardtrust.ca/wp-content/uploads/2016/12/A-Place-to-Call-Home-%E2%80%94-Edmontons-10-Year-Plan-to-End-Homelessness.pdf

Edmonton Joint Planning Committee on Housing. (1991). *A Place to Call Home: The Three Year Plan for Housing in Edmonton's Inner City 1992–1994*. Retrieved October 5, 2019 from https://issuu.com/aesdl/docs/edmonton__alta.__-_a_place_to_call_

Edmonton Joint Planning Committee on Housing. (2000). *Edmonton Community Plan on Homelessness 2000–2003*. Retrieved May 6, 2021 from http://homewardtrust.ca//wp-content/uploads/2016/12/CP-2000-2003.pdf

Edmonton Joint Planning Committee on Housing. (2002). *Review and Update of the Edmonton Community Plan on Homelessness 2000–2003*. Retrieved October 5, 2019 from http://homewardtrust.ca/wp-content/uploads/2016/12/May-1999-Edmonton-Homeless-Count.pdf

Edmonton Task Force on Homelessness. (1999). *Homelessness in Edmonton: A Call to Action*. Retrieved October 5, 2019 from http://homewardtrust.ca/wp-content/uploads/2016/12/May-1999-Edmonton-Homeless-Count.pdf

End Poverty Edmonton. (2015, December). *End Poverty in a Generation: A Strategy*. Retrieved October 5, 2019 from https://static1.squarespace.com/static/54eb5df3e4b0904aceb80bc4/t/56705e1569492e2ff76c46 0a/1450204693098/EPE_Strategy_Dec2015_WEB_v5.pdf

Greater Edmonton Foundation. (2018). *GEF Seniors Housing: About GEF*. Retrieved October 5, 2019 from www.gef.org/AboutGEF.aspx

Goyette, L., & Jakeway Roemmich, C. (2004). *Edmonton In Our Own Words*. Edmonton: University of Alberta Press.

Organisation for Economic Co-Operation and Development. (2002). *OECD Territorial Reviews: Canada 2002*. Paris: OECD Publishing.

Social Housing Regeneration Advisory Group. (2015). *Summary Report*. Edmonton: Social Housing Regeneration Advisory Group.

Suttor, G. (2016). *Still Renovating: A History of Canadian Social Housing Policy*. Montréal and Kingston: McGill-Queen's University Press.

6

RESPONSES TO TORONTO'S AFFORDABLE HOUSING CHALLENGE

Mobilizing for Action

Sean Gadon

Introduction

Toronto is Canada's largest city, the fourth largest city in North America, and home to a diverse population of about 2.9 million people. Over the past decade, Toronto has witnessed an unprecedented residential building boom and a hot housing market for consumers. Toronto leads North American cities in residential construction projects, building on average some 16,000 new residential units annually. Meanwhile, social housing waiting list has grown, with some 100,000 households waiting to access 94,000 social housing homes (Kneebone and Jadidzadeh, 2017). Vacancy rates in market rental housing have declined to 0.7% – the lowest rate in 16 years. Close to half of renters (47%) spend more than 30% of their income on housing – this trend is expected to worsen, with the number of households in core housing need growing by 44,000 by 2030, equivalent to twice the rate over past 12 years. Average home prices have skyrocketed, leaving tenants locked into rental housing and reducing mobility from rental housing. From 2006 to 2018, median household income grew only 30%, while average homeownership costs grew 131% (Canadian Centre for Economic Analysis and Canadian Urban Institute, 2019).

Toronto's Open Door Affordable Housing Program

In 2009, Toronto City Council adopted a ten-year *Housing Opportunities Toronto Action Plan* (HOT) 2010–2020. This plan set out the goal of achieving on average 1,000 new rental units annually, or 10,000 over the ten-year period. By the end of 2015, the number of new affordable rental approvals reached 1,154, and it was clear that the City was falling short of achieving its affordable housing targets (Figure 6.1).

With the support of the new Mayor of Toronto and the City's Housing Advocate, officials were tasked with revamping the City's approach in an effort to meet the annual target of 1,000 units for the period 2016–2020. In 2016, City Council approved a new initiative called the *Open Door Program*. This unilateral City programme set out a consistent approach to the approval of new affordable rental housing through a partnership with non-profit and private sector organizations (City Planning Division, 2018).

The essential elements of the Program provide for a suite of financial incentives, including the waiver of development charges, planning application fees and building permit fees, and the

DOI: 10.4324/9781003172949-6

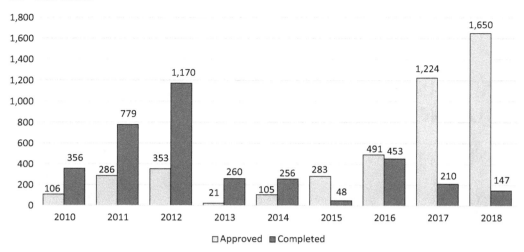

FIGURE 6.1 New Affordable Rental Homes Approved and Completed in Toronto, 2010–2018.
Source: City of Toronto's Affordable Housing Office, August 2018.

waiver of property taxes over the period of operating the affordable housing units. Capital funding has also been added to the Program to ensure project viability. In total, the value of these investments over a five-year period is $222 million. Approved *Open Door* developments were also ensured they get an expedited planning approval process. Further, the Program committed the City to providing select surplus land sites for both affordable rental and ownership housing.

Overall reception to the Program has been positive. Program applications have been robust, and for the years 2017 and 2018, approved projects have exceeded the annual target of 1,000 units. The reasons often cited for the success of the Program include its flexible nature as it provides early certainty to non-profit and private sector organizations on the City's commitments to affordable housing and to their specific project. The approval of projects in the early stages creates a pipeline of developments and eliminates the challenging feature of other affordable housing programmes for developments to be shovel-ready. The Program also provides opportunities throughout the development process to stack other funding to support the construction of the project and/or during the operating phase (CBRE Limited, 2017). Additionally, the Program provides the flexibility to proposed mixed-market and affordable developments, with a requirement that a minimum of 20% of the gross floor area be developed as affordable rental. The Program also has three "portals" through which affordable rental housing development partnerships can be approved. This includes approvals through annual proposal calls, through the final planning application approval process, and through special initiatives such as the *Ontario Affordable Housing Provincial Lands Program*.

At the same time, the *Open Door Program* has also attracted a range of criticisms. Most recently, housing advocates have called for the Program to provide rents on a rent-geared-to-income basis at no more than 30% of a household income. Currently, the Program sets rents at the *City's Official Plan* definition of no more than the average market rent for Toronto as published annually by Canada Mortgage and Housing Corporation (Figure 6.2).

Non-profit groups have also been critical of the fact that the Program does not guarantee affordability in perpetuity. The minimum affordability period for the Program is 25 years. The "pipeline" approach of providing early project approvals rather than shovel-ready projects has increased the risk of some projects not proceeding. The longer development and completion schedules have also resulted in some level of frustration being expressed by local politicians and the public who are looking for immediate results and quick fixes.

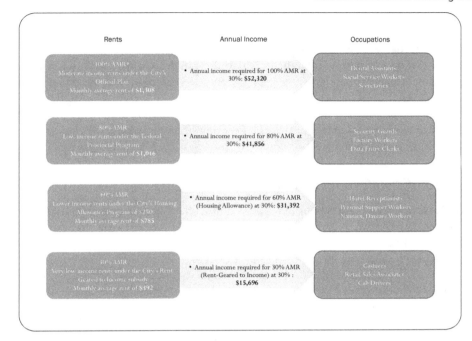

FIGURE 6.2 Toronto Housing Rents and Affordability by Income Band.
Source: City of Toronto's Affordable Housing Office, August 2018.

Leveraging Public Land to Deliver Affordable Housing

It is now some 21 years ago that the new City of Toronto was created through the amalgamation of five local governments and the metropolitan regional government. Over this period of time, a series of public land initiatives impacting the development of affordable housing has emerged.

Leveraging Public Housing Land

Following the municipal amalgamation in Toronto and the provincial transfer (downloading) of housing to Ontario municipalities, the new City was faced with a decision on how to administer the various public housing agencies – specifically the Metro Toronto Housing Company, CityHome, and the Metropolitan Toronto Housing Authority (Golden, 1999). In 2000, City Council amalgamated the three public housing agencies into a new arms-length corporation named Toronto Community Housing Corporation (TCHC). Almost 60,000 residential units were transferred to TCHC, and the new corporation was given broad independent powers to operate.

Immediately following the creation of TCHC, the new leadership developed a public/private sector model of public housing revitalization. This model provided for the replacement of large public housing communities with new mixed-income communities by leveraging profits from the sale of public land to provide for the full replacement of social housing. Most importantly, the revitalization guaranteed the right of return to every social housing resident. The public housing revitalization projects approved by TCHC and City Council were bold, long-term, and unprecedented billion-dollar social and economic investments undertaken in partnership with the private development community and impacted residents.

Today, there are six major revitalization initiatives underway representing the replacement of some 4,805 rent-geared-to-income social housing homes and the addition of 13,500 new market ownership homes. The revitalization sites include Regent Park, Alexandra Park, Lawrence

Heights, Allenbury Gardens, Leslie Nymark, and 250 Davenport Road. In Regent Park, so far some 1,002 new affordable rental homes have been built through leveraging $70 million of federal/provincial affordable housing funding and $37.5 million in City financial incentives. The revitalization of these communities has been achieved through the application of planning and social development principles supporting strong "complete communities". As a result, in addition to the creation of replacement and new housing units, the formerly isolated public housing projects are re-integrated into the adjacent community through reconnecting the street grid, the inclusion of new community facilities, the fostering of new commercial uses, and the employment of public housing residents throughout the process (City Planning Division, 2018).

The West Don Lands Public Lands Affordable Housing Legacy

The West Don Lands are located in downtown Toronto near the west side of the mouth of the Don River (Figure 6.3). The area consists of 80 acres of land and historically supported land uses of heavy industry, stockyards, scrapyards, rail uses, and a distillery. In 1987, in response to the need for new affordable housing, the Province of Ontario and the City of Toronto announced the multimillion-dollar expropriation of all of the businesses within the West Don Lands. The catalyst for change came in 1999 with a federal, provincial, and City tri-government agreement to support Toronto's bid for the 2008 Olympic Games. This effort led to an agreement to establish a new tri-government agency Waterfront Toronto. The new agency was given funding and responsibility to lead the development of 2,000 acres of brownfield lands on Toronto's waterfront into beautiful, accessible, sustainable mixed-use communities and dynamic public spaces. This included the full build out of 40,000 new homes (Marr, 2015). Working with local residents groups and Waterfront Toronto, the City designated the area as *Regeneration Area* and *Parks and Open Space Areas*. This plan placed a requirement that 20% of all new residential housing be required to be developed as affordable rental housing, thus guaranteeing a mix of incomes in the community.

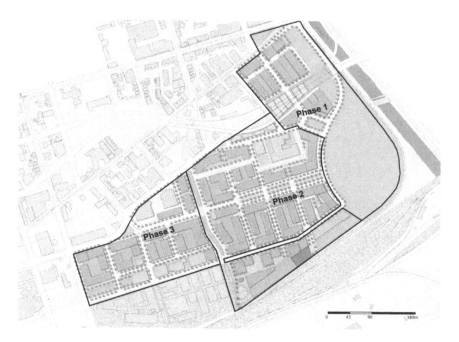

FIGURE 6.3 West Don Lands Phasing Plan.
Source: City of Toronto.

Phase One – New TCHC Homes

While the 2008 Olympic Games were ultimately awarded to Beijing, the City's Olympic bid had created the momentum needed to kick-start the first phase of the West Don Lands redevelopment process. After many years of planning and false starts, by 2014, the first phase of the community was beginning to take shape. Key infrastructure requirements were in place, including the construction of a flood protection berm, the design and build out of the 18 acre Corktown Common Park, and the completion of new residential housing.

Critical to the successful implementation of the first phase of development was the reaching of an agreement in 2009 among Waterfront Toronto, the Ontario government, and the City of Toronto that they would provide serviced and clean land available at no cost to support the development of the affordable rental housing. *The West Don Lands Affordable Housing Agreement* provided the foundation for a partnership among the parties to support TCHC in the construction of 243 new affordable seniors and family TCHC rental homes at River Street and King Street West. Investments from the federal/provincial Affordable Housing Program, the City of Toronto, and TCHC provided the capital to construct the homes. The first phase development of West Don Lands was underway, but what about phases two and three where the majority of the land still remained vacant? A further catalyst was soon on the horizon. That catalyst came in the form of the provincially backed City bid to host the Pan American Games in 2016.

Phase Two – New Non-Profit Homes

Through strong leadership from the Ontario government and the former Premier David Peterson, the City won the bid to host the Pan American Games in 2015. The bid plan called for the creation of a village in the West Don Lands to house the expected 10,000 athletes. As the owners of the West Don Lands, the provincial agency Infrastructure Ontario (IO) assumed the lead in securing a private development partner and ensuring the buildout of the next phase on time and on budget. Through a special Pan Am Office, the City coordinated the involvement of various City divisions throughout and during the Games. Most importantly, IO and the Ontario Ministry of Housing engaged the City's Affordable Housing Office in the detailed planning, approving the specifications and selection of two non-profit organizations who would own and operate 253 units of affordable housing in two rental buildings (City Planning Division, 2018).

This unique arrangement where the master developer of the Pan Am Village and the Province of Ontario would build and turn over the ownership of the buildings to the new owners and operators was the first of its kind in Toronto. This unique partnership resulted in new affordable non-profit housing for Fred Victor Homes to provide housing for low-income and vulnerable residents and Wigwamen to provide housing focused on the needs of indigenous residents.

Phase Three – The Public/Private Partnership

With the Pan Am Games successfully completed, attention turned to how to maintain the momentum in building out the new community. The key issue was how to fund the build out of the affordable rental housing. This time the catalyst came not from a sporting event, but directly from Toronto's overheated housing market. With rapidly rising house prices in the Greater Toronto Area, a shortage of affordable rental accommodation, and cases of evictions from rent increases, the federal, provincial, and City governments all introduced measures to "cool" the housing market and provide new supply (Marr, 2015). In particular, the province introduced the *Ontario Fair Housing Plan* and the *Ontario Affordable Housing Lands Program*.

The first phase of the *Ontario Affordable Housing Lands Program* identified Blocks 3W, 4W, 7W, 8, and 20 in the West Don Lands for new residential development. In working with the City of Toronto, the Province created a new public/private sector development model where

> the primary objective through this premier urban land site offer is to leverage the prized land value of Sites in exchange for a conscientiously designed mixed market and affordable rental housing development. To this effect, the collective vision for the Properties is that they are specifically developed in a manner that effectively marries a broad range of residential unit layouts and accommodates a wide diversity of low to high income residents.

The West Don Lands offering provided a total of 550,000 sq. ft. of residential and mixed-use density where the builder/operator would be required to provide 30% of the residential units (390) at affordable rent levels, 10% at 40% of average market rent, and 40% at 80% of average market rents for a lease term of 99 years. In return for providing the affordable housing, the developer obtained a 99-year discounted leased to reduce upfront land costs. As part of the package, the City pre-approved *Open Door Program* municipal financial incentives for the affordable housing units. The incentives included waiver of planning, building and development charge fees, and property taxes for the duration of the lease. The planning approvals are also being fast-tracked. It has taken some 30 years, but the Toronto-Ontario vision of a new mixed-income community in the West Don Lands is finally being realized. At present, 886 affordable rental homes are being developed due to strong public/private partnerships leveraging the essential value of public lands in delivering affordability.

Municipal governments, compared to other orders of government, do not have the same means to fund housing initiatives. Despite this, cities have been and continue to be leaders in innovation, by using their resources to create the right conditions for other governments to invest (Woetzel et al., 2014). This local leadership is often the catalyst for other governments to act (Hern, 2010). *The Housing Now Initiative* is no different. To meet the public expectations on housing, the City created a programme that takes the first step, the initial leadership, to create new affordable housing in Toronto. The City is using the tools at its disposal, specifically leveraging municipal surplus land at higher-order transit locations to create housing opportunities. This is the genesis behind Toronto's *Housing Now Initiative*, and ultimate success will require investments from all governments.

Housing Now Initiative

Launched by Mayor Tory in October 2018, the initiative focuses on activation of public land for new affordable housing for immediate development. This created a great opportunity for City staff to develop a programme to address affordable housing but also develop mix-income transit-oriented communities. The approach was a distinct break from past business practices where the City's disposition of surplus municipal land sought to achieve the highest financial return.

Housing Now Delivering Affordable Rental Homes

Through the *Housing Now Initiative,* the City is leveraging the value of surplus municipal land, providing municipal financial incentives, and is providing a high level of certainty for the development community by pre-zoning sites. These are real and tangible benefits that help support the business case for the overall development, including the new long-term affordable rental housing. The affordable rental homes are targeted to serve households earning between $21,000

TABLE 6.1 Housing Now, Affordable to Whom?

Market Asking Rent	Annual Income	Annual Income	Housing Now Target (80% AMR)[a]
	$20,000	$20,000	
	$30,000	$30,000	Bachelor $871
	$40,000	$40,000	1-Bedroom $1,106
	$50,000	$50,000	2-Bedroom $1,193
Bachelor $1,399	$60,000	$60,000	3-Bedroom $1,325
1-Bedroom $1,738	$70,000	$70,000	
2-Bedroom $2,026	$80,000	$80,000	
3-Bedroom $2,298	$90,000	$90,000	
Early childhood educator Annual income $33,150	Retired/pensioner Annual income $38,400	Welder Annual income $44,850	Employment counsellor Annual income $52,000

Source: Based on data by CreateTO, September 2019.

a Average market rent (AMR) figures are used to set affordable housing monthly occupancy costs, with different affordable housing programmes charging 100% or 80% of AMR, depending on their agreement.

and $52,000 per year who would pay no more than 30% of their gross income in housing costs (see Table 6.1). These households represent residents who are key workers within the Toronto economy but are unable to find and keep affordable housing in the private rental market where rents for comparable units are $600–$1,000 higher. In addition, some rental homes may be more deeply affordable through working with non-profit organizations who have access to rent-geared-to-income funding programmes and/or though housing allowance programmes (City Manager's Office, 2019).

Building Non-Profit Housing Capacity and Non-Profit Engagement

In approving the *Housing Now Initiative*, the City established a $1 million non-profit capacity building fund. The fund is designed to support non-profit organizations who are bidding themselves, as part of a non-profit consortium or in partnership with a private sector developer. Non-profits have the experience in knowing what works in terms of physical design and building specifications. Non-profit organizations also have a wealth of expertise in the management and operation of housing, including with tenant groups with low-incomes, special needs, and requiring support services. Non-profit housing organizations can also provide a "tenants first" perspective focusing on resident selection, maintaining a residents housing stability, and improving the quality of life of residents (CreateTO, 2019).

Phase One identifies 11 surplus City properties located at higher-order public transit corridors. The City prioritized four sites to be expedited through the planning approval and market offering process in 2019 with construction to start in 2020/2021. The additional seven sites are planned to come forward in 2020 (Richardson, 2019). Extensive public engagement also occurred.

Challenges and Opportunities

The *Housing Now Initiative* represents a new approach to City building and leveraging the value of surplus City properties. The activation of 11 sites is the first phase of a programme intended to support the City's target of providing 40,000 new affordable rental homes between 2018 and 2030. The challenges include:

- Managing public expectations on the speed and delivery of the *Housing Now* sites given that the development and completion of the new affordable housing is a multi-year process – yet the need for affordable housing is immediate.
- Recognizing the limitations of delivering long-term affordable housing rental and mixed-income communities without upfront federal/provincial capital and operating funding – in essence, there is a limit on how much affordable housing can be secured when leveraging the value of surplus municipal land and municipal financial incentives.
- Scaling-up of the *Housing Now Initiative* beyond City sites to achieve a 40,000 affordable rental housing target within 12 years.
- Shifting the focus of the building industry away from a condominium development business model to new mixed-income model that addresses the need for purpose-built rental affordable and market housing.

The opportunities include:

- Restoring public confidence in the role and power of government to use land-use planning and public programmes to deliver urgent public benefits.
- Contributing to providing a range of City-building goals such as creating new mixed-income communities and providing new neighbourhood amenities such as childcare and community hubs.
- Supporting the City's purpose-built private rental housing industry and non-profit housing sectors.
- Kick-starting new affordable and mixed-income housing development with the expectations that the federal and provincial governments will participate through their respective programmes.
- Providing long-term secure and affordable rental homes for low- and moderate-income households who are at the forefront of Toronto's housing crisis.

Conclusion: Developing and Implementing a New Approach

Addressing the affordable housing crisis through strategies to increase the supply of affordable rental housing has emerged as a top priority in Toronto. The City has developed a range of programme and policy tools to stimulate new supply (National Housing and Homelessness Network, 2004). In particular, *Toronto's Open Door Program* provides a range of incentives to eligible non-profit and private builders. In efforts to scale-up new affordable rental housing, governments must look carefully at the importance of public land to leverage affordable rental housing in new developments. This applies to existing land assets and the potential to secure strategic land sites for affordable housing such as through purchase, expropriation, and inclusionary zoning practices (Hulchanski, 2010).

The City of Toronto's experience and track record demonstrate that it is possible to successfully develop new mixed-income communities and new affordable housing on existing and surplus municipal lands. The example of success of leveraging partnerships for affordable rental housing is the 30-year partnership between the Ontario government and the City of Toronto. While not the silver bullet solution to the urban affordable housing crisis, the strategic use of public land has an important role in contributing to solutions today and for generations to come.

Municipal governments play different roles with respect to housing. Traditionally, planning departments direct where housing should be located through *Official Plans* and issue planning approvals; the building department issues permits and inspects construction; the City administers federal and provincial housing infrastructure funds and programmes (Hellyer, 1969). Working in different City divisions, it is often easy to function in silos and continue operating under the status quo. This need not be the case; while municipal resources are scarce, there are ways to break down silos and drive a housing agenda from inside municipal government.

Housing Now was introduced in 2018, but its components are not new – the City has always disposed of land, and planning approvals could be streamlined and fees waived (City Manager's Office, 2019). The opportunity presented itself to align these functions to address a housing crisis in the City while leveraging federal support (Government of Canada, 2017). The mayor and City Council shifted the priority from selling off City land for revenue to using it to build housing. It called for coordination and accountability to get results; thus, a new Housing Secretariat was created to ensure that the work was coordinated and on track. While there have been some challenges along the way, this new coordinated approach that responds to the issues raised by developers and non-profit sector to expedite approvals and provide low-cost land will address housing affordability challenges in Toronto. As Toronto proceeds with the *Housing Now Initiative* and other measures to scale-up towards a achieving a goal of 40,000 affordable rental homes, the real measure of success will be in getting shovels in the ground, having new residents move in, and ultimately producing thriving new healthy mixed-income communities.

Acknowledgements

This chapter has been prepared with input and assistance of Mercedeh Madani and Minha Hassim, Policy Development Officers, Housing Secretariat. Views expressed in this chapter are those of the author.

References

Canadian Centre for Economic Analysis and Canadian Urban Institute (2019). Toronto Housing Market Analysis. City of Toronto. Retrieved October 1, 2019 from www.toronto.ca/legdocs/mmis/2019/ph/bgrd/backgroundfile-124480.pdf.

CBRE Limited (2017). *Land Portfolio Offering for the Provincial Affordable Land Program*. Toronto: CBRE.

City Manager's Office (2019). Implementing the Housing Now Initiative, City of Toronto. Retrieved October 1, 2019 from www.toronto.ca/legdocs/mmis/2019/ex/bgrd/backgroundfile-123663.pdf.

City Planning Division (2018). Rental Housing Market Conditions in Toronto, City of Toronto. Retrieved September 13, 2018 from www.toronto.ca/legdocs/mmis/2018/td/bgrd/backgroundfile-112710.pdf.

CreateTO (2019). *Housing Now Initiative*. Retrieved October 1, 2019 from https://createto.ca/housingnow/

Golden, A. (1999). *Taking Responsibility for Homelessness: An Action Plan for Toronto: Report of the Mayor's Homelessness Action Task Force*. Toronto: City of Toronto.

Government of Canada (2017). Canada's National Housing Strategy. Retrieved September 13, 2018 from www.placetocallhome.ca/pdfs/Canada-National-Housing-Strategy.pdf.

Hellyer, P. (1969). *Report of the Task Force on Housing and Urban Development*. Ottawa: Government of Canada: 41–43.

Hern, M. (2010). *Common Ground in a Liquid City: Essays in Defence of an Urban Future*. Toronto: AK Press, Government of Canada.

Hulchanski, D. (2010). The Three Cities within Toronto Income Polarization among Toronto's Neighbourhoods, 1970–2005, Cities Center, University of Toronto. Retrieved September 13, 2018 from www.urbancentre.utoronto.ca/pdfs/curp/tnrn/Three-Cities-Within-Toronto-2010-Final.pdf.

Kneebone, R., and Jadidzadeh, A. (2017). *An Analysis of Homeless Shelter Use in Toronto, 2011–2016*. Toronto: City of Toronto Shelter, Support and Housing Administration. Retrieved September 13, 2018 from www.toronto.ca/wp-content/uploads/2017/10/97c8-SSHA-Analysis-of-shelter-use2011-2016.pdf.

Marr, G. (2015). Toronto's Residential Land Prices Reach New Highs: "More Condominiums Coming". *Financial Post*. Retrieved September 12, 2018 from https://business.financialpost.com/personal-finance/mortgages-realestate/torontos-residential-land-prices-reach-new-highs-more-condominiums-coming.

National Housing and Homelessness Network (2004). "Ending Homelessness: The One Percent Solution", in Hulchanski, D., and Shapcott, M. (eds). *Finding Room: Policy Options for a Canadian Rental Housing Strategy*. Toronto: Centre for Urban and Community Studies, University of Toronto: 381–387.

Richardson, M. (2019). "Is John Tory's Housing Now Plan Crumbling?" *Spacing*. Retrieved October 5, 2019 from http://spacing.ca/toronto/2019/10/02/is-john-torys-housing-now-plan-crumbling/.

Woetzel, J., Ram, S., Mischke, J., Garemo, N., & Sankhe, Sh. (2014). *A Blueprint for Addressing the Global Affordable Housing Challenge*. Zurich: McKinsey Global Institute (MGI) Report.

PART II

Mixed-Income Affordable Housing and Community Building

7

MIX AND MATCH

A Framework for Understanding Mixed-Income Outcomes

Shomon Shamsuddin

Introduction

Mixed-income housing is a highly prominent approach to housing policy and new housing development in countries and cities around the world. Governments and housing agencies in Australia, Canada, Ireland, the Netherlands, Sweden, the United Kingdom, and the United States, to name a few examples, have proposed or implemented some form of mixed-income housing, in what has been described as "a striking example of international policy transfer" (August, 2008; Bailey et al., 2006; Bridge and Butler, 2011; Chaskin and Joseph, 2015; Darcy, 2010: 1; Musterd and Andersson, 2005; Tsenkova, 2020). In the United States, local and state governments have used regulation and financing tools to construct mixed-income housing since the 1970s; since the early 1990s, the federal government has adopted mixed-income housing as a high-profile strategy for redeveloping public housing through the US Department of Housing and Urban Development's *HOPE VI (Housing Opportunities for People Everywhere)* program (Brophy and Smith, 1997; Epp, 1996; Popkin et al., 2004; Schwartz and Tajbakjsh, 1997; Shamsuddin, 2017; Vale, 2013; Vale and Shamsuddin, 2014).

For a housing strategy, mixed-income housing has a surprisingly wide range of appeal and support. This may be due, in part, to the involvement of the public sector, private sector, and non-profit sector in creating mixed-income housing developments. Elected officials have voiced their support for and belief in the value of creating mixed-income communities through government housing programs (Cisneros and Engdahl, 2009; Cuomo, 1999). Planning and housing advocacy organizations encourage governments to pursue mixed-income housing policies (for example, see Metropolitan Council, 2019). Even private developers and investors have spoken favorably about mixed-income development and its prospects for success (Baron, 2009; Harper, 2017).

Prior scholarly work raises important concerns about mixed-income housing but tends to focus on public (or social) housing redevelopment. Studies of selected mixed-income public housing redevelopment sites in the United States generally find that low-income residents report satisfaction with improvements in housing quality and neighborhood safety but also note few positive social interactions with wealthier neighbors (Chaskin and Joseph, 2015; Kleit, 2005; Shamsuddin and Vale, 2017). Case studies of social mixing involving public housing in Canada and Australia observe that public housing tenants may face stigma and oppression, and miss their

DOI: 10.4324/9781003172949-7

previous homes and the sense of community, which raises questions about the need for social mixes in housing at all (Arthurson, 2002; August, 2016; Ruming et al., 2004). All of these studies draw conclusions about mixed-income housing based on public housing redevelopment but overlook other forms and strategies of the broader phenomenon of residential income mixing.

Additional work suggests that some of the problems observed in mixed-income housing may be due, in part, to the lack of shared understanding of what "mixed income" means. There is no consistent, widely accepted definition of mixed-income housing despite repeated references and discussions of the term over the course of more than 20 years (Brophy and Smith, 1997; Holin et al., 2003; Khadduri and Martin, 1997; Levy et al., 2010; Schwartz and Tajbakjsh, 1997; Vale and Shamsuddin, 2017). Although there is little agreement about how to define the term, mixed-income housing can be characterized by several dimensions: allocation, the proportion of subsidized and unsubsidized units; proximity, the spatial scale of income mixing; tenure, the balance between rental and homeownership units; and duration, the length of time that housing unit affordability is required (Vale and Shamsuddin, 2017). These dimensions directly refer to characteristics of housing, but they do not address residents or the larger geographic context. Further, the dimensions exclusively draw upon public housing redevelopment under the *HOPE VI program*.

Much academic attention has been devoted to mixed-income redevelopment of public (or social) housing, but there are many forms of mixed-income housing. Besides the *HOPE VI*-style approach to public housing redevelopment, and its successor program called Choice Neighborhoods, there are other housing strategies to bring low-income and higher-income residents together. In the USA, these include tenant-based subsidies (e.g. the *Section 8 Housing Choice Voucher program*), financial incentives to build affordable housing (such as the *Low-Income Housing Tax Credit program*), and local regulations that encourage or require affordable housing to be included in new development (e.g. inclusionary zoning). Countries throughout Europe have also developed and implemented a wide variety of housing mix policies that seek to bring different groups of people to live in close proximity to each other (Musterd and Andersson, 2005). Each of these approaches has differences that may have implications for income mixing and expected outcomes.

This chapter presents a new, unified conceptual framework for understanding social mix or mixed-income housing and its potential effects. The framework draws attention to the dynamic process of creating a social or income mix. It identifies several crucial aspects: household income, the moving process, and the neighborhood context, in addition to the housing itself. More specifically, the framework examines which households move to create mixed-income housing, the relative incomes (and other characteristics) of those households, and the neighborhood conditions into which they move. The shorthand description of the framework is "who is moved where." The framework helps distinguish different forms of mixed-income housing and their expected effects. The framework makes several contributions: it draws attention to individual households and neighborhood context, instead of only the physical housing; it integrates households, housing, and neighborhoods into a unified understanding of mixed-income housing; and it applies to multiple forms of income mixing, not just public housing mixed-income redevelopment.

Theory and Literature

Despite the popularity of mixed-income housing, there is little consensus on how to define what it is. More than 20 years ago, a respected housing policy researcher and an official in the U.S. Department of Housing and Urban Development wrote that, "There is no accepted definition of mixed-income housing" (Khadduri and Martin, 1997, 35). They were not alone in their assessment. Analysts and researchers similarly noted that "the term does not carry a formal definition in the housing field" (Brophy and Smith, 1997, 5) and "there is no standard definition in the research literature for what constitutes 'mixed-income' housing" (Holin et al., 2003, 42). An important early article on mixed-income housing presented a series of questions and issues to consider, including that the "term *mixed-income housing* can refer to many different kinds of housing" (Schwartz and Tajbakhsh, 1997, 73). However, the inclusiveness of the term provides little guidance. More recent work has come to the conclusion that "what counts as mixed income varies considerably" (Levy et al., 2010, 16). This work suggests that a definition of mixed-income housing is elusive.

Other housing researchers and practitioners have proposed definitions of mixed-income housing, but little agreement exists here as well. Analysts have suggested that mixed-income housing describes housing developments where 20% or more of families are below 30% of area median income (AMI) and 20% or more are above 50% AMI (Holin et al., 2003). An experienced developer has stated that mixed-income projects can be described by the proportion of units allocated to different groups and typically consist of one-third public housing, one-third affordable housing, and one-third market-rate units (Baron, 2009). In general, scholars and analysts operate under the idea that "mixed-income housing means a deliberate effort to construct and/or own a multifamily development that has the mixing of income groups as a fundamental part of its financial and operational plans" (Brophy and Smith, 1997, 5). But the lack of clear definition raises questions about the implications of creating mixed-income housing.

Theorized Benefits

Many scholars and advocates believe that mixed-income housing will create social and political benefits for residents, especially lower-income residents. Prior work theorizes that the presence of higher-income households may lead to (1) increased social capital for low-income residents; (2) direct or indirect role modeling of social norms for work and behavior; (3) informal social control that produces safer communities for all residents; and (4) gains for the broader community through enhanced engagement of political and market forces (Joseph et al., 2007). Similar expected benefits but somewhat different mechanisms for generating those benefits are attributed to mixed-tenure communities in the United Kingdom (Kearns and Mason, 2007).

Dimensions of Mixed-Income housing

Prior work points to four

> dimensions that apply to mixed-income housing projects: 1) distribution of units by subsidy type (allocation); 2) spatial separation of income mix (proximity); 3) distribution of homeownership versus rental units (tenure); and 4) time limits for subsidies that preserve the income mix (duration).
>
> *(Vale and Shamsuddin, 2017: 59)*

Allocation refers to how housing units are distributed by the type of subsidy in a mixed-income housing project. Allocation encompasses the range of subsidy levels included in the project and the proportions of different income groups represented. The measure of allocation is often expressed in common housing unit subsidy categories: public housing, affordable housing, and market-rate housing. Public housing units are typically occupied by households with incomes that are less than 30% of AMI, affordable housing units are often intended for households with 40–60% of AMI, and market-rate units may house residents with incomes of 100% of AMI or higher (Vale and Shamsuddin, 2017).

Proximity refers to the spatial dimension inherent in mixed-income housing, that is, the spatial area in which residents of different income groups will be living together. Residents of different income groups could live in housing units on the same floor of a building, on different floors of the same building, or in different buildings altogether. Closer proximity is expected to create more opportunities for interaction and social relationships among residents than more spatially distant living arrangements (Vale and Shamsuddin, 2017).

Tenure refers to how housing units are distributed according to rental housing or ownership units. Generally, rental units are expected to have more resident turnover than ownership units. Low-income homeownership units in low-income neighborhoods may appeal to residents with long-standing relationships and ties to the area. However, homeownership units in low-income neighborhoods that are advertised for market-rate households may be more likely to attract people who treat housing as a speculative investment, which could also create resident turnover (Vale and Shamsuddin, 2017).

Duration refers to how long the housing units are required or expected to receive subsidies. The length of time may affect the financial and residential stability of mixed-income housing projects. Some forms of mixed-income housing rely on housing unit subsidies that are programmatically time limited, for example, *Low-Income Housing Tax Credits*. The duration of housing subsidies can have short-term and long-term consequences for those who live in mixed-income housing, how long they live there, what neighborhood opportunities are available, and how well the housing is maintained. Time-limited subsidies may benefit lower-income households in the short-term by providing housing opportunities, while subsidies without time limits may help lower-income households remain in their housing despite neighborhood change (Vale and Shamsuddin, 2017).

These dimensions describe several important factors that housing agencies and housing developers can control when creating mixed-income housing. The dimensions suggest that mixed-income housing can be understood as four types of mixes: (1) socioeconomic mix (allocation of types of subsidy); (2) spatial mix (proximity of different kinds of subsidized units); (3) financial mix (types of tenure made available); and (4) temporal mix (duration of subsidies) (Vale and Shamsuddin, 2017).

It is important to note that this prior work on dimensions was based on administrative *HOPE VI* data obtained from the US Department of Housing and Urban Development. In other words, the dimensions emerged from an examination of HOPE VI redevelopment of public housing only. Of course, these dimensions may be applied to other forms of mixed-income housing. But some mixed-income projects will not have public housing units or extremely low-income residents.

Further, the dimensions focus on physical (e.g. allocation and proximity) or programmatic (e.g. tenure and duration) characteristics of housing. They overlook other inputs into mixed-income housing. Two important considerations for understanding the variety of types and potential effects of mixed-income housing are as follows: (1) individual households living in the development, and (2) the neighborhood context in which the development is located.

Empirical

Prior empirical studies of mixed-income housing find mixed benefits and drawbacks for lower-income and higher-income residents.

Research based on six case studies from Australian public housing estates indicates that housing policy (1) seeks to reduce the concentration of public housing and create mixed-income communities in order to help connect previously socially excluded public housing residents to society; and (2) is predicated on the idea that a balanced social mix is necessary for developing inclusive and cohesive communities. But the case studies suggest that cohesive communities are already in place and predate mixed-income development, which suggests that balanced social mixes are not required (Arthurson, 2002).

In New South Wales, Australia, social mix involves integrating public housing tenants into places that are mostly occupied by private owners and private renters. An in-depth case study finds that public housing tenants face stigma, oppression, and treatment as "the other" (Ruming et al., 2004).

Based on interviews and ethnographic participant observation, a case study of mixed-income housing in Toronto finds some residents were not satisfied with changes in housing quality, neighborhood planning, and social relations (August, 2016). The former Don Mount Court, now named Rivertowne, was the first redevelopment of public housing into mixed-income housing in Canada. Some public housing tenants longed for their previous homes and were unhappy about the loss of previous community connections. They also reported tense social interactions and relationships with higher-income residents.

A study of owners and renters in three Scottish estates finds that they occupy different social worlds. New housing for owner occupation has little effect on social networks of renters (Atkinson and Kintrea, 2000).

A thorough study of selected sites of mixed-income redevelopment of public housing in Chicago finds that low-income residents are pleased with some of the physical aspects of redevelopment, including the substantial improvement in housing quality compared to the previously existing public housing (Chaskin and Joseph, 2015). However, there is little evidence of the type of social interactions associated with the theorized benefits of mixed-income housing. Instead, poor residents report they have developed few meaningful social relationships with their wealthier neighbors. Further, they experience differential treatment from higher-income residents and building management personnel, despite living in the same building, a situation the authors describe as incorporated exclusion.

Framework and Discussion

Mixed-income housing appears to be a simple, straightforward idea, but it encompasses many complicated factors and forces at work. The conceptual framework outlined below helps in understanding mixed-income housing by unpacking some of its constituent elements. A key point is that the framework clearly highlights the importance of considering the dynamic process of creating mixed-income housing.

Households

By construction, mixed-income housing entails bringing households of different income levels together. Some of these households are considered low-income households—in the United States context, the conventional threshold for the low-income category is households with incomes that are less than 80% of the AMI (US HUD, 1998). These households may experience different forms of material hardship, such as not having enough money to pay for basic needs, including food, going to see a doctor or going to the hospital, and paying rent (Shamsuddin and Campbell, 2021). Low-income households may be employed, receiving government benefits, or some combination. However, there is the risk of economic instability due to at-will employment, work schedule changes, and reduction or loss of benefits (Hill et al., 2017). Low incomes may also mean that these households have little or no savings to draw upon in the event of an unexpected event, such as job loss, eviction, or a car breaking down (Board of Governors, 2018). Low-income households may live in low-quality housing, deteriorated units in serious need of repairs, or overcrowded conditions (Watson et al., 2020). Their housing may be located in neighborhoods that are economically declining and distant from employment opportunities. Households that are searching for or already receive a rental housing subsidy may feel constrained to live in public housing or other affordable housing—and the neighborhoods in which they are located—in order to ensure continued receipt of the rent subsidy. For these households, mixed-income housing may be one of the few options available to them.

Higher-income households typically have more resources at their disposal and better access to resources than their low-income counterparts. Although there is no standard litmus test for high income, these households in the United States may have incomes that are 200% of the AMI or even higher. They can comfortably afford to pay market-rate prices for housing and still have plenty of money remaining to pay for basic necessities like food and health care, in addition to purchasing non-essential items. These households are typically employed, often with two wage earners, and may have other sources of income from investments. These households often have high education levels that lead to stable employment positions with many benefits. Higher-income households may live in high-quality housing, new or recently updated units, with spacious accommodations. Their housing is often located in neighborhoods with many educational, cultural, and social amenities. Higher-income households generally have their choice of housing options and neighborhoods in which to live. These households may be motivated to live in mixed-income housing because it is underpriced compared to other market-rate housing or they view themselves as "urban pioneers." In the case of homeownership in mixed-income housing, higher-income households may intend to use the unit as a second home, convert the unit to short- or long-term rental as an additional source of income, or engage in property flipping by quickly reselling the unit after an increase in value.

Moving

In order to bring households of different incomes together, mixed-income housing typically involves households moving. In some cases, low-income households are the ones who move; in other cases, higher-incomes households are the ones who move; sometimes both groups move. Low-income households may feel compelled or forced to move because of the opportunity to obtain or continue receiving a subsidy. Further, there may be few options in the private housing market, and they might be prohibitively expensive. Higher-income households may deliberately elect or voluntarily wish to move for investment purposes or other reasons. The move itself has costs that can be both financial and psychological. For some households, moving can elicit a feeling of uprooting and displacement, which can be heightened if the move is perceived as forced or not by choice. Also, moving may be precipitated by individual circumstances, such as family formation, dissolution, or other changes in family composition. It is also worth noting that some mixed-income housing is developed on sites that previously contained low-income housing that was subsequently demolished, so mixed-income housing may entail multiple moves for some households. Moving may involve relocating to a completely new and unfamiliar area or it may be a move to a neighborhood that is a known quantity. In some cases, moves may result in a return to a neighborhood where the households previously lived. Generally speaking, moves are associated with different types of social relationships that are weakened or severed and expected to be repaired, maintained, or reconstructed.

Housing

Mixed-income housing also involves the physical component of the housing that is constructed and its associated programmatic aspects. As noted earlier, prior work indicates there are four important dimensions in considering mixed-income housing projects: (1) allocation, (2) proximity, (3) tenure, and (4) duration. Allocation refers to the distribution of units by subsidy type. Proximity refers to the spatial separation of income mix. Tenure refers to the distribution of homeownership versus rental units. Duration refers to the time limits for subsidies that preserve the income mix. In addition, there are other housing project factors that are important to consider. These include development size, building type, and rate of resident return.

Neighborhood

Finally, mixed-income housing is situated within the geographic context of a specific place or neighborhood. The neighborhood may have multiple characteristics that are important for residents and can influence the outcomes of mixed-income housing. Some neighborhoods may contain or be close to a wide range of employment options that match the skills and interests of residents. Other neighborhoods may feature education and training opportunities for occupational and personal advancement. Neighborhoods may be distinguished by access to public transportation as an affordable means for travel between home, work, school, and other destinations. The presence of or proximity to community institutions, houses of worship, social organizations, parks, and places for recreation may also be important.

The conceptual framework brings these constitutive elements together. It considers household income, the moving process, and the neighborhood context, in addition to the housing itself. It also forces us to identify and examine key differences between various approaches to mixed-income housing. The framework can be visualized using a diagram. See Figure 7.1.

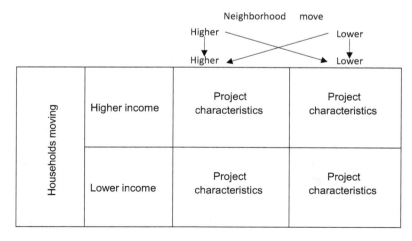

FIGURE 7.1 Income Mixing Conceptual Framework.
Source: Author.

The framework describes how lower-income households may move from higher-income neighborhoods to other higher-income neighborhoods or to lower-income neighborhoods. Or lower-income households may move from lower-income neighborhoods to other lower-income neighborhoods or to higher-income neighborhoods. Similarly, higher-income households may make the same kinds of moves from and to higher- or lower-income neighborhoods.

It is worth pointing out that in the study of mixed-income housing, interest is typically devoted to two types of moves: from lower-income neighborhoods to higher-income neighborhoods or from higher-income neighborhoods to lower-income neighborhoods. However, some families—more often poor households—make moves from one lower-income neighborhood to another lower-income neighborhood. Similarly, other families—mostly wealthy households—make moves from one higher-income neighborhood to another higher-income neighborhood.

As indicated in the figure, project-level variables such as allocation, proximity, tenure, and duration are embedded within the conceptual framework. These building characteristics may influence the frequency and degree of interactions between households. But those dimensions are not the only characteristics that affect the outcomes of mixed-income housing. The framework highlights the importance of considering the characteristics, for example, income of the individual households involved and their position relative to other households. Similarly, the framework makes clear that households and housing projects are situated within a neighborhood context that may influence mixed-income housing outcomes.

A shorthand description of the framework can be formulated as "who is moved where?". This apparently simple question incorporates a series of questions that are expanded upon below:

- What are the incomes of the individual households involved in the mixed-income housing? We would expect households at different income levels to have some differences in their concerns and expectations.
  - Are they relatively high-income households or low-income households? How poor are the poor households? For low-income households, are they considered very low-income (less than 50% of AMI) or extremely low-income (less than 30% of AMI)?
- Which households are the ones moving?
- Why are they moving or being moved? Are the moves completely voluntary or are they forced? How are the moves incentivized, if at all? Are the moves part of a speculative financial investment or due to financial necessity?
- Where are the individual households moving?
  - What is the distribution of units by subsidy type (allocation) in the mixed-income housing project?
  - What is the spatial separation of income mix (proximity) in the mixed-income housing project?
  - What is the distribution of homeownership versus rental units (tenure) in the mixed-income housing project?
  - What are the time limits for subsidies that preserve the income mix (duration) in the mixed-income housing project?
  - How does the median income of the destination neighborhood compare with the median income of the origin neighborhood? Is there a substantial increase or decrease in neighborhood income?

Note that there are many other questions that could be asked related to the framework that may influence household outcomes. For example, how long did the household live in the origin neighborhood prior to moving? At what life cycle stage or age did the household move (e.g.

before having children, with young children, children have left the house, working, retired)? How far (i.e. physical distance) did the household move? For the purposes of this chapter, I treat these as secondary questions.

The attention to moves acknowledges the fact that many types of social relationships are embedded in places. Households often locate in close proximity to family and friends. Residents typically form connections with their immediate (i.e. adjacent) neighbors and other residents in their neighborhood. Residents also attend or participate in local institutions or social organizations, including churches or other houses of worship, community and volunteer groups, ethnic organizations, neighborhood improvement groups, and civic associations. Individuals establish social ties with local providers of goods and services, for example, groceries, beauty and personal care, and retail.

The framework considers the income of households relative to other households and the level of neighborhood income of origin and destination locations for households that move. The attention to income in the framework is a reflection of the attention to income in housing strategies. Affordable housing programs are means tested, that is, eligibility is determined by income level. The construction of mixed-income housing is predicated on the idea of bringing households of different income levels to live together in the same location. In addition, differences in income can be a useful proxy for social distance and are associated with other relevant characteristics.

For various reasons, perhaps including a conscious decision to avoid directly addressing more contentious issues like race, policymakers in the United States have fixated on income. In the United Kingdom and other places, it is more common to discuss social mix instead of mixed-income. The distinction is subtle but has important implications. At one level, social mix explicitly acknowledges that there may be more factors to consider than simply income when encouraging different households to live in close proximity to each other. At another level, social mix emphasizes the importance of social relations that are intended to be fostered between different households. Note that the framework is flexible enough to replace income with other variables. For example, we might be more interested in educational attainment than in income in the housing mix. Then we can simply examine the number of years of schooling for households, as it compares with the population, and the mean or median years of schooling in the origin and destination neighborhoods. Similar substitutions can be made with employment level, occupational status, wealth (as distinct from income), or race and racial composition. In addition, the framework can accommodate indices that combine various measures, such as socioeconomic status.

If housing characteristics are set aside for a moment, then the framework brings households and neighborhood characteristics to the forefront. (For ease of exposition and in the interests of clarity, the following figures focus only on the destination neighborhood and therefore omit the origin neighborhood context.) The various combinations of these characteristics can provide a crosswalk for policy problems and scholarly criticisms that have emerged from prior iterations of housing policies and programs, as well as the stated policy goals of housing programs that seek to address past problems. See Figure 7.2.

Researchers and analysts have raised concerns that higher-income households exclusively moving to higher-income neighborhoods will, over time, lead to increased residential segregation by income. These types of housing practices may reinforce various types of social and political exclusion of low-income households. In many countries, residential income segregation of wealthy households naturally emerges from the operation of the private housing market. In the United States, one concrete and visible manifestation of residential income segregation and exclusion is the existence of gated housing communities.

Neighborhood

		Higher income	Lower income
Households moving	Higher income	(-) Income segregation and exclusion	(+) Reinvestment and revitalization (-) Gentrification and displacement
	Lower income	(+) Access to opportunity (-) Fears of neighborhood tipping and decline	(-) Poverty concentration

FIGURE 7.2 Crosswalk for Housing Policy Goals and Problems.
Source: Author.

Residential income segregation can also operate at the other end of the income spectrum, but this may be less often due to the choice of these households. Observers have suggested that the continual move of lower-income households to lower-income neighborhoods leads to the concentration of poor households. Some policymakers assert that concentrated poverty results in a range of social problems, including unemployment, childbirth out of wedlock, drug use, and crime. Indeed, many forms of mixed-income housing seek to address the social problems associated with the concentration of poor households in public housing.

It is interesting to note that policymakers rarely see any advantages or benefits to lower-income households moving to lower-income neighborhoods, despite decades of public policy—not only housing policy but others too—that have encouraged this very situation. However, academic research has pointed out the deep interpersonal relationships, high levels of social capital, and strong social networks and sense of community found among lower-income households living in lower-income neighborhoods (for example, see Saegert et al., 2002).

Analyzing income mixing in terms of differences between households and between neighborhoods also helps in understanding and predicting the effects on residents of mixed-income housing in its various forms. We can and should expect different effects based on household and neighborhood characteristics, in addition to project-level dimensions.

Households and neighborhood characteristics in the framework can also help distinguish between various forms of housing policy and approaches to creating income mixes in housing. These policies and approaches include public or social housing, *Housing Choice Vouchers* (also known as Section 8), public housing redevelopment into mixed-income housing projects as in the *HOPE VI program*, the *Moving to Opportunity for Fair Housing program*, *Low-Income Housing Tax Credit developments*, inclusionary zoning and inclusionary housing, and others. These policies can be arrayed across the major categories outlined in the framework: (1) lower-income households moving (back) to lower-income neighborhoods, (2) lower-income households moving to higher-income neighborhoods, and (3) higher-income households moving to lower-income neighborhoods. (The fourth category, higher-income households moving to higher-income neighborhoods describes usual activity in the private housing market but does not generally apply to typical, existing mixed-income housing strategies). See Figure 7.3.

Neighborhood

		Higher income	Lower income
Households moving	Higher income	• [Private housing market]	• Conventional view of HOPE VI redevelopment
	Lower income	• Moving to Opportunity treatment group • Inclusionary zoning in strong housing markets	• Traditional Public Housing • Typical Housing Choice Voucher use

FIGURE 7.3 Categorizing Housing Policies.
Source: Author.

Housing policies and programs to create income mixing take different forms even though they are often categorized under the common umbrella term of mixed-income housing. Some of these differences are brought to the foreground when examined in terms of household incomes, who moves, and the neighborhood context. Figure 7.3 enables and suggests how scholars might approach an "apples to apples" comparison of mixed-income housing strategies.

In many academic discussions, the terms "mixed-income housing" or "mixed-income development" have become synonymous with the transformation of deteriorated public housing projects into residential developments that house people with a range of incomes, including low-income, public housing eligible households. However, public housing redevelopment is not the only form of mixed-income housing.

"Mixed-income" is frequently employed as a signal or description of the existence of residential unit subsidies in a given housing development project. Further, the term "mixed-income housing" places emphasis on the building or residential unit as the chief product of the development process. It implies that the physical structure is the end result and primary outcome of interest. All of these combine to suggest a static view of what is involved in mixed-income housing. However, the theorized impact of mixed-income housing crucially depends on how households from different groups interact and mix together. To help redirect our attention to households and the dynamics involved—and to draw a distinction from mixed-income housing—the term "income mixing" is introduced and used. Income mixing (or social mixing) is the process or strategy of bringing households from different income groups to live together in the same location. The process fundamentally depends on moving people of different income levels from one place to another.

The term "income mixing" is also employed because it more easily accommodates different forms of creating mixed-income housing, including tenant-based subsidies, financial incentives for construction, and local regulations about the composition of new development. Income mixing is about the type and nature of interactions between residents. It indicates the importance of social relationships in evaluating housing that brings different income groups together.

There are some limitations and additional considerations to keep in mind with regard to the conceptual framework presented here. As noted earlier, there are many possible variables to consider beyond income. Social relationships are complex and can depend on a complex set of factors. Further, the framework highlights that income mixing is a dynamic process. Similarly, households, housing development composition, and neighborhoods are not static. To take a simple example, resident incomes and neighborhoods can change over time. These changes may affect the nature of content of the social relationships involved.

Despite these limitations, more careful consideration of who is moved where may lead us to revise our expectations about different forms of mixed-income housing and help explain the observed effects on residents.

Acknowledgments

The author would like to thank Mark Joseph for helpful conversations that prompted this chapter, Sasha Tsenkova for creating and organizing the symposium, and Larry Vale for advice and guidance.

References

Arthurson, K. (2002) Creating inclusive communities through balancing social mix: A critical relationship or tenuous link? *Urban Policy and Research*, 20(3): 245–261.

Atkinson, R., and Kintrea, K. (2000) Owner-occupation, social mix and neighbourhood impacts. *Policy & Politics*, 28(1): 93–108.

August, M. (2008) Social mix and Canadian public housing redevelopment: Experiences in Toronto. *Canadian Journal of Urban Research*, 17(1): 82–100.

August, M. (2016) Revitalisation gone wrong: Mixed-income public housing redevelopment in Toronto's Don Mount Court. *Urban Studies*, 53(16): 3405–3422.

Bailey, N., Haworth, A., Manzi, T., et al. (2006) *Creating and sustaining mixed income communities*. Coventry: Chartered Institute of Housing/Joseph Rowntree Foundation.

Baron, R. D. (2009) "The evolution of HOPE VI as a development program." In Cisneros, H. and Engdahl, L. (eds). *From despair to hope: HOPE VI and the new promise of public housing in America's cities*. Washington, DC: Brookings Institution Press, 31–46.

Board of Governors of the Federal Reserve System. (2018) *Report on the economic well-being of U.S. Households in 2017*. Washington, DC: Federal Reserve Board.

Bridge, G., and Butler, T. (eds). (2011) *Mixed communities: Gentrification by stealth?* Bristol: Policy Press.

Brophy, P. C., and Smith, R. N. (1997) Mixed-income housing: Factors for success. *Cityscape*, 3(2): 3–31.

Chaskin, R., and Joseph, M. (2015) *Integrating the inner city: The promise and perils of mixed-income public housing transformation*. Chicago, IL: The University of Chicago Press.

Cisneros, H., and Engdahl, L. (eds). (2009) *From despair to hope: HOPE VI and the new promise of public housing in America's cities*. Washington, DC: Brookings Institution Press.

Cuomo, A. (1999) *HOPE VI: Building communities transforming lives*. Washington, DC: U.S. Department of Housing and Urban Development.

Darcy, M. (2010) De-concentration of disadvantage and mixed income housing: A critical discourse approach. *Housing, Theory and Society*, 27(1): 1–22.

Epp, G. (1996) Emerging strategies for revitalizing public housing communities. *Housing Policy Debate*, 7(3): 563–587.

Harper, J. (2017) How mixed-income housing can benefit both communities and investors. *Urban Land Magazine*. September 18.

Hill, H. D., Romich, J., Mattingly, M. J., Shamsuddin, S., and Wething, H. (2017) An introduction to household economic instability and social policy. *Social Service Review*, 91(3): 371–389.

Holin, M. J., Buron, L., Locke, G., and Cortes, A. (2003) *Interim assessment of the HOPE VI program cross-site report*. Bethesda, MD: Abt Associates Inc.

Joseph, M. L., Chaskin, R. J., and Webber, H. S. (2007) The theoretical basis for addressing poverty through mixed-income development. *Urban Affairs Review*, 42(1): 369–409.

Kearns, A., and Mason, P. (2007) Mixed tenure communities and neighbourhood quality. *Housing Studies*, 22(5): 661–691.

Khadduri, J., and Martin, M. (1997) Mixed-income housing in the HUD multifamily stock. *Cityscape*, 3(2): 33–69.

Kleit, R. G. (2005) HOPE VI new communities: Neighborhood relationships in mixed-income housing. *Environment and Planning A*, 37(8): 1413–1441.

Levy, D. K., McDade, Z., and Dumlao, K. (2010) *Effects from living in mixed-income communities for low-income families: A review of the literature*. Washington, DC: Urban Institute.

Metropolitan Council. (2019) Support for mixed income housing development: Resources for communities to explore mixed income housing possibilities. https://metrocouncil.org/Housing/Projects/Mixed-Income-Housing-Calculator.aspx, accessed June 12, 2019.

Musterd, S., and Andersson, R. (2005) Housing mix, social mix, and social opportunities. *Urban Affairs Review*, 40(6): 761–790.

Popkin, S. J., Katz, B., Cunningham, M. K., Brown, K. D., Gustafson, J., and Turner, M. A. (2004) *A decade of HOPE VI: Research findings and policy challenges*. Washington, DC: Urban Institute.

Ruming, K. J., Mee, K. J., and McGuirk, P. M. (2004) Questioning the rhetoric of social mix: Courteous community or hidden hostility? *Australian Geographical Studies*, 42(2): 234–248.

Saegert, S., Thompson, J. P., and Warren, M. R. (eds). (2002) *Social capital and poor communities*. New York: Russell Sage Foundation.

Schwartz, A., and Tajbakjsh, K. (1997) Mixed-income housing: Unanswered questions. *Cityscape*, 3(2): 71–92.

Shamsuddin, S. (2017) Preserved for posterity: Public housing redevelopment and replacement in HOPE VI. Paper presented at the Association of Collegiate Schools of Planning (ACSP) annual conference. Denver, CO.

Shamsuddin, S., and Campbell, C. (2021) Housing cost burden, material hardship, and well-being. *Housing Policy Debate*.

Shamsuddin, S., and Vale, L. J. (2017) Hoping for more: Redeveloping U.S. public housing without marginalizing low-income residents? *Housing Studies*, 32(2): 225–244.

Tsenkova, S. (2019) Mixed-income affordable housing projects: Experiences in Canadian cities. In Tsenkova, S. (ed) *The Future of Affordable Housing*. Calgary: University of Calgary/SAPL, pp. 171–187.

US Department of Housing and Urban Development. (1998) Transmittal of fiscal year (FY) 1998 public housing/Section 8 income limits. PDR-98-02.

Vale, L. J. (2013) *Purging the poorest: Public housing and the design politics of twice-cleared communities*. Chicago, IL: The University of Chicago Press.

Vale, L. J., and Shamsuddin, S. (2014) All mixed up: Defining mixed-income in public housing redevelopment. Paper presented at ISA World Congress of Sociology. Yokohama, Japan.

Vale, L. J., and Shamsuddin, S. (2017) All mixed up: Making sense of mixed-income housing developments. *Journal of the American Planning Association*, 83(1): 56–67.

Watson, N. E., Steffan, B. L., Martin, M., and Vandenbroucke, D. A. (2020) Worst case housing needs: 2019 report to Congress. Washington, DC: U.S. Department of Housing and Urban Development.

8

MIXED-INCOME PUBLIC HOUSING TRANSFORMATION IN SAN FRANCISCO AND WASHINGTON, D.C.

Joni Hirsch, Mark L. Joseph, and Amy T. Khare

Introduction

Affordable housing crises and the intensified threat of displacement for low- and middle-income residents have become dominant narratives within the context of urban economic growth in the USA, but these dynamics around rapid neighborhood change can overshadow another story: the reality that low-income residents who require public housing face a precarious future. Tens of thousands of residents in major cities including San Francisco, California, and Washington, D.C. use public subsidies to secure housing in thriving neighborhoods but remain marginalized from the increased economic opportunity and changing urban fabric around them (Joint Center for Housing Studies of Harvard University, 2019; Stacy et al., 2019).

In the mid-2000s, amidst accelerating gentrification and dwindling federal funding, the mayors of Washington, D.C. and San Francisco launched high-profile, large-scale public housing redevelopment programs, the New Communities Initiative (NCI) and HOPE SF, which aimed to transform some of the most distressed public housing developments into vibrant mixed-income communities (see dcnewcommunits.org; hope-sf.org). While typically the task of redeveloping public housing had fallen to local public housing authorities under the direction of the U.S. Department of Housing and Urban Development (HUD), these city-driven mixed-income redevelopment efforts represented a major shift in approach. The relatively weak financial and political positioning of the public housing authorities situated these cities' housing and planning departments at the forefront of funding and decision-making. With the aim to address both the physical decay *and* social exclusion of public housing communities, the mixed-income transformation strategies in these two cities promised the much-needed investment to blighted neighborhoods, while aiming to deconcentrate poverty and preserve deeply subsidized housing (Joseph et al., 2007). While neither Washington, D.C. nor San Francisco was the first city to launch large-scale mixed-income public housing redevelopment initiatives, they marked a significant departure from previous efforts – such as those in Atlanta and Chicago – in their explicit social missions, placing goals of success for low-income residents at the center of the design and approach. Given the particular dynamics around city-driven leadership and the rapid gentrification of surrounding neighborhoods in Washington D.C. and San Francisco, NCI and HOPE SF present helpful case studies for examining the effort to promote inclusive and equitable mixed-income transformations in the face of prevailing inequitable market forces.

DOI: 10.4324/9781003172949-8

In this chapter, we use an analytical framework put forth by Amy Khare in her forthcoming book *Poverty, Power, and Profit: Structural Racism in Public Housing Reform* to examine how the city-led public housing redevelopment initiatives in Washington, D.C. and San Francisco have fared in their efforts thus far to promote more equitable development. Khare's analytical frames include (1) creative destruction, (2) urban entrepreneurial governance, (3) devolution, (4) privatization, (5) commodification of public property, (6) contestation, and (7) racial capitalism. We apply them to help situate NCI and HOPE SF both within the contemporary neoliberal urban policy context and also within the specific constraints and opportunities of city-driven housing revitalization amidst gentrification. We are particularly interested in using these frames to examine the inherent tensions between the social goals and market goals of these initiatives. We find that despite the articulation of intentional efforts to promote more equitable outcomes for low-income residents of color, leaders in both cities have experienced significant challenges to operationalizing their equity commitments. We identify strategic implications for future public housing redevelopment efforts.

The Inclusion and Equity Imperative in Mixed-Income Public Housing Transformation

In a recent essay, "Prioritizing Inclusion and Equity in the Next Generation of Mixed-Income Communities," Khare and Joseph (2019) argue that racial and socioeconomic integration is necessary but not sufficient to create inclusion and *equity* through community redevelopment. They define inclusion as the active, intentional, and sustained engagement of traditionally excluded individuals and groups through informal activities and formal decision-making processes in ways that build connections and share power. They believe that inclusion occurs when a social context enables people of diverse backgrounds to interact in mutually respectful ways that reveal their similarities and common ground, honor their social and cultural differences and uniqueness, and value what each individual and group can contribute to the shared environment.

Khare and Joseph suggest that equity entails addressing structural disparities defined by race and class so that people receive a more fair share of resources, opportunities, social supports, and power, given their differential needs and circumstances based on different life experiences. In particular, racial equity places priority on ensuring that people of color, particularly African Americans, are afforded opportunities that they have historically been denied and from which they continue to be excluded. They advance both a fairness case and an economic and social value case for greater inclusion and equity. The imperative for more inclusive mixed-income communities includes recognition of the *value* of people of color and the *value* of people who are economically constrained with a recognition that greater opportunity for marginalized people can actually generate increased and sustained opportunities for all people.

Initiative Background and Context

In D.C., Mayor Anthony Williams launched the NCI in 2005 after the murder of an adolescent girl in Sursum Corda, a formerly low-income housing development. NCI first centered on the neighborhood surrounding Sursum Corda called "Northwest One," which contained several deeply subsidized housing projects and was one of the 14 crime "hot-spots" that the City's police department had identified as priority areas (see, for example, NCI Annual Report, 2014). Williams determined that Northwest One would be redeveloped as a part of his broader plans to revitalize some of the District's most distressed neighborhoods by replacing subsidized housing projects with mixed-income developments. Williams targeted areas where violent crime, concentrated poverty, and distressed housing were located (Northwest One Redevelopment Plan, 2005). Over the next few years, three additional sites were added to the initiative – Lincoln Heights/Richardson Dwellings, Barry Farm, and Park Morton – in reaction to political pressure by council members to address deteriorating, high-crime public housing developments in their wards. The Northwest One and Park Morton developments are in northwest D.C. neighborhoods that are rapidly gentrifying, while Lincoln Heights/Richardson Dwellings and Barry Farm are east of the Anacostia River in neighborhoods that remain predominantly black and will be slower to experience the gentrification pressures sweeping the rest of the city. The initiative is led by a team within the Deputy Mayor's Office of Planning and Economic Development, which works in partnership with the D.C. Housing Authority. The commitment to and investment in NCI has ebbed and flowed significantly under the four mayors who have led D.C. in the 14 years since the initiative was launched. Current Mayor Muriel Bowser made NCI a centerpiece of her first election campaign in 2014, which reinvigorated a focus on the redevelopment effort that she has since sustained (see, for example, "Mayor Bowser Delivers on the Promise of the New Communities Initiative"). Her team is now looking to broaden major redevelopment activity to other public housing developments in her second term.

In San Francisco, HOPE SF was launched in 2006 under Mayor Gavin Newsom and, unlike NCI, has enjoyed a consistent, and in some ways expanded, commitment and focus from the two mayors who have succeeded Newsom, Mayor Ed Lee, and now Mayor London Breed. Both Lee and Breed spent parts of their childhood living in public housing and brought an intuitive commitment for a dramatic and equitable approach to harnessing the burgeoning economic vitality in the city to advance the redevelopment of the four HOPE SF neighborhoods. At the time of the launch of HOPE SF, the San Francisco Housing Authority (SFHA) had redeveloped several public housing sites with HOPE VI funding, but had stalled in its progress in part due to mismanagement and dysfunction, as demonstrated through several years on HUD's troubled housing authorities list. A 2005 study by the San Francisco Department of Human Services revealed that 60% of vulnerable households in San Francisco lived within walking distance of seven street corners in the city, five of which were public housing neighborhoods ("The Seven Key Street Corners for At Risk Families in San Francisco."). At the same time, an assessment found that HOPE VI funding would not be sufficient to transform these neighborhoods. Mayor Newsom appointed a citizen task force to propose a new model for revitalizing public housing. In response to their recommendations, Mayor Newsom and the Board of Supervisors launched HOPE SF and authorized $95 million in local bond funding to initiate the redevelopment of four public housing sites in the Bayview area city: Hunters View, Alice Griffith, Potrero, and Sunnydale.[1]

The basic approach to both NCI and HOPE SF reflects the mixed-income model of the federal HOPE VI and Choice Neighborhoods programs, as well as redevelopment efforts in cities such as Atlanta and Chicago. Private developers are engaged by the city to replace the deteriorating public housing with mixed-income developments, using public funding to leverage private capital for development. Land abatement, infrastructure investments, and other incentives support the development process. One-for-one replacement housing for the original public housing units is complemented by affordable rental housing funded with Low-Income Housing Tax Credits as well as market-rate housing. While in D.C. some of the tax-credit units and market-rate units will be integrated into new buildings with the public housing replacement units, development plans in San Francisco locate the market-rate units in separate buildings. This model combines physical redevelopment and human capital investment, bringing market activity into disinvested neighborhoods to address concentrated poverty, provide higher-quality housing, and offer comprehensive supportive services to residents (Joseph & Miyoung, 2019; Vale & Shamsuddin, 2017).

Dramatically different from previous large-scale public housing redevelopment efforts, however, both NCI and HOPE SF are comprehensive multisite initiatives that articulate a set of clear set of principles aimed to promote neighborhood redevelopment that avoids displacement of original residents and achieves transformative outcomes for those residents. From predevelopment to post-development, these principles are intended to guide a number of decisions from the selection of master developers, the approach to relocation, the human capital and community building strategies, and the metrics of success.

Largely in response to the strident advocacy of resident leaders and housing advocates who were concerned about how NCI's redevelopment efforts would affect existing public housing residents, the NCI established four guiding principles at the outset of the effort (see NCI website):

1. One-for-one replacement
2. Right to return
3. Mixed-income housing
4. Build first.

These principles underscored the city's priority to minimize displacement. More broadly, NCI now touts an overarching goal of "100% resident success," defined as ensuring that the original residents of the developments are stably housed and personally thriving, whether they return to the new mixed-income developments or relocate to another area of the city (see, for example, NCI Stakeholder Report, 2016–2017). This ambitious goal requires a strategy that extends beyond housing redevelopment and includes comprehensive efforts to address human capital needs and promote community building and resident participation.

In its 2006 recommendations for the launch of HOPE SF, the mayor-appointed citizens task force developed a set of eight guiding principles (see HOPE SF website).

1. Ensure no loss of public housing
2. Create an economically integrated community
3. Maximize creation of new affordable housing
4. Involve residents in the highest level of participation in the entire project
5. Provide economic opportunities through rebuilding process
6. Integrate process with neighborhood improvement plans
7. Create environmentally sustainable and accessible communities
8. Build a strong sense of community.

When he stepped in as director of HOPE SF in 2015, Theo Miller branded the initiative as a "reparations effort" to indicate its commitment to acknowledging and redressing the marginalization of low-income African American residents and other residents of color in San Francisco (see, for example, "Low-Income Neighborhoods Approved for Redevelopment").

NCI and HOPE SF also depart from previous public housing redevelopment efforts in other cities in that they are city-led with varying degrees of partnership with the housing authority, rather than managed by the local housing authority. While public housing redevelopment has traditionally fallen under the scope of public housing authorities and has relied on core funding from the federal government, severe decreases in both funding and capacity within the housing authorities provided an opening for city departments to lead the implementation of a mixed-income solution to failed public housing (Kleit & Page, 2015). These initiatives thus fell more directly under the authority of the mayors and served to advance broader political and economic agendas, with the intention of deploying market-oriented development approaches to achieve comprehensive social outcomes including inclusion and equity, a proposition that had limited previous success in these and other cities.

Conceptual Framework: Analyzing Mixed-Income Public Housing Redevelopment in a Neoliberal Urban Policy Context

In her forthcoming book *Poverty, Power and Profit*, Khare examines the multisite public housing redevelopment in Chicago over a 20-year period with particular attention to the trade-offs navigated by a city focused on leveraging the resources and capacity of the private sector and harnessing market forces to drive revitalization for the benefit of low-income communities of color. The detailed evidence shows how and why market-based reforms intended to improve public housing actually furthered the marginalization of low-income, African American communities. At the same time, those in power bolstered a mayoral agenda that largely prioritized reshaping the city's built environment for the benefit of the affluent.

Khare finds that Chicago's reforms resulted in land appropriation, capital accumulation, and the displacement of thousands of low-income African American residents. The financial resources the reforms required, upwards of $8 billion, and the profits generated, nearly $75 million in payments to developers to build 12 mixed-income developments, quantify the massive extent of the market-driven nature of the effort. Ultimately, Chicago's reforms contributed to reproducing racial oppression by furthering the economic interests of elites through decisions made by government officials to repurpose public housing, land, and resources for profit-making and non-public housing uses. *Poverty, Power, and Profit* brings to light the contradictory dynamics at work within a neoliberal framework: competing ideas about the proper partnerships between the public and private sectors, shifting authority among local and national government agencies, and activist struggles for community revitalization on land where public housing projects once stood.

Khare's analysis of the Chicago experience yielded an analytical framework with seven concepts she found key to understanding how mixed-income transformation played out in that city: creative destruction, urban entrepreneurial governance, devolution, privatization, commodification of public property, contestation, and racial capitalism. We introduce this framework briefly here in order to apply the concepts to our examination of NCI and HOPE SF.

Creative Destruction

Khare deploys the Marxist concept of creative destruction to frame the process of reshaping the urban policy environment toward a more market-based system, rolling back collectivist redistributionist systems, such as public housing, while rolling out restructured state institutions, policies, and governing approaches focused on facilitating capital expansion. Within the context of urban redevelopment, the creative destruction process extends beyond the shifting of policy regimes to the literal destruction and rebuilding of inner-city communities. And in a broader sense, the image and function of the entire city can also be seen as being remade for broader economic prominence and appeal (Harvey, 2005).

Urban Entrepreneurial Governance

Khare frames urban entrepreneurial governance as a shift in policy decision-making whereby local urban leaders seek to position their cities at the forefront of a global economic stage by attracting capital, expansion, and investment. Seeking to leverage existing city assets, such as public land and public housing, as a means for expansion and growth, elected leaders and government officials focus policies on maximizing the economic value of these assets. Entrepreneurial governance strategies meant to stimulate economic growth often generate strategies and outcomes that marginalize low-income households of color, instead initiating benefits for whites and people with existing wealth (Clarke & Gaile, 1989; Leitner, 1990).

Devolution

In the process of devolution, local jurisdictions assume greater authority and responsibility over the management of public goods and services, as well as the local allocation of federal subsidies. In the public housing arena specifically, this means a decreased role for HUD and greater influence for cities and public housing authorities (Hackworth, 2000). The federal Moving to Work (MTW) demonstration program, a designation the Chicago Housing Authority was granted in 2000, is a formal manifestation of this devolution which provides for more flexible use of federal funds and waivers from certain regulatory constraints. The D.C. Housing Authority received MTW designation as well. Khare demonstrates that the shift of influence can be partial and inconsistent, with the federal government maintaining a degree of control and exerting its authority episodically.

Privatization

The privatization of public housing redevelopment entails a shift of responsibility away from the public sector to private developers, property managers, investors, social service organizations, for-profit corporations, and non-profit community organizations. Privatization shifts power and decision-making away from a publicly accountable entity and introduces profit-oriented motives. It also introduces the danger of making affordable housing production dependent on market conditions and the availability of private capital (Khare, 2017; Vale & Freemark, 2018). Khare uses this frame to bring into sharp relief the trade-offs between the social mission and economic interests of these redevelopment projects.

Commodification of Public Property

Khare elevates attention to a particular form of privatization that involves the commodification of public property. Publicly owned land is shifted into the private marketplace through government policies that incentivize and increase private investment (Aalbers & Christophers, 2014). The current model of mixed-income housing development requires that public land be made available to private entities to build market-rate and affordable housing. In Chicago, following the Great Recession, the commodification of public property became a controversial issue when mixed-income housing development was no longer profitable. Policymakers shifted their focus away from mixed-income housing and instead made public land available for private retail and recreational development without a clear social purpose.

Contestation

Contestation refers to organized resistance to market-driven and profit-oriented agendas. Khare notes that neoliberalism is a process that evolves and responds to ongoing pressures and resistance. This resistance can promote alternative approaches that reshape specific decisions and the overall political-economic environment (Leitner et al., 2007). In the case of public housing redevelopment in Chicago, contestation reshaped the dynamics of devolution and compelled HUD to exercise its role on key issues.

Racial Capitalism

Khare invokes racial capitalism as the co-production of capitalist exploitation and racial domination. With this frame, the urban landscape in the US cities can be understood as a contested place in which historic and contemporary racist politics and policy processes contribute to producing racialized spaces, such as isolated, disinvested public housing sites (Melamed, 2015). In public housing redevelopment, this frame illuminates the role of racism in shaping how African American communities and households have been further marginalized through housing and community development efforts that have been purported as physical and economic revitalization efforts that will benefit existing residents of color.

Examining the HOPE SF and NCI Efforts to Achieve Greater Equity and Inclusion through Mixed-Income Redevelopment

We now turn to our exploration of the redevelopment efforts in Washington, D.C. and San Francisco. Using Khare's seven frames, we examine whether and how each city attempted to counteract the forces of inequity and exclusion inherent in the public housing redevelopment process, and we consider how those efforts have fared thus far. Then, we draw implications for more effective approaches to promoting equitable, inclusive mixed-income transformations.

Creative Destruction

Relevance of the Frame

In both cities, the public housing redevelopment initiatives emerged in a context of heightened public sensitivity to the inequitable process of "creative destruction" that was radically reshaping the cities' image and identity, altering the priorities and processes of urban policy, and remaking the character of city neighborhoods. An increasing wave of gentrification was sweeping over both cities, resulting in the residential and cultural displacement of African Americans and other low-income households. In Washington, D.C., as Derek Hyra has framed it, along with the urban renaissance it was experiencing, Chocolate City was becoming Cappuccino City (Hyra, 2018). Between 2000 and 2013, D.C. had the highest percentage of gentrifying neighborhoods in the country, leading to the displacement of 20,000 black residents (Richardson et al., 2019). In San Francisco, the disruption and exodus of the African American population was even more drastic, with only one in 20 city residents being black in 2000, down from one in seven in 1970 (Urban Displacement Project). The emergence of San Francisco as a 21st-century global tech hub was only intensifying and accelerating the creative destruction process.

Policymakers and housing advocates in both cities were well aware of the track record of previous public housing redevelopment efforts, most notably through the federal HOPE VI program, which had experienced a median return rate of 18% across almost 259 projects (Gress et al., 2019).

As described earlier, both redevelopment efforts were explicit and intentional about their commitment to minimizing the level of disruption and displacement of the original residents of the public housing sites. Both cities committed to one-for-one replacement of any public housing units that were demolished, ensuring no overall loss of deeply subsidizing housing. Unlike previous redevelopment efforts locally and nationally which started by moving residents off the site in order to commence the demolition and rebuilding process as quickly as possible, both cities committed to a phased, "build first" strategy. This often entailed first constructing new housing on a contiguous off-site parcel, then moving residents from a targeted area of the development to the new housing, and then demolishing the building vacated by the relocatees.

In one case in San Francisco, the Hunters View development, redevelopment started on the site itself, with residents being moved within the site to vacate an initial set of buildings that could be demolished and replaced. The process continued in phases so that no residents would be forced to leave the site during redevelopment. Over time in San Francisco, particularly under the leadership of the second director of HOPE SF, Theo Miller, the label of "legacy residents" was applied to the original residents of the sites to signify the particular commitment that was being made to prioritizing their well-being and positive outcomes through the redevelopment.

There were also specific residents rights protections put in place in both cities. D.C. Housing Authority (DCHA) Resolution 16-06, for example, defines the rights and priorities for residents and stakeholders during the relocation and return process. Among other specifications, it ensures that requirements for eligibility to move back into an NCI property after redevelopment not be any more stringent than existing DCHA policies for residents residing in current public housing units (such as new work requirements, criminal background requirements, or credit or drug screening requirements) (*DCHA Resolution* 16-06). Housing advocates have criticized Resolution 16-06 as being an unenforceable statement of intent without any penalties or ramifications if it is not followed by the private owners and property management corporations.

In San Francisco, the City Council adopted Ordinance 227-12 in October 2012, which established the San Francisco Right to Revitalized Housing Ordinance to set city policy regarding the right to return to revitalized public housing units. The ordinance applies to any redevelopment project in the city that receives financial assistance from the city. It guarantees public housing tenants' relocation rights and the highest priority for tenancy in the new developments. It prevents landlords from submitting public housing tenants to any additional screening to determine their eligibility to return to a redeveloped unit. Notably, unlike in D.C., the ordinance establishes new powers for the San Francisco Residential Rent Stabilization and Arbitration Board to hold revitalization projects accountable to the ordinance.

Emerging Outcomes

In both cities, initiative leaders pronounced early commitments to achieving 100% rates of return of original residents to the new mixed-income developments. In San Francisco, two factors led to a softening of the goal of complete retention of residents in their original neighborhoods. First, preventing residents from leaving the site ran counter to the basic principles of the effort, particularly as delays in redevelopment became more extensive. An initiative that claimed a fundamental commitment to promoting resident choice and opportunity could not restrain residents from using the redevelopment opportunity to move away from the site. Second, the development process itself generated noise, dust. and other inconveniences that required some households, for example those with a family with asthma, to move to another location. Later in the process, opportunities to make replacement units available in new developments in other parts of the city also led to an increase in off-site relocation. In D.C., the commitment to 100% return was replaced with the aspirational commitment to "100 percent resident success," which indicated a commitment that residents would thrive in their new residential location whether or not they returned to the replacement housing. Just as in San Francisco, the slow pace of redevelopment, the desire of some residents to make permanent moves away from the site, and the inconvenience of staying on-site through the redevelopment meant that a 100% return rate was infeasible.

While in San Francisco, the phased, build first approach was fully adhered to, in D.C. there has been mixed follow-through on this commitment. In San Francisco, and to some extent in D.C., this has resulted in a much slower pace of redevelopment, with the additional benefit of extended time to engage residents and prepare them for the coming disruption. In D.C., the Northwest One site was the first to be completely vacated and demolished. While two off-site buildings were indeed constructed and occupied, only about 15–20% of original residents moved into those buildings, with the remainder being, at least temporarily, displaced to other areas of the city. The City proposed to outright demolish Temple Courts, a high-rise building located on the Northwest One site with 211 HUD-subsidized units, because of the particularly egregious building conditions. The City purchased the building from the absentee slumlord with the intention of redeveloping it as a part of NCI. Tearing the building down before new housing had been built on-site threatened the "Build First" promise, and the mayor at the time, Adrian Fenty, provided existing residents with an opportunity to give input on the decision at a community meeting. The prevailing opinion expressed by those that attended the meeting was to tear the buildings down and take vouchers to relocate, and Temple Courts was demolished in late 2008. It has still not been rebuilt!

At the Barry Farm site in D.C., legal challenges and other delays in the redevelopment process, increasing violence and crime on-site, and the rapid deterioration of the buildings resulted in a mass relocation of residents from the site before any replacement housing had been constructed (Giambrone, 2010). At the Park Morton site in D.C., the commitment to building off-site housing first was sustained for well over a decade but has been waylaid by a variety of factors, including legal challenges to the planned off-site development that has generated extensive delays in what was intended to be the first phase of the entire redevelopment process. Since the D.C. Housing Authority has received HUD demolition approval and funds are currently available to issue Housing Choice Vouchers, there are plans emerging to move all residents off-site and skip to the first phase of on-site development. At the fourth NCI site, Lincoln Heights/Richardson Dwellings, two off-site buildings have been completed and occupied and no on-site development has yet been initiated. At a broad scale, the D.C. case shows immense physical destruction of public housing communities without the creation of new homes in which residents were expected to move.

In San Francisco, at two sites, Hunters View and Alice Griffith, all of the replacement public housing has been completed, and, due to the phased redevelopment, return rates of over 70% and over 90%, respectively, have been achieved among original residents. At Alice Griffith, this successful retention of original residents, in large part motivated by the five-year project completion timeframe of a federal Choice Neighborhoods Implementation grant, came at the significant strategic cost of an out-of-sync mixed-income transformation. Due to post-recession market slowdowns and other logistical, financial, and technical challenges, the development of market-rate buildings was put on hold, and the replacement public housing was designed and built as a separate, wholly contained site, thus replicating the housing segregation that had previously existed. Market-rate development was similarly stalled at the Hunters View redevelopment, but unlike Alice Griffith, there are designated parcels for market-rate development integrated throughout the site, and thus the complete physical separation that exists at Alice Griffith will be avoided. The other two HOPE SF sites, Potrero and Sunnydale, completed their first off-site housing in 2019, prior to any demolitions on-site. Both off-site buildings are directly contiguous to the original public housing site.

Implications for More Equitable Policy and Practice

To promote more inclusive outcomes, the creative destruction inherent in a market-driven redevelopment should be complemented by a commitment to "equitable transformation," in which drastic changes in policy approach and community make-up are accepted and even embraced, but with an explicit and disciplined commitment to positive results for original residents of the site and other marginalized populations. It is important to acknowledge and value the ways of life and community history that is being creatively destructed and proactively seek ways to retain the legacy of existing people, history, culture, and traditions. This also requires combating the sense that all that is new — incoming residents, outside norms, and culture — is superior and all that came before — public housing residents and communities — was expendable. Achieving this narrative and strategic shift requires establishing a shared language and commitment, creating spaces and settings for discussion and deliberation, and appointing and positioning leaders and initiative personnel with the natural inclination and operational skill to promote this approach. Even within neoliberal, market-driven framework, a strong vision and process can be established to guide and compel developers to adhere to a more inclusive approach.

Urban Entrepreneurial Governance

Relevance of the Frame

The operational responsibility for the mixed-income efforts in both cities was a significant departure from previous multisite transformations in other cities, including Chicago and Atlanta, where the lead entity was the public housing authority with the mayor as a champion for the effort and city departments acting in support of the effort. In both D.C. and San Francisco, mayors and city government officials play a lead role in the design, funding, and implementation of the initiatives. With the public housing authorities in both cities overwhelmed by shrinking resources and decades of mismanagement, city government, with burgeoning resources in their coffers from their economic vibrancy, stepped in to drive the efforts. This makes the frame of urban entrepreneurial governance even more salient as the initiatives were conducted with high levels of technical competence and transactional efficiency in the context of mayoral agendas to position their cities for economic vitality and global prominence. In D.C., the Mayor's Office of Planning and Economic Development managed NCI alongside other major urban revitalization projects across the district. In San Francisco, HOPE SF was first launched within the San Francisco Redevelopment Agency, also alongside other major revitalization efforts. When all redevelopment agencies across the state were closed in 2012 to promote budget-cutting consolidation, HOPE SF was integrated into the Mayor's Office of Housing and Community Development, with the director of HOPE SF reporting directly to the mayor.

Both initiatives have now been sustained across multiple mayoral administrations, four in D.C. and three in San Francisco.[2] The commitment to NCI waxed and waned considerably with shifts among mayors, with Mayor Muriel Bowser re-elevating NCI as a prominent city commitment in her mayoral campaign. The attention to the initiative seems to parallel the strength of the local housing market, further evidence that an urban entrepreneurial approach is fueled by economic opportunity in the private market. In comparison, the mayoral commitment to HOPE SF as a priority investment and focus in San Francisco has been remarkably consistent, largely undeterred by the slowdown of the market in the years following the Great Recession. Started under Gavin Newsom, who would eventually become governor of

California, HOPE SF benefited from the fact that, as referenced earlier, his successors Mayor Lee and Mayor Breed both lived in public housing during their childhoods and have a personal commitment to resident-centered public housing reform.

There is a striking similarity in how mayor's office leadership has unfolded in both initiatives. Midway through both efforts, African American initiative directors were appointed who brought a deep personal commitment to equity and inclusion, a skepticism about a primarily transactional approach to mixed-income transformation, and the political savvy and personal integrity to position the initiative to forge a different redevelopment path. Angie Rodgers came to NCI with a professional background in affordable housing, with direct experience managing implementation of development projects, underwriting public gap financing, and engaging in policy, research, and advocacy as they relate to affordable housing throughout the D.C. region. She was also a co-convener of the D.C. Affordable Housing Alliance, a coalition of individuals and organizations dedicated to promoting the development, preservation, and operation of affordable housing. Theo Miller stepped into the role of HOPE SF director after having been lured away from his doctoral studies at Harvard to lead Mayor Lee's efforts to design and implement a racial equity strategy for the city.

Emerging Outcomes

Under the parameters set by the respective mayors and with the persistent leadership of Rodgers and Miller, both initiatives established an explicit commitment to prioritizing the well-being and outcomes of original residents. Miller followed-up on the aforementioned "100 percent resident success" by contracting with the Urban Institute to develop a logic model and social service strategy to map out a pathway to ensuring the successful relocation of all residents. However, despite her best efforts, Rodger's ability to maintain social entrepreneurial momentum toward her mantra of "100 percent resident success" has thus far been thwarted by several factors, including resistance and lack of cooperation from the housing authority, the lack of experience in city departments with the complexities of public housing development, legal challenges and other slowdowns to the redevelopment process, and high levels of staff turnover on her team. Ultimately, after more than four years as NCI Director, Rodgers was promoted within the department, to the prominent position of Chief of Staff, and responsibility for the initiative was shifted to Denise Robinson, a newly hired staffer who was charged with managing the initiative along with a broader portfolio of development efforts.

In San Francisco, Miller has successfully positioned HOPE SF for continued priority attention and investment from the city and continues to press for strategic implementation across the sites that center "legacy residents." Like Rodgers, he too has confronted significant challenges to momentum, including dysfunction at the housing authority, delays at the developments, enduring crime and violence at the sites, and high levels of fear and distrust among residents.

Unlike Rodgers, Miller has been able to draw on substantial additional social entrepreneurial leadership from a number of valued partners. The partnership for HOPE SF is a civic alliance led by the San Francisco Foundation, Enterprise Community Partners and the mayor's office, created to provide additional resources and capacity to the transformation effort. To date, the Partnership has raised over $30 million of philanthropic support for HOPE SF and has taken lead responsibility for managing communications, research and evaluation, and best-practice technical assistance on behalf of the initiative (see HOPE SF website). Miller has also benefited from city partners at the Mayor's Office of Housing who have been willing to elevate the social goals of HOPE SF.

Implications for More Equitable Policy and Practice

While both Rodgers and Miller could certainly be characterized as urban entrepreneurs in their energetic and enterprising approach to navigating government bureaucracy to advance implementation, they both added a dimension of *social* entrepreneurship to their priorities and focus. As practiced by both Rodgers and Miller, urban social entrepreneurial governance can be defined as using the resources, tools and influence of city leadership to prioritize and advance social goals as well as economic growth goals.

Avoiding redevelopment that privileges the economic revitalization over inclusive redevelopment requires a broadening of the leadership paradigm from "urban entrepreneurial governance" to "urban social entrepreneurial governance." Mayors, their lead staff, and key public/private partnership leaders need to see themselves not just as economic entrepreneurs but also as social entrepreneurs. This means continuing the imperative for more efficiency, competence, and innovation in implementation of the redevelopment, but adding an expectation of enterprising innovations that achieve a balance of market *and* social goals, not just market goals. This will require the recruitment of personnel with a social entrepreneurial mindset and skills and the ability to galvanize an equity commitment across the initiative. Key staff will need training and support to apply more equitable policies and practices and clear benchmarks and accountability that elevate social goals alongside market goals.

Devolution

Relevance of the Frame

The devolution of responsibility for public housing redevelopment from the federal government to local authorities is a fundamental dimension of the mixed-income transformation efforts in D.C. and San Francisco. Just as in cities across the nation, city and public housing authority leaders in D.C. and San Francisco were faced with dramatically declining federal resources for operating public housing and increased control over decision-making and strategy. However, as HUD stepped back from its federal funding and oversight role, it was unclear how the balance of local responsibility was to be distributed between the public housing authority, which had primary responsibility and control over its land, funds, and residents, and the city government which has broader authority, a public mandate, greater resources, and more efficient infrastructure.

As described earlier, the mayors and their staff in both cities approached the devolution vacuum in the same way, with an assertion of a lead role, creation of the initiative and its transformational aims, and an expectation that the public housing authority would comply with the vision and momentum for change. However, in both cities, officials at the public housing authorities proved resistant to city dominance and, in turn, asserted their own lead responsibility and role in any initiative that involved public housing authority land and residents. In D.C., the housing authority was led by an experienced and respected President/CEO Adrianne Todman who presented a formidable political force. DCHA's designation of federal MTW status granted it considerable flexibility and authority to manage its resources and program strategy. Furthermore, MTW status was normally only granted by HUD to select high-performing PHAs around the country, so the designation alone conferred a certain level of prestige and self-assurance. However, Todman left DCHA partway through the initiative, and her successor has struggled to establish strong leadership and credibility with institutional partners. In San Francisco, where the housing authority has spent several years on HUD's list of most troubled housing authorities and the leader was ousted a few years into HOPE SF in a corruption scandal, city leadership has been steadily working to transition power and responsibility away from the housing authority. The city used the federal Rental Assistance Demonstration (RAD) program to move much of the public housing stock into private ownership with project-based vouchers. Rather than a city-housing authority partnership, HOPE SF has become another element in the gradual shrinking and closing down of the housing authority.

Further complicating devolution dynamics in both cities, HUD's role and decisions about when and how to intervene were inconsistent and often marked by considerable delay before actions. In San Francisco, for example, there was an extensive delay in the approval of allocation of Tenant Protection Vouchers that would transition ownership of the Potrero and Sunnydale units to private property managers.

Emerging Outcomes

Ultimately, devolution has provided broad latitude for both city governments to forge ahead with bold revitalization efforts across the four initiative sites. However, the intransigence of the housing authorities in both cities, along with the inconsistently played role of mediator and arbiter by HUD, has generated considerable delays and impeded decisive, strategic action by the initiative leaders and implementers at numerous critical junctures of the efforts.

As both SFHA and DCHA have resisted relinquishing control or changing their policies, it has generated complex and obstructive power dynamics which manifest at conceptual and operational levels. The cities and housing authorities have fundamentally different goals and priorities, inhibiting collaboration. The city agencies running HOPE SF and NCI emphasize broad goals of neighborhood revitalization and economic development, requiring collaboration with a wide range of public and private stakeholders. The housing authorities, on the other hand, foster a narrower focus on developing, maintaining, and managing public housing specifically, administering the Housing Choice Voucher program and coordinating relocation. In practice, SFHA and DCHA have not gotten on board with a broader place-based approach to the transformation and remained focused on a narrow, people-based approach. The misalignment is compounded at the operational level, leading to the spread of misinformation, confusion among residents, duplication of efforts, administrative complications, as well as an unwillingness to share data about residents' needs and relocation. In both San Francisco and D.C., political tension between City leadership and the local housing authority has had crippling effects on the pace of progress, the ability of residents to navigate these complex systems, the potential for tracking resident success over the short- and long-term, and the ability to ensure a smooth relocation process. In D.C., City Council Legislation introduced in February 2019 would move DCHA from an independent authority to under the purview of the Office of the Mayor (*District of Columbia Housing Authority Amendment Act of 2019*).

Implications for More Equitable Policy and Practice

To facilitate a more consistent and deliberate local effort toward inclusive public housing redevelopment would require a shift from the pattern of relatively hands-off, uneven devolution by HUD to a more "strategic devolution." In this more strategic form of devolution, HUD and key local actors including the city and housing authority would dedicate extensive time early in the initiative to establish clarity about rules of the game and rules of engagement. This would include agreements about the roles of each entity, lines of authority and decision-making, and accountability processes. HUD would retain a clear accountability and mediating role and would be transparent about when and why it was stepping in. HUD would also work to promote local capacity and positioning to ensure local accountability mechanisms are robust and engaged across multiple levels including state government, local government, civic leaders, and community-based organizations.

Privatization

Relevance of the Frame

Both NCI and HOPE SF represent the complete adoption of the neoliberal approach to urban policy wherein the private sector and market-based principles and forces are harnessed to manage and advance efforts in arenas that are usually the province of the government. Private developers have been engaged as the long-term owner-operators of the sites and contracted to manage the real estate redevelopment process and conduct property management for the new buildings. Private non-profit agencies have also been contracted to provide social services and other supports to residents. Considerable public funds have been leveraged to raise millions of dollars in private sector investment in NCI and HOPE SF.

In both initiatives, different teams of for-profit and not-for-profit private developers were selected for each of the four sites. While national not-for-profit developers, The Community Builders and Preservation of Affordable Housing, led the development in some D.C. sites, at Northwest One, a local for-profit development team was chosen for the major on-site redevelopment. For HOPE SF, two for-profit developers (John Stewart Company and McCormack Baron Salazar) and two non-profit developers (BRIDGE and Mercy Housing) were selected. The selection of development teams has proven a key leverage point in maintaining a focus on the success of low-income residents through the relocation process. Developers with experience, expertise, and a commitment to serving low-income communities of color approach these projects differently than those oriented toward market-rate development. In all cases, challenges remain in aligning their mission and approaches with their public partners.

Emerging Outcomes

In NCI, for the most part the development teams have played out their roles in ways that reflect business as usual for mixed-income redevelopment, without any particular actions that indicate any particularly innovative efforts to promote more inclusive or equitable outcomes. POAH was originally in a joint venture with a for-profit developer at Barry Farms, but ultimately the for-profit developer stepped away from the project due to irreconcilable differences with the city and POAH has been left as the sole developer.

In San Francisco, the developers have been subject to far more engagement, direction, and oversight from the HOPE SF team in the mayor's office. This has created some tension, with developers feeling that the city has maintained too much control and has not given them their appropriate positioning as long-term owners of the site.

Implications for Greater Equity and Inclusion

While multisite transformation initiatives as ambitious as NCI and HOPE SF certainly require private sector capacity and resources and sophisticated financing strategies, achieving more equitable outcomes requires a shift from purely "profit-maximizing privatization" to something that might be called "equitable privatization." In this shift, financing schemes and models would be designed and shaped to promote greater inclusion and equity, for example co-operative models that distribute ownership among residents and other stakeholders, land trusts that designate and facilitate commitment to specific goals of affordability and inclusion, affordable home ownership, savings incentive models (like the successful federal Family Self-Sufficiency program) that provide escrow accounts for residents to accrue savings toward home ownership and other personal investments, models that promote entrepreneurship and small businesses. Once again, selection, training, and accountability of initiative personnel are key, with a premium on positioning individuals in asset management and influential roles with the expertise, interest, and commitment to social innovation in the financing space.

Commodification of Public Property

Relevance of the Frame

In the context of rapidly gentrifying cities and skyrocketing land values, a crucial asset in both initiatives was the availability of city and housing authority-owned land that could be made available for market-driven investment and revenue generation. In Chicago, as described by Khare, the commodification of land became a major point of controversy when Mayor Rahm Emanuel pivoted from making the public available land to private developers for a mix of affordable and market-rate housing, to also making the land available for non-housing uses such as a grocery store and a tennis center (Khare, forthcoming). This particular issue has not yet become relevant in either D.C. or San Francisco.

Emerging Outcomes

Thus far in both D.C. and San Francisco, the use of public land has been largely for housing redevelopment. An exception in San Francisco is a planned neighborhood hub in the Sunnydale neighborhood with a community center, YMCA, Boys and Girls Club, daycare, other activities for intergenerational use, and retail establishments. In D.C., a historic theater is undergoing a redevelopment into a mixed-use building.

Implications for Greater Equity and Inclusion

Great equity would entail a shift from "inequitable commodification" to "equitable commodification." City and initiative leaders should articulate a clearer strategic vision upfront about how land is to be used for community benefit. There should be a clear prioritization and commitment to socially beneficial uses of commodified land. Policy and regulatory parameters should be established over how land is used and transferred. A portfolio approach could be designated to track land transfer and use, with specified proportions of the portfolio to be dedicated to largely social uses (for example, affordable housing and parks), purely market uses (for example, luxury condo and high-end retail), and a blend of social and market uses (for example, a community bank).

Contestation

Relevance of the Frame

Contestation involves the organized resistance to neoliberal agendas and the promotion of alternative approaches to restructure the political-economic environment. For example, contestation

can come in the form of political protest, organized activism, and social movements that challenge dominant market-centered practices. Contestation also involves actions by people working within government that shape policies in ways that make them more equitable.

Both initiatives owe their establishment of explicit guiding principles for the initiative to effective early contestation from residents and housing advocates. These principles have remained
relevant over time. In San Francisco, an updated set of principles was recently released.

In both cities, contestation to the public housing redevelopment process has shaped the pace
and direction of the redevelopments, but the political resistance and legal challenges have been
considerably more disruptive in D.C. In both cities, elected city officials have exerted significant influence over the process, but both city teams have generally found ways to secure the
support of these elected officials for the broad strategic direction of the effort. Examples include
unanimous support for the DCHA relocation rights resolution by the D.C. City Council and
the approval of bond financing by the San Francisco Board of Supervisors.

Emerging Outcomes

In D.C., before the establishment of Resolution 16-06, there was active contestation by housing
advocates around legislating the right to return. NCI had articulated a right to return principle
in theory, but no one could say what that meant and the initiative had not operationalized it. As
the initial replacement housing was coming online and private property managers were taking
on their roles, they were not acting differently, nor was any agency forcing them to. This led to
a buildup of unaddressed complaints about residents not able to get back into units for reasons
such as criminal background checks.

While HOPE SF has proceeded without any major or long-standing lawsuits or other legal roadblocks, NCI has been severely hampered and delayed by multiple lawsuits. In D.C.,
contestation against redevelopment plans has arisen from public housing residents, advocates
and organizers, neighboring renters, and home-owners. Despite intentional efforts to include
community input early on in decision-making, a number of aspects of various redevelopment
plans and policies have been fought through lawsuits and planning tools. In some cases, this
opposition had the effect of reshaping planning decisions, and in others has resulted in major
delays in construction, with few concrete changes to show for it. During these years of delay,
residents continue to move to other public housing properties or take vouchers to move into
private market housing, thereby forgoing their right to return to the redeveloped property. New
residents have continued to lease up, further complicating the right to return.

Barry Farm in NCI is an example where major contestation through a lawsuit filed by the
Barry Farm Tenant Allies and Empower D.C. has had the impact of reshaping the plans for
redevelopment, though it has so far failed to ultimately block the project. A litany of protests
and lawsuits in Barry Farm has delayed redevelopment for many years. In 2018, the D.C. Court
of Appeals demanded that the city and DHCA go back to residents and engage them more
thoroughly around what their redevelopment preferences. As a result, the city proposed amendments to the plan, which decreased on-site density and increased the size of units. There will
also be greater attention to historic preservation in the design and construction process.

The same advocates behind Barry Farm are now involved in the lawsuit against the Bruce
Monroe site, the first off-site development to be built in the Park Morton neighborhood. The
Park Morton redevelopment initially appeared to be a development scenario that was set up
for a successful and timely process – the funding was in place, the development team was in
alignment with DMPED's goals, and City Council members and advisory neighborhood commission members were supportive of the development plans. But local community members,

concerned about the plans to use public park land to create off-site replacement public housing in a mixed-income building, have blocked the plans.

Implications for Greater Equity and Inclusion

Given the momentum of market forces and the influence of profit-seeking private actors, even under the most enlightened and equity-oriented city leadership, it is likely that some degree of contestation and external accountability will be needed to aid the balancing of market goals with social goals. Thus, the implication for achieving greater equity and inclusion is to seek a level and form of contestation that is strategically disruptive and ultimately generative of equitable outcomes without completely stalling or derailing progress and creating long-term harm for low-income residents. This could be framed as moving from "periodic contestation of limited effectiveness" to "transformative contestation."

Transformative contestation would entail a strategic blend of oppositional and constructive resistance. It would require city and initiative leadership that sees contestation as opportunity for strengthening policy, practice, and outcomes and ultimately gaining support for and inclusion in the change process. Transformative contestation would involve a wide variety of actors in accountability and contestation, not just community residents, grassroots activists, and housing advocates, but also policy actors, business actors, philanthropy, and, as mentioned above, internal actors within the system at multiple levels who use lower profile decisions and actions to promote more equitable processes. Transformative contestation would require capacity building and positioning for advocates and other accountability actors, strategies for durable contestation over the decades-long initiative lifespan, and transparent accountability to clearly established equity and inclusion goals.

Racial Capitalism

Relevance of the Frame

Racial capitalism, as defined by Cedric J. Robinson, refers to the racialism that influenced the formation of capitalism as it emerged as a primary political-economic structure. Racial capitalism provides the analytical key for understanding how racism undergirds the accumulation of wealth – not how class relations within capitalism led to or further heightened existing prejudice and power based on race relations. Racial capitalism helps to explain how public housing transformation creates negative consequences for low-income communities and benefits for majority-white institutions and actors.

The redevelopment efforts in both cities have emerged with a heightened awareness of the historical marginalization of African Americans that has characterized both cities' approaches to public housing investment and management. One central impetus for both initiatives was the recognition of the continued failure of public housing to provide a quality and safe environment for low-income households of color. In D.C., the encroaching gentrification with rapid real estate development geared toward the return of a white population in neighborhoods throughout the city made readily the way in which market-driven development was reinforcing racial disparity.

In San Francisco, the dramatic exodus of the African American population presented an even more stark demonstration of market forces exacerbating the alienation of already-marginalized households. In both cities, the "mixed-income" redevelopment solution portends a "mixed-race" reality, and thus raises deep concern among existing residents and advocates about who the redevelopment efforts will benefit and how the new communities will be experienced by those African American and low-income households of color that are able to remain. While a black-white racial framing is largely appropriate for the D.C. context, in San Francisco it is important to acknowledge the complexity of the long-standing multiracial context in public housing with a substantial Asian population in some of the developments along with Latino households and a Samoan population. Samoan residents, in particular, share with African Americans deep concerns about long-standing marginalization and discrimination. And this multiracial context means both friction on a white, non-white dimension and, sometime more relevantly, friction between populations of color.

Emerging Outcomes

In the NCI initiative, there has been little explicit engagement by initiative leaders on the racialized dimension of the challenges at hand and no expression of race-focused strategies for initiative implementation. In San Francisco, under the leadership of Miller, there has been a very different story. As previously noted, soon after taking the helm of HOPE SF, Miller rebranded the initiative as a "reparations effort" and encouraged explicit naming of the past trauma and isolation experienced by African Americans and other low-income households of color in San Francisco public housing. Until 2019, this branding largely served to invoke a clear spirit of a prevailing commitment to ensure the centering of African Americans and other households of color in initiative activities. In 2019, Miller began to lay out in writing more specifics about his reparations framework, including articulation of four phases of the process: truth, restitution, reconciliation, and liberation.

Implications for Greater Equity and Inclusion

Given the limited and emergent progress thus far in NCI and HOPE SF, to name and address the realities and pitfalls of racial capitalism, there are some fundamental implications for greater momentum on this front. The task here can be understood as a shift from enduring and transmitted "structural racism" to what might be called "antiracist development." This would include an explicit acknowledgment of the historical and contemporary racialized context in which the initiatives are taking place, including the naming of race and racism, not just class and income. There could be an identification of specific decision and action points in redevelopment process that often lend themselves to reinforcing structural racism, for example, the establishment of house rules and lease agreements. There would then be an implementation of "antiracist practice and policy" – procedures and actions to disrupt the natural racism that inevitably is carried out through implicit bias on the part of actors and baked into existing systems. Progress will entail the selection and training of leaders and personnel with the commitment, comfort, and ability to name and address racism as an actionable component of the overall redevelopment effort.

Overarching Implications

Using Khare's frames to examine these two initiatives has generated numerous implications for how mixed-income redevelopment efforts can adhere more effectively to a commitment to greater inclusion and equity.

Vision and Principles

There should be a clear articulation of the vision for creating communities that retain those original residents who wish to stay and that promote belonging and influence for those residents. Explicit principles should be established to guide redevelopment decisions. In particular, the commitment to racial equity and a recognition of the demands and trade-offs required by an antiracist approach to development should be made abundantly clear.

Elevate Commitment to Social Goals

While the commitment to promoting economic growth and the engagement of the private sector are integral elements of the neoliberal urban policy context, there should be more vigilance by public and civic actors to strive for a greater balance of social and market goals.

Strategic Collaboration and Role Alignment

It is critical that there be more effective collaboration and role alignment among the numerous actors involved in multisite public-private partnerships.

Innovation and Social Entrepreneurship

Unlike many facets of real estate development that are well-developed with broadly accepted techniques and processes that can be deployed across various contexts, designing, creating, and sustaining inclusive and equitable mixed-income communities remain highly complex, context-specific endeavors that require high levels of innovation and entrepreneurial drive. Any reliance on "business as usual" will likely replicate existing structural disparities.

Personnel Selection and Management

Ultimately the success of these efforts will depend on the vision, commitment, and capacity of the leadership and key personnel. This places a high premium on thorough recruitment and hiring procedures along with strong orientation, training, and management processes.

Accountability

Even with the best of intentions from initiative leaders and personnel, the pull of market forces, status quo procedures and practices, and existing power dynamics present formidable pressure toward accepted and familiar ways of doing business. Achieving a more inclusive and equitable results will require effective accountability mechanisms at all levels of the effort.

Conclusion

The NCI in Washington, D.C. and HOPE SF in San Francisco set out to chart a more inclusive, equitable approach to transforming public housing developments into mixed-income communities. This has been a daunting aspiration in the face of the full-on commitment to neoliberal urban policy at all levels of government and overwhelming market forces that are rapidly transforming the form and demographics of the urban environment. While we found numerous examples of policy and practice in both cities that were deployed to help achieve better social outcomes for the original residents of the public housing communities being redeveloped, ultimately it has been extremely difficult to do so in both the cities. Despite the shortcomings and challenges, there is no question that but for the principles, policies, strategies, and political compromises put in place by the urban social entrepreneurs tapped to lead both efforts, the outcomes would have been far less favorable for the original residents of the developments. Furthermore, we find enough evidence of serious intent toward principle-driven development by city leaders and initiative practitioners to warrant continued persistence in determining ways to leverage mixed-income development processes for more equitable social outcomes. Using an analytical lens that elevates a focus on race and spotlights the strategic trade-offs associated with issues such as privatization, devolution and entrepreneurial governance can be a useful and practical device for promoting greater strategic action and stronger accountability.

Notes

1 There were originally eight public housing sites planned for inclusion in HOPE SF. Alice Griffith was added as a priority site in response to the opportunity and criteria of the federal Choice Neighborhoods Initiative when it was launched in 2010.
2 In San Francisco, there have technically been five mayors: upon the sudden death of Mayor Lee in December 2017, Mayor London Breed assumed office in her role as President of the Board of Supervisors. She subsequently was forced to step down to run in the special election, and Mark Farrell served as temporary mayor until Breed won her official position as mayor.

References

Aalbers, M. and Christophers, B. (2014) Centering housing in political economy. *Housing, Theory & Society, 31*(4), 373–394.

City and County of San Francisco Human Services Agency (2005) *The Seven Key Street Corners for at- Risk Families in San Francisco.* Unpublished report.

Clarke, S. and Gaile, G. (1989) Moving toward entrepreneurial economic development policies: Opportunities and barriers. *Policy Studies Journal, 17*(3), 574.

DCHA Resolution 16-06. Retrieved from www.dchousing.org/docs/res16_06.pdf

District of Columbia Housing Authority Amendment Act of 2019. Retrieved from http://lims.dccouncil.us/Download/41812/B23-0125-Introduction.pdf

Giambrone, A. (2010) D.C. resets Barry Farm redevelopment after unfavorable court decision. Retrieved from: https://dc.curbed.com/2018/8/4/17648968/dc-barry-farm-redevelopment-court-decision-public-housing-new-communities-initiative

Gress, T.G., Joseph, M.L., and Cho, S. (2019) Confirmations, new insights, and future implications for HOPE VI mixed-income redevelopment. *Cityscape, 21*(2), 185–212.

Hackworth, J. (2000) State devolution, urban regimes, and the production of geographic scale: The case of New Brunswick, NJ. *Urban Geography, 21*, 450–458.

Harvey, D. (2005) *A brief history of neoliberalism.* New York: Oxford University Press.

Hope SF. Website. Retrieved from www.hope-sf.org/timeline/

Hyra, D. (2018) *Race, Class and Politics in the Cappuccino City.* Chicago, IL: The University of Chicago Press.

Joint Center for Housing Studies of Harvard University (2019) *The State of the Nation's Housing.* Cambridge, MA: Harvard University.

Joseph, M.L., Chaskin, R.J., and Webber, H.S. (2007) The theoretical basis for addressing poverty through mixed-income development. *Urban Affairs Review, 42*(3), 369–409.

Joseph, M.L. and Miyoung, M. (2019). Mixed-income development. In Orum, A. (ed.), *Wiley-Blackwell Encyclopedia of Urban and Regional Studies.* John Wiley & Sons Ltd.

Khare, A.T. (2017) Privatization in an era of economic crisis: Using market-based policies to remedy market failures. *Housing Policy Debate, 28*(1), 6–28.

Khare, A.T. (forthcoming). *Poverty, Power, and Profit: Structural Racism in Public Housing Reform.*

Khare, A.T. and Joseph, M.L. (2019) Prioritizing inclusion and equity in the next generation of mixed-income communities. In Joseph, M.L. and Khare, A.T. (eds)., *What Works to Promote Inclusive, Equitable Mixed-Income Communities*. San Francisco, CA: Federal Reserve Bank of San Francisco, pp. 10–19.

Kleit, R.G. and Page, S.B. (2015) The changing role of public housing authorities in the affordable housing delivery system. *Housing Studies, 30*(4), 621–644.

Leitner, H. (1990) Cities in pursuit of economic growth: The local state as entrepreneur. *Political Geography Quarterly, 9*(2), 146–170.

Leitner, H., Sheppard, S.E., Sziarto, K., and Maringanti, A. (2007) Contesting urban futures: Decentering neoliberalism. In Leitner, H., Peck, J., and Sheppard, S.E. (eds)., *Contesting Neoliberalism: Urban Frontiers*. New York: The Guilford Press, pp. 1–25.

Melamed, J. (2015) Racial capitalism. *Journal of the Critical Ethnic Studies Association, 1*(1), 76–85.

New Communities Initiative Annual Report (NCI) (2014) Retrieved from https://dcnewcommunities.org/wp-content/uploads/2014/06/FINAL-FOR-PRINT_NCI-Annual-Report_1140513-2.pdf

New Communities Initiative Stakeholder Report (NCI) (2016–2017). Retrieved from https://dcnewcommunities.org/wp-content/uploads/2018/04/NCI-2016-AnnualReport-03.22.18-v3b-PREVIEW.pdf

New Communities Initiative. Retrieved from dcnewcommunities.org

Northwest One Redevelopment Plan (2005) Retrieved from: https://dcnewcommunities.org/wp-content/uploads/2014/06/Northwest-One-Plan.pdf

Office of the Mayor (2016) "Mayor Bowser Delivers on the Promise of the New Communities Initiative. Retrieved from https://mayor.dc.gov/release/mayor-bowser-delivers-promise-new-communities-initiative

Peck, J., Theodore, N., and Brenner, N. (2009) Neoliberal urbanism: Models, moments, mutations. *SAIS Review of International Affairs, 29*(1), 49–66.

Richardson, J., Mitchell, B., and Franco, J. (2019) Shifting neighborhoods: Gentrification and cultural displacement in American cities. National Reinvestment Coalition. Retrieved from https://ncrc.org/gentrification/

San Francisco Board of Supervisors Resolution 227-12. Retrieved from https://sfbos.org/ftp/uploadedfiles/bdsupvrs/ordinances12/o0227-12.pdf

San Francisco News Staff (2017) Low-income neighborhoods approved for redevelopment. *San Francisco News* (February 2). Retrieved from www.thesfnews.com/low-income-neighborhoods-approved-redevelopment/34787

Stacy, C., Meixell, B., and Srini, T. (2019) Inequality versus inclusion in US cities. *Social Indicators Research, 145*(1), 117.

UC Berkeley's Urban Displacement Project (n.d.) Rising housing costs and re-segregation in San Francisco. Retrieved from www.urbandisplacement.org/.

Vale, J.L. and Freemark, Y. (2018) The privatization of American public housing: Leaving the poorest of the poor behind. In Anacker, K.B., Nguyen, M.T., and Varady, D.P. (eds)., *Routledge Handbook of Housing Policy and Planning*. Abingdon: Routledge, pp. 184–202.

Vale, J.L. and Shamsuddin, S. (2017) All mixed up: Making sense of mixed-income housing developments. *Journal of the American Planning Association, 83*(1), 56–67.

9

PARIS HABITAT'S EXPERIENCE OF URBAN REGENERATION TO CREATE AFFORDABLE HOUSING

Stéphane Dauphin and Hélène Schwoerer

Introduction: Living in Paris

Like the world's other great capital cities, the housing market in the heart of Paris is under great strain, with purchase prices exceeding €10,000/m² and average monthly rent reaching €27/m². The development of tourism through Airbnb and second homes, which take thousands of homes away from families, and the many empty accommodation units are aggravating the situation, while the regulatory tools to control the housing market are inadequate. Inspired by Vienna's achievements in social housing—a city that all social classes can call home—the local authorities in Paris are committed to design and build an inclusive city with diverse housing opportunities. A long-term strategy and strong intervention in housing markets are required if these goals are to succeed. In particular, this entails a command of real estate performance, price regulation instruments (for rental properties as well as those related to affordable home ownership) and the market.

Many cities in Europe (London, Berlin, Budapest, Riga) and Asia (Taipei) which sold off their social housing stock and relied on market regulation alone in the 1980s and 1990s are now reassessing those decisions given the current situation (gentrification of cities, exclusion of lower and middle classes, etc.). They are investing massively in affordable housing and are adopting market regulation instruments (rent control, Airbnb prohibition, etc.) (Figure 9.1).

Today, 21% of the 1,160,000 primary residences in Paris are public housing units. Given the financialisation of the housing sector, the attractiveness of Paris and its soaring property prices, the city's low-income and middle-class families can only continue to live there if the local authorities demonstrate a strong desire to intervene and if market regulation is established. Quality of life, wealth, the variety of its heritage and economic momentum make Paris an attractive city for most people: from the richest to the most vulnerable. Such a high level of attractiveness and numerous potential investors—housing seen as a safe investment—combined with the rarity of both real estate and land opportunities, mean that available accommodation in Paris is under great strain.

Therefore, in 2001, the City of Paris authorities committed to an ambitious, interventionist policy to reshape the housing market and ensure that low-income and middle-class households can access decent housing. However, the metropolis' housing crisis and its consequences for

DOI: 10.4324/9781003172949-9

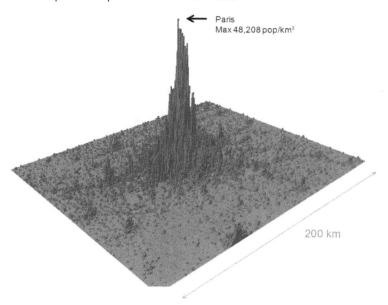

FIGURE 9.1 Paris – High-Density City.
Note: Calculations of OCDE based on Landscan database, 2009.
Source: City of Paris/Paris Habitat.

society remain a serious concern. Hence, the City of Paris authorities and Paris Habitat, the capital's main social housing provider, continue to promote social diversity. The aim is to act along the housing spectrum, from housing for the most impoverished to intermediary housing, paying particular attention to the social mix (Houdard, 2009). Finding effective answers to the demand for housing in Paris is a considerable challenge given the compounded physical and financial constraints in a very high-density area. And yet, Paris remains attractive for young adults, students, executives, low-income and even impoverished families who work there but live far away. Indeed, to this day, more than 249,000 households are waiting for social housing in Paris, nearly 135,000 of which already live in the city (APUR, 2014).

Adapting Provision to the Diverse Needs of Households

Since 2001, particular effort has been made to support the development of social housing; nearly 110,000 accommodation units were funded between 2001 and 2018. And given the issues surrounding social diversity and unmet demand, the city authorities intend to exceed the goals set down in the *SRU Law on Urban Solidarity and Renewal* whereby 25% of main residences should be in the form of social housing (Bacqué & Gauthier, 2011). They seek to achieve 30% between now and 2030.

To meet the expectations of all households, the social housing units funded since 2001 can be split into three distinct categories based on the applicable rent and on the income ceilings the households must meet to could qualify for them:

- PLAI (*Prêt Locatif Aidé d'Intégration* or Assisted Integration Rental Loan): average rent of €6/m²/month; annual income for one person: €13,000; and for a couple with one child: €28,000;

- PLUS (*Prêt Locatif à Usage Social* or Rental Loan for Social Housing Purposes): average rent of €7/m²/month; annual income for one person: €23,700; and for a couple with one child: €46,500;
- PLS (*Prêt Locatif Social* or Social Housing Rental Loan): average rent of €13.40/m²/month; annual income for one person: €30,800; and for a couple with one child: €60,500.

These income ceilings are set by the State and can be adapted depending on the region, residents' incomes and the situation in the different housing markets (Driant, 2014). All accommodation units are allocated to households whose incomes are 60–80% below the ceilings indicated (PLAI, PLUS, PLS).

To respond to the diversity of households—families with children, students, dependent elderly people and the vulnerable—68% of the housing units funded represent family accommodation units and 32% specific accommodation units. The latter category includes accommodation for dependent elderly people, temporary accommodation, guest houses, accommodation for young workers, Emergency Housing Centres and so forth. The balance of the three main categories is 40% to PLUS, 30% to PLAI and 30% to PLS. Further, more than 50% of Paris' residential housing stock consists of small units. This makes it very difficult for families with children to find accommodation suited to their family and their income. Therefore, all social housing development projects include more than 50% of 2+ bedroom apartments.

On the other hand, the so-called 'upper' middle class also faces increasing problems to find affordable housing. Combined with the public goal to promote social diversity, this situation has led local authorities to develop intermediary accommodation units. These developments have been located in chosen geographical areas in order to balance the social mix (Houdard, 2009). These housing units targeted to upper-middle-class households are called 'PLI – Prêt Locatif Intermédiaire' or Intermediary Rental Loan- units):

- PLI: average rent of €17/m²/month; annual income for one person: €42,400; and for a couple with one child: €76,700.

Levers for Developing Social Housing

The City of Paris authorities activate all possible legal provisions to encourage the creation of affordable housing to as many people as possible (Driant, 2014). These provisions include:

- Exercising pre-emption and priority rights;
- Development of public construction projects where at least 60% of the housing is put aside for the creation of social and intermediary accommodation units (new urban areas on the east side of Paris, near the Seine, and on the northwest, both using land created above railroad tracks);
- Conditions imposed in the *Local Urban Development Plan* which identify the specific land lots needed to be dedicated to social and intermediary housing;
- Conditions imposed for all private projects greater than 800m² located in areas with insufficient social housing to include 30% of all housing built as social housing or to include 30% of intermediary housing in the areas without a social housing deficit;
- Encouragement to transform obsolete office buildings and public buildings into social and intermediary housing;
- In the near future, the creation of a community land trust (in French, 'Organisme de foncier solidaire', or socially responsible real estate entity) to develop affordable home ownership.

A diversity of housing is sought for all projects within each *arrondissement (Paris' district)*. Thus, in *arrondissements* which already have a large proportion of social housing, PLS, PLI or specific rental accommodation projects will be given preference. The distribution and integration of all the funding categories within a given housing project takes into account the 'SRU [urban solidarity and renewal] rate' of the *arrondissement* and local rebalancing issues (APUR, 2017). Still, the need for housing cannot be resolved at the scale of Paris alone; answers have to be found within the Greater Paris.

Moreover, the climate emergency and the need to take collective action to confront climate change force us to reassess how we live our lives, in every sense, and how we make cities. We need to reconsider urban density, materials and even the place of nature in the city. These paradigmatic changes are being imposed on us, but they cannot divert us from our goal: the city must be shared and must be accessible to everyone in all our diversity.

An Ambitious Policy in Terms of Quality and Sustainable Housing

To implement this proactive social and affordable housing policy, the City of Paris authorities rely mainly on three housing providers: Régie Immobilière de la ville de Paris – RIVP (60,000 housing units), Elogie/Siemp (27,000 housing units) and Paris Habitat.

Paris Habitat is the largest Public Housing Office (*office public de l'habitat* or OPH) in France, with nearly 125,000 housing units. Created in 1914, it houses more than one in nine Parisians. It invests nearly half of its average budget of approximately €1 billion in developing, renovating and maintaining its properties. On average, Paris Habitat's properties are 74 years old. They are strongly committed to their upkeep: adapting themselves to climate change, updating their facilities, reducing their energy consumption and combating the economic vulnerability of tenants. The potential value of these properties, which are for the use and enjoyment of all Parisians, is very high, greater than €50 billion. Paris Habitat also owns 4,000 stores, more than 50,000 parking lots and over a 100 ha of gardens and green spaces. Paris Habitat has a deliberate policy of maintaining ownership of these properties.

Development of social and intermediary housing goes hand in hand with high standards in terms of architectural quality. Hence, Paris Habitat systematically selects projects through architectural competitions and competitive bids. Since 2007, with Paris' first Climate Plan, environmental criteria have become priority goals in new housing projects and regeneration projects: these goals target energy consumption, reduced greenhouse gas effect, creation of green roofs, development of renewable energy, and are formalised in certifications (ISO 50 001, NF Habitat HQE) and charters such as *Démoclès and Bois*.

Since 2018, the City of Paris has intensified its effort to tackle the climate emergency. In all its construction and renovation programmes, Paris Habitat has undertaken to comply with nine of the 17 *UN Sustainable Development Goals* to be achieved by 2030. Indeed, all Paris Habitat's development programmes are affected by the issues related to the creation of a post-carbon city by 2050.

- *Energy*: be a player in energy transition, thermal renovation and renewable energy;
- *Sustainable city*: ecological transition of the area; limit the excavation of land, encourage non-carbon movement and transport materials, compensation of residual emissions locally or over another area;
- *Climate change*: propose solutions to reduce greenhouse gas emissions and adjust to global warming. Reversible building, dry construction, maximise permeable surfaces. Work on improving summer comfort;

- *Resources*: engage in responsible consumer practices, circular economy, waste reduction;
- *Water*: develop sustainable water resources, use of non-drinking water;
- *Innovation*: use BIM/CIM or optimise performance at a lower cost;
- *Life on Earth*: create green roofs and walls on buildings, demineralisation of free spaces, preservation of biodiversity;
- *Health*: clean site, air quality, materials, and so forth;
- *Partnership*: discuss, pool energy and assess energy production facilities.

Rising to the Challenge: Transformation of the Reuilly Barracks

Owned by the Ministry of Defence, the Reuilly Barracks (Figure 9.2) occupied two hectares of land in the heart of Paris between Place de la Bastille and Place de la Nation, a well-connected area, served by a dense public transport network (bus, metro) and cycle paths.

Like a hundred other real estate and property lots in Paris, in 2006, these Barracks had been tagged for the development of 50% social housing in the *Local Urban Development Plan*. As time went by, the Barracks no longer met the needs of the army. Hence, the State decided to sell them in order to rationalise its real estate holdings.

In 2013, the government adopted *The Duflot Law*, requesting State-owned real estate to facilitate the creation of social housing in France. This law enabled the State and other large public operators to sell real estate at prices below their market value in order to encourage the creation of social housing. This specific cut allows social housing providers to acquire land or buildings below the local market price and therefore make their projects economically sound (Bacqué & Gauthier, 2011). The Reuilly Barracks were part of this plan. After extensive nego-tiations between the City of Paris authorities, the State and Paris Habitat, a memorandum of understanding was agreed upon. It defined the housing programme to be achieved on the parcel

FIGURE 9.2 Historical Military Barracks in Paris.
Source: Paris Habitat, by Cyril Bruneau.

and the financial conditions for the purchase of this property. The programme stipulated that in order to avoid any speculation, it was agreed that only rental properties would be developed. Given its location, the historical qualities of the existing buildings and the parade ground and its transformation potential, it was decided that the project would include:

- 50% social housing (family accommodation, PLUS, PLS and PLAI, student accommodation);
- 20% intermediary housing (PLI); and
- 30% private, rent-controlled accommodation units.

Specific premises for activities including artists' workshops, retail space, a nursery for 66 children and a public garden measuring nearly 5,000m² completed the programme.

Financial Arrangement to Develop Sustainable Housing

First of all, it is essential to recall that access to housing is the responsibility of the State, and mobilisation of its real estate to develop accessible housing programmes was one of its priorities. As early as 2004, the State agreed to sell or rent property in Paris at prices compatible with the financial equilibrium of projects in order to ensure the development of housing and social housing. In the case of the Reuilly barracks, the purchase price was defined taking into account the nature of the various programmes, their respective costs and projected income to reach a global financial equilibrium. Four components were identified:

- Social housing programmes built by refurbishing existing buildings and constructing new ones: €958m²,
- Intermediary housing programmes through refurbishing and construction: €900m²;
- Rent-controlled private rental accommodation units: €1,400m²; and
- Public facilities, retail space: €1,700m².

Paris Habitat purchased the Reuilly barracks for €40 million. The agreement provided that, in the event the income generated by Paris Habitat on the project was higher than expected, Paris Habitat would pay 75% of this extra income to the State, keeping 25% as an incentive and/or reimbursement for front-end costs for environmental cleaning of polluted land and partial demolition of existing buildings. This purchase was also bound by an obligation to comply with a precise schedule for the various urban development procedures (impact study, filing of construction permits, etc.) and competitive bidding with regard to the private portion.

In the time that went by between the purchase of this property by Paris Habitat and the beginning of the project itself, the law changed and made it possible for Paris Habitat to sell part of the project to a private investor 'once-completed' (*vente sur plans* or VEFA). It was the first time a social housing provider, publicly regulated, was going to sell housing units to a private investor. This requires an explanation. In France, many development projects are carried through private promotion, and this is increasingly the case in the construction of social and intermediary housing. The landlord buys the property 'once-completed' and takes no part in the construction project; its sole role is to buy and then manage the property. The new law changed the role of the social housing provider who could thereafter engage in large-scale programmes, guarantee their overall consistency and environmental goals, *construct* the properties and then in turn sell them, 'once-completed', to a private landlord. Note that it is possible for a social housing provider to undertake this role akin to the one of a private promoter only when private accommodation units account for less than 30% of the housing units to be developed.

In order to find the investor that would acquire the rent-controlled, private accommodation units, Paris Habitat organised an open call for tender. This competitive bid laid out clearly the sale conditions, the quality level of the accommodation sold and the requirements set by Paris Habitat both in terms of their management and their future use. Potential buyers had to commit to keep these accommodation units in the private rental sector for a 20-year period. After these 20 years, Paris Habitat will have the option to purchase the housing units. In the meantime, these accommodation units will be rented out at between 20% and 30% below the market rate.

The project was undertaken by Paris Habitat based on this memorandum of understanding which set a constructability goal of 37,163m², that is, around 500 accommodation units. This constructability was below the theoretical, maximum constructability that could have been reached according to the *Local Urban Development Plan*. But this theoretical level would have entailed total demolition of the existing buildings, which was unthinkable. In fact, it was imperative to preserve the historical buildings and the large central space which formed the parade ground. Total demolition of the existing buildings would not have been compatible with the opinion of the 'Architectes des Bâtiments de France', State architects in charge of preserving historical heritage. Paris Habitat undertook a long process of negotiation with this entity. This resulted in a project that protects the legacy of heritage resources and yet allows a higher than expected constructability for 600 accommodation units. Local authorities granted all the urban development permits needed.

In the end, the extra income generated by the project and due to the State exceeded €12 million:

- €4 million earned thanks to the additional constructability that Paris Habitat managed to reach, while still respecting architectural and historical heritage requirements; and
- €8 million thanks to the sale of the 'once-completed' private, rent-controlled rental units: Paris Habitat found an investor for the private units at a better than expected price.

Cooperation and Co-Design to Transform the Reuilly Barracks

For decades, these military barracks were an enclave in the city, and access was completely denied to the public. Protected by thick walls, the area was cut off from the rest of the neighbourhood. Therefore, before launching the transformation of the site to turn it into a new neighbourhood, it was decided that it should be opened up to the public. Various spaces were entrusted to partners and collectives of artists until construction work began. For nearly two years, the buildings and external spaces have been occupied by:

- Le Centre d'Action Social Protestant which housed 120–180 homeless people and refugees;
- Artistic groups, Gare XP and le Jardin d'Alice, which produced and organised exhibitions and activities;
- The Romanès circus; and
- Hip Hop Citoyen and the Astral theatre.

Through their creativity and their work, these different partners have fully contributed to the opening up of this historical place to the neighbourhood. Today, this is known as 'transitional urban development' or 'transitional urban arrangements'. We expect this model of occupation to develop markedly in the years to come. While it allows spaces to be occupied during the often long and protracted period before the transformation project begins, the unoccupied premises provide a response to emergency situations (accommodation for the homeless, refugees, etc.). The City of Paris authorities have adopted a charter to support and encourage this type of transitional arrangements. It was signed in August 2019 by the main operators in the sector (developers, promoters and social housing landlords) working in this area (APUR, 2017).

Construction projects usually coincide with a refusal by residents to accept the transformation of their local environment, particularly when it involves creating social housing. Therefore, this large-scale project required not only to transform existing historical buildings while taking advantage of their intrinsic qualities but also to rethink how a new neighbourhood should be created.

The process involved several steps. First, Paris Habitat organised a competitive bid to select the 'main architect' that would coordinate all the others ('l'architecte coordinateur'). This bid was won by H20 team who was therefore entrusted with the development of this new neighbourhood and had the task of guaranteeing the correct delivery of the project goals – be they urban, environmental or historical preservation. These main goals had then to be shared with the City of Paris authorities and the various players involved such as the Architectes de Bâtiment de France. Then, six project management teams of architects were chosen for the different projects that compose the whole programme.

Given the scheduling challenges and the ambitious time frame, it was decided to select these architects through a competitive dialogue instead of a regular bid where they would have presented finished projects, which could not have been adapted to guarantee the global harmony of the programme. The competitive dialogue process ensured that projects could be developed simultaneously in a workshop format in collaboration with the various players and residents. In all the construction and renovation programmes it undertakes, Paris Habitat always endeavours to select project management teams of architects with different experiences and backgrounds, each with its unique architectural style. This was the case for the transformation of the Reuilly barracks which was entrusted to six different design and project management teams:

- Lin Architects Urbanits (German team), Package A;
- Lacroix Chessex (Swiss team), Package F;
- Mir (French team), Package D/E;
- Anyoji Beltrando (French team), Package B;
- Charles Henri Tachon (French team), Package B1; and
- NP2F and Office Kersten Geers and David Van Severen (French/Belgian team).

Workshops and co-design between project management teams made it possible to develop the urban project, the positioning of buildings and the relationship between what already existed and the new buildings. This collaborative work resulted in agreement on sizes, materials and colours. Overall coherence was reached through diversity.

Throughout the project development process and until its delivery, a specific place, a 'project house', was put aside for collaborative work and discussions between the project's players and the residents. As needed, the project house could alternatively be used as a design workshop, a conference venue, an exhibition site and an area for negotiation. The various project development phases were presented at public meetings. All the programmes, such as the garden or the future of the retail spaces, were subject to consultation, co-design and local walks with residents and Parisians. Joint development of this project meant that it was possible to go beyond the anticipated constructability with nearly 40,000m^2 created and renovated spaces. All the urban development regulatory procedures (development permit, public consultation, environmental authorisations and the six construction permits) were met favourably and no legal action was taken against them by local residents. This is truly unheard of in Paris.

Ecological and Social Transformation

The Reuilly barracks project undoubtedly provides a response to critics of 'Paris being covered in concrete' – critics which also condemn the housing conditions of the most vulnerable and the exodus of families with children who can no longer be housed in Paris for financial reasons. Parisians who demand that the city's population be reduced and only green spaces be developed. Indeed, in our opinion, the Reuilly Barracks project truly reconciles environmental and social emergency concerns.

For many years, private investors impatiently awaited the sale of these Barracks to demolish the existing buildings and 'pour concrete' over this plot of land in the very heart of Paris. Little attention was paid to the intrinsic quality of the buildings, their transformation potential, the urban singularity of the military site and the sensitivity of local residents to their environment (Donzelat, 2012). These property players did not consider the necessity to create a sustainable city (Figure 9.3).

Promotion of the Site's Heritage and History

For Paris Habitat, preservation of the central empty space and transformation of the old buildings, even if the latter were not exceptional, were obvious. It was a necessity with regard to the sustainable development goals of the project. These buildings were not seen as a constraint, but rather, and for many reasons, as an opportunity. It was an opportunity to use those buildings which had a real identity in this part of the 12th *arrondissement*, to invent a new neighbourhood, to find the right balance between transformation of the old and creation of new buildings and to achieve acceptable density in a very dense city. It was an opportunity to invent new types of housing and new uses while limiting the carbon footprint of the development operation.

FIGURE 9.3 The New Vision for The Reuilly Barracks.
Source: Paris Habitat, TU VERRAS.

Using the old buildings and the existing urban shape, while 'gently' inventing a new landscape and new buildings, no doubt led to increase the neighbourhood's population. However, the density remains a lot lower than the Parisian average. Only the buildings from the 1970s and 1980s – logistics, the army mail sorting facility and the officers' mess (a prefabricated building containing asbestos located in the middle of the parade ground) – were demolished.

With the preservation of the buildings and the demolition of those which could not be transformed, issues surrounding 'reuse' had to be considered by us and the project management teams from the design phase onwards. Paris Habitat enlisted the talents of a young Belgian agency, Rotor, to draw up an inventory of the site and analyse the life cycle of its components, the deconstruction of some elements and the conditions for their reuse with the same usage or their 'hijacking' for other purpose. Rotor worked in partnership with the different architect teams, and managed to integrate old materials into the new project while effectively contributing to improve the quality of the accommodation units and to the positive image of social housing.

Thanks to their work, it was possible to require the companies selected to do the construction works to consider reusing materials whenever possible. Here are a few examples of reuse on-site and off-site:

- The old iron radiators were refurnished and used in the new accommodation units;
- The oak cupboards from the old military offices were reconditioned and used as storage in the new accommodation units;
- The glass from the old windows was recycled as car windscreens by Saint Gobain;
- Concrete from demolition of the Barracks' mail sorting facility was crushed and partly used on-site for levelling the work sites;- the rest was sold to construction companies; and
- Recovery and adaptation of old cobblestones for public passageways and garden paths.

In short, in this reuse approach, waste was seen as a resource. With this project, Paris Habitat won a European award project, 'Charm', and received funding to roll out reuse in all its development projects: from construction to refurbishment of existing accommodation units and their reletting. The ecological transition of the Barracks, beyond developing buildings which encourage bioclimatic housing, also involved work to minimise the carbon impact of the project through the use of bio-sourced materials and decarbonised products for thermal insulation or the choice of wooden floors for some accommodation units and the nursery.

Like all programmes developed by Paris Habitat, it also required compliance with the City of Paris authorities' *Energy Air Climate Plan* which sets energy consumption goals. The City of Paris authorities allocate specific grants to help reach the goals of achieving 50 kWhpe/m²FA/year for new buildings and 80 kWhpe/m²FA/year for renovations. To achieve these ambitious goals, renewable energy and recycling, such as recycling grey water, form a considerable part of the programmes.

The Place of Nature: Green and Public Spaces

In many respects, preservation of the central empty space and reclaiming it as a real ecological opportunity for this new neighbourhood and for its future environmental quality was an important component of the redevelopment (Figure 9.4). Before even considering the creation of a public garden measuring nearly 5,000m², the asbestos-contaminated asphalt and the soil polluted by various activities performed on this site over many years had to be removed. The landscape designer and contractors took particular care to preserve the 11 existing plane trees in the ecological restoration.

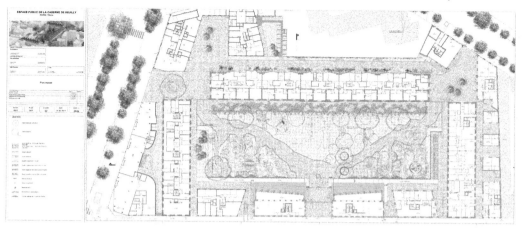

FIGURE 9.4 Site Plan and Urban Green Spaces.
Source: City of Paris/Paris Habitat.

In the months to come, this garden and the many trees it will house will ensure that warming and heat islands can be combated efficiently. The garden is complemented by the systematic re-vegetation of all the areas between the various buildings. Some of them will be for residents through the creation of a shared garden. Green flat roofs and areas within the student accommodation block will be taken care of by a not-for-profit organisation, Quartier Maraicher, to support the City of Paris authorities with their urban agriculture projects. They will grow vegetables and herbs, which will be sold to greengrocers and restaurants in the neighbourhood. They will also run workshops to raise awareness about agriculture with residents and children who attend the nearby schools. In total, more than 6,600m² are transformed into a public garden, Paris Habitat green spaces and green roofs.

The Reuilly Barracks is also home to a pair of common falcons (kestrels) who have been nesting there for a very long time. The presence of these protected birds had to be taken into account during the construction and renovation work. It was a real headache for the contractors when it came to defining the crane clearance areas during the nesting period or when the young kestrels were flying off the nest! Many were concerned that this space for the birds could be preserved, but expectations were met and at least 20 chicks were born during the operation.

Housing Accessible to Diverse Households

In total, 582 new accommodation units will be delivered between September 2019 and spring 2020:

- 209 social housing units divided into 100 PLUS, 61 PLAI and 48 PLS, and 129 student accommodation units funded via PLUS (studio flats) to house 140 young people;
- 110 PLI family accommodation units;
- 133 rent-controlled, private family accommodation units;
- A garden and public passageways covering more than 4,800m²;
- A nursery for 66 children;
- Seven artist/artisan workshops; and
- Nine retail plots in the first round.

TABLE 9.1 Monthly Rents per Square Metre

Operations	Local Increases (%)	Rent in € per M² per Month Depending on Category[a]			
		Category PLUS	Category PLAI	Category PLS	Category PLI
Lot A – Logement Familial	20	8.15	7.3	13.13	
Lot A – Etudiant	20	11.12			
Lot C – Logement Familial	20	8.28	7.35	12.96	
Lot C – PLI – Logement Familial					16.81
Lot F – Logement Familial	20	8.23	7.38	13.06	
Lot B1 – Logement Familial	20	7.89	7.18	13.09	

Source: City of Paris/Paris Habitat.
a   Excluding charges, based on the building and the funding category.

Family accommodation range from studios to four bedrooms:

- 97 studio flats (from 18m² to 27m²);
- 20 large studio flats (from 27m² to 40m²);
- 56 1-bedroom flats (from 40m² to 48m²);
- 158 2-bedroom flats (from 60m² to 70m²);
- 107 3-bedroom flats (from 70m² to 85m²); and
- 14 4-bedroom flats (from 83m² to 95m²).

It should be underlined that all the accommodation units can be accessed by people with reduced mobility. In view of the historic nature of Parisian property and the related accessibility problems, social housing stock plays an essential role in housing those with disabilities or reduced mobility. As mentioned above, the goal of the City of Paris authorities and of Paris Habitat is to develop housing with rents compatible with the incomes of a range of households, from the most vulnerable (those leaving the care system, those with a statutory right to housing, etc.) to the middle classes (teachers, civil servants, employees, etc.) (Table 9.1). Further, average fees for a student accommodation unit (from 18m² to 27m²) amount to €384/month. These fees cover the rent, charges, furniture and availability of the communal areas (study room, launderette, etc.).

Funding Social Housing: A French Model

As detailed earlier, the project benefitted from a discounted purchase price. Moreover, the State and the City of Paris granted investment subsidies to make this program possible. Although social housing remains the responsibility of the State, this level of State support could no longer be achieved for a similar project. Since 2018, the French social housing system and its funding scheme are being revisited by the government, endangering the whole system. For instance, the State imposed a cut of up to 6.5% on the rent collected by social housing providers in order to reduce its own expenditures. Likewise, the Ile de France region has reduced its financial support for creating social housing (Taffin & Amzallag, 2010). However, since 2001, the City of Paris authorities have made housing one of their priorities and have allocated a considerable budget to fund construction and renovation programmes and purchase real estate and property. Thus, between 2014 and the end of 2019, nearly €3 billion will have been mobilised for housing, including over 18 million euro for Reuilly Barracks (Table 9.2).

TABLE 9.2 Funding Conditions for the Project

Reilly Barracks	Number of Units							Cost in Thousand €									
	PLUS	PLAI	PLS	PLI	Total	Others	Pkg	Unit Size (m²)	Unit Cost	Retail Units Cost	Equity	Grants State and City of Paris	Regional Grant	Action Logement	CDC Loan	PR/SU	PRHIP Cost per Unit
Package A	27	44	20		91	2		5,746	25,267	4,717	1,496	5,870	558	3,504	13,839	4,229	278
Package A Student	140				140			2,660	14,775			5,600	1,120		8,055	5,498	106
Package C	4	9	6		19	2		1,197	5,268	2,539	489	1,060	72	848	2,799	4,324	277
Package C – PLI				111	111			6,490	32,599					2,310	30,289	4,662	294
Package F	23	39	17		79	2	100	4,851	21,168	3,894	1,365	4,917	493	3,238	11,155	4,231	268
Package B1	6	10	6		22			1,499	6,736	597	179	1,258	139	778	4,382	4,371	306
Total	20	102	49	111	462	6	100	19,783	91,038	11,747	3,529	18,705	2,382	1,0678	70,519	4,602	197

Source: City of Paris/Paris Habitat.

Since 2004, the City of Paris authorities set out annually their quantitative and qualitative goals in terms of development of new housing and renovation of existing buildings. They also spell out their requirements in terms of improvement in energy consumption. All these goals are laid out in an annual framework which also defines the investment subsidies the City will grant to the housing providers to meet these goals. This framework specifies the level of subsidies granted depending on the nature and location of the projects (Donzelat, 2012). The level of subsidies also depends on the category of social housing: a PLAI with very low rent will be more subsidised than a PLS with higher rent / more middle-class tenants, and PLI will not get any additional support.

Additional grants may be available, if, for instance, the project is located in an *arrondissement* with a social housing shortage or if it involves the regeneration of a substandard and unsafe property (insalubrious properties). Other considerations might include ambitious goals in terms of energy consumption or sustainable development. These grants make it possible to develop housing with accessible rents in a city where the cost of accommodation is prohibitive.

Note that the French social housing funding system is multilayered. The project therefore also benefitted from the other, traditional levers in the system: reduced VAT, reduced property tax during 25 years and a preferred funding mechanism via the French development bank, the CDC. (Refer to Table 9.2).

Local Facilities

Quality of life in Paris also depends upon the availability of retail spaces with stores and cafés. All housing development programmes therefore include retail premises. These spaces are designed to meet the needs and expectations of local and future residents. The choice of establishments depends on the location in Paris and is made with local partners. Some of these premises may be dedicated to non-commercial activities: not-for-profit, start-ups, cultural or craft-based, or community-oriented projects. However, in some areas, especially where property prices are very expensive, these premises are rented at market prices – the income generated contributes to the equilibrium of the project for the social housing provider. For the Reuilly Barracks, Paris Habitat worked with Semaest, an entity dedicated to economic development and also linked to the City of Paris. Semaest analysed the needs of local businesses, the neighbourhood and the uses of its inhabitants and held thereby what should be the priorities for the 4,000m² retail space of the project. The type of spaces and their purposes were defined through discussions with councillors, local residents and retailers in the neighbourhood (see Figure 9.5).

On this basis, calls for projects are being organised to choose the new businesses. A food court and a bookshop have already been chosen. The development of food trade apprenticeships and a partnership with training colleges in the area proposed by the future retailer were a determining factor. Therefore, the spaces located on rue de Chaligny, which are less commercially attractive, will be given over to not-for-profit organisations and institutional partners. Although not a medical desert like many places in France, rental costs for medical practices, doctor specialisation and prices above the State pricing system have reduced low-income residents' access to healthcare. Therefore, there are plans to use some spaces to set up a medical practice which, thanks to below-market rents, will enable doctors and paediatricians to practice and offer low fees. The Reuilly Barracks are located on the edge of Faubourg Saint Antoine, the historic artistic neighbourhood known for its cabinetmaking, and near the Boulle school (which teaches fine arts and crafts). It has therefore been decided to use some spaces to develop five artist and artisan workshops whose rents will help young people launch their careers.

In parallel with housing developments, the City of Paris authorities also aim to create facilities for young children. Given the lack of affordable real estate opportunities, these nurseries

FIGURE 9.5   Nursery and Retail Stores.
Source: Paris Habitat, by Frédéric Delangle.

are often done together with the social housing projects. After studying the needs of the neighbourhood, the City instructed Paris Habitat to build a nursery for 66 children aged three months to three years. It was decided that the nursery would be established within the social housing programme (Package F) and developed on the second and third floors of the building. The facilities benefit from their own entrance from the courtyard, above street-level, away from the hustle and bustle of the street. The production cost of the nursery is €5,800K, paid for by the City of Paris.

Conclusion: Paris Habitat Is a Local Player

A diversity of housing is sought for all projects within each *arrondissement (Paris' district)*. This case study responds to the ambitious goals of the City of Paris to increase its share of social housing. The development provides a mix of housing types to respond to different needs of residents, but also a sensitive integration of a variety of housing opportunities for low- and middle-income renters and homeowners. The funding model for social housing is an important defining element for the success of such developments, as is the regulatory and planning framework for the realisation of the 'SRU [urban solidarity and renewal] rate' in each *arrondissement* and local rebalancing issues (Taffin & Amzallag, 2010).

For Paris Habitat, the preservation and the adaptive reuse of the Reuilly Barracks was a challenge, but also an opportunity to transform a historic place in a sustainable way, with an emphasis on social and environmental aspects. It was an opportunity to use those buildings which had a real identity in the 12th *arrondissement*, to invent a new neighbourhood, to find the right balance in the transformation of old buildings and to achieve density through high-quality design. It was an opportunity to invent new types of housing and new uses while limiting the carbon footprint of the development operation.

All programmes for adaptive reuse, such as the common garden, retail spaces and nursery, were the result of public engagement and co-design, leading to a shared vision for the place. With the preservation of the buildings and the sensitive new additions of housing with high energy-efficient performance, green roofs and diversity of opportunities for neighbourhood interaction, Reuilly Barracks is a new diverse community. Paris Habitat's commitment does not end with the construction project. We want to participate in the creation of a living community, bringing together current residents and future tenants and enable them to really feel part of their new neighbourhood. To do so, we organised various events to welcome everyone on the site, get them to know each other and meet Paris Habitat's staff who will be working there. As the first tenants move in, this beautiful project will become a lively neighbourhood.

Acknowledgement

This chapter was originally presented as a paper at an international symposium at the University of Calgary in 2019. We have used Paris Habitat materials and project documents to illustrate this unique example of award-winning redevelopment of heritage resources to accommodate the diverse housing needs of people in the city. Additional resources are available at www.parishabitat.fr/. Our thanks to Dr Tsenkova for the invitation to the symposium and for her kind support in the development of this chapter.

References

Atelier Parisien d'Urbanisme (APUR) (2014). *L'évolution du logement social à Paris (Social Housing Development in Paris)*. Paris: Paris Urbanism Agency, www.apur.org/fr/nos-travaux/derniers-chiffres-logement-social-paris.

Atelier Parisien d'Urbanisme (APUR) (2017). *La ville autrement (The City By Other Means)*. Paris: Paris Urbanism Agency, www.apur.org/fr/nos-travaux/chiffres-logement-social-paris-2016-edition-2017

Bacqué, M. H. & Gauthier, M. (2011) Participation, urbanisme et études urbaines. Quatre décennies de débats et d'expériences depuis. *Participations*, vol. 1: 36–66.

Donzelat, J. (2012) *A quoi sert la rénovation urbaine? (What Purpose Does Urban Renewal Serve?)*, Paris: PUF, collection La ville en débat.

Driant, J. Cl. (2014). Enjeux et débats des politiques du logement en France, Revue d'économie financière. *Association d'économie financière*, vol. 0(3): 189–208.

Houdard, N. (2009) *Droit au logement et mixité sociale (Right to Housing and Social Mix)*. Paris: L' Harmattan Collection, Habitat et Sociétés.

Taffin, C. & Amzallag, M. (2010). *Le logement social (Social Housing in France)*. Paris: Dexia L.G.D.J.

10

TORONTO

Revitalization in Regent Park 12 Years Later

Vincent Tong

Introduction

Toronto Community Housing Corporation (TCHC) started its revitalization program as a way to leverage public assets to address a growing capital repair backlog, improve the living conditions for tenants and correct some of the planning mistakes of the past. After almost 20 years of experience with revitalization efforts and redevelopment of public housing sites into mixed-income communities, we can reflect on valuable lessons learned and share what has worked. The development process has created a lot of challenges, but also many opportunities to create social housing communities. This chapter outlines the lessons learned from planning and implementing the revitalization program, particularly focusing on the Regent Park community.

Regent Park was one of the oldest public housing communities in Canada (Figure 10.1). Built between 1948 and 1959, Regent Park was home to 2,083 units of rent-geared to income (RGI) housing spread over 69 acres. Similar to other developments, which occurred during that time, Regent Park was designed as a self-contained community with no through traffic and buildings located in open field settings (GHK International, 2003).

Regent Park Revitalization Plan

In 2002, the TCHC Board of Directors approved proceeding with a due diligence process to explore the feasibility of redeveloping the Regent Park community along with the development of a planning and engagement framework to guide the redevelopment process. In 2003, the *Revitalization Plan for Regent Park* was approved. The plan was developed around 12 principles:

1. Renew the Regent Park neighbourhood
2. Re-introduce pedestrian-friendly streets and park spaces
3. Design a safe and accessible neighbourhood
4. Involve the community in the process
5. Build on cultural diversity, youth, skills and energy
6. Create a diverse neighbourhood with a mix of uses
7. Keep the same number of rent-geared to income

DOI: 10.4324/9781003172949-10

FIGURE 10.1 Regent Park in 2005.
Source: Toronto Community Housing.

8. Minimize disruption for residents from relocation
9. Design a clean, healthy and environmentally responsible neighbourhood
10. Develop a financially responsible strategy
11. Create a successful Toronto neighbourhood
12. Improve and maintain existing parts of Regent Park as redevelopment occurs.

TCHC began implementing the revitalization in 2006, with the first phase consisting of 10 acres at the southwest corner of the community, which included four development parcels. One of these parcels is currently the site of the Regent Park Management Office and Sales Centre to be developed in the future. Since the start of the revitalization process, TCHC has rebuilt approximately 1,350 social housing units. Of the 1,353 units, 364 are affordable rental (rents at 80% of AMR) and 989 RGI rental replacement units. In addition, TCHC with our private sector developer partner has added 1,769 market units (rental and ownership). Of the housing completed, 43% of the units are at below-market rates and 57% of the units are at market rates. Figure 10.2 illustrates the progress achieved, the built form of new residential developments and their integration with the existing communities in downtown Toronto.

The Original Plan, 2005

The *Revitalization Plan for Regent Park* was developed through extensive consultation with tenants, stakeholders and surrounding communities. The original six-phase plan proposed 1,779 RGI units be replaced on site, 304 RGI units to be replaced in other buildings in the Downtown East area and the addition of approximately 3,300 new market units. As part of the City

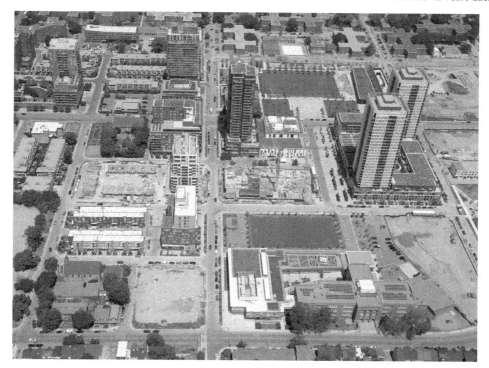

FIGURE 10.2 Regent Park Phase Two Development.
Source: Toronto Community Housing.

planning approvals process, 65% of RGI units and 85% of the social housing had to be replaced on site. Social housing was defined as rental housing units owned by the TCHC, or on their behalf by a non-profit corporation, or a non-profit housing co-operative, and operated by or on their behalf to provide accommodation primarily to persons of low and moderate income. The intent was that no less than 25% of all units in Regent Park would be RGI and no less than 32% of all units would be non-profit rental.

Updates to the Plan, 2007–2013

Beginning in 2007, TCHC began exploring revisions to the existing phasing for Regent Park to deliver the park sooner (planned for phase 5) and to consolidate a number of smaller parks located throughout the community into a central green space. Central to this move was the advancement of capital funding for a new aquatic centre which would be located within the central park space. A rezoning was granted by Toronto City Council in 2009.

In 2013, Maple Leaf Sports and Entertainment began discussions with TCHC to build a sports and athletic field within the footprint of Regent Park. To facilitate the development of this new sports field, TCHC submitted a rezoning application, which was approved in 2014. As part of the rezoning, TCHC proposed reducing the number of phases from six to five and increasing the number of housing units from 5,400 to 7,500 (Figure 10.3). The increase in density allowed TCHC to offset costs for replacing the rental housing, which was seeing significant cost increases year over year due to rising construction costs.

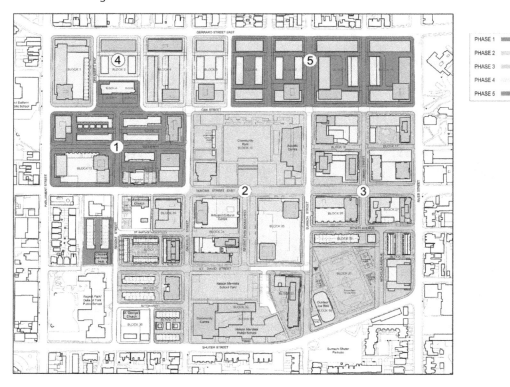

FIGURE 10.3 Current Master Plan for Regent Park.

Note: Regent Park Target Phasing Plan, Scale 1:2,500; Regent Park Revitalization Project, Diamond Architects, August 15, 2016.

Source: Toronto Community Housing.

Regent Park is now past the halfway point in its implementation. The new buildings in Regent Park dominate the landscape, although a small segment of the original buildings was retained.

Lessons Learned 12 Years Later

The following are the key lessons learned, not necessarily in the order of priority, from 12 years of implementing revitalization in Regent Park. Now past the halfway point and prior to starting the implementation of the final phases of the plan, it is the perfect opportunity to reflect on what worked and what has not in the first three phases.

Shorten Timelines

Revitalization is about improving the lives for those who are presently living there, the social housing tenants. Tenants' lives are improved through brand new homes and transforming the socio-economic reality in which they live (Regent Park Collaborative Team, 2002).

In 2003, it was recognized there would be a shortfall of approximately 79%, with the majority of funding coming from operating savings. TCHC was open to the possibility of revitalization because it would transform the neighbourhood and help reduce operating costs. Since then, the shortfall has been reduced to 50% as a result of higher revenues from profit shares on the condominium units. Despite this, decision makers and politicians see less value in continuing to invest in the project. They are balancing competing demands and priorities on shrinking municipal funds. A 20+ years project is a long time. While the goals and objectives were clear when the project started, a decade later, that clarity becomes less prevalent. Many of those who were involved with making the original decisions are no longer involved in project management and execution. Many tenants no longer remember what it was like to live in the old Regent Park, or may only know the new Regent Park moving to the community after revitalization was already underway. For comparison, the majority of the St. Lawrence neighbourhood, which is long-touted as one of the most successful mixed-use mixed-income communities in Toronto, was completed within a decade, providing enough time to reflect on whether the plan is working, but not taking too long that its implementation becomes less of a priority due to competing interests (Gordon, n.d.).

Adapt, Remain Flexible and Embrace Opportunity

Part of the success of Regent Park thus far has been the public and cultural amenities that have added to the vibrancy of the community. Not all of these were in the original plan. As opportunities presented themselves, TCHC adapted and changed its plans to ensure they could be accommodated. This happened early on with consolidation and delivery of the central park to not only accommodate the new aquatic centre but to also provide a key community amenity earlier on in the revitalization as opposed to near the end as originally planned.

In 2013, another opportunity presented itself when Maple Leaf Sports Entertainment Foundation (MLSE) approached TCHC to locate a basketball court, soccer/cricket pitch, running track, hockey rink and field house within the Regent Park community (Figure 10.4).

FIGURE 10.4 Maple Leaf Sports Entertainment Athletic Grounds in Regent Park.
Source: Toronto Community Housing.

FIGURE 10.5 Daniels Spectrum Arts & Cultural Centre.
Source: Toronto Community Housing.

The Regent Park Athletic Grounds, the central park and the aquatic centre have all been vital to the transformation of this neighbourhood. More than any other business or service, these amenities, along with the Daniels Spectrum Arts & Cultural Centre (Figure 10.5), have been the main draw for people across the City visiting this community. Part of removing the stigma of the old Regent Park is about reconnecting this neighbourhood to the fabric of the City.

Pre-Zoning Not Necessarily Faster

TCHC is in the process of rebuilding close to 5,000 RGI social housing units across the City of Toronto. In three instances, TCHC undertook the required entitlements work to implement its revitalizations. What TCHC has found is that pre-zoning sites prior to seeking a private sector partner does not provide the certainty and expediency that pre-zoning strives to achieve. More often than not, once a developer partner is brought on board, they provide a lens that the public sector may not have considered, such as how to maximize revenues through built form and siting. In every instance where TCHC has undertaken the regulatory amendments required, TCHC has had to go back and amend those plans adding both time and cost.

What TCHC has found across its seven revitalization initiatives is the private sector knows what the market is seeking in terms of size of buildings, and the types of units and amenities being offered. The market insight is critical in order to maximize value, which in the case of TCHC is reinvested in rebuilding social housing units.

TCHC's revitalization programme is also structured on partnerships as opposed to land disposition. Having a private sector partner engaged from the beginning co-developing a development plan generates buy-in and ownership from all parties involved. In TCHC's experience, when partnering on a site that has already been zoned, the private sector is bidding on land with entitlements with the assumption the land is clean from contamination and no further approvals are required. The onus has fallen on TCHC to rectify any issues through minor variances and to ensure all site plan and subdivision conditions are satisfied along with all soil remediation. When a partner is brought in at the outset, many of those responsibilities, risks and costs are shared rather than borne by the landowner.

Skin in the Game

The public sector is increasingly risk averse as municipal governments and public sector entities are facing budget pressures. The same is true for TCHC, and the revitalization programme has had to adapt to the changing public sector landscape. The common approach has been to move away from partnerships with the private sector to a land sale model, whereby the market risk is borne solely by the private sector. TCHC took this approach when implementing phase 3 where a land sale model was seen as mitigating a projected downturn in the market. The downturn never happened and went in the opposite direction where the price per square foot for real estate has increased 36% from 2013 to today. The funding gap has widened, and TCHC was not able to benefit from the upswing in the real estate market.

The lesson learned for TCHC has been that in order to leverage its assets (land) to the fullest, it has to take on some of the risk. The added benefit to partnerships as opposed to land sales has been that TCHC has a seat at the table on decisions around the market buildings and can ensure greater integration with community in terms of public realm and architecture.

Diversity of Landowners

One element originally envisioned but yet to implement in Regent Park has been diversifying the social housing ownership. To date, all social housing replacement units within the Regent Park footprint are owned and managed by TCHC. Many have argued that a diversity of landowners and non-profit housing providers is why the St. Lawrence neighbourhood has been so successful (Gordon, n.d., p. 6), ensuring a true mix of incomes and socio-economic backgrounds is represented in the new community (Preville, 2018).

While RGI and affordable housing make up 32% of the revitalized neighbourhood where it used to be 100%, TCHC still remains the largest landowner in Regent Park. Vacancies are filled using the City of Toronto social housing waitlist as opposed to co-operative housing, which use both the social housing waitlist and their own waitlists providing a diversity of incomes and socio-economic backgrounds.

Urban Design Best Practices Need to Reflect Reality

Regent Park was planned using urban design best practices – primarily focused on reintroducing the historic Toronto street grid, providing a pedestrian scale to buildings and properly framing streets and public spaces with buildings to provide what Jane Jacobs called passive surveillance with "eyes on the street".

A different reality has emerged that was never truly contemplated. For example, urban design best practices have been used to locate garbage and loading areas away from street view. Loading and servicing areas have been located in laneways in the newly built parts of Regent Park. Vehicular laneways reduce curb cuts from multiple driveways interrupting the street, creating a safer pedestrian environment. In some instances, these laneways have become difficult for surveillance as they typically do not have active uses fronting on to these spaces and have proven difficult for TCHC's Community Safety Unit to monitor.

Toronto has seen increasing incidents of gun violence over the past few years, and TCHC has been seeking design interventions to deal with the rise. While TCHC recognizes the importance of grade-related units and units with multilevel living for families, rebuilding social housing in a townhouse form is not responsible from both a cost or land use perspective. TCHC also finds it more difficult to secure blocks of townhouses spread across a neighbourhood rather than having units located within a building. For these reasons, TCHC has moved towards grade-related multilevel units within the podiums of buildings rather than rebuilding low-rise townhouses.

Another reason why TCHC is moving away from townhouses is the operating costs and staffing efficiencies. Townhouses, which are spread over a wider area, require operations staff to oversee a larger footprint. In Regent Park, due to the large scale of the development, this is making it more time-consuming to do regular duties such as managing waste or landscaping.

Scale

At approximately 69 acres, Regent Park is able to deliver the public and institutional amenities along with neighbourhood amenities such as retail that deliver a truly mixed-use neighbourhood. The St. Lawrence development was also successful in delivering these amenities across a 56-acre site. TCHC has rebuilt social housing in communities as small as 2.6 acres, and while they are still important to undertake and improve the living conditions for social housing tenants, their ability to deliver transformative change at a broader level is more limited. Smaller sites do not have enough land to provide for spaces which serve as regional nodes of activity, drawing in populations near and far.

Mix at Different Scales

The success at Regent Park can be attributed to mixing at various scales – within buildings, at street level and across the entire neighbourhood. One of the lessons learned from the St. Lawrence neighbourhood is the idea that mixing of RGI units and market units in the same building provides integration and stability, with more residents wanting to stay and live in those buildings (GHK International, 2003). Details around why residents of St. Lawrence found the integration to be a stabilizing force were not provided, but it is a concept that TCHC has implemented in Regent Park, with approximately 25–33% of all units in TCHC rental buildings being rented at 80% of average market rents. Rebuilding rental buildings that are not 100% RGI does provide a mix of people from different socio-economic backgrounds and does contribute to a more diverse neighbourhood that is not only RGI tenants and residents of market buildings.

The revitalization has also ensured there is a mix of built form and affordability at street level. The *Master Plan for Regent Park* was designed to mix market and rental replacement buildings in alternating blocks so there is never a concentration of one type in any given part of the neighbourhood. Both market and rental replacement units also ensure there are grade-related units for both, so there is a consistency to the streetscape, making both types indistinguishable from one another. This is to remove the stigma that has long been associated with living in social housing.

FIGURE 10.6   Regent Park Boulevard Mews with Retail.
Source: Toronto Community Housing.

Vital to the success of Regent Park has also been the mix of uses throughout the neighbourhood. Significant efforts continue to be made to ensure the right balance of commercial retail,
services, institutional and cultural amenities to serve Regent Park residents (see Figure 10.6).
To date, Regent Park has successfully added grocery stores, restaurants, banks and a barbershop
to name a few. Second-floor spaces have been leased out to institutions and agencies such as
George Brown College. A birthing centre and the Regent Park Arts and Cultural Centre also
serve different needs in the community. TCHC and its current developer partner have also
formed a retail committee to explore ideas for future tenants that residents would like in the
community. The difficulty, moving forward, will be the state of the retail industry itself which
is struggling in many communities around the world as more people move to online shopping.
The master plan will need to adapt to ensure the revitalization principles are met and that
Regent Park continues to have thriving streets with grade-level animation.

Social Infrastructure

Revitalization is about more than just housing. Revitalization is about improving both the
physical and social aspects of a community. Considerations should be made to relocate community amenities such as a community centre or library to the new community. One of the most
transformative parts of Regent Park has been the new aquatic centre. It has become a destination in the community and well used by residents of Toronto near and far.

TCHC has also made economic development a priority in the community. The developer
partner has a commitment to provide a minimum 10% of all job opportunities for Regent Park
tenants.

Today, over 1,600 jobs have been filled by tenants since revitalization began. Opportunities were also created with retailers who have opened in the neighbourhood. Investments have also been made in education and training for tenants to ensure they are prepared for the job opportunities offered in the community. TCHC and its partners leverage their relationships to extract benefits for tenants in this regard. As part of the procurement process, economic benefits to tenants is a priority, and TCHC seeks out proposals, which provide robust plans to connect tenants with jobs and training.

Community Engagement

Community engagement has been a cornerstone from the beginning of the planning stages for revitalization of the Regent Park community, and TCHC's goal is to engage as many people as possible throughout the revitalization process. The corporation recognizes that revitalization is an enormous change for residents that creates uncertainty and affects their ties to the community. To ensure the broadest reach possible, TCHC has employed a variety of methods such as using community animators, who are TCHC tenants, to facilitate the exchange of information between TCHC and tenants. This has proven to be extremely effective, as many tenants may feel intimidated speaking directly to their landlord about certain issues. It also helps that these tenants are usually known in the community and easily accessible to others that may have concerns or questions.

TCHC has also employed other methods of communication such as lobby intercepts and door-knocking in addition to more traditional methods such as meeting notices, flyers and newsletters. TCHC has found lobby intercepts and door-knocking to be two of the most effective means of outreach to tenants. Many tenants do not feel comfortable asking questions in front of their neighbours at larger community meetings or they may ignore paper mail and miss critical information. By interacting with tenants in person, it allows tenants to recognize the engagement team and allows the teams to identify potential barriers that will need to be addressed in future communications and/or outreach (e.g., translation and language services, accessibility requirements). As the revitalization progresses, the engagement process has become more complicated due to the fact that new residents, who are not TCHC tenants, are being included in the conversations. TCHC has had to adapt to ensure all voices are being considered, even though it has an obligation to engage with its own tenants and ensure their needs are being met.

TCHC released a request for proposals (RFP) process to seek a developer partner for the remaining phases of Regent Park in early 2019. After hearing from residents who felt they did not have a voice in the process, the procurement practices were adapted to include residents through:

1. An RFP procurement committee made up of TCHC tenants and condominium residents to review the terms of the RFP and ensure the community vision and resident expectations were reflected in the terms of reference;
2. A revitalization working group was created and tasked with the co-creation of the community engagement strategy around the RFP. Many of the recommendations have been incorporated into the process;
3. Two RFP informational open house were held where the community could do a page-turn review of the final document prior to it being issued;
4. TCHC held two "community conversations" which were forums where the community could share their priorities and recommendations for the revitalization of the phase 4 and 5

lands. The priorities were compiled into a Community Conversations Report, which was shared with the proponents via an RFP addendum;

5. A presentation to the community by the shortlisted proponents was incorporated into the process, where residents will hear the different visions and community economic development plans and evaluate those parts of the proposal. The final scores make up 20% of the proponents' overall score; and

6. Once the developer partner has been selected, a plan for community benefits will be entered into by TCHC, the successful proponent and representatives of the community. The plan will secure the benefits to residents and hold the developer partner and TCHC accountable for delivering on those commitments.

References

GHK International (Canada) (2003). *Lessons from St. Lawrence for the Regent Park redevelopment process*. Toronto: Author.

Gordon, D.L.A. (n.d.). *CIP/ ACUPP Case study series: Directions for new urban neighbourhoods: Learning from St.Lawrence*. Calgary: University of Calgary.

Preville, P. (2018). The secrets to a lasting mixed-income neighborhood. Retrieved September 25, 2019, from www.sidewalklabs.com/blog/the-secrets-to-a-lasting-mixed-income-neighborhood/.

The Regent Park Collaborative Team (2002). *Regent Park revitalization study*. Toronto: Author.

PART III

Affordable Housing Partnerships in Practice

11

MIXED-INCOME HOUSING IN NEW YORK CITY

Achievements, Challenges, and Lessons of an Enduring Mayoral Commitment[1]

Alex F. Schwartz and Sasha Tsenkova

Introduction

New York City has long been a laboratory for mixed-income housing. For decades, in collaboration with nonprofit and for-profit organizations, New York has built thousands of housing units in mixed-income developments under many different programs and formats. New York is also distinctive among other cities in the United States in that its mixed-income housing is not contingent on the redevelopment of public housing or on inclusionary zoning. Whereas much, if not most, mixed-income housing built elsewhere in the country since the 1990s is connected to the demolition and redevelopment of public housing, often leading to a net loss of public housing, this is not the case for New York City. New York has had some form of inclusionary zoning since the 1980s, but it is a minor source of the city's mixed-income housing.

In this essay, we describe the breadth of mixed-income housing in New York City. We situate mixed-income housing within the history of New York's affordable housing programs, and emphasize the variety of forms it takes and the neighborhood contexts in which it occurs. We show how New York's mixed-income housing ranges from luxury housing that includes some units designated for lower-income households, to developments with a larger proportion of low- and moderate-income units and a much smaller share of market-rate units. We argue that New York City's case, including its experimentation with many forms of mixed-income housing, shows that:

- Mixed-income housing can be much more diverse in terms of its income composition, funding sources and programmatic design than one might presume from a reading of the literature.
- Mixed-income housing is an ordinary, even mundane, part of the city's landscape; notwithstanding occasional controversies sparked by particular buildings or programs, it is commonplace for people with widely varied incomes and other characteristics to reside in the same building or on the same block. In fact, the mixed-income quality of mixed-income housing may not be what defines or distinguishes the housing in the eyes of residents.
- Mixed-income housing nearly always requires government subsidy; the notion that income from market-rate units will fully subsidize the "affordable" units is rarely viable.

DOI: 10.4324/9781003172949-11

- The city's chronic shortage of affordable housing and broad-based support for public investment in many forms of affordable housing may allow for more creative, ambitious and durable approaches to mixed-income housing than anywhere else in the USA.

We conclude with a brief discussion of lessons and unresolved questions about New York's experience with mixed-income housing and implications for policy and practice in the mixed-income field.

The Relationship between Public Housing and Mixed-Income Housing in New York City

In the rest of the United States, mixed-income housing is strongly associated with the redevelopment of public housing. Under HOPE VI and other programs, public housing authorities demolished more than 150,000 public housing developments, replacing many with mixed-income housing that includes a smaller number of public housing units and varying blends of other subsidized and market-rate housing, sometimes including owner-occupied housing (Chaskin and Joseph 2015; Gress et al. 2019; Vale and Shamsuddin 2017; Vale et al. 2018).

New York has not demolished any of its public housing developments, however; its two HOPE VI projects upgraded the physical plants and remained 100% public housing.

New York's public housing encompasses aspects of mixed-income housing that are found in few other cities. First, many of New York's public housing developments have been home to households with a wider range of incomes than elsewhere. As with public housing in the rest of the country, New York's public housing accommodates many people with extremely low incomes. But unlike other places, New York's public housing has also attracted many people, including teachers and civil servants, with higher incomes. This attraction reflects the relatively high quality of many public housing developments at the time of their construction, their affordability and in many cases their proximity to transit and other urban resources (Bloom 2008). It also reflects the fact that public housing in New York City is widely dispersed, with developments located in 46 of the city's 59 community districts. While fewer moderate- and middle-income residents currently live in New York's public housing than in years past, they are still more prevalent in New York than in the public housing of other cities. For example, in 2018, wages were the most important source of income for 40% of New York's public housing residents, compared to an average of 29% in the ten next-largest housing authorities in the continental USA, and 40% of New York's public housing households earned at least $20,000 annually, compared to 23% in that comparison group (U.S. Department of Housing and Urban Development 2019).

The second aspect of mixed-income public housing in New York City stems from the fact that many developments are situated in middle-class and affluent neighborhoods. While many public housing developments are located in relatively isolated low-income neighborhoods, others are found in the midst of some of New York's wealthiest areas (NYU Furman Center 2019). It is not hard to find public housing located next door or across the street from condominium towers, with apartments costing several million dollars each. For example, Amsterdam Houses is located across Amsterdam Avenue from Lincoln Center for the Performing Arts and the 54-storey Hawthorne Parke luxury rental building, where the average rent for apartments leased from January 2018 to June 2019 was $7,218.[2] The Chelsea Elliot Houses and Fulton Homes are located in close proximity to the Highline, the elevated park that has stimulated the construction of numerous luxury condos. Among them is 520 West 28th Street, designed by internationally renowned architect Zaha Hadid, where the sales price of apartments sold from

January 2018 to March 2019 averaged \$10.3 million.[3] New York University's Furman Center found that nearly 60% of New York's public housing units, as of 2017, were located in gentrifying neighborhoods and an additional 27% in higher-income neighborhoods (NYU Furman Center 2019: 3). The close proximity of public housing with various tiers of market-rate housing illustrates what Vale and Shamsuddin (2017) have called the "mixing-around" form of mixed-income housing.

In an effort to generate much-needed revenue to help finance essential renovations and other capital improvements, New York City has started to lease vacant land on selected public housing campuses for the development of high-rise housing developments—some 100% market-rate and others that combine luxury housing with units priced for lower-income households (New York City Housing Authority 2018). These efforts have been controversial, both because of the loss of open space, light, and views and because of fears that the development of market-rate housing will ultimately lead to the displacement of public housing residents (Kim 2019). That said, the fact that private developers will build luxury market-rate housing cheek by jowl with public housing underscores that public housing need not be demolished or downsized in order to make mixed-income communities possible.

Mixed-Income Housing Produced under Mayoral Housing Plans

Most of New York City's mixed-income housing originated from the various affordable housing programs launched by the city since the late 1980s. Starting with Mayor Koch's *Ten-year housing plan of 1987,* New York City has invested, after inflation, more than \$18.9 billion on the construction and preservation[4] of more than 450,000 units of affordable housing. Every subsequent mayor, Democrat and Republican, has allocated hundreds of millions of dollars each year for this purpose (see Figure 11.1). The current mayor, Bill de Blasio, set a goal of building

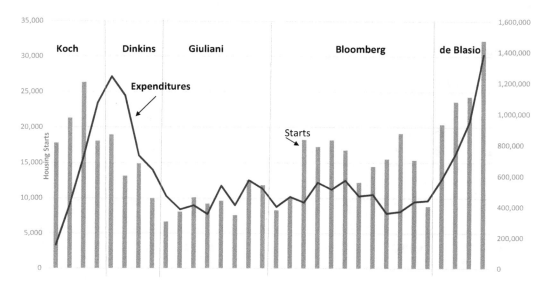

FIGURE 11.1 Capital Budget Expenditures (in Thousands of 2017 Dollars) and Affordable Housing Starts, 1987–2018.
Source: Mayor's Management Report and Comptroller's Budget Report.

120,000 units and preserving 180,000 from 2014 to 2026; as of April 2019, the city had completed or started work on nearly 124,000 units (Schwartz 2019). De Blasio's initiative builds on Mayor Michael Bloomberg's *12-year New Housing Marketplace plan*, which produced 165,000 affordable units.

New York's housing plans are assemblages of various programs that target different income groups and residents; they involve new construction, physical renovations, and the renewal of existing subsidies. The plans involve a range of partners, including for-profit housing developers, large nonprofit organizations, and smaller community-based organizations. The plans are funded through the city's capital budget (in the form of general obligation bonds), and also from tax-exempt and taxable private activity bonds issued by the city's Housing Development Corporation, federal Low-Income Housing Tax Credits, and other sources. The plans also make use of property tax abatements and inclusionary zoning, which provide private developers with financial incentives to allocate a portion of otherwise market-rate housing developments to lower-income occupancy. Under Mayor de Blasio, the city expanded its previous voluntary inclusionary zoning program with the establishment of mandatory inclusionary zoning in neighborhoods that complete a rezoning process to permit higher-density housing.

New York's housing plans have produced several forms of mixed-income housing. These vary from luxury apartment buildings in prime Manhattan neighborhoods that include some units for low- and/or moderate-income households, to developments situated in far less affluent communities that designate a higher percentage of units for such households. Virtually all mixed-income housing built over the past several decades involves some form of public subsidy. With the development of affordable housing often involving the purchase of expensive privately owned land, New York's housing programs increasingly include units for higher-income households to reduce the amount of public subsidy necessary to support low-income units.

As discussed below, the mixed-income housing produced under mayoral plans varies widely in terms of the share of housing allocated to various income bands and the degree to which the housing is affordable to very-low-income people. Some mixed-income programs, especially under Mayors Koch and Dinkins, designated most units to very-low-income households (earning up to 50% of the area median family income), including the formerly homeless, and allocated most of the rest to moderate- and middle-income families. Other programs produced predominantly market-rate housing, with a small share earmarked for low- or moderate-income tenants. Except for formerly homeless individuals and families, who almost always receive federal *Housing Choice Vouchers* or other rent subsidies, the lowest-income band in New York's mixed-income programs has ranged between 40% and 60% of average median income (AMI). Unfortunately, there is no information available on the racial and ethnic composition of the mixed-income housing produced in New York City.

Most of the mixed-income housing developed over the past three decades occasioned minimal, if any, opposition or controversy. However, this is less true today. Some opposition involves the real estate tax exemptions given to developers of ultra-luxury housing. The city has provided more than $1 billion in exemptions for high-end housing, some but not all of which included affordable units. A more recent debate has centered around the rezoning of selected neighborhoods, mostly minority and low-income, for higher density (Schwartz 1999). Although these rezonings trigger mandatory inclusionary zoning that requires 20–40% of new units to be affordable to households at various income levels, critics contend that the affordability levels are not affordable enough given the low incomes of most residents, and that new market-rate development resulting from the rezoning will exacerbate the neighborhoods' affordability problems by stimulating gentrification (Greenberg 2019; Stein 2018; Tsenkova and Witwer 2011) and displacing low-income residents. Finally, a few mixed-income developments elicited public outrage by requiring the residents of the affordable units to enter the building through a separate door and barring them from using some of the buildings' amenities (Joseph 2019; Satow 2019).

Selected Examples of Mixed-Income Housing in New York City

Luxury Housing with a Low- or Moderate-Income Component

Private developers have built hundreds of market-rate apartment buildings in prime sections of Manhattan and, more recently, Brooklyn that include some amount of units for people with low or moderate income. Whether through below-market-rate financing, property tax exemptions, the opportunity to build at higher densities than otherwise allowed, or a combination thereof, developers have used these incentives to build apartment buildings that are mostly market-rate but reserve up to 25% of units for lower-income tenants. Sometimes these developments receive two or more such incentives. The affordable units are assigned to eligible households by lottery. The number of people who apply for affordable units in these mixed-income units typically exceed the number of available units available by a ratio of several hundreds to one (Navarro 2015; Satow 2019).

The so-called *80-20 program* used tax-exempt bond financing to underwrite below-market-rate mortgages for housing that reserved 20% of units for households with incomes up to 60% of AMI, while the remaining 80% were market-rate. Most buildings financed under the 80-20 program also received property tax exemptions. The *421a tax abatement program*, created in the 1970s and modified several times to include buildings located in particular areas of New York City,[5] required developers to designate a portion of units for low- or moderate-income tenants. An example is a project at 505 West 37th Street, Manhattan. Completed in 2009, the 835–unit doorman building is located in the Hudson Yards district on the far-west-side of Manhattan. Average market-rate rents in 2019 amounted to $3,533, but 168 units are designated for low-income households earning no more than 60% of AMI.

Generally, the affordable units within *80-20 and 421a buildings* are intermixed with market-rate units, although units with the best views and other amenities usually are reserved for market-rate tenants. An exception is the small number of buildings that partitioned affordable units within separate sections. This issue became particularly contentious when news came out that a mixed-income building on the west side of Manhattan had installed separate entrances for market-rate and affordable units; the latter soon became known as the "poor door." The developer structured the building as two condominiums, each with its own entrance; in effect, a market-rate building situated next to a subsidized building. The physical segregation of income groups within a development, symbolized by separate entrances and amenities, raised concerns that this form of mixed-income housing can stigmatize lower-income residents and undermine the potential for community building across income groups (Joseph 2019; Navarro 2014).

In 2015, the city issued regulations requiring all entrances in mixed-income projects that receive tax exemptions or other subsidies to be open to all residents regardless of income (Moyer 2015). However, some mixed-income buildings prohibit residents of affordable units from using amenities (e.g., gyms, storage spaces) available to market-rate residents. The physical separation of income groups is characteristic of some luxury buildings that include a component of affordable units; it is much less common in other forms of mixed-income housing (Lamberg 2019).

Mixed-Income Housing with Larger Proportions of Lower-Income Units

New York has sponsored many mixed-income developments that feature substantially larger percentages of low- and moderate-income units, with the top-income tier targeted to households earning much less than the market-rate tenants in *80-20 or 421a* buildings. Because these buildings tend to designate more units for lower-income households, they often involve larger amounts of subsidy than *80-20* buildings and the like.

Mayor Koch's Construction Management Program. One of the earlier mixed-income programs instituted in New York City was the *Construction Management* program. Created as part of Mayor Koch's original initial ten-year plan, *Construction Management* involved the gut rehabilitation of large assemblages of vacant and highly deteriorated housing in the Bronx and Harlem. There were six *Construction Management* developments, each involving several hundred housing units (Schwartz and Tajbakhsh 2005). One of these projects was the *New Settlement Apartments*, sponsored by the Settlement Housing Fund, one of New York's largest nonprofit sponsors of low-income housing. Located in the Mount Eden section of the Bronx, the complex currently has 1,082 units. In all, 30% of the units were originally allocated to formerly homeless families, who received Section 8 vouchers to cover the rent; 40% were allocated to low-income families; 20% to moderate-income families; and 10% to households paying market-rate rents. Interestingly, the rents paid for the market-rate units were less than the rents paid by Section 8 vouchers. Every floor in the development includes households from all targeted income groups (Lamberg 2018).

The Construction Management program is one of the very few mixed-income initiatives in New York City to be examined from the tenants' perspective. In focus groups with residents in two *Construction Management* developments in the Bronx, Schwartz and Tajbakhsh explored resident satisfaction with the developments, awareness of the mixed-income character of the developments, and degree of social interaction within and across income categories. The researchers found that while the residents were fully aware of the mixed-income character of the developments, they did not consider it to be a defining feature. More salient were the affordability of the apartments, the location of the developments, the high physical quality of apartments, the responsiveness of property managers to their concerns, and the availability of on-site social services (Schwartz and Tajbakhsh 2005). Lamberg detailed the challenges in building and managing one of the *Construction Management* developments, as well as provided profiles of several long-time residents. Lamberg was the Executive Director of the Settlement Housing Fund, the sponsor of the development (Lamberg 2018).

Mayor Bloomberg's Mixed-Income Programs. These included three types of mixed-income projects: *low- to moderate-income (80% AMI or below), New HOP (81% AMI or above),* and *50/30/20 mixed-income* (replacing the previous 80-20 program). Developments were located mostly in Manhattan, to capitalize on demand for mid- and higher-income housing. Newly built mixed-income, affordable housing set an example for sustainability, design innovation, and institutional partnerships. The Hunter's Point South development on the Queens waterfront is the largest new affordable housing complex built in New York City since the 1970s. Envisioned as part of the City's 2012 Olympic bid, the first phase, co-developed by Related Companies, Phipps Houses, and Monadnock Construction, included 925 permanently affordable apartments and 17,000 square feet of new retail space, key infrastructure installations, a new five-acre waterfront park, and a new 1,100-seat school, while meeting national green building criteria (see Figure 11.2).

Another mixed-income project to come out of the Bloomberg era is Navy Green, co-developed by Dunn Development, L&M Development Partners, and the Pratt Area Community Council. Consisting of 433 units in four multi-family buildings and 23 townhouses,

FIGURE 11.2 Hunter Point in New York City: The Largest Affordable Housing Development.
Source: New York City Housing Development Corporation.

FIGURE 11.3 Via Verde Sustainable Mixed-Income Housing in New York City.
Source: New York City Housing Development Corporation.

the development combines supportive housing for formerly homeless families, owner–occupied housing, and rental housing for several income groups. Located across from the former Brooklyn Navy Yards, the complex also includes retail space, children's play area, open lawn, patios, and gardens.

Via Verde is a sustainable residential development, with 222 units of mixed-income housing in the South Bronx co-developed by Phipps Houses and Jonathan Rose Companies (see Figure 11.3). The project received the U.S Department of Housing and Urban Development's Award for Excellence in Affordable Housing Design in 2013. The ground floor features 11,000 square feet of retail, a community health center, and live-work units. With a 66-kilowatt, building-integrated photovoltaic system, on-site cogeneration, green roof, community vegetable gardens, green interior finishes, rainwater harvesting, and drought-tolerant vegetation, the complex is LEED NC Gold certified (Tsenkova 2014).

Mayor de Blasio's Mixed-Income Housing Programs. Mixed-income programs rolled out by the de Blasio administration vary widely in terms of the top- and bottom-income levels that are targeted, the number of income tiers represented, and the distribution of units across income tiers. Two programs allow some units to be rented to market-rate tenants of any income, but three programs cap the maximum income at a specified percentage of the area median family income (from 100% to 165%). The lowest-income households eligible for the programs vary from formerly homeless people with incomes well below the poverty level to those earning 60% of AMI. The percentage of units allocated to the top-income tier varies from 30% to 75%.

For example, the *Extremely Low- and Low-Income Affordability* (ELLA) program's income tiers include formerly homeless and other extremely low-income households. In one option, units must be allocated as follows: 10% to formerly homeless households, 10% to households earning up to 30% of AMI, 10% to households earning up to 40% of AMI, 10% to households earning up to 50% of AMI, and 30% to households earning up to 60% of AMI. Developers have the option of designating some or all of the remaining 30% of the units to households earning 70% to 100% of AMI; otherwise, they must be slated for households earning up to 60% (Tsenkova and Schwartz 2019). In the second option, 30% of the units are allocated to formerly homeless households, 5% to households earning up to 40% of AMI, and 5% to households earning up to 50% of AMI. As with the first option, the remaining 60% must go to households earning up to 60% of AMI, although developers may allocate up to 30% of the units to households earning 70% to 100% of AMI. The city provides $130,000 to $150,000 in subsidy per unit, depending on the overall income mix in the development. City subsidies, federal *Low-Income Housing Tax Credit*, and property tax exemptions, combined with the cash flow from the higher-income units, make it financially viable to charge lower-income households affordable rents.

One of the first *ELLA* projects to be developed, by Dunn Development and L&M Development Partners, is Livonia Commons. Located in the East New York section of Brooklyn, the development includes 278 apartment in four buildings. Fifty-one units consist of supportive housing for formerly homeless families who receive services on-site from two nonprofit organizations. More than half of the units are designated for families earning below 50% or 40% of AMI. The development also includes an arts center, a legal services office, a supermarket, a pharmacy, and other retail space (see Figure 11.4).

In the *Mix and Match* program, eligible developments must have a minimum of four income tiers. In all, 40% to 60% of the units must be affordable to households earning up to 60% of AMI, including at least 10% of units serving formerly homeless households. A minimum of 10% of units must be affordable to households earning 30% to 50% of AMI, and the remaining 40% to 60% of the units must be affordable to households earning up to 130% of AMI. Units receive $10,000 to $225,000 from the city's capital fund, depending on the income designation. Developments may also receive federal *Low-Income Housing Tax Credit* and property tax exemptions.

New York's Mandatory Inclusionary Housing Program. This mixed-income housing program allocates the majority of units to households able to pay market-rate rents. However, it also includes households with incomes that are lower than those permitted in nearly all other inclusionary zoning programs in the United States. Moreover, the program allocates a larger proportion of units to low- and moderate-income households, and it requires affordable units to remain so permanently (i.e., affordability is not time-limited). The program takes effect

FIGURE 11.4 Livonia Commons.
Source: Dunn Development Corp.

whenever a neighborhood (or land parcel) is rezoned for higher densities. As of January 2019, five neighborhoods, starting with East New York, had been rezoned at higher densities, thereby effectuating mandatory inclusionary housing. Rezoning proposals were in process or anticipated for six additional neighborhoods. All but one of the neighborhoods with rezoning completed or in process are located outside Manhattan, and most are predominantly low-income neighborhoods (Kully 2019).

There are two basic options in the mandatory inclusionary housing program (*Inclusionary Housing Program* 2020). Under one, developers can designate 75% of total floor area for market-rate units, while the remaining 25% must go to households with an average income of 60% of AMI, including 10% that are allocated to households earning up to 30% of AMI. In the second option, 60% of the floor area is reserved for market-rate units, and the remaining 40% goes to households with an average income of 80% of AMI. If developers choose to build the affordable units off-site at a separate location, they must allocate an additional 5% of total floor area to households with an average income (depending on the option) of 60% or 80% of AMI. Mixed-income housing properties are underwritten so they do not require direct city subsidy, although they may be eligible for federal *Low-Income Housing Tax Credit* and city property tax exemptions. However, buildings financed under other subsidy programs may be, and are, located in rezoned neighborhoods.

Mandatory inclusionary housing is the most controversial of the de Blasio administration's affordable housing programs. Although it accounts for less than 4% of the 39,949 units of new construction started under the plan from 2014 through the first quarter of 2019, the program has attracted far more attention and criticism than all other aspects of the *de Blasio plan* (Schwartz 2019). One criticism is that even the lowest-rent apartments are unaffordable to most low-income residents. This is because the rents are set in relation to the New York metro area's median family income, which is much higher than the median income in the neighborhoods that have been upzoned (Schwartz 2019). A second criticism is that, while the new buildings in the rezoned neighborhoods will provide some affordable units (notwithstanding the first criticism), the construction of taller, mostly market-rate buildings will exacerbate affordability problems by driving up land prices and rents throughout the neighborhood (Dulchin 2019; Savitch-Law 2017). The fact that the residents of most of the neighborhoods slated for rezoning tend to have low incomes and to be predominantly non-White has no doubt contributed to the plan's hostile reception. Some observers have suggested that the plan might have received more support if the city had also included more affluent and more White neighborhoods among those to be rezoned (Savitch-Law 2017). In any case, there is little evidence to show that the affordability pressures in the rezoned neighborhoods are any greater than in other neighborhoods of the city. On the other hand, rental pressures are acute in many neighborhoods, including many that have not been rezoned.

Conclusions

The New York City experience leads us to the following conclusions:

Mixed-income Housing Can Be a Financially and Socially Viable Form of Housing That Leverages the Private Sector to Finance a Limited Amount of Affordable Housing. The city's experience with public housing and, most especially, with the many housing programs that have been instituted under mayoral housing plans since 1986 illustrates the many ways in which mixed-income housing can be configured. It includes luxury housing located in prime Manhattan and Brooklyn neighborhoods in which about 20% of the units are designated for relatively low- and/or moderate-income households. It also includes developments located in lower-income neighborhoods with a larger percentage of low-income units and in which the rents charged to tenants at the top of the income tier tend to be considerably less than the market-rate rents of other mixed-income developments.

Mixed-income housing also has limitations as a vehicle for producing and financing affordable housing, however. The inclusion of market-rate units can generate a "cross-subsidy" to supplement the lower rents paid by lower-income residents. But only in limited circumstances is this cross-subsidy sufficient by itself to make the development financially viable. It may be sufficient when 80% of the units are reserved for market-rate units charging more than, say, $4,000 per month, and when few, if any, affordable units are designated for households with extremely low incomes. Even in these cases, the developments receive low-interest financing and tax exemptions.

Ambitious Design That Set the Bar High in Terms of Sustainable Design and Green Elements Can Be Achieved. New York projects have won design awards for excellence, innovation, incorporation of public realm, and mixed-use components that contribute to neighborhood qualities (Honan 2019; Tsenkova 2014). Such experiences create an image of affordable housing projects that is remarkably different from the stigma associated with public housing of the 1960s.

Mixed-income Housing Can Take Many Forms and Be Situated in Many Different Types of Neighborhoods. Physically, mixed-income housing can involve rehabilitation of existing buildings as well as new construction. It can involve walk-up buildings of six stories to towers of 30 stories or more. It can be limited to single buildings or encompass multiple structures. Mixed-income projects can be entirely residential, and they can include various types of nonresidential components too, including retail, medical offices, schools, and libraries. As noted above, New York's mixed-income housing programs feature various combinations of income groups, with the representation of market-rate units varying from 80% to less than 20%. And while it is true that mixed-income housing typically requires less subsidy in more affluent neighborhoods that command relatively high rents—rents that can "cross-subsidize" units occupied by low- and moderate-income households—with sufficient government subsidy, mixed-income housing also is viable in low-income neighborhoods.

There Is No One Way to Finance Mixed-income Housing. Nearly all of the city's mixed-income developments have received some form of subsidy from New York City; very few have been underwritten entirely from private sources. Subsidies include property tax exemptions, grants, low- or zero-interest mortgages, federal *Low-Income Housing Tax Credit*, and project-based *Housing Choice Vouchers.* One challenge for financing mixed-income housing is the difficulty of providing subsidies for households with incomes that exceed the eligibility limits for the *Federal Low-Income Housing Tax Credit* (60% of AMI) but are too low to afford market-rate rents.

Notes

1 This essay was previously published in *What Works to Promote Inclusive, Equitable Mixed-Income Communities*, eds. Mark L. Joseph and Amy T. Khare (Cleveland, OH: National Institute for Mixed Income Communities, 2020). To access the volume, go to https://case.edu/socialwork/nimc/resources/what-works-volume.
2 The real estate service StreetEasy listed 57 apartments that were leased in this building from January 25, 2018 to June 6, 2019. The lowest rent was $3,295 for a studio apartment and the highest was $16,900 for a 3-bedroom unit.
3 Sales data from StreetEasy, which listed 28 open-market transactions during this period.
4 Preservation refers to physical renovation and other capital improvements of existing affordable housing and to commitments to extend or renew existing subsidies so that housing can remain affordable.
5 Originally Manhattan below 96th Street; later extended to parts of other boroughs.

References

Bach, V., and Waters, T. (2015) "Why We Need to End New York City's Most Expensive Housing Program: Time to End 421-a." New York: Community Service Society. Policy Brief (May), https://-smhttp-ssl-58547.nexcesscdn.net/nycss/images/uploads/pubs/421aReportFinal.pdf

Bloom, N. D. (2008) *Public Housing that Worked.* Philadelphia: University of Pennsylvania Press.

Chaskin, R. J., and Joseph, M. L. (2015) *Integrating the Inner City: The Promise and Perils of Mixed-Income Public Housing Transformation.* Chicago, IL: The University of Chicago Press.

Dulchin, B. (2019) "Does Trickle-Down Affordability Justify the Mayor's Zoning Policy?" New York: Association for Neighborhood and Housing Development (blog, January 24), https://anhd.org/blog/does-trickle-down-affordability-justify-mayors-zoning-policy

Greenberg, M. (2019) "Tenants Under Siege: Inside New York City's Housing Crisis," *New York Review of Books* (August 17), www.nybooks.com/articles/2017/08/17/tenants-under-siege-inside-new-york-city-housing-crisis/

Gress, T., Joseph, M. L., and Cho, S. (2019) "Confirmations, New Insights, and Future Implications for HOPE VI Mixed-Income Redevelopment," *Cityscape* 21, 2: 185–212.

Honan, K. (2019) "New York City Selects Designers with Big Ideas for Small Lots," *The Wall Street Journal* (May 13), www.wsj.com/articles/new-york-city-selects-designers-with-big-ideas-for-small-lots-11557793868

Joseph, M. L. (2019) "Separate but Equal Redux: Resolving and Transcending the Poor Door Conundrum," in *The Dream Revisited: Contemporary Debates about Housing, Segregation, and Opportunity*, eds. Ingrid Gould Ellen and Justin Peter Steil. New York: Columbia University Press, 292–294.

Kim, E. (2019) "Facing Opposition to Redevelopment Plan, City Establishes Working Group to Decide Future of NYCHA's Chelsea Complex," *Gothamist* (October 11), https://gothamist.com/news/facing-opposition-redevelopment-plan-city-establishes-working-group-decide-future-nychas-chelsea-complex

Kully, S. A. (2019) "De Blasio's Sixth Year in Office Could Feature Three Neighborhood Rezonings," *City Limits* (January 7), https://citylimits.org/2019/01/07/de-blasios-sixth-year-in-office-could-feature-three-neighborhood-rezonings/

Lamberg, C. (2018) *Neighborhood Success Stories: Creating and Sustaining Affordable Housing in New York.* New York: Fordham University Press.

Lamberg, C. (2019) "Housing Priorities: Quality Is More Important Than the Number of Entrances," in *The Dream Revisited: Contemporary Debates about Housing, Segregation, and Opportunity*, eds. Ingrid Gould Ellen and Justin Peter Steil. New York: Columbia University Press, 295–297

Moyer, J. W. (2015) "NYC Bans 'Poor Doors' – Separate Entrances for Low-Income Tenants," *Washington Post* (June 30), www.washingtonpost.com/news/morning-mix/wp/2015/06/30/nyc-bans-poor-doors-separate-entrances-for-low-income-tenants/

Navarro, M. (2014) "'Poor Door' in a New York Tower Opens a Fight over Affordable Housing," *New York Times* (August 26), www.nytimes.com/2014/08/27/nyregion/separate-entryways-for-new-york-condo-buyers-and-renters-create-an-affordable-housing-dilemma.html?searchResultPosition=2

Navarro, M. (2015) "88,000 Applicants and Counting for 55 Units in 'Poor Door' Building," *New York Times* (April 20), www.nytimes.com/2015/04/21/nyregion/poor-door-building-draws-88000-applicants-for-55-rental-units.html

New York City Department of Housing Preservation and Development (2010) *New Housing Marketplace Plan*. New York: New York City Department of Housing Preservation and Development.

New York City Department of Planning (2020) *Inclusionary Housing Program*. New York: New York City Department of Planning, www1.nyc.gov/site/planning/zoning/districts-tools/inclusionary-housing.page

New York City Housing Authority (2018). *NYCHA 2.0: Part 1– Invest to Preserve*. New York: New York City Housing Authority, www1.nyc.gov/assets/nycha/downloads/pdf/NYCHA-2.0-Part1.pdf

NYU Furman Center (2019) "How NYCHA Preserves Diversity in NYC's Changing Neighborhoods," http://furmancenter.org/research/publication/how-nycha-preserves-diversity-in-new-york8217s-changing-neighborhoods

Satow, J. (2019) "Better Than the Powerball: For New Yorkers Looking for an Affordable Home, the Odds of Winning a Housing Lottery are 1 in 592," *New York Times* (January 11), www.nytimes.com/2019/01/11/realestate/better-than-the-powerball.html

Savitch-Law, A. (2017) "Will Rezoning Cause or Resist Displacement? Data Paints an Incomplete Picture," *City Limits* (January 10), https://citylimits.org/2017/01/10/will-rezoning-cause-or-resist-displacement-data-paints-an-incomplete-picture/

Schwartz, A. (1999) "New York City and Subsidized Housing: Impacts and Lessons of the City's $5 billion Capital Budget Housing Plan," *Housing Policy Debate* 10, 4: 839–877.

Schwartz, A. (2019) "New York City's Affordable Housing Plans and the Limits of Local Initiative," *Cityscape* 21, 3: 355–388.

Schwartz, A., and Tajbakhsh, K. (2005) "Mixed-Income Housing," in *Revitalizing the City: Strategies to Contain Sprawl and Revive the Core*, eds. Fritz E. Wagner, Timothy E. Joder, Anthony J. Mumphrey, Jr., Krishna M. Akundi, and Alan F. J. Artibise. Armonk, NY: M.E. Sharpe.

Stein, S. (2018) "Progress for Whom, toward What? Progressive Politics and New York City's Mandatory Inclusionary Zoning Program," *Journal of Urban Affairs* 40, 6: 770–781.

Thaden, E., and Wang, V. (2017) "Inclusionary Zoning in the United States: Prevalence, Impact, and Practices" (Working Paper WP17ET1, September). Cambridge, MA: Lincoln Land Institute (September), www.lincolninst.edu/sites/default/files/pubfiles/thaden_wp17et1_0.pdf

Tsenkova, S. (2014) "Investing in New York's Future: Affordable Rental Housing in Mixed Income Projects," *Plan Canada* 53, 3: 32–40.

Tsenkova, S., and Schwartz, A. (2019) "Partnerships for Affordable Rental Housing in New York City," in *Housing Partnerships*, ed. Sasha Tsenkova. Calgary: University of Calgary, 37–46.

Tsenkova, S., and Witwer, M. (2011) "Bridging the Gap: Policy Instruments to Encourage Private Sector Provision of Affordable Rental Housing in Alberta," *Canadian Journal of Urban Research* 20, 1: 52–80.

U.S. Department of Housing and Urban Development (2019) Picture of Subsidized Households, www.huduser.gov/portal/datasets/assthsg.html

Vale, L. J., and Shamsuddin, S. (2017) "All Mixed Up: Making Sense of Mixed-Income Housing Developments," *Journal of the American Planning Association* 83, 1: 56–67.

Vale, L. J., Shamsuddin, S., and Kelly, N. (2018) "Broken Promises or Selective Memory Planning? A National Picture of HOPE VI Plans and Realities," *Housing Policy Debate* 28, 5: 746–769.

Waters, T. J., and Bach, V. (2013) *Good Place to Work Hard Place to Live: The Housing Challenge for New York City's Next Mayor*. New York: Community Service Society, www.cssny.org/publications/entry/good-place-to-work-hard-place-to-live

12

PARTNERSHIPS FOR AFFORDABLE HOUSING IN ENGLAND

Kath Scanlon

Introduction

As housing has become more expensive in England, and particularly in London and the south-east, the pressure of housing affordability has moved up the income scale. Housing—and particularly housing affordability for young people—is now the top political issue in London local politics. Middle-income groups that previously had no need to turn to the state for housing assistance now demand action, and London's businesses and politicians fear that the city's economy could suffer serious damage from a lack of affordable housing. The key question is, 'Affordable for whom?': it is not only very low-income households that cannot access housing, but even accountants and doctors. In London, the household income limit for some types of affordable housing is £90,000/year (150,000 CAD).

Who can build the enormous number of new homes needed? A generation ago, many local authorities boasted their own architecture departments and construction teams, but this institutional expertise has been almost entirely eroded in the decades since 1979. Housing associations are the obvious candidates; the largest associations are already among the country's biggest developers. Increasingly, public bodies and housing associations are entering into partnerships to produce affordable housing. These partnerships are based on their comparative advantages: the public bodies often supply low-cost land, while the housing associations bring development expertise. This chapter examines the elements of the English policy framework that—usually unintentionally—has permitted such partnerships to emerge.

What Is 'Affordable' Housing?

In writing about national housing systems, one of the potential snags is that words do not necessarily mean the same thing in every country—even in countries that share a language. We therefore start by exploring the meaning of the term 'affordable housing' in England.

In England, there have traditionally been three officially recognised tenures: owner occupation, private renting and social renting. Social housing[1] was owned by local authorities or housing associations and rented at (usually) below-market prices to (usually) low-income households. Until recently, affordable housing was simply a catch-all term for any low-cost accommodation, whether public or private. Since 2011, 'affordable housing' has been a government-recognised

DOI: 10.4324/9781003172949-12

category, but the official meaning of the term does not always align with its common usage, and may not correspond with the meaning of the term in other countries.

As defined in planning regulations and guidance, 'affordable' housing now spans a range from traditional social housing at very low rents (less than 50% of market in some areas) to homes renting for up to 80% of local market rates. In the past, social housing was synonymous with rented housing, but the wider affordable-housing offer includes various home ownership products including shared ownership and shared equity. Current national planning guidance suggests that at least 10% of homes on major developments should be affordable home ownership.

Officially recognised, affordable housing is almost always cheaper than market-price housing (though there are some exceptions in very low-cost areas of the country). However, not all of it is affordable for low-income households, nor is it designed to be. The so-called intermediate housing is targeted at middle- or even higher-income households (Figure 12.3), who face particular problems accessing housing in London and surrounding areas.

The Evolution of Affordable-Housing Provision in England

Early provision of affordable housing responded to the miserable conditions in the slums of London and northern industrial cities, documented by Charles Booth and fictionalised by writers such as Charles Dickens. The first providers were not public bodies but rather charitable organisations and wealthy philanthropists such as George Peabody, whose name lives on in one of the country's largest housing associations. These efforts drew on even earlier private initiatives by industrialists to build model towns for their workers including New Lanark (built in the late 18th century for Scottish mill workers), Saltaire (built in the 1850s for textile mill workers in Yorkshire) and Bourneville (built by the Quaker owners of Cadbury Chocolates around 1900).

At the start of the 20th century, about 90% of English households rented their homes from private landlords; there was no social housing sector as we now know it. Although charitable institutions were the first providers of affordable housing, the 20th-century picture was dominated by council housing—that is, housing built and operated by local authorities (municipal governments). They started building homes in the 1920s for soldiers returning from the First World War. This housing was meant to accommodate low- and middle-income working people, not the very poorest, who typically lived in overcrowded, poor-quality homes rented from private landlords. After the First World War, but especially after the Second World War, local authorities became increasingly active in the provision of housing and were the country's most important house builders by far for some decades after 1945 (Figure 12.1). Central government built no housing itself but provided generous construction and operational subsidies to councils.

Throughout much of the 1960s and 1970s, local authorities built most of the country's new homes and carried out associated slum-clearance programmes. When these homes were built, they were considered modern, desirable, even aspirational. They later became stigmatised, and serious problems arose because of poor-quality construction, insufficient maintenance and high concentrations of vulnerable households. Some such estates are now being demolished and redeveloped at higher densities as mixed-tenure communities.

Over the course of the 20th century, the tenure composition of the housing stock changed, with a long-term decline in private renting accompanied by a growth in owner occupation (both trends that were later reversed). By 1979, when Conservative Prime Minister Margaret Thatcher took office, 57% of English households owned their own homes. Within the rented sector, private renting had fallen to 12%, while 31% of homes were rented from social landlords—mainly local authorities (Figure 12.2). Housing associations were minor players, controlling just 2% of the housing stock.

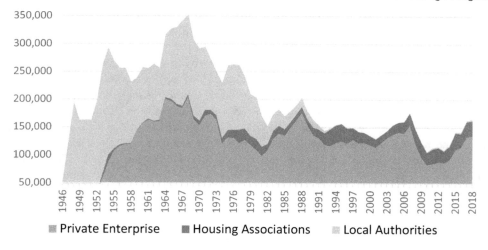

FIGURE 12.1   New Home Construction in England by Type of Developer, 1946–2019.
Source: MHCLG Live Table 244: Permanent Dwellings Started and Completed by Tenure, England.

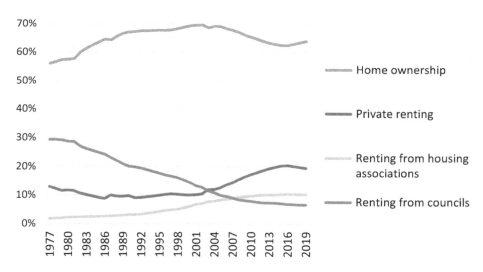

FIGURE 12.2   Housing Tenure in England, 1977–2019.
Source: MHCLG Live Table 104: Dwelling Stock by Tenure, England.

Under the British constitution, local authorities can only carry out those functions for which the parliament officially grants permission—and the parliament can at any time rescind or change those permissions. Mrs Thatcher believed that home ownership should be radically expanded and that local authorities should not be major housing providers; her government therefore made two radical changes to local-authority powers and responsibilities for housing.

First, sitting tenants in council-owned properties (but not housing association homes) were given the right to buy their homes at a discount. Local authorities were required to remit the sales receipts to central government rather than using them to build new homes, and restrictions on their use of other funds made it almost impossible for them to build new homes to replace those sold.

Second, local authorities were required to hold tenant ballots on whether to transfer their stock to housing associations. In practice, this usually meant hiving off part of the local-authority housing department to create a new housing association. Many authorities transferred some or all their stock, and now a number of local authorities own no housing at all.

These changes meant local authorities were no longer major builders of new housing. As Figure 12.1 shows, since the early 1990s, most new social homes have been built by housing associations (the remainder were mainly built by private developers who then sold them to housing associations—see below). The proportion of social rented homes in the housing stock has been in decline since 1979 (Figure 12.2), as the loss of stock through right to buy has not been entirely made up for by new construction.

Importantly, the traditional tripartite tenure distinction between owner occupation, private renting and social renting no longer captures the increasingly nuanced housing system, as a number of new forms of 'affordable' housing sit uncomfortably across these definitions. However, official statistics are still based on the three main tenures and fail to capture many of the newer variations of affordable housing.

Current Varieties of Affordable Housing

Historically, construction of most new social and affordable housing was subsidised with government grant. The amount of grant available has been reduced since 2011, and that which remained was redirected to 'affordable rent' and home ownership products rather than social housing. Figure 12.3 illustrates these trends: a fall in overall grant funding, and a change in targeting.

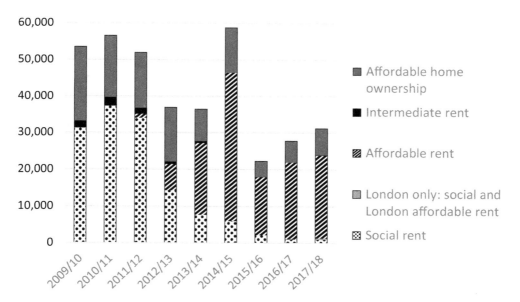

FIGURE 12.3   New Affordable Housing Units Built with Government Subsidy, 2009–2017.
Source: MHCLG Live Table 1012: Affordable Housing Starts and Completions Funded by Homes England and the GLA.

In 2016/2017, some 42,200 new 'affordable homes' were constructed or rehabilitated in England (MHCLG live table 1011), or about 19% of all new additional dwellings that year. Just 14% of new affordable homes were at social rents, so traditional social housing, with its low rents and tenure security, now represents only a small proportion of new affordable housing. Some 58% were at officially designated affordable rents, a category introduced in 2011.

While common usage of the word 'affordable' relates cost to a household's ability to pay, England's affordable rents are benchmarked to market rents rather than to tenant income. Affordable-rent homes can be let at up to 80% of market rates, although providers and local authorities can agree to lower proportions. Affordable-rent homes are legally regarded as social housing, but unlike traditional social homes, they are let on fixed term rather than indefinite leases. Recognising the Newspeak overtones of the term 'affordable rent', some providers and local authorities have developed their own 'genuinely affordable' products that fit within the legal definitions of affordable rent, for example, London Living Rent and London Affordable Rent. Wilson and Barton (2018) provide a good summary of the current meaning of affordable housing in England.

The Main Partners

Until 1980, councils were the main providers of affordable housing, but the Thatcher government's policies ended their dominance, and subsidies for new social housing were redirected to housing associations. Since then, the associations have dominated the market for *new* social housing, although many local authorities retained the housing they already owned. The two groups thus operated in parallel, but largely separately.

Recently though there has been an increasing trend towards partnership. This has been driven by a strong political imperative, both nationally and locally, to increase affordable housing provision, and by the recognition by the public sector and housing associations alike that they have complementary strengths. Other public bodies such as hospitals, transport authorities and prisons may also form partnerships with housing associations, especially where the public sector owns land. Profit-seeking private companies, including for-profit developers, private landlords and financial institutions, may also participate but usually require incentives—either carrots or sticks—to do so, as almost by definition building affordable housing is not a profitable activity (although operating it subsequently can be).

Local Authorities

Local authorities in England own 1.6 million homes which they must maintain and operate. They have other legal duties in regard to housing: they must find housing for local homeless families, and they are given government targets for the number of new homes to be built in their areas, of which a proportion must be affordable.

Councils of all political colours take seriously their responsibility for ensuring enough affordable homes are built. In post-war Britain, providing good-quality housing for working people was a proud achievement of the welfare state. Up to the 1970s, most new low-cost housing was built by councils, but the Thatcher reforms put an end to this model. Almost all new affordable housing is now built by the private sector (whether for-profit or not-for-profit).

While local authorities' existing housing stock is mostly let at low social rents to low-income households, some authorities have recently set up companies to build market-priced housing. This is a reflection of the financial pressures on municipalities. England's highly centralised system of government affords local authorities very little fiscal autonomy: most of the tax revenue they collect is remitted to the Treasury and is redistributed to local authorities based on a formula. The amount of central funding for local government has been radically reduced in the last decade, but authorities' statutory responsibilities have not; this has created a strong pressure for them to look for new revenue sources. Recent changes in the law have opened the possibility for councils to generate funds from some commercial activities including developing housing on their own land. The so-called local housing companies (LHCs) are legally and financially separate from the authorities' housing departments and do not build social housing. In these cases, there is a tension between developing affordable housing and maximising profits. Some LHCs are pure profit maximisers, trying to generate money for other local-authority services (especially adult social care, which is hugely costly); other local authorities have prioritised affordable housing (Hackett 2017).

Housing Associations[2]

As of September 2018, the government recognises 1681 housing associations in England (officially known as 'registered' providers). Most are tiny organisations that operate only a handful of homes and do not build new housing (e.g. the Polish Retired Persons' Housing Association or the Reverend Rowland Hill Almshouse Charity). At the other end of the spectrum, consolidations over the past few decades and a recent wave of mergers among the larger players has resulted in a few mega organisations. Clarion, the biggest, has 12,500 units across much of England; L&Q merged with East Thames and has 90,000 units, mostly in London; and the Peabody/Family Mosaic merger owns 111,000 homes. Members of the G15, an association of London's largest housing associations, build a quarter of London's new homes.

The operations of English social landlords—housing associations as well as councils—are subject to strong government control. Regulations channel and constrain their activities in myriad ways. Central government dictates how social rents are set, how councils may spend rent receipts and what types of leases must be used. For local authorities, this degree of control is a given; as creations of the Parliament, they can only carry out those activities that the Parliament permits, in housing as in any other field. Housing associations by contrast are in principle private bodies.

The public/private distinction is in fact not clear-cut. In 2015, the Office of National Statistics reclassified housing associations as public-sector organisations, citing the degree of government control over their activities.[3] In the most dramatic exercise of that control, the government decreed in 2015 that all social landlords would be required to cut rents by 1% per annum for four years until 2020. This abrogated a formal rent settlement allowing for CPI + 1% rent increases that had been agreed only the year before. The rent cut had nothing to do with housing policy; the goal was to reduce the government's expenditure on housing benefit (some 59% of social tenants receive housing benefit, according to the English Housing Survey 2016/2017, and most housing-association revenue comes from government). Housing associations pointed out that the reduction in rents had a knock-on effect on their ability to borrow to finance new development, and an official government analysis indicated that 14,000 fewer social rented properties would be built by 2020/2021 as a consequence of the rent cut (OBR 2015). In 2018, the government indicated it would allow rents to rise after 2020 to better support housing association borrowing against future income (MHCLG 2019).

The post-2011 cuts in grant forced housing associations to modify their business models, and many of the larger associations have become more commercial and market-facing. Those associations that build new homes (a minority) now rely more on bank loans, bonds and cross-subsidies from market activities than on government grants (Manzi & Morrison 2018).

The Housing and Planning Act 2016 contained a number of policies that would have damaged housing associations' balance sheets and ability to plan (Scanlon 2017). However, the government has since rethought these proposals as part of the national re-examination of attitudes to social housing brought about by the June 2017 fire at Grenfell Tower, and the expectation now is that these provisions will never be implemented.

How Policy Shapes Partnerships

In principle, housing associations should need no external incentives to develop affordable housing, because providing such housing is the main reason they exist. But many things have changed since the original housing associations were established; while their mission statements may refer to housing poor people,[4] the direction of incentives is not so clear. Some of the established truths of a few decades ago have been overturned, and the recent government policy has created a muddled tangle of incentives. These sometimes contradictory policy directions reflect the different priorities of different government departments, which have not been satisfactorily resolved.

Housing associations have for the last 30 years been the main developers of new affordable housing. Such development was previously supported by rather generous government grants, but these have been whittled away (especially in the post-crisis period since 2010) and redirected towards affordable rent homes rather than social homes. This gradual withdrawal of government subsidy has forced associations to rework their financial and operational models: with less government grant available, associations that want to build new affordable homes must find subsidy elsewhere. There are two main possibilities. The first is to cross-subsidise from their own profits, and this strategy has led many of the larger associations to become major developers of for-profit homes (Manzi & Morrison 2018). The other way to replace the lost subsidy is to work with public-sector partners, especially those with access to low-cost land. We look at four case studies of this approach in the following section.

Partnerships between Public Bodies and Housing Associations: Four Case Studies

The following case studies look at four partnerships between public bodies and housing associations in England. Housing partnerships are very much in vogue in the English housing-association sector: one professional body recently published a handbook about how to make them work (Fraser et al. 2017). The word 'partnership' should not disguise the fact that the various actors can have rather different motivations and priorities, and there is always some tension in the relations. Even so, the goals of the public sector and housing associations are largely aligned, in that the affordable housing is a key goal for both.

The first case study highlights the importance of national policy (see Fraser et al. 2017 for more details). In the English system, central government policy shapes much of what can be accomplished locally. Partners with ambitious ideas often cannot move straight into development but first must prepare the ground with central government departments and agencies. Local authorities and housing associations feel their voice is stronger if they work together.

For several decades, since they stopped being major builders themselves, local authorities have worked with housing associations to produce affordable housing. Typically, the local authority sold land to a housing association at less than market value, in exchange for nomination rights to the resulting housing. However, this meant housing associations alone benefitted from any subsequent increase in capital values, so local authorities now increasingly enter into joint ventures or long-term leases. This enables them to retain some control over their assets and benefit from the income stream they generate. The second case study describes a joint venture partnership between a local authority and a major housing association to produce affordable homes

BOX 12.1: GREATER MANCHESTER HOUSING PROVIDERS

Partnership between Metropolitan Authority and Housing Associations Strengthens Voice at National Level

Greater Manchester is one of a handful of city regions that has been granted greater powers of self-government under England's ongoing policy of local devolution. The Greater Manchester Combined Authority (GMCA) was created in 2011 and is now led by elected Labour Mayor Andy Burnham. Each 'devolution deal' is individually negotiated, and greater Manchester has secured additional powers over housing and particularly over housing investment. GMCA has been granted £300 million in direct funding from central government as an investment fund to support development of affordable housing on a revolving, repayable basis.

The new authority has formally established a partnership with housing associations working in the area. Greater Manchester Housing Providers, set up in 2012, is a partnership between 24 housing associations, three arms-length management organisation (non-profit bodies that manage council housing) and one local-authority housing department that still owns stock. Together, the members house one in five people in Greater Manchester. In 2016, GHMP signed a memorandum of understanding with GMCA. This memorandum formalised some existing joint working arrangements and set out new areas for work. The partnership has set up a joint venture called Athena to deliver commercial activities, job training and apprenticeships, and is working on a residential development joint venture. The group has been able to influence on the authority's policy on housing, health and social care, and joins GMCA in lobbying national government about these issues.

Having secured the £300 million investment pot, the GMCA is also seeking more control over the allocation of central government funding for affordable housing within its area (these funds are controlled nationally, except in London). They propose that GMHP housing associations in receipt of grant through this programme should be permitted to switch sites, products and priorities with prior approval, allowing flexibility to respond to changes in land availability, land price and local need. To make the case for greater local control and additional money, they need to demonstrate that they have ambitious and achievable plans for housing delivery. The local-authority members have land (together they could release about £280 million worth of brownfield sites for housing in the next five years), but the housing association members have the development expertise; in recent years, they have been responsible for about 40% of new homes across greater Manchester. Strong partnership with housing associations is central to achieving the GMCA's delivery plans, which are only possible with their enthusiastic participation.

The GMHP itself is bullish about what it can offer—its ambition is to double the delivery of new homes for greater Manchester, and according to its website:

> We know that we can be the 'go to' partners to tackle some of the key challenges facing the region and play a major role in delivering the 227,000 more homes needed across the city region over the next 20 years. We have the capacity, determination and infrastructure to build even more homes, create more jobs, tackle homelessness (and) connect health and housing… Together we can achieve our city region's ambitions for housing. Supporting the right conditions for collaboration is key, and we are committed to continuing the positive relationships we have developed.

.... Only we can provide the future homes that people can truly afford and that meet everyone's needs. ***The key to unlocking this ambition is land.*** We want to work in partnership with all public sector agencies to explore new and equitable ways to allocate land to housing associations in Greater Manchester (author's emphasis). (Greater Manchester Housing Providers 2020)

Source: Greater Manchester Housing Providers, 2020.

The third case study describes a partnership between a housing association and a forward-thinking hospital to provide accommodation for its workers. Healthcare workers in high-cost areas face huge problems accessing housing. Given the pressures on the National Health Service to retain staff, this sort of partnership would seem an obvious solution, but, to date, there are only a few examples in operation.

BOX 12.2: HOMES FOR THE CITY OF BRIGHTON AND HOVE

Brighton City Council and Hyde Group Joint Venture to Produce New Homes at Affordable Rents

Brighton, a lively coastal city 60 miles south of London, has one of the most pressured housing markets in southern England and a severe deficit of affordable housing. The city plan looks for at least 13,200 new homes by 2030. The local authority, Brighton & Hove City Council, would like to maximise the amount of affordable housing within this total, but national restrictions on how local authorities can spend certain funds mean the council cannot build affordable homes itself, and housing associations have not recently built much affordable rented housing in the city.

In December 2017, the council entered a joint venture with the Hyde Group, a housing association that owns and manages more than 50,000 mostly affordable homes in South East England. Hyde builds about 1,500 new homes each year and is one of Brighton's largest developers. The two organisations' aims dovetail: both want to meet housing need and generate revenue to enable more house-building in future. The council wants to generate economic development, and Hyde hopes to develop a rental model that works for local low-income households.

The joint venture will acquire sites in the area (including some currently in council ownership) and build homes for sub-market rent and shared ownership. Rents will be income-linked, averaging 37% of gross take-home pay for households earning the National Living Wage, and homes will be let or sold to people with a connection to the area. The five-year goal is to provide 1,000 genuinely affordable homes for employed people who currently cannot afford to live in the city or must commute to work: half for rent and half shared ownership. Each partner will contribute up to £60 million to enable the joint venture to buy sites and build housing. The council's share will come partly from the sites (some will be offered on a first-refusal basis to the partnership at 'best consideration'—market value, roughly speaking), and partly from borrowing from the Public Works Loan Board, which lends at

(Continued)

favourable rates to public-sector borrowers. The council will use the loans to fund its equity investment in the partnership and make repayments out of the partnership's earnings. The joint venture partners are open to the idea of institutional investment in the vehicle in future (Bevan Brittan 2018).

Lessons

The structure of the partnership responds to the particularities of UK constitutional framework; the legal device of the joint venture allows councils to skirt around central government restrictions on some types of local-authority expenditure and activity. In most federal systems, these restrictions would not be present, so a different type of partnership vehicle, or a different relationship altogether, might be more appropriate.

Source: Bevan Brittan, 2018.

BOX 12.3: THAMES VALLEY HOUSING AND FRIMLEY HOSPITAL

Building Housing for Medical Workers on NHS Land

Because most public-sector workers are on pay scales that do not vary geographically, key workers in expensive areas like southern England are often seriously affected by the lack of affordable housing. At the same time, many of their employers (hospitals, prisons, transport providers) own large amounts of under- or unused land. This public-sector land could be given or sold cheaply to housing associations, who could build affordable housing for workers at the sites.

It seems an obvious win-win arrangement, but in practice few such partnerships have been created. There are two main reasons for this: first, asset rationalisation has historically not been a high priority in many public sector organisations, some of which have portfolios of land that date back generations or even hundreds of years. This is now changing: austerity has exacerbated the financial pressures on these bodies and driven them to look forensically at how they could realise the value of their assets. Land disposal is an obvious strategy, and outright sale to the highest bidder is the default approach: financial imperatives often favour capital receipts. In addition, most public bodies have a legal responsibility to secure 'best value' for any asset they sell, and lawyers often interpret this to mean the highest monetary value, even though the courts have made clear that wider social and environmental values can also be taken into account.

One example of successful partnership between a public-sector landowner and a housing association is at Woodbridge, near Frimley Hospital, in an upmarket and high-cost area of Surrey, southwest of London. Thames Valley Housing Association converted a former children's centre building that was owned by the hospital but had been vacant for some time. The new homes include both self-contained flats and 'cluster homes', where residents rent a bedroom and bathroom, and share kitchen and living space with other tenants. The cluster flats and some of the self-contained flats are let out to doctors, nurses and other workers at Frimley Park Hospital, and the remainder are for market sale. This is one of the nine relatively small joint projects between TVHA and hospitals in London and southern England.

The final case study looks at how Transport for London (TfL), the capital's metropolitan transport body, developed a partnership framework with developers, including four housing associations, to build on its land. The resulting schemes will include at least 50% affordable housing; this high proportion is required by mayoral policy for land in public ownership.

BOX 12.4: HOUSING ASSOCIATIONS IN PARTNERSHIP WITH TRANSPORT FOR LONDON

Major Public-sector Landowner Partners with 13 Developers, Including Four Housing Associations

TfL, the transport authority for greater London, is one of the city's biggest landowners with a portfolio of 5,700 acres. TfL is facing financial pressures and needs cash to make up for the budget shortfalls left by long-term withdrawal of government transport subsidy. Its large financial team is focused on maximising the value of its assets and generating extra revenue. As discussed earlier, many public-sector landowners have little incentive to sell their surplus land to affordable housing providers, since they could maximise receipts by selling to the highest bidder (normally a speculative developer).

London Mayor Sadiq Khan was elected in 2016 on a manifesto that emphasised provision of affordable housing. As well as being mayor, Khan is chairman of TfL's board. After taking office, Khan changed TfL's incentive framework by decreeing that in future, an average of 50% of the new homes built on former TfL land would have to be affordable. This had the effect of reducing the capital value of TfL's developable land, as the gross development value of schemes with 50% affordable housing is lower than that of standard speculative schemes (which in London generally are required to provide 20–35% affordable housing). This change made it more likely that TfL would decide not to sell the land outright but rather would enter into joint ventures and retain an equity stake, and would look to housing associations, rather than for-profit developers, to partner for development.

In 2016, TfL announced that it had appointed a panel of 13 developers (out of 50 applicants) to its Property Partnership Framework (Transport for London 2016). Four of the final framework partners are housing associations: L&Q, Notting Hill Housing, Peabody and Hyde. These developers will serve as a short-list of approved potential partners for new schemes on TfL land. One criterion for selecting developer partners was that they had net assets of at least £100 million, which excluded smaller players. Each framework partner will be eligible to bid to work with TfL in individual joint ventures to develop specific sites; in the first year, 75 sites were to be released. TfL will rely on the expertise of the successful partner to secure detailed planning permission, consult with local communities and so forth.

These (potential) partnerships may turn out to be tremendously productive, given the extent of TfL's landholdings and their location, and the clear strategic aim of maximising the quantum of affordable housing produced. But it is early days: as of December 2020, five residential sites were under construction and planning permission had been secured for a further six (Transport for London 2020), but none were yet completed. The history of major

(Continued)

developments on public land in London shows that even relatively straightforward schemes can become enmired for decades in political, legal and financial wrangles.

One of the first concrete plans to emerge from the framework agreement was at Kidbrooke Station Square. The scheme will be built on 1.7 hectares of redundant TfL land adjoining a rail line in southeast London; the housing association partner is Notting Hill Genesis.

Lessons

TfL is one of London's biggest landowners, and only the largest and best resourced housing associations can work with it because of the time and resources required to prepare the framework bid, the uncertain timeline for eventual developments and the requirement for framework members to prepare 'mini bids' for specific projects. The specific framework mechanism fulfils the requirements of European Union procurement rules [known as OJEU (Official Journal of the European Union]). Such a mechanism would not necessarily be appropriate elsewhere (see also London Assembly Housing Committee 2016).

Source: Consultation documents for Kidbrooke Station Square, September 2018.

Planning Gain: Partnership or Quid Pro Quo?

Much new affordable housing in England is produced through a system known as 'planning gain'. This shares some features with inclusionary zoning in the USA and Canada, although the mechanism is very different, reflecting the different bundles of rights conferred by land ownership in these countries. Ownership of land in England does not confer the right to develop that land: development rights were nationalised in 1947, so almost all new construction or major modification of existing structures requires permission from the relevant planning authority (usually the local authority). Canada's planning system is based on zoning system, with defined spatial areas that that give *a priori* permission for certain types of construction; in England, by contrast, planning authorities negotiate permissions individually with developers based on principles set out in the statutory local plan.

Planning permission covers the uses, size and design of the proposed development. Because there is no automatic right to develop land, the granting of planning permission confers (sometimes enormous) value. In return, local authorities almost always require some *quid pro quo* in the form of 'developer contributions' (usually known as S106 contributions, for the relevant provision of the 1990 Town and Country Planning Act). Developer contributions may include new schools, improved transport facilities, doctor's surgeries, improvement of local parks and so forth, but the main element is normally affordable housing.

Currently, 43% of all new affordable housing and nearly half of new social rented housing is built by private developers as a condition of planning permission for private residential or office schemes. Such homes may or may not benefit from government subsidy (Table 12.1). The resulting new affordable homes are then generally purchased by housing associations. New social housing is thus largely a by-product of commercial development; looked at another way, it is funded by a tax in kind on developers and landowners.

TABLE 12.1 New Affordable Housing Units by Lead Producer, 2016

Totals by Lead Producer	Number	Percentage
Section 106 without grant	18,219	43
Housing associations with grant from central or London government	10,810	26
Local authorities	4,108	10
Housing associations without grant from central or London government	1,310	3
Other	7,776	18

Source: MHCLG live tables 1000 and 1011; author's analysis.

The current national document governing planning policy is the National Planning Policy Framework, which sets out the expectations for how local plans should treat the question of affordable housing in new developments. It says:

> Plans should set out the contributions expected from development. ***This should include setting out the levels and types of affordable housing provision required***, along with other infrastructure (such as that needed for education, health, transport, flood and water management, green and digital infrastructure). Such policies should not undermine the deliverability of the plan. (author's emphasis)
>
> *(MHCLG 2018)*

All new residential developments of ten units or more are expected to include some affordable housing, as a condition of receiving planning permission. Broadly speaking, new residential schemes in England are expected to include at least 20% affordable housing. The guidelines are more demanding in London; Mayor Sadiq Khan has indicated that developers who agree to provide 35% affordable housing (or 50% if the scheme is on public land) should have their applications fast-tracked (Mayor of London 2017). The details—the proportion of affordable housing, the breakdown between different types of affordable product, the location within the scheme—are matters for negotiation between planning authority and developer. Planning authorities usually push for the maximum amount of affordable housing and will treat planning applications from housing associations the same as those from for-profit developers, with similar requirements for affordable housing. The difference is that while for-profit developers generally want to minimise the amount of affordable housing provided, housing associations usually look for ways to maximise it.

Section 106 channels resources from private developers to affordable housing and is therefore basically a hypothecated (ring-fenced) tax on development. Taxes like this are in principle borne by the landowner—that is, the price of the land should fall to reflect the eventual tax on the finished development. However, this is the case only if the market can correctly forecast the final S106 affordable housing requirement. In practice, these forecasts have large margins of error because affordable housing contributions are negotiated rather than fixed (although there are signs that the Mayor's threshold of 35% affordable housing is starting to be priced into land in London).

In the period before the global financial crisis, many schemes were granted planning permission with ambitious affordable housing contributions. Developers agreed to these in the expectation that house prices would continue to rise and that profits from the high-price units would be sufficient to subsidise the affordable homes. But when house prices turned down, profits were squeezed. Many developers argued that providing the original amount of affordable housing would reduce their profits unacceptably, or even result in losses. Until 2016, the government therefore permitted renegotiation of some S106 agreements on 'viability' grounds.

English planning policy strongly favours mixed communities, with affordable units located within or directly adjacent to market-price blocks. The NPPF says,

> Where a need for affordable housing is identified, planning policies should specify the type of affordable housing required, and expect it to be met on-site unless: a) off-site provision or an appropriate financial contribution in lieu can be robustly justified; and b) the agreed approach contributes to the objective of creating mixed and balanced communities.
>
> *(MHCLG 2018)*

A Triumph of Policy Design?

There is an increasing number of well-functioning, productive relationships between local authorities and private partners—mostly housing associations—around affordable housing. But these partnerships have generally not come about in response to specific policy initiatives at central or local level. Many varieties of partnership started as small-scale, local innovations; the policy and planning framework permitted such partnerships to exist but was not designed with that in mind. In fact, the policy that contributed most to the formation of partnerships in recent years was a negative one: the reduction in grant funding for affordable housing. This forced organisations to pair up to take advantage of each other's strengths, rather than trying to go it alone. Even S106, the inclusionary zoning-type mechanism that forces private developers to build affordable housing, was not conceived of primarily as a housing tool: the original intention was that developers should be required to mitigate any negative effects of their schemes on their immediate localities (by, say, paying for expanding local schools). Only later did it become focused on affordable housing

Partnership working has enabled the various actors to do more than they could individually, and enthusiasm for the approach is spreading; indeed, some housing associations are now advertising for local-authority partners (see for example Hyde undated). From a fiscal point of view, the gradual reduction of housing-construction subsidies has arguably led to more efficient use of the public money that does remain. Pushed by the tighter funding situation, housing associations have become more professional and tightly run, and are better leveraging the substantial value of their existing stock to borrow funds to build more. The implicit government guarantee allows them to access market funding at very low interest rates, reducing the requirement for public funds. On the other hand, the biggest associations, driven by the logic of cross-subsidy, have become increasingly market-focused, and some critics say there is now little to differentiate them from major commercial housebuilders.

There are different degrees and types of partnership, depending largely on the degree to which partner organisations' overall interests are aligned. Because their housing goals are largely shared, local authorities and housing associations are natural partners. Councils' relationships with profit-seeking organisations, on the other hand, usually involve straightforward commercial transactions (e.g., where councils contract with private landlords to accommodate homeless households) or requirements that the private actor might prefer to avoid but cannot (S106).

Of course, for partnerships to be formed, there must be a pool of suitable partner organisations, and English housing and planning policy has (largely unintentionally) created such an ecosystem. There can be a sort of symbiotic relationship: local authorities have planning authority, housing responsibilities and land, but not much money and little ability to build; housing associations have development expertise and access to money but need planning permission and sites.

The characteristics that allow housing associations to be effective partners did not develop overnight: many of the biggest organisations were founded more than 100 years ago (the Peabody Trust, for example, dates from 1862). The major associations have substantial asset bases underpinned by decades of generous government subsidy and employ teams of well-qualified finance and development professionals. The largest groups have reached a critical mass and would be able to function and indeed thrive without any external subsidy at all. But if these organisations did not exist already, it is very unlikely they would develop under the current regulatory and financial system.

On the other hand, the emergence of mega-associations has made partnerships with councils more challenging in some ways. Until recently, most housing associations had strong local ties, having been founded originally to deal with poor housing in a specific place. The recent wave of mergers and consolidations has loosened local bonds and local knowledge within housing associations. It can be difficult for local authorities, especially small ones, to engage at high level with an association that covers the whole country. Conversely, local authorities do not have the staff or resources to deal separately with large numbers of housing associations operating on their areas. One recent study concluded that 'Unless there is substantive change in government policy, many of the underlying issues that make partnership working difficult will continue' (Fraser, Perry, and Duggan 2017, p. 40).

Internationally, England and the Netherlands stand out for having housing associations that effectively function like major corporations. But in many countries, housing associations are typically small, poorly resourced local organisations. In these places, partnerships will inevitably take a very different form from that seen in England.

Notes

1 The term 'social housing' is little used outside the housing sector; the general public tends to refer to 'council housing' even when the homes in question belong to a housing association.
2 This section draws heavily on Scanlon 2017.
3 The government quickly made changes to its supervisory framework to ensure the reclassification was reversed.
4 In fact, not all do—see Scanlon, Whitehead and Blanc 2017.

References

Bevan Brittan (2018) Living wage joint venture to deliver 1,000 affordable new homes. www.bevanbrittan.com/insights/news/2018/living-wage-joint-venture-to-deliver-1-000-affordable-newhomes/, accessed December 31, 2020.

Fraser, R., Perry, J., and Duggan, G. (2017) Building bridges: A guide to better partnership working between local authorities and housing associations. Chartered Institute of Housing. www.cih.org/resources/PDF/Policy%20free%20download%20pdfs/Building%20Bridges%20Full%20Report.pdf, accessed September 5, 2018.

Greater Manchester Housing Providers (2020) Our ambition to deliver. https://gmhousing.co.uk/our-ambition-to-deliver/, accessed December 31, 2020.

Hackett, P. (2017) Delivering the renaissance in council-built homes: The rise of local housing companies. The Smith Institute. www.smith-institute.org.uk/book/delivering-renaissance-council-built-homes-rise-local-housing-companies/, accessed June 4, 2021.

Hyde (undated). Working with our partners. www.hyde-housing.co.uk/partnership/, accessed December 31, 2020.

Kidbrooke Station Square (2018) Consultation documents. http://kidbrookestationsquare.org/wp-content/uploads/2018/09/Kidbrooke-banners1.pdf, accessed September 1, 2018.

Manzi, T., and Morrison, N. (2018) Risk, commercialism and social purpose: Repositioning the English housing association sector. *Urban Studies*, 55(9): 1924–1942.

Mayor of London (2017) Homes for Londoners: Affordable housing and viability supplementary planning guidance. Greater London Authority. www.london.gov.uk/sites/default/files/ah_viability_spg_20170816.pdf, accessed December 31, 2020.

Ministry for Housing, Communities and Local Government (2018) A new deal for social housing: Social housing green paper. https://assets.publishing.service.gov.uk/government/uploads/system/uploads/attachment_data/file/733605/A_new_deal_for_social_housing_web_accessible.pdf, accessed December 31, 2020.

Ministry of Housing, Communities and Local Government (2019) National planning policy framework. https://assets.publishing.service.gov.uk/government/uploads/system/uploads/attachment_data/file/810197/NPPF_Feb_2019_revised.pdf, accessed December 31, 2020.

Office for Budget Responsibility (2015) Economic and Fiscal Outlook, November. London: Williams Lea Group/Controller of Her Majesty's Stationery Office.

Scanlon, K. (2017) Social housing in England: affordable vs "affordable". *Critical Housing Analysis*, 4(1): 21–30.

Scanlon, K., Whitehead, C., and Blanc, F. (2017) *The future social housing provider*. London: Flagship Group/LSE London. www.lse.ac.uk/geography-and-environment/research/lse-london/documents/Reports/The-future-social-housing-provider-full-report.pdf, accessed December 31, 2020.

Transport for London (2016) TFL selects 13 property partners to help it deliver thousands of homes for London. https://tfl.gov.uk/info-for/media/press-releases/2016/february/tfl-selects-13-property-partners-to-help-itdeliver-thousands-of-homes-for-lond, accessed December 31, 2020.

Transport for London (2020) Projects and communities. https://tfl.gov.uk/info-for/business-and-commercial/communities, accessed December 31, 2020.

Wilson, W., and Barton, C. (2018) What is affordable housing? House of Commons Library BRIEFING PAPER Number 07747. https://researchbriefings.files.parliament.uk/documents/CBP-7747/CBP-7747.pdf, accessed December 31, 2020.

13

RESILIENCE OF SOCIAL HOUSING SYSTEMS IN VIENNA, AMSTERDAM, AND COPENHAGEN

Sasha Tsenkova

Introduction, Objectives and Methodology

The crisis that started in the mortgage markets of the United States in 2007–2008 has had dramatic and sustained impacts on people and housing systems throughout the world. These complex and interlinked crises exposed vulnerabilities of housing markets and low-income households, pointing to the need to build resilience through better policy tools and sustainable provision of social housing. In the context of fiscal austerity and budget cuts in all European countries, the future, purpose and form of social housing are being questioned and re-examined. This is of great importance to society and to our cities, where over 80% of the people live and work, particularly given the rapid growth of urban poverty and vulnerability. Comparative studies indicate a renewed emphasis on the supply of social housing in some European countries and city-wide initiatives to encourage private and non-profit provision to minimise 'poverty trap' effects (CECODHAS, 2012; Scanlon et al., 2015). In the post-crisis era, countries with unitary models and a strong social housing legacy have introduced a range of policy instruments and economic stimulus packages to promote supply-side responses in large metropolitan areas.

Housing providers and funding regimes have adjusted to the new environment, and some innovative entrepreneurial models have emerged in European cities (Pogglio and Whitehead, 2017). The emphasis is very much on diversifying social housing suppliers, public/private partnerships and the development of mixed communities in the context of urban regeneration. While there is a growing commitment to social housing in the political rhetoric, few countries, mostly with unitary systems, have identified new policy instruments to ensure that the investment necessary to meet the need for affordable housing will actually occur (Bardhan et al., 2012; CECODHAS, 2012).

This chapter aims at exploring the resilience of social housing systems in times of crisis. It focuses on the policy and practice of three conceptually appropriate case studies—the Netherlands, Austria and Denmark. These are examples of unitary housing systems with sustained investment in new social housing provision, a range of private and non-profit housing providers and a wide range of fiscal and regulatory instruments enhancing the competitive performance of the social housing sector (Kemeny et al., 2005; Matznetter, 2002). The emphasis is on housing policy and social housing system performance in the capital cities, where the impact of the fiscal crisis is more visible. The hypothesis is that unitary social housing systems, despite their

DOI: 10.4324/9781003172949-13

unique characteristics and institutional legacy, are more resilient in institutional, economic and social terms. This may be attributed to the robustness and the resourcefulness of social housing institutions and/or to better policy intervention in the post-crisis period. The research has three interrelated objectives:

- To develop a framework for comparative analysis of system resilience of social housing;
- To identify fiscal, financial and regulatory instruments implemented to ensure growth in the system and its resilience
- To identify patterns of resilience in institutional, economic, social and environmental terms.

The research methodology, which employs both qualitative and quantitative techniques, was structured in *two parts*. First, country-specific reform strategies were explored more broadly through review of the literature—country monographs on social housing, officially published documents, reports, working paper series and journal articles. Second, the collection of quantitative indicators (time-series data) was carried out though a survey instrument. Data on social housing at the city level (Vienna, Amsterdam and Copenhagen) were organised in four thematic blocks: (i) new housing construction and investment, (ii) financial indicators, (iii) affordability indicators and (iv) quality indicators.

Additional data on supply-side responses by social housing providers were collected through primary research to illustrate the diversity of experiences. The emphasis was on output, quality and diversity of social housing as well as business strategies to access land and long-term finance. Key informant interviews in Vienna, Amsterdam and Copenhagen were carried out in 2009 with close to 40 housing policy-makers, social housing providers and municipal planners with pertinent expertise and immediate involvement in social housing policy implementation. A follow-up process of data validation took place in March 2013.

Theoretical Context: Models of Social Housing Provision and Policy Instruments

The research is informed by the convergence-divergence paradigm for comparative housing studies (Kemeny and Lowe, 1998) and advances the notion that European systems of social housing provision have become less similar over time, with diverging experiences likely to accelerate in the future. The core idea of the convergence theory is that similarity of economic and demographic development in different countries will lead to converging housing policies, despite differences in ideology, politics and institutional structures (see Tsenkova 2009 for discussion on these issues). Esping-Andersen (1990) made perhaps the most significant attempt to identify patterns of dissimilarity based on distinct welfare state regimes. The approach has been refined through the comparative housing studies of Kemeny (1995), with the development of typologies of 'housing policy regimes'. In the spirit of divergence debates, scholars argued that despite similarities, European countries have distinctive housing systems and there is no evidence of convergence (Doling, 1997; Donner, 2000).

The research focuses on comparative analysis of countries with unitary systems of social rented housing where the sector operates like a 'social market' in direct competition with other tenures. The institutional arrangements favour non-state ownership by non-profit landlords, rents are set below-market level but tend to be sensitive to demand and allocation extends access to a more diverse income group. Distortions in pricing are less prevalent, since rental systems not only ensure cost recovery for services, but also allow rent-setting to be adjusted to a range of property attributes (Kemeny, 1997; Kemeny et al., 2005). In Western Europe, the Netherlands, Sweden, Denmark and Austria exemplify the characteristics of unitary systems. These relationships sketched in broad strokes reflect very general aspects of the role of social housing in unitary systems. The supply of new social housing, in particular, is dependent on the availability of fiscal, financial and regulatory instruments to encourage provision and to deal with the front-end loaded nature of housing costs (Carmona et al., 2003; Tsenkova, 2009).

Different countries have experimented with a range of *fiscal instruments* requiring direct expenditures of the government (grants, subsidies, tax incentives), or indirect, such as depreciation allowances or rent control. England and Austria rely on capital grants, Denmark on interest rate subsidies and the Netherlands has abolished direct subsidies, having first provided the housing associations with payments designed to relieve them of debt (Boelhouwer et al., 2006). Some countries (e.g. Austria, England and France) subsidise a range of housing suppliers directly (with conditions on production levels and rents), reducing house builders' and landlords' costs in social housing (Angel, 200; Donner, 2000). A second major stream of subsidies, as the main instrument of housing policy, is applied in all countries through housing vouchers, rent supplements or housing benefits. These fiscal instruments in unitary systems operate with various levels of efficiency, transparency and distributional equity (Oxley, 1995; Scanlon et al., 2015).

Financial instruments to encourage new supply of social housing relate to the availability of long-term finance and the diversity of mortgage products. In most countries with unitary models, private finance has become a dominant source of low-cost finance and is obtained mainly from banking intermediaries. Borrowing costs from private sector institutions are subsidised in Denmark and England, while borrowing is guaranteed in the Netherlands (Scanlon and Whitehead, 2007). Finally, tenants provide up to 2% of the funds for new social housing in Denmark and up to 10% in Austria, with additional grants available from local municipalities (Tsenkova, 2014).

A wide range of regulatory policies define housing standards in the social housing sector and the way social landlords and providers operate through supervision, auditing and control over allocation procedures. *Regulatory instruments* and operational practices allow the physical production, allocation and consumption of housing without imposing restrictions on main institutions and agents in the market (see Tsenkova, 2021). The regulatory environment has evolved to enhance efficiency in production and allocation decisions by making social providers more responsive to household preferences (e.g. the Delft model of allocation). Second, policies in this category include reduction in land costs to promote housing investment in social housing. Inclusionary zoning, planning agreements, provision of free public land and development land taxes have been used to extract some of the 'excess profit' of the landowner and/or provide incentives to developers, particularly in the context of regeneration projects (Buitelaar and De Kam, 2011). The Dutch planning system provides the most comprehensive 'solution' in Europe, while in England and France planning negotiations may lead to a provision of 20–50% of social housing in large-scale projects.

Conceptual Framework

The conceptual framework brings more established concepts of housing policy analysis with concepts related to resilience thinking (Tsenkova, 2021). More specifically, it is designed to explore the resilience of unitary social housing provision systems focusing on new supply—the most dynamic element of the system. It applies the concept of resilience, which has a well-established history in environmental research, engineering, psychology, sociology and economics, but has not been explored in housing studies. In this way of thinking, resilient systems have the ability to thrive, improve or reorganise themselves in a healthy way in response to stress

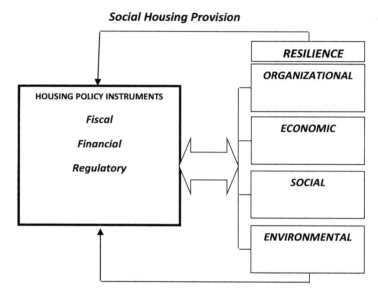

FIGURE 13.1 Conceptual Framework: Resilient Social Housing Systems.
Source: Sasha Tsenkova.

(Vale et al., 2014). Such systems demonstrate greater adaptive capacity and can maintain system function in the event of disturbances. Understanding complex adaptive systems, such as social housing in large urban centres, and their resilience, can be defined as the ability to withstand, recover from and reorganise in response to crises. Function is maintained, but system structure may not be. Key properties that contribute to resilience are diversity and redundancy, the presence of multiple smaller systems that are relatively independent and responsive regulatory feedbacks (Walker et al., 2006).

Defining Resilience. Most discussions of resilience agree that it is a multifaceted concept and should be understood and measured across multiple dimensions, including physical, social, economic, institutional and ecological fronts. The conceptual framework (Figure 13.1) explores the impact of housing policy packages combining fiscal, financial and regulatory policy instruments on the social housing system and its performance during the times of financial crisis since 2008. The comparative analysis focuses on four dimensions of systems resilience—institutional, economic, social and environmental—to quantify various types of social housing system responses (see Walker and Salt, 2012). Resilience is the ability of a system to withstand stresses and to adapt to sudden shocks. For the purposes of this research, resilience of the social housing system is defined as the ability of social providers to contain the effects of financial and fiscal stress during times of crisis, and to carry out maintenance and redevelopment activities in their social housing portfolio in a manner that minimises disruption to affordability and mitigates the impact on housing quality. Enhancing the resilience of social housing systems minimises economic and social losses during a crisis and allows moderate growth in the system. It can be achieved by the ability of a social provider to perform more efficiently and effectively to absorb a shock, if it occurs, and to recover quickly after a shock.

More specifically, a resilient system is one that shows the following attributes:

• Robustness: strength, or the ability of the system to withstand a given level of stress without suffering degradation or loss of function;

- Resourcefulness: the capacity to identify problems and mobilise resources (financial, technical, physical) to counteract disruption in the system;
- Redundancy: the extent to which systems/subsystems are substitutable, that is, capable of satisfying functional requirements in the event of disruption, degradation or loss of functionality.

(Walker et al., 2006)

Notwithstanding the importance of this *institutional* dimension, resilience encompasses three interrelated dimensions—economic, social and environmental (McCarthy et al., 2011). The *economic* dimension of resilience refers to the capacity to reduce both direct and indirect economic losses resulting from reduced financial and fiscal support and continue to grow. Housing providers adopt different business strategies for land acquisition and capital mobilisation and that influence important outcomes in terms of output, costs and quality. The *social* dimension of resilience consists of measures specifically designed to address communities' need for affordable housing through better access, social integration, affordability and choice. Important measure of affordability is the share of households receiving demand-based support in new social housing: a higher share implies greater vulnerability and potential for social exclusion. The *environmental* dimension of resilience refers to the ability of the social housing portfolio to provide access to affordable, good-quality housing through sensitive integration in neighbourhoods, access to transit, community facilities, jobs and schools. It also refers to standards and innovation to improve environmental performance and the energy efficiency of new social housing. Further, housing provision is examined as a dynamic process of interaction between public and private institutions with a focus on the performance of major social housing developers. The approach recognises the importance of institutional structures in defining patterns of economic, environmental and social resilience and diverging responses to policy intervention.

Comparative Analysis of Policy Instruments

The following sections explore fiscal, financial and regulatory instruments implemented to ensure growth in the system and its resilience. The focus is on the most dynamic aspect of the system—the provision of new housing in Vienna, Amsterdam and Copenhagen.

Fiscal and Financial Instruments

In principle, affordability in the Austrian system is ensured by brick-and-mortar subsidies in the form of discounted land, public loans, grants and tax relief. Housing programmes, and the new supply of social housing, enjoy a relatively long-term stability and support from federal resources on the basis of housing policy commitments of the provinces (Länder).[1] These are complemented by local grants to ensure adequate supply of new social housing. Vienna, with the status of a federal state, has a long-standing tradition of social housing provision, demonstrated in stable financial support. Typical financing of new social housing is based on a system of five interacting layers of low-interest, long-term commercial loans (50–70%), subsidies (grants, low-cost loans) (20–60%), equity contributions by developers (5–15%) and future tenants (0–10%) (Mundt and Amann, 2019). Loan repayments ensure revolving funds at the provincial and non-profit association levels. To enable low borrowing rates for commercial loans and to channel private investment in to new social housing development, housing banks (*Wohnbaubanken*), which are subsidiaries of the five major commercial banks, offer tax-privileged housing construction bonds to housing providers. Purchasers of the bonds are required to hold them for ten to 15 years, and, in return, capital income tax relief is offered on the first 4% of investment returns.

The system contributes to stabilisation of the housing market and lowers borrowing costs. The annual city budget for direct subsidies (new construction and renovation) has fluctuated between €505 million and €735 million since 1997. Fiscal austerity measures since 2009 affected these allocations and reduced the output of new social housing by Limited Profit Housing Associations (LPHA).

In the Netherlands, the Dutch government abolished the supply-side subsidies in 1993 and promoted a more enabling and financially self-sufficient approach to social housing provision. Within this framework, housing associations are free to sell, invest and choose the way to allocate their revolving funds to fulfil their social mandate. Housing associations finance new social housing with capital market loans, own equity and revenue from sales of newly built housing and/or sale of rental dwellings. Commercial loans are guaranteed by the national *Social Housing Guarantee Fund,* which reduces the capital costs (van Kempen and Priemus, 2002). In the last few years, policy changes have attempted to redefine 'social housing'. An income limit was placed on social housing units, requiring housing associations to provide 90% of their housing stock to households with taxable income of €33,000 or less. These changes resulted in increased capital pressure on the housing associations, as capital from private market development after the start of the financial crisis became more restricted, coupled with a new government requirement introducing corporate taxation. While both measures further decreased available funds, the City of Amsterdam, which owns 80% of the land, continued to subsidise the provision of new social housing through reduced land lease fees on City-owned land (about 50% lower compared to regular market developments).

Danish housing policies have gone through a phase of retrenchment, gradually transitioning from support to housing supply to demand-based subsidies to households (Nielsen, 2010). The social housing sector is subsidised through central government co-payment of the interest rates on mortgages financing construction of new dwellings. Other supply-side subsidies are also provided through the urban renewal programmes and interest-free loan for capital costs by local governments. Social housing is exempt from income tax and real-estate tax. A reform in the financial system in 2002 introduced an increased degree of self-financing for housing associations and an obligation to reimburse more than half of total state subsidies for new social housing. The cost of new social housing provision (91%) is financed by a mortgage (30-year variable-rate loan) by *Landsbyggefonden,* an independent organisation established in 1967 by non-profit housing associations. It guarantees mortgage loans in collaboration with the municipality. The municipality covers 7% in the form of an interest-free loan for base capital (*grundkapitallån*), while the remaining 2% is covered by tenants' deposits (Scanlon and Vestergaard, 2007; Tsenkova and Vestegaard, 2011).

In the three countries, low-income tenants receive demand assistance to defray housing costs. In the Netherlands, an income limit is applied when allocating new housing. At least 90% of the rental housing with a rent below the maximum rental supply limit (€648 in 2009, €711 in 2015) must be allocated to households with an income up to €33,000 (€35,000 in 2015). This means that more than 40% of Dutch households qualify for social housing. In Austria, demand assistance is not a dominant feature of the social housing system, and its expansion has been resisted by the sector (Mundt and Amann, 2019). It is estimated that 60% of all Viennese households live in subsidised housing (municipal, non-profit and private rental). Although the crisis has created pressures in the system increasing the share of households receiving demand-based support, it starts from a very low base of 3%. Housing allowances have a broad coverage in Denmark and are granted to more than 530,000 housing in the social and private rental housing, equivalent to more than one-fifth of all Danish households. There are two main housing allowance schemes: (i) for low-income households and persons receiving disability pension, and

(ii) for old age pensioners (Nielsen, 2010). Data indicate that housing allowances make up 50% of the rent in social housing in general and in the case of newly built projects, 55% (Interview data, June 2013).

Regulatory Instruments

In Austria, a wide range of regulatory instruments ensures the supervision of social housing providers and defines their allocation and rent-setting policies. LPHA operate on a cost recovery basis and needs to keep separate accounting for each project. Profits are capped at 6% and need to be reinvested in the housing portfolio. Regulations specify the conditions, which must be met in order to receive subsidies (cost, size of dwellings and target households) (Bauer, 2004). Supply-side subsidies finance about 30% of development costs (land and construction). City Council supports new social housing through the provision of land by *Vienna's Land procurement and Urban Renewal Fund—Wohnfond*—a non-profit financially independent land banking and development organisation preparing sites for social housing development since 1984. As a way to reduce construction costs, encourage high-quality and innovative design and achieve energy-efficiency targets, the City of Vienna introduced compulsory tender procedures and mandatory developer competitions for developments larger than 200 units. Proposed development plans are judged by a panel on the basis of quality, cost, energy efficiency and social sustainability. Approved proposals are granted subsidies and land by the City (Förster and Menking, 2019).

In most of the cases, new housing requires a contribution from tenants in the range of 10% of development costs. Since 1993, national regulation introduced 'the right to buy option', which enables tenants to purchase their dwellings after ten years in cases of such contributions. It is unclear how 'the right to buy model' will affect the sector in the future. Rents are calculated on a cost-rent basis in accordance with *Limited Profit Housing Act*. The Act establishes maximum and minimum allowable rent to cover the cost of land acquisition, construction, capital costs of the project, administration and investment in maintenance. Initial rents can be increased each year with the consumer price index (CPI), and revenues should be sufficient to repay the annuity of the capital loan as well as the interest on the public loan.

In the Netherlands, the supervision is less prescriptive, and housing associations are supervised on the basis of general 'fields of performance' (Boelhouwer et al., 2006). They are driven by portfolio management considerations and operate in a more business-like manner. Given their financial self-reliance, housing associations in Amsterdam sell existing housing (2 for 1 rule) to build new housing and reinvest profits and own equity to ensure a tenure and social mix in new projects. Sales as well as levels of new social housing provision in Amsterdam are subject to negotiation with the City administration and specified in three-year agreements, but both sales and new social housing output have failed to meet recent targets (Amsterdamse Federatie van Woningcorporaties, 2010). Housing associations are required to give priority to accommodating low-income and disadvantaged households, but are also driven by considerations of balancing revenue and expenditures. In Amsterdam, the allocations are centrally managed by the municipality, with over 100,000 households registered in the system. The implementation of the 'Delft model' allows prospective tenants to react on vacancies published every two weeks (Gruis et al., 2005). Specific rules apply to determine eligibility for relatively cheaper social rented homes (rent under €548 per month as of July 2009). In terms of rent-setting, social landlords have the freedom to pool rents across their portfolio and address priority tasks. This autonomy, however, is confined by rent regulations defining rents by the central government with prescriptive annual rent increases, usually adjusted by CPI (van der Veer and Schuiling, 2005).

In Denmark, municipalities supervise the housing associations and, since 1994, must approve their decisions for investment in new housing, which implies a financial commitment of 7% to capital costs. Each of the 7,750 housing estates (or 'member sections' in Danish) must balance its books—there is not supposed to be any cross-subsidisation between housing associations, or between estates that belong to the same association. The municipalities approve housing associations' budgets and accounts (Jensen, 2013). In 2004, an attempt to privatise social housing essentially delivered limited results. Out of the 5,000 apartments, fewer than 800 have been privatised, and this figure for Copenhagen is lower than 70 (Interview data, June 2010). The boards of tenants generally oppose privatisation, and tenants have been reluctant to take on such risks, despite a 30% discount of the market price. Social housing must be rented on cost recovery principles. The rent is expected to cover the cost of development (based on mortgage repayment costs) as well as maintenance and management charges. The average rents are 600–700 DKK/m^2 in estates/sections constructed before 1920, falling to 515 DKK/m^2 in estates constructed in 1960–1964 and then increasing to over 750 DKK/m^2 in the most recent estates.[2] Access is managed by housing associations on the basis of time on the waiting list and household size. There are no restrictions on who may join a waiting list, and the social housing sector is open to all income groups. Municipalities have the right to assign tenants to at least 25% of vacant housing association units. Waiting times in Copenhagen in attractive older estates exceed 15 years, but new housing due to its higher cost may be readily available (Interview data, June 2010).

Social Housing System Responses: Patterns of Resilience

Partnerships and Institutional Resilience

Social housing systems are path-dependent, so it is important to position the patterns of institutional transformation in the context of outcomes attributed to past housing policies and market conditions affecting the start of the crisis. The tenure distribution and the relative share of social housing operated by major providers/institutions in 2009 are important starting points. Data in Table 13.1 indicate that social housing was dominant in Amsterdam (50%) and Vienna (44%), but it also accounted for a sizeable share of the housing stock in Copenhagen.

Social housing in Austria is developed and owned by LPHA. The institutional ownership could be municipal, cooperative or private. There were more than 190 LPHA owning about 22.5% of housing in Austria and 20% in Vienna in 2009. The City of Vienna owned another 24%, while owner-occupied housing, mostly apartments, constituted 19% (see Table 13.1). In the Netherlands, social housing is managed by private non-profit housing associations

TABLE 13.1 Housing Tenure in Vienna, Amsterdam, and Copenhagen, 2009

Housing Tenure Share of Total Housing	Vienna (%)	Amsterdam (%)	Copenhagen (%)
Social (non-profit) housing	20	50	16
Social (municipal) housing	24		
Private rental housing	36	24	21
Owner-occupied housing	19	26	25
Cooperative housing			31
Other housing	1		7
Total	100	100	100

Source: Interview data, 2011.

operating under a range of public regulations for over 100 years. The social landlords owned 35% of the total stock in the Netherlands and 50% in Amsterdam in 2009. Private renting in the city was less significant compared to Vienna and accounted for 24% of the housing stock, but rent-setting and demand-based subsidies are applied in a tenure-neutral way to social and private rental. The financial reforms in the last 20 years have resulted in a large number of mergers reducing the number of housing associations from 767 in 1997 to 492 in 2005, with only seven operating in Amsterdam in 2010 (Amsterdamse Federatie van Woningcorporaties, 2010).

The Danish social housing sector (*almene boliger*) comprises housing owned by non-profit housing associations (20% of total housing stock) and a small amount of public stock (about 2%), mostly used for short-term emergency housing. There were about 760 housing associations, which own 7,750 estates with 541,500 dwellings (Ministry of Wefare, 2009). The associations are self-governing units and the dwellings are not entirely public nor privately owned, hence the concept of third-sector housing. The tenants are organised through a model of internal democracy, which ensures that there are representatives from the tenants parallel to the administrative levels within the sector. In Copenhagen, the share of social housing was 16% managed by 28 housing associations. All sectors, including private rental, social and cooperative housing, are subject to rent regulation.

With the external economic shocks experienced by all European countries since 2008, tightening of mortgage lending and fiscal austerity measures, the investment in the housing in general has declined, but the impact on the social housing sector has been particularly significant (CECODHAS, 2012; Scanlon et al., 2015). The private limited profit associations in Vienna and the housing associations in Amsterdam are extremely professional, knowledgeable and able to withstand stresses and to adapt to sudden shocks. While they contained the effects of financial and fiscal stress during the times of crisis, there were significant disruptions to their portfolio and ability to continue to invest in new high-quality affordable housing. Social housing providers in both cities enhanced their efficiency through mergers and acquisitions of smaller associations to optimise asset management and consolidate properties across different portfolios. Redundancy was not a viable strategy (Interview Data, 2013). These private market agents are very resourceful in navigating the system of finance, development control and planning regulations, but due to the capital-intensive nature of new social housing provision, their ability to mobilise resources (financial, technical, physical) to counteract disruption was system-dependent. In Amsterdam, the lack of supply-side support resulted in a shrinking portfolio reaching 47% of total housing in 2013, while in Vienna due to a more limited but still ongoing flow of subsidies, the share social housing has grown to 23%.

In Copenhagen, the third-sector model was more vulnerable to market fluctuations in capital and mortgage markets, affecting the ability to mobilise funds for new social housing provision. However, more proactive City strategies to assist with access to low-cost land and ability to acquire projects from bankrupt private housing developers provided a small boost to a sector that for years was struggling to deliver new affordable housing due to high costs. In the financial crisis period, a public-private partnership (PPP) model for a new type of affordable housing (*Almenbolig*) with a tenure-mix strategy appeared in Copenhagen. The goal of these partnerships is a mixed neighbourhood where non-profit housing associations collaborate with cooperatives and private developers to deliver new housing, often on brownfield sites. On the development side, housing associations are represented by six very professional organisations well versed in the planning and construction management process. Despite these positive shifts, data indicate that the share of non-profit housing in Copenhagen declined by 0.7%, while private rental increased (Ministry of Housing, Urban and Rural Affairs, 2013).

Overall, the institutional transformation has responded to three similar drivers: state/provincial decline of subsidies to social housing production, collaboration with private sector to finance new housing while increasing the role of public/private partnerships and, finally, growing authority of municipalities/cities. The partnerships were embedded in the provision system of Vienna and Amsterdam for decades, but are relatively new in Copenhagen. The three European cities have joined their efforts with non-profit and private organisations to provide social housing in mixed-income, mixed-tenure projects. A model of public, private and not-for-profit (PPNP) partnerships has evolved over time, capitalising on the strengths of each sector. The public sector (federal, provincial, municipal) is effective in the mobilisation of much-needed resources, while the private sector (designers, developers, construction companies) is efficient in managing the construction process by maximising economies of scale, tapping into technological innovation and marketing strategies. Not-for-profit housing institutions are more effective in managing and operating social housing due to the extensive knowledge of the people they service. In large-scale developments, such synergies are important in the provision process (design, build, finance, operate), as insights from projects in Vienna, Amsterdam and Copenhagen demonstrate. In Vienna and Amsterdam, these partnerships are led by the social housing providers—private organisations—operating with a high degree of efficiency and autonomy to design-build-finance-manage/operate social housing. They have a strong legacy and significant institutional resilience, which is a real strength of the sector.

Economic and Environmental Resilience

The overall restructuring of the social housing systems in economic terms implies that the institutions are able to minimise economic and social losses during a crisis to allow moderate growth in the system. It can be achieved by the ability of a social provider to perform more efficiently and effectively to absorb a shock, and to recover quickly without compromising affordability and quality. As the focus is on the most dynamic component of the system, the comparative analysis in this section highlights important similarities and differences in two areas: output/investment and strategies to develop new social housing at the city level. The projects illustrate important aspects of environmental resilience in terms of location, design qualities and environmental characteristics to enhance energy/water performance.

Housing production levels in Vienna have been relatively stable since 2003, with a peak in 2007 due to a growing share of social rental housing with the option to buy. Supply subsidies in Vienna declined sharply in 2000, reducing production from 12,000 to 6,000 dwellings under the conservative coalition government, but output increased to 9,000 dwellings in 2007. LPHA accounted roughly for half of the new production in the city. The impact of the financial crisis on output was significant in 2011, but later trends stabilised (see Figure 13.2).

The City of Vienna is actively steering the production of new housing into areas of brownfield development and other secondary nodes in support of its planning and urban development priorities. The City also operates an evaluation system to rank projects for new sites sold through Wohnfond. Land is sold by competitive tender, which aims to reduce building costs and focuses developers on quality outcomes (Förster and Menking, 2019). In the redevelopment of brownfield sites (Gasometer, Kabelwerk), the social housing providers establish joint companies with private developers to meet City's requirements of mixed-tenure, mixed-income communities (Figure 13.3). Kabelwerk, a former industrial factory, was reinvented as a new neighbourhood with 950 dwellings, with a mix of social rental and owner-occupied housing, shopping, offices, kindergarten, green spaces and cultural facilities (Tsenkova, 2014). In other strategic urban regeneration sites, such as the new quarters along the Danube River, LPHA

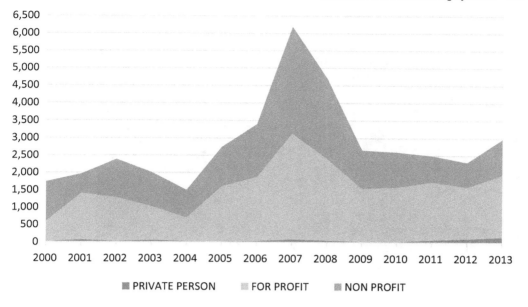

FIGURE 13.2 New Housing Construction in Vienna and Amsterdam, 2001–2013.

Source: Author's estimates based on data from Austrian Federation of Limited-Profit Housing Associations (GBV); Centraal bureau voor de Statistiek, 2013 (statline.cbs.nl/StatWeb/publication); Ministry of Housing, Urban and Rural Affairs (n.d.); the Danish social housing sector (www.mbbl.dk/sites/mbblv2.omega.oitudv. dk/files/dokumenter/publikationer/the_danish_social_housing_sector.pdf).

FIGURE 13.3 Brownfield Developments in Kabelwerk, Vienna.
Source: Sasha Tsenkova.

FIGURE 13.4 Mixed-Income Housing in Urban Regeneration Quarter in Vienna.
Source: Sasha Tsenkova.

built new social housing in developments with high-quality services, schools, public amenities and transit to initiate the process of neighbourhood rebuilding (see Figure 13.4). Due to the mixed-income, mixed-tenure models, it is not possible to distinguish social housing from the other housing developments. In terms of business strategy, when LPHA reach a critical mass of investment in the local area, private developers follow with market housing that may be more conservative in terms of design and quality.

There are many examples of innovative sustainable housing, passive housing, car-free developments and ethnic integration through design innovation fostered by the City's competitive bidding process and sustainable development guidelines for project evaluation. Eurogate is the world's largest passive housing development, with 2,000 flats achieving energy demands between 7 and 15 kWh/m^2. Through solar orientation and technology that improves exterior wall and window insulation and air supply, the energy-efficient design contributes to the reduction of carbon emissions, as well as to lower heating costs for residents. Located in Aspang-Gründe on a 20 ha former railway area, the development involves six different property developers and seven different architects, who were awarded the right to build and the supply-side subsidies through City-administered developer competitions. The development accommodates about 5,000 residents and 8,300 jobs (Förster and Menking, 2019).

Nordbahnhof is a residential complex located in Vienna, constructed with prefabricated concrete; the building is lifted above the service facilities to offer covered exterior open spaces on the ground level that are connected to site amenities such as walkways and green spaces. Designed by Synn Architekten, the concept behind the development is based on providing units that are affordable, flexible and offer functional interior and exterior spaces for communication. The development includes mini-lofts (one- or two-room units) and one- or two- room family units with a flexible open concept design that can be modified based on the needs of the resident.

In Amsterdam, contrary to Vienna, the production by housing associations has tripled since 2000, reaching 3,045 in 2007, but about a half or more is geared to the homeownership market (see Figure 13.2). Recent years have seen a wave of mergers and acquisitions of housing associations driven by risk reduction and portfolio management strategies. Housing associations focus on better quality of services, efficiency gains and neighbourhoods where they have a dominant position. New social housing is built on brownfield sites, and in the new greenfield development of Ijberg on land reclaimed from the sea (Gilderbloom et al., 2009). Production levels in 2007 reportedly responded to high pent-up demand for new ownership housing. The output of housing associations in the city accounts for 40% of the completions, which are in the range of 1,-200–1,700 in the last five years. Social housing for rent—about 25–30% of this output—is used to achieve social and tenure mix in priority development areas for the housing associations, with 70% of the housing targeting the homeownership market and 30% retained as social housing. This is also perceived to be a revenue neutral model in terms of development costs. The impact of the financial crisis was significant, but levels of production bounced back in 2013.

Housing associations in Amsterdam have the historical role of city builders with increasing responsibilities to improve liveability of deprived neighbourhoods as well as to provide social infrastructure. The sale of social housing is encouraged by the municipal administration in order to create more tenure choices and attract middle-class families to the city. Overrepresentation of social rented housing in some parts of Amsterdam is perceived to contribute to the concentration of socio-economic problems and ethnic minorities (Van der Veer and Schuiling, 2005). In these neighbourhoods, such as the New West, housing associations created strategic partnerships to demolish parts of the social housing and develop new medium-density, tenure-mixed communities (Amsterdamse Federatie van Woningcorporaties, 2010).

The New West in Amsterdam is an example of a housing estate built in post-war years where 10,000 social housing apartments, mostly home to low-income ethnic communities, were subject to major energy-efficiency retrofits to improve the environmental performance and the quality of housing. Other major improvements to the neighbourhood focused on high-quality public spaces, urban playgrounds, provision of local work opportunities and new housing (see Figure 13.5). In the process of social engineering of the neighbourhood, a consortium of housing associations demolished 3,000 social housing units, provided 5,500 new private housing apartments and sold about 1,600 social housing units to tenants under very favourable financial conditions. This transformation from 2009 to 2015 is impressive in social and economic terms:

- Social housing: from 75% to 45%
- Market rental housing: from 10% to 15%
- Privately owned housing: from 15% to 40%.

(Tsenkova, New West Project office Interview, 2013)

Housing associations have taken the lead in the redevelopment of Amsterdam's Docklands. These brownfield sites are centrally located, with access to water amenities and transit. The process is part of a long-term planning strategy for sustainable regeneration of Amsterdam using a model of integrated jobs, retail, community facilities and green + blue recreation with a mix of social, market rental and ownership housing. In many cases, the design strategy includes the adaptive reuse of industrial heritage reinvented as mixed-use hubs to encourage social interaction between residents (see Figure 13.6).

The new development strategies by housing associations in Amsterdam pioneer a lot of design innovation, often the outcome of architectural competitions run by the large associations. The implementation of sustainability by design is systematic, in addition to newly adopted co-design approaches to facilitate the integration of tenants and owners in one building and complex. The new projects in Ijburg demonstrate these outcomes. Located about 10 km east of the

FIGURE 13.5 Redevelopment of the New West in Amsterdam.
Source: Sasha Tsenkova.

city of Amsterdam, Ijburg is an archipelago of artificial islands planned to have 18,000 homes. After the completion of the first three islands, Ijburg included 30% social housing integrated in the community, with 15% designated as 'very low rent' (Gilderbloom et al., 2009). Planners emphasised social integration that has seen the mix of all housing tenure types within individual blocks, and even within buildings, all with little differentiation between the units. The incorporation of mixed incomes throughout the community facilitates the use of common space by all households and prevents the segregation of certain groups (Buitelaar and De Kam, 2011).

FIGURE 13.6 New Mixed-Income Housing Development in the Amsterdam Docklands and Ijburg.
Source: Sasha Tsenkova.

In Denmark, levels of new social housing output declined dramatically since 2006 as a result of a policy changes reducing subsidies to housing associations and emphasising a higher degree of self-reliance (see Tsenkova and Vestegaard, 2011). In Copenhagen, the decline in output was exacerbated by high construction costs and growing land prices related to the housebuilding boom in the owner-occupied market. An important factor affecting the supply of social housing was the regulatory cap on construction costs introduced in 2004. The limits increased steadily and reached DKK 20,710 for family housing and DKK 25,710 for seniors in 2010, but these limits exceeded the costs in Copenhagen. Despite some regional variation of such costs, the central regulations affect substantially where housing associations can build, and how much. Given the high land prices in Copenhagen, this led to a collapse in new social housing provision in the mid-2000. The global financial crisis provided some opportunities to invest and expand the sector due to availability of land, acquisition of housing projects (private sector developers under bankruptcy) and overall stability of financing for social housing, but the output per year was limited and even non-existent in 2009 and 2010 (Interview data, June 2010).

City policies set targets for social housing output for the 2009–2013 period: 700 flats for families and 200 homes for the disabled.[3] The City's investment in total amounted to 120 million DKK (interview data, June 2010). The City of Copenhagen announces annual competitions to reach its target for new social housing construction. The six largest administrative organisations managing the social housing portfolio of the housing associations compete on the basis of quality, innovative design, sustainable features and energy-efficient solutions (such as passive housing, 'zero' energy housing). In the financial crisis period, a local PPP for a new type of affordable housing production (*Almenbolig*) with a tenure-mix strategy emerged in Copenhagen. The Emiljhaven project brought together non-profit, cooperative and private developers to build 193 units. Compared to Vienna and Amsterdam, completions of new social housing were modest, in the range of 150–200 dwellings per year (less than 0.5% growth in the existing portfolio). During the post-financial crisis period, the City approved four to five projects on an annual basis and channelled some of these investments into urban regeneration areas such as the old Copenhagen harbour (see Figure 13.7).

Sluseholmen is a residential area in the Copenhagen harbour with 1,800 apartments on eight islands. The design is inspired by the Dutch city model with canals running between the blocks with interconnected courtyards. A leading principle in the development was to create a coherent area with a lot of diversity and unique identity for each island. Twenty-five different architectural firms were involved in the design. The developments have a mix of uses and a diversity of housing and tenure types, range from four to seven storeys, depending on whether they face the harbour, the promenade or the canals. Units have a central heating system and local amenities—bicycle pathways, water features and generous public spaces. Another innovation to increase the supply of social housing was associated with the provision of prefabricated housing. A *Non-profit Fund for Cheap Housing* was created to ordered 800 modular, prefabricated units from Estonia, where they could be built for 30–40% less; another 7,200 prefabricated units were delivered by producers in Sweden, Norway and Denmark (Figure 13.7). Only 5,000 of the 8,000 units were designated as low-rent housing (Scanlon and Vestegaard, 2007).

Social Resilience

The social resilience of the social housing systems implies that it retains its ability to deliver high-quality affordable housing with a fair amount of choice to tenants. This is associated with costs of new housing, the flow of services it provides in terms of access to transit, neighbourhood amenities and social integration. The comparative analysis focuses on rents in new social housing, allocation processes and affordability constraints reflected in the share of households needing housing allowances to support rental payments. The insights from projects illustrate the path-dependent nature of the system and the fact that social resilience during the time of crisis is highly dependent on policies and wider regulatory aspects affecting the ability of housing providers to influence affordability and choice.

Average housing costs in LPHA housing in Austria are lower compared to those in the Netherlands and Denmark. The sector also has a much lower share of low-income households.

FIGURE 13.7 New Social Housing in Sluseholmen and Prefabricated Units in Copenhagen Central Areas.

Source: Sasha Tsenkova.

These characteristics of the national system have implications for the affordability of social housing in the capital cities. With income limits high enough to accommodate 80–90% of the population, access to social housing in Austria is more universal in comparison to many other European countries. While eligibility rules are defined at the federal level, housing providers are responsible for assessing eligibility and allocation of units. Social housing is not limited to low-income households, and the supply-side subsidies have contributed to its affordability.

Rents are regulated based on unit area and quality of accommodation and are cost-based. The average cost for rent in Vienna was €452 or €6.45 per square metre of useful floor space in 2012 (Statistics Austria, 2012). The financial crisis did not change these conditions, but it affected the ability of tenants to contribute €15,000–€30,000 as a downpayment to project costs in new social housing. Interviews with major social housing providers of new developments indicated that tenants were increasingly young and ethnically diverse; about a third were migrants from Central and Eastern Europe, the Middle East and Asia. Problems with non-payment were almost non-existent, and vacancies were below 1%.[4] Less than 5% of the tenants received housing allowances.

By contrast, rents in the Netherlands are not cost-based but politically determined with little variation across locations within the city. The central government sets expenditure levels, eligibility criteria, rent-setting rules and annual rent increases. Social rents are set according to a 'formula rent' for each property, calculated on the relative value of the property, its size, energy efficiency and relative local income levels. The average monthly rent in the social housing sector in 2007 was €398. Subsequent regulations limited the maximum rent for social housing to 4.5% of the property's valuation, which translated into a maximum rent of €664 per month in 2012 (CBS Statistics Netherlands, 2012). Across the Netherlands, 15% of the households living in social rented housing received housing allowances; in Amsterdam, this share exceeded 20% in 2011, indicating the presence of a larger share of low-income and vulnerable households in the sector, compared to Vienna. While social and private rental housing are treated in a tenure-neutral way in terms of policy support, private rental is less affordable.[5]

Paradoxically, social housing in Denmark is not necessarily synonymous with affordable provision. A recent response by the Minister of Social Affairs to the Parliamentary Standing Committee on Housing indicates that there are 59,000 affordable rental apartments in Copenhagen (rent of less than 4,000 DKK per month, average size 58 m^2). Only 20,000 are social and 39,000 are private rental. High construction and land costs, as well as a less generous subsidy regime, make new social housing less attractive to prospective tenants. In Copenhagen, social housing administrators reported problems with leasing new schemes, particularly when costs go beyond DKK 25,000/m^2.

In terms of choice and allocation, the target group in Austria is rather broad, and reportedly close to 80% of the households can qualify for access to new housing. Households without sufficient capital or unable to access commercial loans can apply for a public loan at zero interest rates to pay the required 10% contribution. In Vienna, 25% of tenants are nominated by the City's Housing Service, half are offered externally to prospective tenants on the waiting list and the rest to existing tenants. Waiting lists are managed by individual LPHA, but the average waiting period is less than one year. By contrast, the centrally managed allocation system in Amsterdam provides a one-stop shopping opportunity for households, but the waiting time to get into a desirable neighbourhood is reportedly over six to seven years. Households in areas subject to major renewal programmes and demolition have a priority to return to the area and/or receive dwellings in the neighbourhood of their choice. The waiting time is attributed to the relatively flat rent structures that do not take into account location. Some of the historic properties in the most attractive parts of old Amsterdam reportedly have rent levels three to four times lower compared to market rates, and the situation may be similar in the case of new infill social housing along the canals (Tsenkova, 2014).

In Copenhagen, housing associations manage their own waiting lists, and the waiting period can be as long as ten to 15 years. When tenants move in, they have to pay a deposit that corresponds to 2% of the original construction cost of their unit. Housing associations also operate internal waiting lists, so tenants can move up the housing ladder within a housing association, from an expensive dwelling to a cheaper and more attractive one, which may explain the high number of households on the waiting lists in the City of Copenhagen (estimated at over 150,000). Social housing used to be considered a tenure for all, and in general there is still no stigma attached to living in social housing.

Discussion: Crisis and Opportunity

The global housing finance crisis in 2008 has had dramatic and sustained impacts on people and housing systems throughout the world (Tsenkova, 2021). This research explores housing policy strategies in the post-crisis period, focusing on three European countries with unitary housing systems and a strong social housing sector. The conceptual framework provides important insights into the dynamic relationships between housing policies and patterns of resilience in three capital cities. Findings point out that despite similar challenges and pressures to cope with increasing production costs, different countries and cities made different policy choices. The diverging experiences are exarcerbated by the institutional set-up defining the system of social housing provision. The complex and interlinked crises in housing finance, public subsidies and housing markets leads to diverging coping strategies by social housing providers. The institutional resilience and the ability to capitalise on partnerships with public, private and not-for-profit organisations are considered as strength in Vienna and Amsterdam. The partnerships have an important legacy and define the robustness and the adjustment of business operations.

Better policy tools and alignment of fiscal, financial and regulatory instruments result in more robust institutional and economic performance (see Tsenkova, 2019 for discussion). The Dutch *'Revolving Fund Model'* is an example of a financial model for social housing that can withstand global financial and regional policy pressures. The Guarantee Fund for Social Housing acts as a solidarity fund that enables housing associations to benefit from favourable conditions and interest rates on the open capital market. The triple guarantee of security has allowed housing associations to remain in strong financial position throughout the economic crisis. In Austria, long-term commercial loans provide most of the capital funding, supported by *Wohnbaubanken* and tax-privileged housing construction bonds to housing providers. In Copenhagen, housing finance is much more market-driven, leading to higher borrowing costs and lower output of new social housing.

While Austria retained its brick-and-mortar support for a strongly regulated limited profit, cost-capped and cost-rent regime, in the Netherlands the elimination of supply-side support has led to financial self-reliance, organisational change, sales and more entrepreneurial strategies by housing associations. Both systems demonstrate a high degree of economic resilience and are essential in pursuing national and city development objectives (neighbourhood renewal, brownfield redevelopment, sustainable practices). Dutch housing associations have a lot more freedom to pursue own policies in terms of new development, sales and other commercial activities. In Amsterdam, they dominate the market for new housing but produce predominantly for homeownership with significant exposure to market risks, which makes them more vulnerable during recessions when sales are not brisk and market prices are declining. This exposure to the fluctuations in the owner-occupied housing market makes the system more vulnerable to external shocks and places significant limits on innovation (Tsenkova, 2014). In Austria, the existence of public grants and loans influences production levels and shields the sector from market fluctuations, providing more stability for its operation. Although public finance has declined in proportion to other forms of investment, it remained essential as collateral for securing commercial loans.

In terms of environmental resilience and ability to build new housing in mixed-income, mixed-tenure communities on priority urban sites, LPHA in Vienna perform better. Social housing landlords are extensively regulated through the cost-rent model and limitations on profits in Austria, while in the Netherlands the centrally determined rents provide stability in the rental market, but may constrain investment in innovation and quality improvements. Levels of output are influenced through voluntary agreements with Amsterdam municipality and below-market land leases, but have been in general lower compared to Vienna, resulting in net losses in the portfolio. In Vienna, new social housing pioneers design innovation, sustainable living and consistently deliver high standards, in part steered by the City of Vienna competitive bidding process for land allocation through the Wohnfond. This is not necessarily the case in Amsterdam, where housing associations claim that every new social dwelling results in a loss of over €100,000 for the organisation, with obvious limitations for such experiments. In both cities, partnerships are an important legacy of the system and an area of institutional strength.

The Danish system is less resilient in institutional and economic terms. Denmark has a different institutional model of third-sector social housing, owned by the tenants and serviced by professional administration responsible for new development and management of the existing stock. Danish housing policies have gone through a phase of retrenchment, transitioning from 'brick-and-mortar' support to demand-based support. The sector is also changing from providing affordable housing to all groups in society, towards a more selective role of provider for groups with special needs and the elderly. Finally, housing associations seem to be less influential, given the declining share of new output and limited growth prospects in Copenhagen. Although since 2011 new social housing construction has gained some momentum, production costs remain high and rent levels ensuring cost recovery tend to be highly dependent on demand-based support through housing allowances.

In terms of social resilience, affordability and choice are much more significant in Vienna, manifested in shorter waiting lists (less than two years, compared to seven in Amsterdam) and a much lower dependence on housing allowances to pay cost recovery/controlled rents. In all, 5% of tenants in Vienna receive housing allowances versus over 30% in Amsterdam, although the required tenant contribution may present a barrier for some socially vulnerable groups. Access to social housing is universally accessible, while in Amsterdam some income limits steer the allocation to low- and mid-income housing. In Copenhagen, despite the high quality of new social housing, due to its high costs, this is not a preferred choice and in some cases it is difficult to rent.

Concluding Comments

The three cities have a strong system of social housing provision that responds to similar pressure in the post-crisis period: decline in public finance due to austerity measures and growing shortage of affordable housing in local markets. Patterns of institutional resilience indicate a move towards more self-reliance, entrepreneurial strategies and partnerships for the provision of new social housing. Social housing plays a critical role in Amsterdam and in Vienna and has a long history of support instruments to ensure its stability in city building. While direct government subsidies have declined, the role of cities has grown (Tsenkova, 2021). Cities and planning play an important role in regulating the supply of new social housing through inclusionary zoning, provision of land and design control. All three cities provide excellent examples of mixed-income, mixed-tenure neighbourhoods with emphasis on sustainable design and high environmental performance. On the social side, rent control and housing allowances ensure opportunities for social integration and stability in the social rental sector, so social housing provision can bounce back and recover from the external shocks.

As cities recover from the biggest health and economic crisis the world has collectively ever faced, the resilience of social housing systems will be extremely important. The crisis has exposed major gaps and inequalities in urban housing markets, particularly for low-income households. As we chart the road to recovery, we can learn from the success of other cities where better housing policy leads to a more resilient performance with better results for local communities. This is the time to invest in better tools and work towards building a more effective, equitable and more robust social housing response system.

Acknowledgement

The research is supported by the Social Sciences and Humanities Research Council of Canada.

Notes

1 The level of subsidization in Austria is high in comparison to other European countries with 80% of housing receiving subsidies. Direct expenditures by provincial governments, which amounted to 0.9% of Austria's GDP in 2010, included subsidies for new construction (60%), building refurbishments (25%) and allowances (14%) (Interview data, 2012).
2 The average exchange rate in 2010 for 1 Danish krone (DKK) was €0.1344.
3 This was still short of a target set by Copenhagen's mayor elected in 2006 on a promise of providing 5,000 new homes at a rent of DKK 5,000 (approximately €670) per month. It was clear that housing associations could not build these homes since the building standards they must comply with are so costly that rents would necessarily be much higher.
4 In 2007, the average rent burden in Vienna, across both private and limited profit sector, for couples with children was only 20% of household income (Czasny and Bständig, 2008), which is considered low compared to other European capital cities.
5 Tenants are spending a larger proportion of their income on housing—up from 34% in 2009 to 38% in 2018; social housing rents have gone up 26% over the past ten years, rents in the non-rent-controlled sector have risen 44%.

References

Amann, W., Lawson, J., and Mundt, A. (2009) Structured Finance Allows for Affordable Housing in Austria, *Housing Finance International*, July, pp. 14–18.

Amsterdamse Federatie van Woningcorporaties (2010) *Jaarboek 2010*. Amsterdam.

Angel, Sh. (2000) *Housing Policy Matters—A Global Analysis*. New York: Oxford University Press.

Austrian Federation of Limited-Profit Housing Associations—Audit Federation (GBV) (2013) *Organization Summary*. Vienna: GBV. Retrieved February 28, 2012 from www.gbv.at/Document/View/4104

Bardhan, A., Edelstein, R., and Kroll, C. (2012) *Global Housing Markets. Crises, Policies and Institutions.* Hoboken, NJ: Wiley & Sons.

Bauer, E. (2004) Austria. In V. Gruis and N. Nieboer (eds)., *Asset Management in the Social Rented Sector; Policy and Practice in Europe and Australia*. Dordrecht: Kluwer Academic Publishers, 39–59.

Boelhouwer, P., Boumeester, H., and van der Heijden, H. (2006) Stagnation in Dutch Housing Production and Suggestions for a Way Forward. *Journal of Housing and the Built Environment*, 21 (3), 299–314.

Buitelaar, E., and De Kam, G. (2011) The Emergence of Inclusionary Housing: Continuity and Change in the Provision of Land for Social Housing in the Netherlands. *Housing, Theory and Society*, 29 (1), 56–74.

Carmona, M., Carmona, S., and Gallent, N. (2003) *Delivering New Homes. Processes, Planners and Providers.* London: Routledge.

CBS Statistics Netherlands. (July 2012) Over a Quarter of Tenants in Housing Association Stock Earn more than 33 Thousand Euro. www.cbs.nl/en-GB/menu/themas/bouwen-wonen/publicaties/artikelen/archief/2012/2012-3652-wm.html

CECODHAS (2012) Impact of the Crisis and Austerity Measures on the Social Housing Sector. Brussels: CECODHAS Housing Europe Observatory Research Briefing, 5 (2).

Czasny, M., and Bständig, T. (2008) Housing Conditions in Vienna—Changes as Mirrored in the Austrian Micro Census, Vienna Housing Research. www.wohnbauforschung.at/en/Projekt_Mikrozensus.html

Doling, J. (1997) *Comparative Housing Policy: Government and Housing in Advanced Industrialised Countries.* New York: St. Martin's Press, Inc.

Donner, C. (2000) *Housing Policies in the European Union: Theory and Practice.* Vienna: Donner.

Esping-Andersen, G. (1990) *The Three Worlds of Welfare Capitalism.* Cambridge: Polity Press.

Förster, W., and Menking, W. (eds). (2019) *The Vienna Model 2: Housing for the City of the 21st.* Berlin: Jovis.

Gilderbloom, J. G., Hanka, M., and Lasley, C. B. (2009) Amsterdam: The Ideal City, Policy and Planning. *Local Environment: The International Journal of Justice and Sustainability,* 14 (6), 373–392.

Gruis, V., Elsinga, M., Wolters, A., and Priemus, H. (2005). Tenant Empowerment through Innovative Tenures: An Analysis of Woonbron Maasoevers' Client Choice Programme. *Housing Studies,* 20 (1), 127–147.

Jensen, L. (2013). Housing Welfare Policies in Scandinavia: A Comparative Perspective on a Transition Era. *LHI Journal of Land, Housing, and Urban Affairs,* 4 (2), 133–144.

Kemeny, J. (1995) *From Public Housing to the Social Market: Rental Policy Strategies in Comparative Perspective.* London and New York: Routledge.

Kemeny, J., Kersloot, J., and Thalmann, P. (2005) Non-Profit Housing Influencing, Leading and Dominating the Unitary Rental Market: Three Case Studies. *Housing Studies,* 20 (6), 855–872.

Kemeny, J., and Lowe, S. (1998) Schools of Comparative Housing Research: From Convergence to Divergence. *Housing Studies,* 13 (2), 161–176.

Matznetter, W. (2002) Social Housing Policy in a Conservative Welfare State: Austria as an Example. *Urban Studies,* 39 (2), 265–282.

McCarthy, D., Crandall, D., Whitelaw, G., General, Z., and Tsuji, L. (2011). A Critical Systems Approach to Social Learning: Building Adaptive Capacity in Social, Ecological, Epistemological (SEE) Systems. *Ecology and Society,* 16 (3), 18.

Ministry of Welfare. (2009). Committee Report on the Financing of Third-Sector Housing. www.vfm.dk/Publikationer/Sider/VisPublikation.aspx?Publication=356

Mundt, A., and Amann, W. (2019) "Wiener Wohnbauinitiative": A New Financing Vehicle for Affordable Housing in Vienna, Austria. In G. van Bortel, V. Gruis, J. Nieuwenhuijzen, and B. Pluijmers (eds)., *Affordable Housing Governance and Finance: Innovations, Partnerships and Comparative Perspectives.* Abingdon: Routledge, pp. 187–209.

Nielsen, B. G. (2010). Is Breaking Up Still Hard to Do?—Policy Retrenchment and Housing Policy Change in a Path Dependent Context. *Housing, Theory and Society,* 27 (3), 241–257.

Oxley, M. (1995) Private and Social Rented Housing in Europe: Distinctions, Comparisons and Resource Allocation. *Scandinavian Housing and Planning Research,* 12, 59–72.

Poggio, T., and Whitehead, Ch. (2017) Social Housing in Europe: Legacies, New Trends and the Crisis. *Critical Housing Analysis,* 4 (1), 1–10.

Scanlon, K., Fernández Arrigoitia, M., and Whitehead, C. M. (2015). Social Housing in Europe. *European Policy Analysis,* 17, 1–12.

Scanlon, K., and Vestegaard, H. (2007). Social Housing in Denmark. In C. M. E. Whitehead & K. Scanlon (eds)., *Social Housing in Europe.* London: London School of Economics and Political Sciences, pp. 44–54.

Statistics Austria. (2012). Housing Costs. Vienna: National Statistical Institute. www.statistik.at/web_en/statistics/dwellings_buildings/housing_costs/index.html

Tsenkova, S. (2009) *Housing Reforms in Post-socialist Europe. Lost In Transition.* Heidelberg: Springer-Verlag.

Tsenkova, S. (2014) A Tale of Two Cities: Resilience of Social Housing in Vienna and Amsterdam [Krisenfestigkeit der sozialen Wohnungssektoren in Wien und Amsterdam]. In, W. Amann, H. Pernsteiner, and Ch. Struber (eds)., *Wohnbau in Osterreich in Europaischer Perspective.* Vienna: Manz Verlag and Universitatsbuchhandlung, pp. 95–105.

Tsenkova, S. (2019) Social Housing on Trial: Institutions + Policy Design. *Urban Research and Practice*, 12 (1), 1–6.

Tsenkova, S. (2021) *Transforming Social Housing: International Perspectives*. Abingdon: Routledge.

Tsenkova, S., and Vestegaard, H. (2011) Social Housing Provision in Copenhagen, ENHR Conference, University of Toulouse, July 3–8, Workshop 7, p. 16.

Vale, L., Shamsuddin, S., Gray, A., and Bertumen, K. (2014). What Affordable Housing Should Afford: Housing for Resilient Cities. *Cityscape*, 16 (2), 21–50.

van der Veer, J., and Schuiling, D. (2005) The Amsterdam Housing Market and the Role of Housing Associations. *Journal of Housing and the Built Environment*, 20, 167–181.

van Kempen, R., and Priemus, H. (2002) Revolution in Social Housing in the Netherlands: Possible Effects of New Housing Policies. *Urban Studies*, 39 (2), 237–253.

Walker, B., and Salt, D. (2012) *Resilience Practice: Building Capacity to Absorb Disturbance and Maintain Function*. Washington, DC: Island Press.

Walker, B., Salt, D., and Reid, W. (2006) *Resilience Thinking: Sustaining Ecosystems and People in a Changing World*. Washington, DC: Island Press.

PART IV

Design Innovation in Affordable Housing

14

THINKING "OUTSIDE THE BOX" ABOUT AFFORDABLE HOMES AND COMMUNITIES

Avi Friedman

A Need for a New Paradigm

The Next Home demonstration project was proposed as a direct response to contemporary North American households with their diversity of interior design needs and affordability constraints (Figure 14.1). The project extends the research undertaken by the author on the Grow Home project: an affordable, narrow-front, row house prototype of which over 10,000 units were subsequently built in Canada (Rybczynski et al., 1990). A primary consideration in the approach of these prototypes is the economic and demographic changes that have rendered many notions inherent in the traditional design and marketing of housing obsolete.

Old-home ownership models are weakening. The traditional mortgage system requires the borrower to possess a long-term job – a basic security which many people no longer have. Rising costs for land and urban infrastructure justify the building of houses on smaller plots of land in denser communities, while financial insecurity on the part of the homeowners validates a need to purchase an affordable and compact housing unit and consider other paradigms for housing design and marketing.

For many first-time buyers, affordability is a major – if not the only – impediment to home-ownership, since the relative cost of housing has doubled in recent decades (Filion and Bunting, 1990). In a situation where housing prices rise much more steeply than household earnings, purchasing a compact amount of space at a relatively low cost is a means of coping with the housing affordability crisis.[1]

Under strained conditions – both global and personal – potential homeowners are finding that committing a smaller portion of their earnings to housing is a distinctly desirable, if not unavoidable, option. Therefore, buying unpartitioned and unfinished space, with the intention to upgrade and expand at a later date when finances permit, is another affordability strategy that was used in the past and is currently considered by wary homeowners. A parallel, increasingly popular trend has been the opening of home renovation "supermarkets" where homeowners are able to select from a wide range of tools and products that are easy to use and install. It enables them to renovate and expand their homes: a trend that directly complements the idea of user involvement in their unit design.

The new economic landscape has similarly led to dramatic demographic responses. Significantly, while the number of families and households in Canada (and similarly in the U.S.) is

DOI: 10.4324/9781003172949-14

FIGURE 14.1 The Next Home: Full-Scale Prototype.
Source: Author.

increasing, the size of these domestic arrangements is decreasing. This trend towards greater numbers of households is relevant not only to the family dynamic but to an additional note-worthy phenomenon: fewer people are living within families[2] (Statistics Canada, 2001). The effect of these demographics is found in the need for homes that are designed flexibly to reflect the changing nature of a diverse range of occupant groups. At the same time, baby boomers are continuing to have the largest impact on the age structure of the population. Inevitably, fewer numbers of young people will be "supporting" a greater number of older people, a prospect which creates incentives for the elderly to take active measures to safeguard against a precarious future of insufficient or non-existent government pensions, and shortages of suitable institu-tional care housing.

Furthermore, another household type which has gained in numbers over the years is the household composed of only one person. In previous years, young, single people were not considered potential homebuyers. Nowadays, there are not only many young male and female singles who purchase homes on their own before marriage but many who buy homes without the specific intention of marrying in the near future (Friedman, 2001; Friedman and Krawitz, 2002). Homebuilders who neglect to market their products to single people are sacrificing a considerable portion of first-time buyers, as are architects and planners who fail to design hous-ing units and communities with single owners in mind. Flexible design strategies, whereby both traditional and non-traditional households may reside in the very same structure need, therefore, need to be considered.

These socio-economic phenomena were the catalysts for the author's quest for a new housing paradigm, one that will foster a better fit between homebuyers and their chosen accommodation.

The thrust of the approach was to regard the buying procedure as a process of selection from a menu. The author recognized that this choice and flexibility must be reflected in all aspects of housing design and marketing. It has to be factored into the composition of varied households within a single structure, the component choices available and the minimal inconvenience with respect to future modifications to facilitate changes in the occupant's space needs.

This approach stands in stark contrast to current marketing practices of homes whereby only a small number of options, primarily in interior layouts and finishes, are offered to buyers. Having a variety of prototypes – either single- or multi-family dwellings – within the same development, enabling buyers to purchase the amount of space that they need and can afford and permitting them to actively take part in the interior design of their home (e.g. choose kitchen types, locate partitions), is not common in today's housing market. The Next Home intended to demonstrate that a flexible approach to the design, construction and marketing of dwellings can contribute to lowering the financial burden that buyers assume at the outset, thus making housing more affordable.

The Next Home – Flexibility and Cost Reduction

One of the fundamental distinguishing features of the Next Home was the option extended to prospective buyers of purchasing the type and "quantity" of house they presently need and can afford. The feasibility of this option was attained by designing a three-storey structure which can be built, sold and inhabited as a single-family house, duplex or a triplex at a construction cost of $26 per square foot ($380 CAN per square metre). The interior of the units can also be configured according to the wishes of the occupants. Some, as noted in Figure 14.2, may choose to have a home office as part of their unit.

The dimensions of the Next Home have been chosen by adhering to modular sizes and by balancing the advantages and critical limitations of various unit widths. In order to reduce waste of materials, the framing dimensions were subsequently adjusted to a 2-foot (610mm) module to enable sub-floor material which has been cut to be used elsewhere in the frame. A 20-foot (6.1m) width produces spaces of comfortable dimensions and compatibility with municipal regulations while liberating the interior of load-bearing partitions. With diligent planning and material selection, the same principle was implemented to accommodate interior finishes such as drywall and floor tiles. Furthermore, cost savings were achieved not only through efficient use of materials but also through reduced labour requirements as a result of less on-site cutting and fitting (CMHC, 1995). The flexible choice of interior components combined with the efficient design reduces the cost of each 750 square feet (75 square metres) floor to an average of $37,000 ($50,000 CAN) (including serviced land at a cost of $7.50 per square foot [$108 CAN per square metre]) in Montréal.

The Next Home was designed to be subdivided and rearranged in both the pre- and post-occupancy stages in order to accommodate change from one housing type to another, with minimal inconvenience and cost. In order to facilitate future transformation of the dwelling units and to maximize the impression of open space, the stairs were placed along the side longitudinal wall in the middle of the unit and adjacent to the front entrance. By positioning the stairs lengthwise against the side wall, the available floor space was more efficiently increased (Figure 14.3).

The stairs were placed along the side wall, leaving the floor space open.

Another characteristic of the dynamic and flexible design was the confining of the mechanical systems to a vertical shaft and horizontal chaser. The vertical shaft enclosed the water supply, drainage, venting (including heat recovery ventilator – HRV), as well as electrical, telephone and cable. The horizontal chaser was installed to run the length of each floor and facilitated

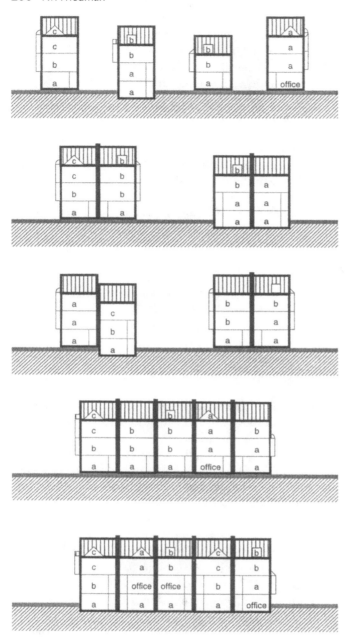

FIGURE 14.2 Subdivision and Volume Options.
Source: Author.

future relocation of rooms. Such an arrangement of chasers permits access to the building systems through the floor – not the ceiling or the walls – thus facilitating all changes without disrupting the neighbouring units. Consequently, regardless of the initial configuration of a Next Home design, the household and its evolving nature are accommodated with minimal renovation work and expense.

The owner of the ground-floor unit is a widower, age 57, who has worked as a civil servant for many years and has been offered an early retirement package due to budget cuts.

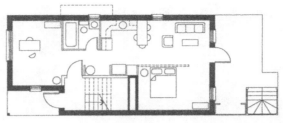

Ground-floor layout plan

The owners of the second-floor unit are a young couple without children who have been married for three years and who, until the purchase of their Next Home unit, rented a one-bedroom apartment in a suburb not far from the city centre.

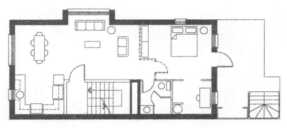

Second-floor layout plan

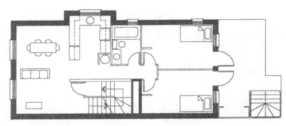

Third-floor layout plan

The owner of the unit on the third floor and the mezzanine at the top of the house is a single mother, age 41, with two school-age children.

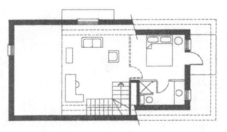

Fourth-floor (mezzanine) layout plan

FIGURE 14.3 Demonstration Unit Plans.
Source: Author.

Components à La Carte

In the interest of responding to today's diverse demographic, lifestyles and the economic capabilities of buyers, the Next Home included a menu of preoccupancy choices. Prospective occupants choose from a catalogue of interior components designed by an architect, determined and made available by the builder (Figure 14.4). User choice enables occupants

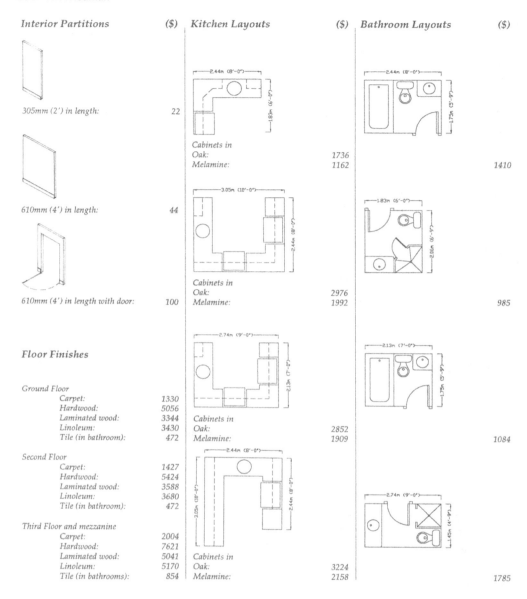

Interior Partitions	($)
305mm (2') in length:	22
610mm (4') in length:	44
610mm (4') in length with door:	100

Floor Finishes

Ground Floor

Carpet:	1330
Hardwood:	5056
Laminated wood:	3344
Linoleum:	3430
Tile (in bathroom):	472

Second Floor

Carpet:	1427
Hardwood:	5424
Laminated wood:	3588
Linoleum:	3680
Tile (in bathroom):	472

Third Floor and mezzanine

Carpet:	2004
Hardwood:	7621
Laminated wood:	5041
Linoleum:	5170
Tile (in bathrooms):	854

Kitchen Layouts	($)
Cabinets in Oak:	1736
Melamine:	1162
Cabinets in Oak:	2976
Melamine:	1992
Cabinets in Oak:	2852
Melamine:	1909
Cabinets in Oak:	3224
Melamine:	2158

Bathroom Layouts	($)
	1410
	985
	1084
	1785

FIGURE 14.4 Menu of Interior Elements and their Costs.
Note: Costs in 1996 $CAN.
Source: Author.

to "consume" only the type and quantity of features they currently require or can afford. These options also include a range of components to assist physically challenged occupants to live independently.

Despite the large number of potential lifestyles that the Next Home aims to accommodate, current trends indicate that the average time spent by an adult on productive activities is

7.8 hours per day, compared with 5.7 hours spent on free time (Lindsay, Devereaux, and Bergob, 1994). Such reduced leisure time is acknowledged and applied directly to the variety of configurations of Next Home units. For example, the preoccupancy flexibility and the capacity for post-occupancy modification of the Next Home have inspired the design of a variety of kitchen layouts to suit a wide range of household configurations. These kitchen arrangements cater to desires for increased work surfaces, space economy and the inclusion of washer, dryer and recycling facilities within this area (Friedman et al., 1993). Moreover, due to the prefabricated nature of kitchen cabinetry, builders can offer a wide selection of layouts without significantly increasing the administrative costs that are incurred by allowing these choices.

Similarly, bathroom choices also vary according to the occupants and their individual needs. Living in a small home does not mean being restricted to a single bathroom: if the number of occupants and their schedules justify a second bathroom, one can be included. Consequently, the bathroom options offered by the Next Home builders will range in size from powder rooms to complete bathrooms with shower, bath, toilet and sink.

An analysis of the layouts of the three units of the Next Home demonstration house, which was displayed on the McGill University campus, illustrates the manner in which various preoccupancy selections of interior components formed three highly personalized, versatile living spaces. Household scenarios have been created for the three units in order to account for choices made at the preoccupancy design stage of each unit and to illustrate the potential inherent to such flexibility.

Flexibility of Building Exterior

Façades of housing developments where identical units are built are often repeated for reasons of economy. Using the same size of window openings and the same style of windows gets a builder a volume discount from his framing team and manufacturer. The effect of such a streetscape, primarily one with row housing, is frequently unpleasant and sterile. In conversation with builders, the author has found that when a carpenter is alerted in advance (i.e. prior to the construction of the frame), he generally does not mind alterations in façade openings as long as the variations are not radically different from one another. With regard to the opening sizes and to the windows themselves, small numbers can be selected and alternated within the composition.

The principles underlying the design of the Next Home façades are the same as those governing the design of the structure and plan: flexibility, individual identity and affordability. The three basic formal strategies for the location and treatment of windows (the essential component in the articulation of residential façades) are systematic repetition, random order and composition. The strategy of systematic repetition accommodates the concept of flexibility by allowing the application of a universal standard of window placement, which could accommodate any function, but such a strategy eliminates the potential for personal expression and must therefore be considered unsuitable. The second option, of random placement of windows based on user preferences and plan consideration, accommodates a high degree of individual identity but runs the risk of undermining the reading of a single module as a unified whole. The result of absolute random placement of windows would be visual chaos. Some vertical emphasis is required to carry the eye upward and indicate the importance of a single unit over the row. The second strategy has therefore been applied to the Next Home façade in combination with the third strategy – that of composition – to obtain a balance between flexibility and unit identity. While compositional concerns impose some measure of constraint on the sizing and placement of windows, they impart a sense of stability and recognizability to the façade. The element of personalization in the placement and the specific sizing of windows reduce flexibility in the long term, in the sense that interior modifications could also lead to changes in the façade. While this aspect may be considered as an obstacle to flexibility, the appropriate choice of façade materials (such as stucco) makes such façade changes relatively easy.

Application of the Next Home Concept

The Next Home concept was implemented in the design and construction of several communities in the greater Montréal area. The builders' main objective, although different in each site, was to take advantage of the flexibility that the design offers both in the unit and the urban levels. Attracting a variety of households with a range of socio-economic backgrounds was meant to expand the builders' profit opportunities. In collaboration with the author, the builders adopted the principles of the demonstration unit to their site as per their specific marketing needs. Affordability through flexibility remained a key factor in all the built projects. The units were sold at an average cost of $48,000 ($65,000 CAN) per 800 sq. ft. of floor area, a price equivalent to 50% of the median price in the Montréal area. The sites were all infill, and the projects benefitted from existing infrastructure and access to civic amenities. Descriptions of three of the projects' main features follow.

Le Faubourg Du Cerf

Le Faubourg du Cerf is a 130-unit project in Longueuil, a suburban town near Montréal. In 1998, the builder, Cleary Construction, sold each floor for $44,000 ($59,900 CAN) in a relatively affluent area of town. The structures faced a communal green space and were built without a basement. The outdoor parking was designed for a ratio of one parking space per unit.

Units of two dimensions were designed in the three-storey structure and mezzanine: 20 feet by 37 feet (6.15 metres by 11.6 metres) and 25 feet by 43 feet (7.7 metres by 13.2 metres) (Figure 14.5). It led to the creation of a floor plate with an average footprint of 800 square feet (80 square metres). The developer offered the option to purchase one, two or all three floors as was proposed in the original concept. He subsequently commented in a conversation with the author that buyers like the flexibility offered to them, which became a significant draw for clients with smaller means. This was demonstrated by the large number of single-storey units sold compared to two- or three-storey units, which enabled many young households to become homeowners.

As part of the marketing process, the developer constructed a temporary sales office near the site. In it, there was a display of drawn floor plans and scale models of possible interior layout options. In addition to preconceived designs, the developer permitted buyers who were interested to participate in the design of their chosen floor. His firm's technicians assisted these clients for a modest administrative fee. The offered unit and those designed by the occupants demonstrate a wide variation of interior arrangements. Some of the units have one bedroom and others two. There is also a variety in the interior components (e.g. kitchens, bathrooms) chosen by the occupants and the placement of these components on the floor. The choices made and their location were an outcome of the household's demographic composition, lifestyle and affordability level.

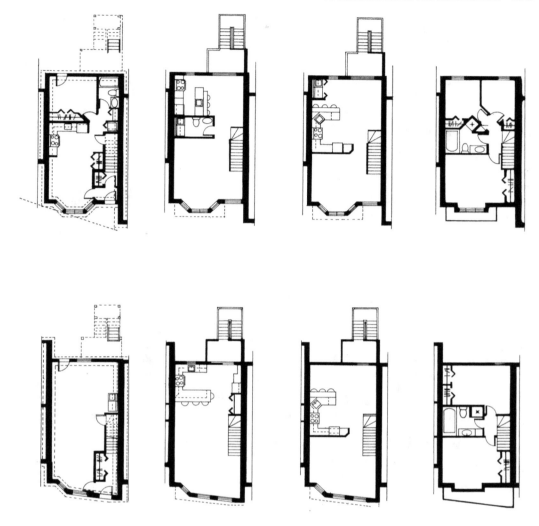

FIGURE 14.5 Plan Options in the Le Faubourg Saint-Michel Project.
Source: Author.

Conclusion

The evolutionary nature of the Next Home – the notion that housing be designed to evolve in layout and use – requires a thoughtfully developed urban design code which balances individual expression with the overall continuity of the street or neighbourhood. Another essential design element is the realization that lifestyle – as one of the defining characteristics of people's lives as citizens, consumers and householders – is a feature that shifts in accordance with a dynamic life cycle process. A home that can be altered with a minimum of effort and expense at a time of change in the lives of its owners is a home that evolves with the life cycles of its household rather than becoming restrictive.

The assessment of the application of the Next Home principles in building sites demonstrated that they responded to the two underlying objectives: affordability and flexibility. Although the builders had to invest more time in the marketing process, buyers were willing to pay the small administrative cost in return for having their choices built. It is no doubt a change to current approaches to home-building and marketing. The flexible, affordable and sustainable design principles of the Next Home respond sensitively to the urgent need to accommodate a wide diversity of contemporary users and household types and to extend affordability to a wider portion of the population.

Notes

1 The "affordability gap" – a much-used phrase with regard to contemporary housing – refers to a situation where the rate of increase of shelter costs far outstrips the rate of increase of income: in the USA, during the 1980s, the median price of a new home rose by over 23%, while median income went up by only 8%; gross rents increased by 14%, while renters' income rose by only 5%.
2 In the USA, married couples with children make up less than one quarter of all households, a significant drop from almost half in 1960 (American Demographics: www.demographics.com).

References

Canada Mortgage and Housing Corporation (CMHC) (1995) *Canada's Exportable Housing*. Ottawa: CMHC.

Filion, P., and Bunting, T.E. (1990) *Affordability of Housing in Canada*. Ottawa: Supply and Services Canada.

Friedman, A. (2001) *The Grow Home*. Montréal: McGill-Queen's University Press.

Friedman, A., Cammalleri, V., Nicell, J., Dufaux, F., and Green, J. (1993) *Sustainable Residential Developments: Planning, Design and Construction Principles («Greening» the Grow Home)*. Montréal: McGill School of Architecture Affordable Homes Program.

Friedman, A., and Krawitz, D. (2002) *Peeking through the Keyhole*. Montréal: McGill-Queen's University Press.

Lindsay, C., Devereaux, M.S., and Bergob, M. (1994) *Youth in Canada*. 2nd Edn, Target Groups Project. Ottawa: Statistics Canada, Catalogue no. 89–511E.

Rybczynski, W., et al. (1990) *The Grow Home*. Montréal: McGill School of Architecture Affordable Homes Program.

Statistics Canada (2001) *Annual Demographic Statistics*. Ottawa: Statistics Canada. Catalogue no. 91–213.

15

AFFORDABLE HOUSING AND DESIGN INNOVATION

A View from Paris

Christelle Avenier and Sasha Tsenkova

Design Quality in Affordable and Social Housing

Decent, affordable housing is critical to the social and economic well-being of any nation. Different housing systems respond to this challenge in different ways. In countries with more diverse housing systems, sustained investment in social, non-market housing continues to provide significant additions to the stock to address affordability challenges and the needs of low-income residents. A number of European countries fall in this category where a diversity of housing providers—public, private and non-profit—operate with substantial government support to finance, build and manage affordable/social housing allocated on the basis of need (Tsenkova, 2019). France is a country where such long-term commitment is supported by urban policies for social inclusion, social mix and inclusive neighbourhood redevelopment. While the need for such housing continues to outstrip supply, particularly in large cities, the social housing projects, being built aim to promote design excellence, create places of community interaction that meet the needs of residents, but also allow them to live with pride and dignity, avoiding physical and social isolation. Good-quality design—often considered an expensive amenity in many other countries with more restrictive housing policies—is promoted through design competitions for social housing projects and programme requirements that allow developments to integrate successfully in the neighbourhood and contribute to its evolving urban fabric. The result is a country dotted with projects that meet and exceed affordable housing requirements and raise the bar in terms of well-planned, well-designed environments. This approach is a departure from the strategies of mass-produced social housing in high-density peripheral housing estates that dominated the social housing developments of the 1960s and 1970s, not just in France but also in many other European countries (Tsenkova, 2014).

Good design in recent housing policies in France, but also globally, is considered to be a critical component for successful social housing development essential for its residents and the community where it is built for years to come. Good design may be the most viable strategy available to improve the quality, functionality, asset value and acceptance of affordable housing. The literature articulates the value of good design principles to address issues of higher-density, appropriate construction materials, building massing and siting strategies. Good design is considered essential; it is much more than aesthetics and a process much more than a product

DOI: 10.4324/9781003172949-15

defined by innovation, expertise, community engagement and user/client feedback (Evans and Beck, 2005). Studies posit that the goal of a good design process is to create developments that (1) meet the needs of the occupants, (2) respond to the building's physical context, (3) enhance their neighbourhoods and (4) are built to last. A number of sustainability design guidelines provide case studies of affordable and social housing developments that are both well-designed and green incorporating environmental and social features. New Jersey Institute of Technology (2003) highlights ten criteria that can be used, such as community context, site design, building design, water conservation and management, energy efficiency and indoor environmental quality. "Designing New York: Quality Affordable Housing" (2018) lays out best practices in planning affordable housing that contribute to the quality, character, diversity and experience of New York City's communities while improving equity and sustainability for residents and neighbourhoods. The developments should foster density and encourage interaction while presenting inviting, warm, safe and dignified living spaces that are durable, easy to maintain, attractive and accessible by transit.

Design Strategies for Affordable Housing

The following design strategies are identified for the successful development of affordable housing and its integration in the neighbourhood:

Create Synergies of Uses

Many affordable and social housing developments serve people that need extra support, such as seniors, formerly homeless individuals or low-income families. Creative use of space, careful attention to architectural detail and thoughtful integration of open spaces, common areas and public art can make a huge difference in the experience and perception of a building.

Projects need to be designed inside-out and outside-in. A strong relationship between community rooms and individual housing units is important. Ensuring that the development provides opportunities for social interaction, community events that can spill out in the courtyard or sidewalk can enhance social activities and help residents feel part of the local community. Incorporating amenities, such as day care, community centres, urban gardens, small-scale retail and business premises at the ground level, can provide an important catalyst for local economic development and integration.

Reweave and Integrate in the Urban Fabric

Affordable housing projects in the past were often isolated from the rest of the city, which often created stigma and exclusion. Good design requires new developments to be 'knit into the urban fabric' so residents have access to transportation, jobs and all community resources. It means that projects in such attractive locations with high land value might have higher density, so a focus on building massing, access and circulation is particularly important to contextualize the design.

An understanding of the orientation and nature of the nearby urban typologies is key to successful integration in the urban landscape (Prevost et al., 2015). Projects should connect to existing typologies and use materials and style that contextualize and enhance integration in the streetscape and the neighbourhood. The design could orient views strategically, perhaps to a nearby landmark or public park, "borrowing" green space or visually connecting interior courtyard or community room which can create a more animated pedestrian realm (Baker and Patel, 2015).

Design Flexible Housing Spaces

Affordable housing is often built with constrained budgets for people with a variety of housing needs. It is important to consider the social aspects, changing life circumstances and needs and provide thoughtful design solutions that allow people to age in place, adjust to changing lifestyles and health challenges while remaining in the place they call home. Flexibility of individual units is a socially and economically efficient way of designing social housing. This may include diversity of housing types to allow a transition through a continuum of units with various supports, accessible design considerations and specific requirements related to the design of kitchens, bathrooms and balconies.

Implement Sustainable Design + Form

The first step to provide an efficient concept for sustainable and affordable housing is through optimal architectural design (Praznik, Butala & Zbašnik-Senegačnik, 2014). The architectural design process involves considering all factors that influence a specific site and performing background research to determine the best possible solution or design. When considering sustainable design, the research phase of the design process will determine where the building should be placed on the site to ensure optimal sun exposure, connectivity, passive air circulation and minimal impacts to existing landscapes (Martty, 2015). Affordable housing design should survive the test of time and remain a positive feature/landmark in the neighbourhood.

Select Green Materials + Assemblies

Once the site and mass of the housing is determined, materials then need to be sourced and building assemblies need to be detailed as we move forward to a more sustainable future (Rothrock, 2014). Green strategies for affordable housing promote the use of materials that are local, renewable, recycled or that have specific life-cycle assessment ratings (Canadian Mortgage and Housing Corporation, 2016). The way that materials are assembled in the building can also have an impact on the efficiency of the housing and contribute to passive efforts supported by the envelope design. Insulation combined with thermal mass installations can work with passive heating and cooling strategies to further decrease energy needs (Glossner, Adhikari & Chapman, 2015; Scheatzle, 2006). With regards to structural assemblies, studies states that wood is one of the oldest and most sustainable materials for building as it is abundant, locally available and versatile (Araujo et al., 2016). Concrete forms and bricks can also be efficient structural materials, providing durable stability and opportunities as a thermal mass (Scheatzle, 2006).

Introduce Energy Efficient Systems + Technology

For conventional buildings, only 5–15% of the total building life-cycle cost is accounted for in the design and construction phase, and therefore the operation of the building accounts for most of the energy and consumption of resources over time. Some of the more popular new technologies for heating and cooling involve ultra-efficient heat pumps, natural gas and low-cost gas heat pumps, which can reduce home energy consumption by more than 30% (U. S. Department of Energy, N.D.). Combining efficient fuel-burning heat-generation methods with advanced insulation, high-efficiency window assemblies, and passive technologies can be very efficient—reducing heat loss through the envelope and loads on mechanical systems (Silverman & Mydin, 2014). There are also opportunities to reduce water use with low-flow fixtures and rain water recycling systems, offsetting 80% of water used in the home (Prevost et al, 2015).

Design Innovation: A View from Paris

In the following sections we provide specific case studies from the practice of Avenier Cornejo Architects in Paris, France, that illustrate the implementation of these design strategies in five award-winning projects. The agency has many achievements in the field of social housing and is a recognized leader in design innovation.

Zac des Lilas, Paris

Social housing with 240 units, 2013
Client: RIVP (Paris Public Housing Agency)
Architects: Avenier Cornejo & Chartier-Dalix
Cost: €19.9m
Surface 9,300m² (SHON)
HQE Labels: Paris Climate Plan, BBC Effinergie
H & E Profile A
Profile: Performance Option

The housing development includes a hostel for immigrants, a hostel for young workers, a day care on the ground floor, as well as communal facilities. Located in the 20th *arrondissement* of Paris, the building is part of an area undergoing immense change including the beltway and the art-house cinema. The structure's homogeneity is due to the building's symbolic nature; it is visible from the area's new public spaces. The high density of the services offered translates into very carefully planned housing, offset by two breaks, which divide the building both horizontally and vertically. The third floor is open, providing a view of Paris and a common space for residents. The vertical rift, a source of light for the circulation facing the street, offers a visual link between hostel life and the area around it (Refer to Figures 15.1 and 15.2).

The Hostel's common amenities (media centre, sport hall, group kitchen) are located on one level (third floor). This area offers the residents of the two hostels the possibility to "live together." It allows them to get to know each other as they participate in different activities. The goal of mixing diverse groups together responds to the desire to bring people from different walks of life under one roof. The vertical rift hollows out the building, creating areas for people to come together and relax on each floor. *The Day Care is* located on the ground floor facing south. The rooms enjoy generous light and extend to the outside play areas. An aerial canopy made from a light metallic mesh covers the play areas, giving a sense of protection without blocking any light. A combination of delicate and rustic plants borders the playground. *The Flats* are compact 18 m² with 2x2 m windows for each studio, designed to maximize the use of the space and to provide a flexible living area. Custom-made furniture is designed by the architect. Shutters mean the kitchenette can be closed off; there are two sleeping options—a pull-out bed or a trundle bed. A bench and wardrobe maximize space and comfort, while the bathrooms are naturally lit using a light well.

The entire building is covered with a homogeneous skin. It is cladded in brick, which is long-lasting and easy to maintain. The bricks are handmade and placed using a square edged joint cut. This semi-industrial manufacturing method gives the brick infinite shades in its anthracite tones. In order to bring out the sensual pleasure of this material, the two caesuras are dressed in copper. The setback of floors 7–9 allows space for some small terraces in varnished aluminum.

Two wind turbines installed on the roof supply energy to the day care during the day and the hostel at night. This choice of energy supply, still in its infancy in an urban setting, is particularly justified here. The building is located in an elevated position and is in a wind corridor. Solar panels located on the roof meet 30% of the building's energy needs.

FIGURE 15.1   Porte des Lilas Urban Development Zone.
Source: Avenier Cornejo Architects.

FIGURE 15.2   Porte des Lilas Young Workers' Hostel and Day Care.
Source: Avenier Cornejo Architects.

Rue Saint-Maur, Paris

Social housing with 14 units and activity space, 2016
Client: elogie-SIEMP
Architects: Avenier Cornejo
Labels: HQE Plan climat de Paris, BBC Effinergie, H&E Profil A Option Performance, RT2012

The social housing apartments at 179 rue Saint-Maur are located on the site of a former well-known space "Nine Billiards". The unhealthy conditions of the structure forced a demolition and reconstruction of the building. Each element of the project reinterprets the dense and complex "faubourien" fabric in order to blend in the existing urban landscape, while emphasizing originality that creates the real identity of the project. The building takes advantage of the narrow plot to develop into a compact and efficient six-storey high shape. The front façade integrates with the street by a raw and minimalist materiality: stained concrete that unfolds from the sidewalk up to the roof curb. A subtle series of diagonal lines cuts the façade in three sections to align with adjacent buildings. This is not just a symbolic gesture to the urban landscape, but a spatial synergy with the existing context (Refer to Figure 15.3).

The plot has a small garden of 47 m² facing south. Each of the 14 units, ranging from studios to 3-bedroom apartments, is flooded with light and has a balcony with a unique place next to the kitchen. The balcony on the sixth floor offers a frame over the Paris rooftops and grants an unexpected one-on-one with the city. The design orients the living room and the kitchen towards the garden, while bedrooms face Rue Saint-Maur. The interior of the apartments is atypical and contradicts the rigidity of the façade by integrating non-standard, daring elements: rounded walls in the living room, folded wall sections and square openings where a wall meets the ceiling, thus creating a contemporary composition of forms that interact with the natural light.

Each architectural element is a detail treated with attention: large casement windows in every room, opening from floor to ceiling in each living room and kitchen, full-height closets with customized hinged doors and perforated louvered shutters along the windows facing the garden. The materials used are of good quality: solid wood windows and enamel sinks.

FIGURE 15.3 Social Housing: A New Version of the Faubourien Style.
Source: Avenier Cornejo Architects.

Rue Bonnet Clichy: The Ambivalence of a Beacon to Reconnect a City

Social housing with 38 units, 2016
Client: Efidis
Architects: Avenier Cornejo
Surface: 2,900 m² (SHON)
Labels: HQE BBC Effinergie
H&E Profil A, RT2012

The 38 social housing units at 10/12 rue Bonnet in Clichy-la-Garenne completed for Efidis are located at the doorstep of Paris, along the périphérique beltway. At the edge of the capital and its inner suburbs, the development looks towards the Clichy-Batignolles district and the new regional court de Renzo Piano. Inside and out, the design approach embodies a strategy that eliminates borders in the city through a building that connects two different urban entities towards a common future (Refer to Figures 15.4).

The multifamily housing sets a unique standard of a new neighbourhood, which will mark the threshold of Clichy-la-Garenne, aptly named "ZAC entrance of the city". It can reach ten stories, allowing the building to make a statement and overlook a large part of its surroundings. The southeast façade on perforated metal vibrates with its louvered shutters and echoes the activity of the city and the speed of the périphérique.

The project responds to the composite fabric of Clichy-la-Garenne, starting a dialogue with its brick landmarks. The northwest and southwest façades feature a dark red 'Lucca' brick full with vivid joints. To render this brick façade even more vibrant, an array of ornamentation connects two expressions of the city, that of the capital and that of the suburbs. A motif in Art

FIGURE 15.4 Social Housing in Paris, Rue Bonnet.
Source: Avenier Cornejo Architects.

Deco tones, two crossing diamonds, originates from the overhanging and recessing of brick headers on one side, and through large-scale metal perforations on the other. On the ground floor facing the street, the façade alternates large spans of brick with glass-covered surfaces such as the entrance and the commercial space. The wall spacing between bricks creates a feeling for intimate spaces and ensures ventilation while maintaining privacy allowing glancing in from certain angles. The hall acts as a transition between the exterior and the interior by a view from the sidewalk into the garden.

The units also entertain this ambiguity of rapport to the city by opening to the heart of the lot through balconies and loggias, which hide behind the perforated metal, or through loggias cut into the brick facing the street. Each apartment has a double exposure transforming the natural light. This also multiplies the viewpoints on an ever-changing city that extends its borders to regenerate its identity.

Rue de Charenton, Paris 12

BEPOS building with 22 dwellings and business premises, 2019
Client: Habitat Social Français
Architects: Avenier Cornejo
Surface: 1,795m² (SDP)
Labels: HQE BEPOS Effinergie 2013, Certified NF Habitat HQE (eight stars), RT2012, Climate Plan of the City of Paris

FIGURE 15.5 BEPOS Energy Efficient Social Housing, Paris.
Source: Avenier Cornejo Architects.

Rue de Charenton is one of the oldest and longest in Paris with a very diverse streetscape. The site is close to Paris City Hall, and a design competition by Habitat Social Français required a replacement of the existing structure. Each element of the project advances the vision for 22 social housing units with sustainability features that reinterpret the unique urban fabric while creating a real identity of the project (Refer to Figures 15.5).

Our approach for the design of "BEPOS", which produces more energy than it consumes, was to think first of maximizing the natural efficiency of the site. The team proposed a compact U-typology building, with a large frontage on the garden, facing southwest. Building massing capitalizes on three successive withdrawals on the street side as well as on overflow on the road carried over from the existing structure. The brick cladding of the façade ensures coherence and a harmonious relation with the immediate environment. The sun-drenched garden façade vibrates with perforated aluminum shutters. This system allows thermal regulation and intimacy of the terraces and interiors. The two gable walls outline a geometric design thanks to bricks of different nature (glazed, enamel blue, glass). Larger apartments have natural ventilation, private outdoor area, terraces or loggias.

The entrance extends the continuity of Rue Bignon. Framed by the windows of the business premises and common areas, it creates a "visual breakthrough" to the garden. A garden is located in heart of islet, a cool and natural place in balance with the housing. Selected vegetation, left free, allows easy and occasional maintenance.

Rue Dareau, Paris 14

Student Housing & Music Facilities
Status: in progress
Client: RIVP
Architects: Avenier Cornejo
Surface: 2,857m² (SDP)
Labels: HQE Label E + C level E2C1, Effinergie +

The Ourcq Canal, steeped in history, is a testimony to a continuous evolution. It has precious historical buildings, while it continues to evolve to adapt to the needs of urban life. The three buildings, property of ZAC Grands Moulin de Pantin, built by Emerige and Semip, are located on the canal. The design approach respected the exceptional location and its industrial heritage, while capitalizing on contemporary architecture for the layout of the buildings. The programme includes a cultural/music facility for the association La Sirène and 50 student housing units at 18–20 rue Dareau. One of the features of the project is the creation of a breakthrough, visible from the square. It acts as a breath, a visual extension of the plant party, extending the island's heart. This opening creates a unique sense of place, integrating the three buildings and a garden of 878 m². An interior and exterior link is made possible with a large number of terraces, loggias and balconies (Refer to Figure 15.6).

The project is conceived as a homogeneous whole—sober and refined. Each of the brick buildings has a specific hue that identifies them. The windows as well as the shutters are in metal-coloured aluminium, as well as the guards and the underside of the balconies. In the same spirit as the brick, a metallic shade identifies each frame. Strong elements emerge to animate the façades of the project following the orientation and bringing a reading of district and an urban visibility. The green roofs, treated as a "5th façade", preserve the visual comfort of the residents. The greening of the roof promotes landscaping and helps to fight against the heat island effect. These roofs also provide a refuge for insects and birds and fight against fragmentation of the environment. The inertia

FIGURE 15.6   Student Social Housing and Music Facilities, Paris.
Source: Avenier Cornejo Architects.

of the earth mass makes it possible to manage rainwater and to protect the building against large temperature variations. It greatly increases the insulation of the roof, usually a source of heat losses.

This design approach leads to transversal approaches that mix scales. In a journey from the general to the particular, the morphology, the materiality, the spatiality, the systems and the uses are considered. This approach favours simplicity and architectural quality in order to be part of a sustainable strategy.

Concluding Comments

Social housing projects in Paris are embedded in a dense interconnected urban environment, often close to the historic city centre. The planning and design requirements are complex and the myriad approvals and community consultations are challenging to navigate. Design competitions are a standard process to identify the best and the most innovative solution for new social housing developments in the context of urban regeneration. The new sites become an important urban portal for social integration and perform a role of a hub within the Parisian system of interconnected neighbourhoods; they work from the inside-out to connect people to jobs, parks and community spaces and reinforce urban, social and cultural transfer (Gausa et al., 2019). Resonating with neighbourhood buildings and streetscapes, the projects prioritize urban dialogue, elegance in building massing and use of materials in a sensitive way. Schools, day care, community spaces and pocket parks often become part of the social housing projects. The goal is to create dynamic movement and rhythm associated with the rich architecture of the past in the immediate environment, optimization of planning rules and design with sustainability and environemntal performance in mind. This design puzzle often integrates the layering of a variety of strategies to enhance sustainability— from the quest for compact form and housing diversity, to incorporation of green roofs, grey water heat recovery, rainwater harvesting, solar energy and solar filters in the new addition to the historic landscape. Excellence by design is essential for the long-term success of social housing and its good vibrations in the Parisian neighbourhood.

References

Baker, D., and Patel, A. (2015). 11 Strategies for Building Community with Affordable Housing. *Urban Land Magazine*, February 13. Washington, DC: Urban Land Institute.

Canadian Mortgage and Housing Corporation. (2016). Sustainable Building: A Materials Perspective. Retrieved from http://aanb.org/wp-content/uploads/2016/08/sustainable_materials.pdf

Evans, D., and Beck, J. (2005). *Good Design: The Best Kept Secret in Community Development*. New York: Local Initiatives Support Corporation.

Gausa & Raveau Actarquitectura and Avenier-Cornejo Architects. (2019). *Good Vibrations. Clichy Batignolles*. Paris: Gausa & Raveau Actarquitectura and Avenier-Cornejo Architects.

Glossner, S. J., Adhikari, S., and Chapman, H. (2015). Assessing the Cost Effectiveness of LEED Certified Homes in Kentucky. *Journal of Technology Studies*, 41(1), 10–19.

Martty, M. (2015). The Difference between Green and Sustainable. Sourceable. Retrieved from https://-sourceable.net/difference-green-sustainable/

New Jersey Institute of Technology, Center for Architecture and Building Science Research (NJIT). (2003). *Bringing the Power of Design to Affordable Housing: An Evaluation of the Affordable Housing Design Advisor*. Washington, DC: U.S. Department of Housing and Urban Development, Office of Policy Development and Research.

New York City Design/AAA Housing. (2018). *Designing New York: Quality Affordable Housing*. New York: NYC Public Design Commission City Hall.

Praznik, M., Butala, V., and Zbašnik-Senegačnik, M. A. (2014). Simple Method for Evaluating the Sustainable Design of Energy Efficient Family Houses. *Strojniski Vestnik / Journal of Mechanical Engineering* [serial online], 60(6), 425–436.

Prevost, G., Baetz, B. W., Razavi, S., and El-Dakhakhni, W. (2015). Retrofitting Suburban Homes for Resiliency: Design Principles. *Journal of Urban Planning & Development*, 141(3), 1–10.

Rothrock, H. (2014). Sustainable Housing: Energy Evaluation of an Off-Grid Residence. *Energy & Buildings*, 85287–85292.

Scheatzle, D. (2006). Combining Radiant and Convective Systems with Thermal Mass for a More Comfortable Home. *ASHRAE Transactions*, 112(1), 253–268.

Silverman, N., and Mydin, A. O. (2014). Green Technologies for Sustainable Building. *Acta Technica Corvininesis – Bulletin of Engineering*, 7(3), 87–94.

Tsenkova, S. (2014). A Tale of Two Cities: Resilience of Social Housing in Vienna and Amsterdam [Krisenfestigkeit der sozialen Wohnungssektoren in Wien and Amsterdam]. In Amann, W., Pernsteiner, H., and Struber, Ch. (eds)., *Wohnbau in Österreich in Europäischer Perspective*. Vienna: Manz Verlag and Universitatsbuchhandlung, pp. 95–105.

Tsenkova, S. (2019). Social Housing on Trial: Institutions + Policy Design. *Urban Research and Practice*, 12(1), 1–6.

16

AFFORDABLE HOUSING DESIGN + A NEW URBAN ERA IN EUROPEAN CITIES

Paul Karakusevic

Introduction

In cities across Europe, a new generation of practices is transforming affordable housing. Responding to ongoing demand and working with a set of newly energised public and community-focused clients, architects are once again playing a crucial role in addressing how homes are delivered at scale and advancing high standards of design ushering in a new urban era.

Across Europe, definitions of affordable and social housing vary from city to city. Each has its own municipal tradition, political landscape, architectural preferences and, alongside them, often complex funding cultures (Fezer et al., 2015). In London, there is a revival in direct public-led delivery; in Vienna and Berlin, cooperative and community projects are strongly supported; while in the cities of the Netherlands, a range of intermediate options is routinely pursued (Power, 1997). Each housing response and delivery methodology stems from its own context, but common to all is the idea that there are alternatives to a purely market-oriented system of provision, and that these are all crucial in delivering high quality, using resources sustainably and addressing equality of cities everywhere.

In 2015, Karakusevic Carson Architects was commissioned by the Royal Institute of British Architects (RIBA) to survey this emerging landscape and take stock of the range of different approaches being pursued by a range of practices across Europe. The result was a book *Social Housing – Definitions and Design Exemplars* published in 2017, which formed the basis of a touring design exhibition shown in London, New York and Calgary. Adopting a selection of criteria, with an emphasis upon exemplar processes with clients and communities, it features 24 case studies from 20 practices in seven countries. The international scope of the research highlights the variety of affordable and public housing projects being pursued and the range of innovative and sustainable design strategies that make them possible (Karakusevic and Batchelor, 2017). This chapter incorporates some of these examples and offers insights on the innovative ways in which affordable housing is being delivered in Rotterdam, Vienna and London. These projects pursue excellence through design, challenge how homes are created today and inform the design of affordable housing in future cities. Among the schemes discussed are public projects led by local authorities in London and collective schemes led by residents in Vienna and in Rotterdam. The projects of Karakusevic Carson Architects illustrate how design-led responses are

DOI: 10.4324/9781003172949-16

enabling the implementation of new housing programmes and delivering affordable housing for communities in mixed-use, medium-density developments. These design and planning strategies are a vital part of ushering in a new era for affordable housing in cities.

Renovation Strategies

In the years following the Second World War, many of Europe's cities were left in a state of ruin and nearly all pursued programmes of reconstruction, with new housing embracing principles of modernist design and concrete construction. In the 1930s, pioneering projects in France and Germany did much to establish an appetite for a bold new architectural approach, and the outcome across the continent were ambitious variations on the tower or slab block in the urban landscape. While there are many celebrated and iconic examples of this approach, there are many more that have suffered badly in structural terms as the buildings reached the end of their life cycle. In some cases, housing became socially obsolete in the types of homes provided due to its inability to respond to changing demographics. Lack of integration in the urban landscape reinforced patterns of social and spatial segregation. Across many cities, the fabric of large post-war estates proved difficult to maintain, pushing municipal budgets amplified by economic change to the limits and leading to neglect and decline in the 1980s. Addressing the physical legacy of this period is one of the unifying architectural themes of European affordable housing today.

Knikflats, Oommord, Rotterdam, The Netherlands BIQ / Hans van der Heijden

In Rotterdam in the Netherlands, one district created in the post-war period is that of Ommoord on the northern outskirts of the city. Designed by Bauhaus urban planner Lotte Stam-Beese in 1968, the ambitious project was built to house 35,000 people at a variety of scales and densities, with the largest type of housing including 15 eight-storey L-shaped blocks in a wide-open landscaped setting. The denser part of the district was constructed as a series of high-rise slab block to accommodate a typically low-income community. BIQ's scheme dealt with four of the eight-storey blocks, which required renovation and updating. The estate's size means that any intervention in an individual block is also a strategic response to the whole, so the architect became a strategic member of the estate management team (van Der Heijden and Wessels, 2013).

The Knikflats project by BIQ / Hans van der Heijden was initiated in 2006 (Figure 16.1). The architect became part of the estate management team and worked closely with residents and client Woonbron Prins Alexander – one of around 425 registered housing associations who manage the bulk of the affordable housing stock in the Netherlands. In reconsidering the estate's future, demolition was not considered an option, partly due to the fact that many of the problems which have arisen over time could be traced back to the design of the communal access system and layout. In each of the huge concrete buildings, the 176 dwellings shared just two lifts and one entrance, putting the spaces under intense pressure. Residents had over half a century appropriated the neighbourhood as best they could, but the estate's abstract design made meaningful interaction between the buildings and the public spaces alongside them very challenging.

Two of the buildings were redeveloped as accommodation for the elderly people with the addition of a medical centre at the ground floor. In others, new homes were added to the bases of the blocks, purposefully expanding the original envelopes to create new inhabitable space

FIGURE 16.1 Architectural Intervention to the Blocks.
Source: Hans van der Heijden by Stefan Muller.

and employing earth red bricks to create warmth and texture in contrast to hard concrete above (Karakusevic and Batchelor, 2017). Two further blocks were redeveloped within the so-called 'customer choice' concept, a Dutch scheme similar to that of the 'Right to Buy' in the United Kingdom, but with tighter controls on occupation and sale. This means that the socio-economic diversity of the residents will be greater, along with the existing ethnic diversity among the occupants across the blocks. BIQ's intervention is the result of a ten-year process to implement careful organisational changes to the blocks, avoiding unnecessary cosmetic changes in favour of meaningful, long-term alterations to adapt the blocks to a contemporary way of living.

Kings Crescent Estate, London, Karakusevic Carson Architects

In London, the Kings Crescent Estate renovation, led by Karakusevic Carson Architects in collaboration with Henley Halebrown for Hackney Council, similarly adopts a strategic approach to the reinvention of a post-war estate with a master plan providing 750+ mixed-tenure homes with circa 500 new dwellings created alongside the retention and refurbishment of 175 existing homes (see Figure 16.2). Common to much comprehensive inner-city redevelopment across the United Kingdom, the 1970s era estate had suffered as a result of its disconnect from the wider historic neighbourhood, with a set of defensive linear blocks severing connections and the creation of a closed-off network of mono-cultural buildings and spaces within.

Started in 2012, our approach includes the intensive refurbishment of retained homes, residential infill of garage spaces and the introduction of new homes at its heart. Responding to the geometry of older blocks, new buildings work to form a series of rectilinear courtyards either

FIGURE 16.2 Kings Crescent Estate Model and Street View.
Source: Karakusevic Carson Architects, street view by Jim Stephenson.

side of a broad and open central street, with new workspace, community and retail uses introducing new life and activity. Completed in 2017, the first new buildings take their form from London's traditional urban 'mansion block' typologies and anchor the estate within the area with materials that complement the grain of nearby Victorian villas and terraces. Phases three and four received planning approval in 2019 and will be completed in 2023.

At Kings Crescent, one of the greatest challenges faced by our studio was how to engage with a community left frustrated after 18 years of false starts. In 2001, approximately half of the estate had been demolished leaving a large hoarded-off wasteland of rubble. Later attempts to redevelop the area in 2007 and 2011 had both failed. Through regular steering group meetings and consultation events, residents were involved from the start on everything, from developing a site-wide strategy and the planning of new streets, right through to the internal specification of materials and the details of new homes. The role of people in the successful development of new affordable and public housing is crucial for cities everywhere. Consultation and engagement have been the core part of London's development process for many years, but there have been notable instances where processes have lacked sincerity and outcomes have not reflected local need in terms of the type of housing delivered. To promote a new level of transparency in the city, the Greater London Authority has introduced compulsory ballots with residents on grant-funded projects to ensure consultation when demolition of existing affordable housing is proposed. Introduced in 2016, it seeks to set a new benchmark for how engagement, participation and co-design processes work.

New Processes with Residents

Wohnprojekt Wien, Vienna, Austria, by Einszueins

Vienna has a long history of government-driven innovation in social housing provision as part of its strong tradition of welfare provision. Even today, Austria's biggest landlord remains the City of Vienna, which owns around 220,000 rental apartments, while 60% of all Vienna households live in subsidised apartments. Throughout its post-war history, Austria has been particularly resistant to market forces, resulting in a stable housing market. Housing co-operatives form part of this history and the Einszueins' project in Vienna continue these themes in a contemporary context.

Located in the newly master planned neighbourhood of Nordbahnhofgelände, an area which for many years was the site of a railway freight yard, the 'Wohnprojekt Wien' by architects Einszueins follows in the new tradition of Vienna development. In this process, the city authorities purchase land, determine a new layout for the area and then tender out plots for development according to a sustainability framework. Plots are then sold to qualifying developers on the merits of the design proposals who receive subsidies to offset the development costs. Einszueins worked closely with the 'Wohnprojekt Wien' housing group to create 39 co-housing units which accommodate a wide mix of generations, languages and cultures including 67 adults and 25 children in a single building (Figure 16.3). The project is funded through a complex system of membership and 'asset pooling' which aims to keep the cost of housing permanently low. This model requires residents to commit to long-term investment and to engage proactively in the financial management of the building, as well as to maintain a 10% liquidity fund for maintenance of the building. This comparatively large co-housing organisation has an advantage of being able to retain a funding structure which smaller groups do not always have the capacity to pursue (Karakusevic and Batchelor, 2017).

The main emphasis of the project is the will of a self-organised community with the common aim to live together in the city in a sustainable, collaborative and open-minded way. The group describes itself as 'sociocratically organised', meaning that decisions are not based on a vote system but on the entire group openly discussing issues until a unanimous verdict is reached. This attitude is mirrored by that of the architects' proposals to maintain a level of simplicity in the structure to allow for user specification. Unit sizes range from 35 m² studios

FIGURE 16.3 Wohnprojekt Wien Co-Housing.
Source: Einszueins by Hertha Hurnaus.

to 150 m^2 shared apartments. Generous community and commercial spaces are managed by residents, which allows facilities such as a bike repair workshop and communal kitchens to create a lively and activated ground floor. Electric vehicles are used for residents to share trips, a weekly market is organised on the forecourt and vegetable gardens form part of the communal property.

The design strategy was initiated from the outset as a participatory process for the planning of the communal spaces and individual apartment units. This continued with the car sharing, a communal garden for the neighbourhood and ends with the common ownership of the building, resulting in active participation during all stages of the project's development. One of the fundamental aims of the project was to achieve a high level of individualisation inside the building envelope and to express this in terms of architectural design. For example, the void which runs alongside the main staircase facilitates spontaneous communication between residents, while the individual apartment units can act as spaces for retreat.

Some of the common spaces are located on the top floor, including a sauna, library and guest rooms, whereas on the lower floors, there is a communal kitchen, workshops and event rooms including a playroom for children and adults (Figure 16.4). The community also contributes to a fund, which allows two housing units to be used to accommodate people particularly in need of social care in the local community. The ground-floor commercial space is occupied by a small grocery store, which provides locally sourced produce to the community as well as hosting weekly performances and exhibitions. The notion of sustainability within the built environment is one which is often misused as a term for a developer's sales pitch or merely a blanket requirement placed on all new developments. However, in this model of co-housing, the term signifies a different meaning, specifically as a deliberate choice to live in a restrained and cooperative way.

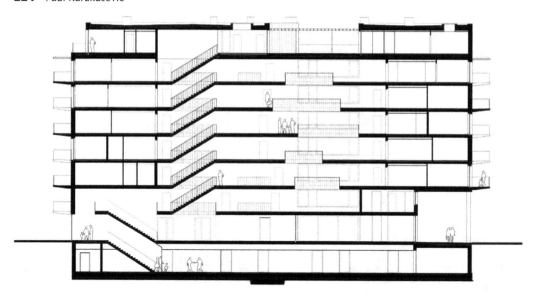

FIGURE 16.4 Wohnprojekt Wien Co-Housing – Common Spaces.
Source: Einszueins.

Council Housing Reinvented

In London, the re-establishment of a strong new public culture has been the key story of the past 20 years. At the end of the 19th century, London pioneered public housing and new dwelling standards. However, as funding was drastically cut in the 1980s, the abilities of local authorities or councils to plan their own affordable housing with any autonomy were curtailed. Shifting to a market-oriented system, the UK's urban public housing estates became neglected, with land sold off for redevelopment by the market, with very few terms and conditions attached about what types of dwellings should follow. In recent years, as a result of legislation allowing local government to lead council housing projects and borrow money, more new public projects are emerging that are setting new standards. In London, direct delivery of public housing is devolved to 32 Boroughs or municipalities. These local authorities or councils have their own housing portfolios, their own tenants and their own holdings, which they can put to use directly to create the type of housing and sustainable mixed urban neighbourhoods they want to see.

Located in the east of the city, The London Borough of Hackney was among the first to embrace a new housing programme of scale in 2008. Adopting a range of strategies including stock refurbishment, strategic infill on small sites as well as large housing estate redevelopment, the borough today uses its own land to reverse years of underinvestment. It has developed a new ambition for design within an expanded housing team, a process supported by London's upper tier of government, the Greater London Authority, through planning, training and enabling of affordable housing through provision of funds and subsidies.

Colville Estate, London, United Kingdom, by Karakusevic Carson Architects

One of the earliest and largest projects taken on by the council is the Colville Estate by Karakusevic Carson Architects. Adopted in 2012, the master plan for a worn-out 1950s estate consists of

FIGURE 16.5 Colville Estate Master Plan Model.
Source: Karakusevic Carson Architects.

eight phases that will create a new neighbourhood of 925 homes with new amenities set amidst a network of humanely scaled public spaces and streets (Figure 16.5). As part of the design, we worked closely with an active and articulate community to realise a shared vision for comprehensive redevelopment and a totally reconceived piece of the city. The old estate consisted of 438 homes organised in rows of linear blocks typical of the post-war period, with inward-looking service-dominated streets and courtyards, car parks and inaccessible or unused green spaces, which had little relationship with the wider area. Embracing the wishes of the existing community to live in low- to medium-rise housing, our approach creates a new townscape with a range of building types containing a mix of public, affordable and market sale homes and new amenities set amidst a network of accessible streets and humanely scaled public spaces.

Phase one was completed early in the programme in 2011 and enabled the process of rehousing existing residents. Phase two (Figure 16.6) was completed in 2017, and at its heart is a courtyard block with terraced and apartment buildings which were inspired by nearby historic forms that coalesce around a generous communal space at its core. Behind its various street facades are a series of interlocking and stacked homes that enables a wide variety of accommodation types and helps achieve a high density of homes. Brick colours and the textures of openings and balconies were chosen with the community and are used to create architectural order, but also vibrancy with recessed private terraces at roof level breaking the roofline line at regular intervals to create further character and generating exceptional living spaces.

Phase three (Figure 16.6) was completed in 2017 and includes Hoxton Press, two taller buildings designed in collaboration with David Chipperfield and taken forward for market

FIGURE 16.6 Colville Estate Developments in Phases Two and Three.
Source: Karakusevic Carson Architects by Peter Landers.

sale by a commercial developer to provide extensive cross-subsidy for affordable homes in the scheme. To ensure the architectural vision created for these elements was seen through, the developer was selected by the council after detailed planning with full design intent drawings and specifications had been achieved.

Dujardin Mews, London, United Kingdom, by Karakusevic Carson Architects

In Enfield, North London, we worked in a similar way to help the council realise Dujardin Mews, the first housing delivered directly by the borough in nearly four decades. Completed in 2017, the 38-home project forms the first phase of the Ponders End district rebuilding programme tasked to provide replacement homes for the neighbouring Alma Estate. Designed in collaboration with Maccreanor Lavington Architects, the project makes use of a narrow 0.70 hectare site that was formerly part of a nearby gas works (petroleum facility/station). This remediated land, next to the Oasis Academy School and a wider two-storey suburban neighbourhood, is now home to a new street of high-quality housing arranged in two terraces, establishing permeability through the site and important pedestrian connections between north and south. The development is a mix of 1-, 2-, 3- and 4-bedroom homes including dual aspect dwellings, with entrance doors facing the street to encourage activity, natural surveillance and create opportunities for neighbours to meet. The scale and massing of the street reflects the urban grain of the surrounding area to create a domestic and intimate character (Figure 16.7).

The eastern terrace comprises predominantly three-storey family homes, with an apartment building to the south. Houses are orientated west to the street, with sheltered first-floor terraces facing to the south, creating a layout where no habitable rooms overlook the neighbouring school. The design of the townhouses featuring pitched and mono-pitched roofs creates an articulated and varied street profile, which allows daylight to flood the street. The west terrace consists mainly of two-storey houses, with three-storey homes to the north, creating a mix of family-sized houses – maisonettes and apartments – in addition to hidden courtyards oriented behind brick street facades (Figure 16.8).

FIGURE 16.7 Council Housing Dujardin Mews – Street Profile.
Source: Karakusevic Carson Architects.

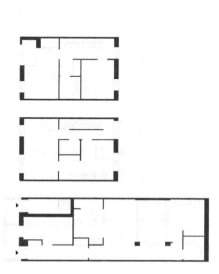

FIGURE 16.8 Council Housing Dujardin Mews – The Scheme.
Source: Karakusevic Carson Architects.

Internal layouts for all homes exceed the London Housing Design Guide with generous spaces, substantial floor-to-ceiling heights, natural light and ventilation. The use of high-quality materials and detailing in the form of textured brickwork, combined with pearl composite windows and matching metalwork, creates a sophisticated palette, which draws inspiration from the typical London street. Articulated brickwork predominantly featured on homes on the western terrace is designed to create interest up-close (see Althorpe and Batchelor, 2019). The project also enhances wider neighbourhood connections, ensuring the new homes are rooted in the ecology of the area and are an active part of the urban whole. New public spaces create a landscaped route through the street and areas for social activities. Community amenity to the north of the site buffers the Academy School's car drop-off area and provides a new play area and seating for residents and a pedestrian entrance to the new street. The success of Dujardin Mews is unprecedented for a local authority-led public housing project and is the result of an ambitious and cohesive client and design team.

Learning From European Affordable Housing Projects

Cities are many years in the making. To address the dual challenges of housing affordability and sustainability in the 21st century, urban leaders and clients need to take a long-term view, and, as the examples from Europe illustrate, they need to be increasingly ambitious in their thinking. Uniting many of the innovative social and affordable housing projects is a revitalised and robust public sector. Cities need strong civic cultures and proactive leadership that can act with autonomy and who are enthusiastic about design quality and working with communities. This means understanding neighbourhoods and knowing what great housing looks like, new and historically. But it also means implementing rigorous procurement processes and holding design teams to account throughout the process of development to maintain design intent, build quality and uphold environmental standards. To support these outcomes, robust spatial frameworks and a nuanced view to development have strong roles to play.

In many cities, the public sector or municipal body owns and may acquire large volumes of land. Rather than selling it off, it can put this asset to use to develop housing not only for and by itself, but in partnership with others as part of progressive good growth strategies. The examples of Vienna and in London demonstrate how local government can embed criteria at master planning stages to blend strategies between new build, infill and refurbishment and to promote better mix and a broader range of urban design responses, tenures and typologies.

Over the past 15 years, the United Kingdom has absorbed many lessons, and a growing number of urban councils are embracing new approaches. Momentum is now building around direct delivery even in cities where there was historic reluctance to develop public housing and pioneer programmes. New York, Sydney and Melbourne are starting to consider such approaches to respond to a growing shortage of affordable housing. To ensure these become reality, housing professionals of all kinds will need to think differently about city making and embrace the full cannon of alternative methods to create truly affordable and sustainable cities that can thrive and belong to everyone. Notwithstanding immense diversity of design approaches to affordable housing across European cities today, a few key strategies remain important.

Regionalism

Housing in most European countries is a devolved issue and is able to work independently of central government. In the case of the United Kingdom, after years of a strongly centralised state in terms of policy, new housing teams operating within local governments today are devising their own plans and borrowing to create public housing, often in ways that have to circumnavigate central government policy. Affordable housing needs ambitious and proactive local government that can work closely with communities and with the knowledge of local need (Förster and Menking, 2017, 2019).

Client

Great housing design needs clients that are ambitious about quality. This means knowing what great housing looks like, new and historically, but also about implementing rigorous and open procurement processes and holding design teams and value engineers/surveyors to account throughout the process to maintain quality and design intent.

Public Land

In the UK and in many other European states, the public sector owns and may acquire large volumes of land (University of the West of England, 2019). Rather than selling it off, it can put this asset to use to develop housing not only for and by itself, but as part of a nuanced and wide-ranging planning strategy. In Vienna and now in London, local or city government can develop a master plan for a site and release land for sale to a range of developers on a conditional basis in order to get the tenure mix and design quality it wants.

Funding

Public housing needs direct funding to enable its development. Government grants and seed funding can work to prepare sites and guarantee additional borrowing to keep prices low and offset risk to local authorities. Small funding in these areas can yield long-term benefits (Kubey, 2018).

Nuance

Refurbishment of old housing estates and neighbourhoods must be responsive to need and what is desirable and achievable on site. One size does not fit all. Developments across Europe actively blend strategies on site with new build supporting infill and refurbishment (Boughton, 2018).

Long Termism

New housing rarely happens at speed. Projects across Europe have been years in the making and they are the result of long-held plans that embed long-term environmental + retrofit objectives, for example, Passivhaus and strategies of land assembly and phased development. A long-term project requires ring-fenced funding and political commitment so that communities are not blighted by stalled processes and disputes (Housing Europe, 2019).

People

In various parts of Europe, people-led housing is a strong part of delivery. Elsewhere, notably in the UK, co-design processes are taking forward schemes that have previously been resisted by communities. New affordable housing on public land requires an open and upfront dialogue with their future inhabitant and those in the neighbourhoods they adjoin (Swenarton, 2018).

References

Althorpe, M. and A. Batchelor (2019). Revolutionary Low Rise – Informing London's Suburban Densification. http://karakusevic-carson.com/system/dragonfly/production/2019/10/28/8bt67uvljt_Revolutionary_Low_Rise_PDF_071019.pdf, accessed October 5, 2019.

Boughton, J. (2018). *Municipal Dreams: The Rise and Fall of Council Housing.* London: Verso.

Fezer, J., C. Hiller, and N. Hirsch (2015). *Housing after the Neoliberal Turn: International Case Studies.* Berlin: Spector Books & HKW.

Förster, W. and W. Menking (2017). *The Vienna Model: Housing for the Twenty-First Century City.* Berlin: Jovis.

Förster, W. and W. Menking (2019). *The Vienna Model 2.* Berlin: Jovis.

Housing Europe (2019). Website. www.housingeurope.eu/, accessed October 21, 2019.

Karakusevic, P. and A. Batchelor (2017). *Social Housing: Definitions and Design Exemplars.* Newcastle upon Tyne: RIBA Publishing.

Kubey, K. (2018). *Housing as Intervention: Architecture towards Social Equity.* West Sussex: John Wiley & Sons Ltd.

Power, A. (1997). *Estates on the Edge: Social Consequences of Mass Housing in Northern Europe.* New York: St. Martin's Press.

Swenarton, M. (2018). *Cook's Camden: The Making of Modern Housing.* London: Lund Humphries.

University of the West of England (2019). *History of Council Housing (UK).* Bristol: University of the West of England. https://fet.uwe.ac.uk/conweb/house_ages/council_housing/print.htm, accessed October 6, 2019.

van Der Heijden, H., & Wessels, R. (2013). *Habitat: Biq bouwt de stad / biq Builds the City.* In Woodman, E. (ed). Rotterdam: Nai Uitgevers Publishers: 4–8.

17

AMSTERDAM

More than a Social Housing Project

Jeroen Atteveld and Bas Liesker

Social Housing in the Netherlands

heren 5 architecten creates living environments where dreams can take flight, where sustainability and durability are key factors, where residents and users feel safe and that we are proud to call ours. Each project we take on is different in terms of design, location and programme. But the underlying theme in all of our work is the desire to understand the minds, requirements and needs of the users. heren 5 is an architectural firm with a wealth of experience in the private and social housing sector. Approximately a third of our current client base is made up of housing associations, and most of these projects are located in Amsterdam. In this chapter, we briefly describe the history and development of social housing in the Netherlands and talk about our study into the living preferences of various target groups. Then we illustrate how these ideas are implemented in designs of social housing projects.

Amsterdam has been characterised as the "Mecca of Social Housing" since the beginning of the last century. Since *1901 the Housing Act,* the construction of social rented housing has been a main policy target of Amsterdam municipality, which owns most of the land within its boundaries and leases it to real estate owners. After the Second World War, the size of the social rental housing increased rapidly in Amsterdam, from 18% in 1950 to 58% in 1995, replacing the private-rented as the dominant sector. Like in several European countries, the restructuring of the welfare state in the Netherlands has led to a decline of the social rented housing sector and a change from a broadly accessible system to a means-tested system. But of all member states in the European Union, the Netherlands still has the highest percentage of social housing of 30%. It is owned by independent housing associations, not by local governments. Middle-income groups also live in social housing; however, we seem to be in a new era now. At the national level, the Dutch government is trying to reduce the social rented housing sector in favour of the market sector. Housing associations, so the idea goes, should confine themselves to their core task of providing housing for people with low incomes. In Amsterdam, social housing has declined to 44%, while homeownership (24%) and private rental (32%) have increased in the last decade (Van der Veer, 2019).

Since May 2018, Amsterdam has had a local government consisting of the Green Left, D66 (Liberal Democrats), Socialist Party and PvdA (Social Democrats). The affordability of new housing is now a central theme. The local government strives to build 7,500 new housing units

DOI: 10.4324/9781003172949-17

annually, of which 2,500 are social housing units constructed by housing associations and 1,670 are medium-rent dwellings. In 2017, Amsterdam housing associations acquired six municipal buildings including former schools, health care centres and office buildings, with the intention of transforming them into more than 200 social housing units. These are also intended primarily for young households and refugees with a residence status. They are housed in a mixed manner to facilitate integration in the immediate environment. The housing associations and the municipality inform and involve residents in the surrounding neighbourhoods during development of the transformation plans through meetings between the current and new residents, creation of common meeting spaces and programming activities (Van der Veer, 2019).

For Whom?

"For whom do we build?" is a question we continually ask ourselves.

Since we do not work for private clients but for housing associations and private developers, we have little or no contact with the future residents of our projects. Future residents have first-hand experience and assess the quality of the dwelling differently than housing associations. Besides, no two residents are alike, and what works for one might not work for another.

At Home

Residential architects play a large role in shaping people's lives and sense of home. Therefore, it is important to develop an understanding of what "home" means to people (heren 5 architecten, 2005).

In 2005, we issued a publication titled *Thuis, At Home*, which explores what home means to future residents as an attempt to bundle the range of different meanings that could be found. In this book, the residents of heren 5's housing projects are the main characters. It is a personal story of seven residents, portrayed in a unique and intimate way. The residents talk about their housing experiences and aspirations, and comment on our ideas and plans. In turn, we explain how we analyse the emotion of "feeling at home" and how it serves as a source of inspiration in the design process. The striking portraits in *Thuis, At Home* provide an easy, almost casual insight into the capabilities and incapabilities of architecture (refer to Figures 17.1 and 17.2).

Families and City Life

In 2011, we discovered that many young families living in the city are not satisfied with their home and living environment. As a result, young families are leaving or considering to leave the city. This is a huge problem. First, because young families have a huge influence on urban economy through their use of services, their departure impacts this negatively. Second, as a result of the departure of young families, the population diversity in cities is decreasing. Families are important because they often belong to tight-knit communities and social networks. You could say that families are the glue that holds the city together.

The publication *Het alledaagse gezin in de stad* [*Everyday Families in the City*] is a report of our study on the ideal family apartment for middle-income families. heren 5 architecten, together with BNA Onderzoek (2013), the research group of the Dutch Architecture Association, fellow architects, municipalities, project developers and housing corporations, initiated a collaborative study into the preconditions for designing attractive family apartments in the city. Our study showed that the traditional Dutch apartment does not meet the housing requirements of Dutch families. The main obstacle is the open-plan layout: a spacious living room that incorporates a

FIGURE 17.1 Residents at Home.

Source: heren 5 architects by Kees Hummel.

★*Question from the residents' survey for Thuis, At Home*: "How do you describe your house to someone who hasn't seen it?" Answer: "I say that I live in a house that's just like a holiday park".

FIGURE 17.2 Resident's Perception about Home.

Source: heren 5 architects by Kees Hummel.

★*Question from the residents' survey for Thuis, At Home*: "What is it about the surroundings of your house that makes you proud?" Captain Schouten in his old and new home: "A new neighbourhood that feels like home".

kitchen, dining and living space. We discovered that family members need a space, a bedroom or separate living area, where they can retreat when they want to get away from hectic family life. The width of the traditional Dutch apartment (7.50 metres) is based on the space required to park three cars. In other words, the rules for parking dimensions determine the size of the home. But does this make for a good layout?

Unlike cities like Paris, London and New York, the cultural "norm" in the Netherlands towards raising children is in houses rather than apartment buildings. In our search for good design solutions for family apartments, we came up with the idea to draw inspiration from floor plans in other countries. So, we approached our non-native, former trainees. Francesca, who is originally from Genoa in Italy, was delighted to contribute and sent us a mental map of the apartment she grew up in. Unlike the traditional Dutch apartment, her parental home had many small rooms where each member of the family could find some peace and quiet. We also noticed that the entrance hall was big enough to serve as a small room. This space was used by Francesca to do her make-up or have a drink with friends before going out on the weekends.

We also learned a great deal from talking to city-minded families closer to home, such as the Bora family in Amsterdam. The Bora family is not particularly happy with their rented social housing apartment in Amsterdam. Besides the small size of the entrance hall, which makes it impossible for the whole family to welcome or say goodbye to friends, they are most dissatisfied with the layout of the apartment. The living room and kitchen are located adjacent to the bedrooms and bathroom, which leads to a lack of privacy when visitors are present. According to the family, their apartment in Turkey has a better, much smarter layout because the night zone, the bedrooms and bathroom, is spatially separated from the day zone, the living room and kitchen. Thanks to our conversations with the Bora family and many other families, we now have a fuller understanding of the living preferences of families in cities (Atteveld and Liesker, 2010).

Investigating the living preferences of foreign families has resulted in various design solutions for the layout of family apartments, circulation spaces, outdoor spaces and various other aspects that can make life more comfortable for urban families in compact homes. The results of the study have been compiled in a book titled *Nestelen in de stad – Appartementen voor gezinnen* [Nesting in the city – Apartments for families]. (Refer to Figure 17.3).

City Veterans

Our most recent study, conducted in 2016, is *Stadsveteranen* [City veterans], a collection of stories on growing old happily in the city. The last few years, the number of nursing homes in Dutch cities has been steadily decreasing. This is not necessarily a problem, as the current generation of city veterans would rather not live in nursing homes anyway. This generation wants to have control over how they live and grow old. For this study, heren 5 architecten interviewed city veterans about what they expect and need from their neighbourhoods and homes to grow old in the city. The study involved five workshops held in various locations in Amsterdam. During these workshops, groups of city veterans were interviewed about what they expect from their neighbourhood, street, apartment building and home. The "veterans" stories were then translated into trends and represented as illustrations in a book. Nine locations that came out on top were visited and documented. The study was conducted in cooperation with seven co-financiers, including a housing association, a demographer, Jan Latten, and a philosopher, Dort Spierings. We identified three important design strategies for elderly residents:

Spontaneous Interactions: "Having an obligatory coffee in the communal living room is not for me. I might be old, but I'm not dead yet". This was the response we got from a city veteran

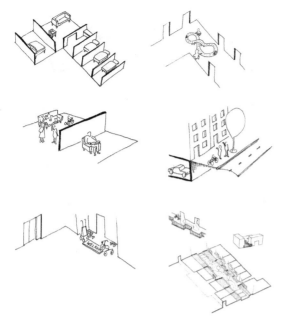

FIGURE 17.3 Creating Family Apartments.

1. Create as many rooms as possible. 2. A hallway is also a room and can double as a study, office, playroom and so forth. 3. Create separate spaces where residents can escape to. 4. Make it easy to go outside. 5. Create a safe and child-friendly living environment. 6. Incorporate sufficient storage spaces into the design (e.g. for strollers and children's bicycles).

Source: Atteveld and Liesker, 2010.

when we asked her about meeting other seniors. City veterans prefer to meet each other spontaneously while collecting their mail, on the spacious corridor on their way home or while tending the vegetable garden in the courtyard. This inspired us to include in our recent project in *Zeeheldenbuurt*, a working class neighbourhood in Leiden, a building that has street-facing living rooms, an inner court with gardens and galleries wide enough for benches where residents can socialise, wave to friends or simply sit and enjoy people strolling by.

Grey Economy: Seniors today are more active and independent than ever before – nothing like Statler and Waldorf, the pair of characters known for their grumbling on the Muppet Show balcony. In fact, the city veterans we have met are living the third half of their lives to the fullest. Start-ups from strong, sassy seniors doing what they do best are shooting up like mushrooms. Take, for instance, social catering company and commissary kitchen "Tante Tosti", or Auntie Toast providing home-cooked food and her specialties to local residents. This is what we call the "grey economy". Where possible, we incorporate spaces in our designs that provide opportunities for stimulating the grey economy.

Active Ageing: A striking finding of our study was that seniors prefer walking to cycling, and that they often opt for the "scenic route" rather than the shortest route. Wide footpaths, ample space for passing each other and safe and clear crossing points are some of the issues and amenities that seniors find important. For seniors, getting from one destination to the other has become a leisure pursuit (Figure 17.4). Another finding was that they attach particular importance to cultural activities and the availability of sufficient sports facilities.

FIGURE 17.4 Olga in Her Walkable City.
Source: heren 5 architects by Herman Stukker.

Our study identifies eight opportunities for successful ageing in the city:

1. City veterans make extensive use of the city's amenities, so it is important to create walkable cities.
2. No other target group is more active than city veterans. Therefore, cities should offer ample cultural activities.
3. In terms of safety, there are many spatial improvement opportunities that can be seized. For example, courtyards provide an intimate and safe place for seniors to sit and socialise.
4. The power of the grey social economy: most city veterans like to share their knowledge and experience with younger people.
5. Designs of buildings should include spaces that encourage people to gather and interact.
6. City veterans like living in mixed-age settings.
7. City veterans like living in apartments with a street view, preferably not located on the ground floor.
8. Senior apartments can be compact. Sweeping views are more important than floor space.

(Delisse and Liesker, 2016)

Recent Work

A number of social housing projects that we designed incorporate the findings from our studies. At heren 5, we very much like to work in multidisciplinary teams. We view each project as multilayered, and this approach enables us to contribute to the identity of the living environment and to incorporate art. These aspects are important in creating dwellings and living environments that people love and value. Four projects discussed below were realised in cooperation with a landscape architect and various artists.

Kolenkithuis, 37 Dwellings in Amsterdam

The *Nestelen in de stad - Appartementen voor gezinnen* [Nestling in the city - Apartments for families] study served as the basis for designing the *Kolenkithuis*. The design is a mix of apartments, maisonettes and raised homes for large families in one social housing block. Family wishes and requirements, as reflected in the study's findings, have been taken into consideration in designing the dwellings. We focused on creating multiroom spaces, spacious entrance halls, living rooms with annexes and a nice flow between areas for private use and areas for entertaining friends and family.

A daycare and out-of-school centre are located at each end of the *Kolenkithuis*. Both are important facilities for the community. Car-free residential streets have been incorporated into the design, allowing children the necessary space to play. The outdoor spaces provide a safe, child-friendly environment. For parents, the large windows offer clear views of the streets and the playing children. The smallest of children can safely crawl around and play in the raised residential street (Refer to Figure 17.5). Brick garden beds soften the border between private property and public space. Just as each family is unique, so is each apartment in the *Kolenkithuis*. The walls are composed of a patchwork of different brick patterns, forming a decorative collage of texture and colour.

FIGURE 17.5   Car-Free Living for Children in Kolenkithuis.
Source: heren 5 architects.

Dieselbuurt, 178 Dwellings in Amsterdam

In our endeavour to design houses for the future with a focus on social sustainability and compact living, boosted by our studies on this subject, we joined forces with housing association Ymere, building company Era Contour to develop 178 rented social dwellings divided over two buildings, creating a positive environment for tenants of all ages. First-time renters, families with children and city veterans will be the residents of this future-proof residential area, where sharing and socialising will be a natural part of everyday life.

There is an increasing demand for smaller and more economical units by increasingly smaller households, and this trend will only pick up in the coming years. Housing association Ymere can only keep the price of housing in popular districts affordable if units are smaller and residents share the use of various facilities. These two residential buildings will house apartments that are smaller than traditional social rented dwellings, by combining smaller private living spaces with shared communal facilities. For example, significant floor space is saved by creating units without a washing machine connection and investing in a communal laundry room. High-density compact housing becomes an amazing collective experience through sharing. Residents can relax in the lobby after their day at work, celebrate birthdays in the lounge area and do their DIY tasks in the bike storage area. Collectivity is the key word in this project.

A lot of attention is paid to the interior of the communal spaces and to the circulation routes, connecting the communal spaces and facilities to the living spaces (Figure 17.6). The design stimulates a sense of community, encourages residents to take care of the building and promotes

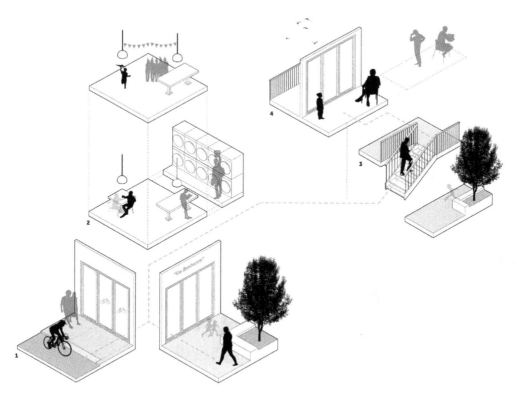

FIGURE 17.6 Two Buildings Where Several Target Groups Live Side by Side.
Source: heren 5 architects. Dieselbuurt. Amsterdam.

FIGURE 17.7 Living in the Heart of the City in a Green, Car-Free Environment.
Source: heren 5 architects.

social interaction and trust between neighbours. The compact dwellings allow users to make optimal use of the environment. All new residents will have a view of the street, and each apartment, however small, will have a private outdoor area. The *Dieselbuurt* is being developed as a place where neighbours live in close harmony along child-friendly, car-free roads dotted with family homes. A place where children can frolic and play in the streets while their parents watch (Figure 17.7). Raised houses around open courtyards provide city veterans with a comfortable, safe place to live. Also, routes encourage first-time renters to traverse through the building to their homes with a view and a private balcony.

Polderweg, 72 Dwellings in Amsterdam

The unique location of the *Polderweg* inspired us to design a residential block with two faces. The building is strongly connected to the hustle and bustle of the railway, and yet the residents are worlds away within the peace and quiet of the courtyard on the other side. The *Polderweg* housing complex features 72 social rented apartments spread over a total of six floors, a central hall and covered parking. By dividing the block to look like six buildings, the complex was designed to be fitted within the scale and character of the Oostpoort neighbourhood. The building folds outwards on both sides and is ornamented with fronton. The façades of the building created an undulating rhythm and accentuate the divided blocks by different reliefs and figures. Our design is an ode to and an interpretation of Isaac Gosschalk's work, an Amsterdam architect who invested heavily in beautiful brickwork. Two stained glass façades by artist Stefan Glerum, spanning all six floors of the complex, are incorporated into the entrance halls to the front and rear of the building (Figures 17.8). The two colossal compositions depict the colourful history of the Oostpoort area. Residents and visitors are welcomed into the complex with a richly adorned entrance – an entrance to be proud of.

FIGURE 17.8 Polderweg Artwork and Design.
Source: heren 5 architects by Luuk Kramer.

The *Polderweg* complex features two types of apartments: south-facing units situated over the width of the building, and see-through units that extend from the railway side to the south side of the building. On each floor, the apartments can be accessed by folded corridors offering varied views of the surrounding area. The parlour-floor apartments have a stoop and steps leading up to a private front door. This mixture makes for lively street life and ensures a good transition between private and public spaces.

Huis van Hendrik, 106 Dwellings in Haarlem

The *Huis van Hendrik* complex is a mix of social housing, private-sector rented housing and owner-occupied homes. The project was designed in cooperation with landscape architect Buro Mien Ruys and artist Boris Tellegen. The *House of Hendrik* forms the entrance to the redevelopment district of Parkwijk in Haarlem. The curve in the street and the neighbouring block gave rise to the folded form that the plan is based on. On the spacious Prins-Bernhardlaan, this shape is folded into three large houses. On Berlagelaan, a smaller residential street on the other side, the building volume is reduced to five smaller houses. The apartments and houses are intertwined into one residential building on the upper floors and corners. This scales the building according to the different levels of the city. The residential building encloses the introverted garden, designed by Buro Mien Ruys, which occupies a central position in the plan (Figure 17.9).

FIGURE 17.9 Huis van Hendrik, Haarlem.
Source: heren 5 architects by B. Uterwijk.

The building manifests itself as a unified whole with a mix of masonry façades of yellow, grey and blue-green bricks, reinforcing the character of both the apartments as the complex. The artwork on the façades of surrounding buildings dating from the period of reconstruction following the Second World War inspired us to work with fine artist Boris Tellegen. On the street side, on the folded entrance, jagged brick artwork extends over the façade across all seven floors (Figure 17.10).

FIGURE 17.10 Brick Artwork by Boris Tellegen on Façade.
Source: heren 5 architects by B. Uterwijk.

Concluding Comments

heren 5 architecten sees as our mission to improve neighbourhoods, build healthier environments and create spaces that people can identify with and want to relate to. At the same time, we want our living environments to provide answers to issues relating to mobility, demographics, inclusiveness, energy conservation and climate change. Creating designs that make complexity manageable, with the human dimension as a benchmark, is what heren 5 architecten excels at. Turning dreams into tangible realities makes our hearts beat faster. Every project represents a story. But it is people who tell that story, who live that story. Each story is made up of different layers. We listen to residents and users, we analyse trends and developments, we closely examine the location and design challenges, we uncover motivations and dreams. Integrating all these elements in a single design provides a baseline that guides the design process forward and allows us to breathe life into the environments we design. We dream along with people, in search of emotions, excitement, meaning. This is how we translate stories into compelling architecture. heren 5 was founded based on the conviction that designing urban environments comes with a great social responsibility. We design buildings and public spaces, but, more importantly, we create a context for healthy and enjoyable daily living. To us, the link between architectural and social challenges presents beautiful opportunities.

Acknowledgement

Jeroen van der Veer from de Amsterdamse Federatie van Woning Corporaties contributed to our chapter, sharing his article on social housing, published in Baumeister 2019, and providing insights on most recent developments. Jeroen was a man with a sense of humour and a positive outlook, a true ambassador of social housing in the Netherlands and far beyond. We will miss you!

References

Atteveld, J. and Liesker, B. (2010, June). *Het gezin in de stad (Families and City Life)*. Amsterdam, the Netherlands. heren 5.

BNA Onderzoek (2013). *Nestelen in de stad (Nestling in the City)*. Amsterdam, the Netherlands. BNA Onderzoek.

Delisse, M. and Liesker, B. (2016, July). *Stadsveteranen (City Veterans)*. Amsterdam, the Netherlands. heren 5.

heren 5 architecten (2005). *Thuis, At Home*. Amsterdam, the Netherlands. Valiz.

van der Veer, J. (2019, June). "One Among Many – Amsterdam in the 21st Century", *Baumeister*, 6, pp. 74–83.

PART V

Perspectives on Policy Design for Affordable Housing

18

PATHWAYS OF DUTCH AND GERMAN SOCIAL RENTING

Marietta E.A. Haffner

Introduction

After the Second World War, the private rental sector dominated the housing stock of the Northwestern European countries (Haffner et al., 2008, 2009). In the post-war period, the market share of private renting declined because of multiple reasons. On the one hand, the shares of owner-occupation and/or social rental units increased, while on the other hand, regulation of rents and security of tenure characterized the private rental sector, sometimes up until the 1980s (Hoekstra et al., 2012; Haffner et al., 2018). As an exponent of this development, the Netherlands reached one of the lowest market shares of private renting (9% in 2012). Germany will be the atypical case, where private renting amounts to more than 40% or even 50% of stock, depending on the definition (2011), one of the highest market shares (Haffner, 2018a, 2018b). In both countries, in recent decades the share of affordable (Dutch social and German subsidized) rental stock has lost ground. Both countries have been coping with affordability problems in the rental sector in this century (Elsinga and Haffner, 2020).

The contribution aims to develop an understanding of the pathways of Dutch and German housing policies resulting in two different housing markets and housing systems, while coping with affordability problems in the rental sector since the early 2000s. These affordability problems are briefly sketched in the next section. Thereafter, the term 'social' in the sense of affordable rental housing is framed in each country's context with a focus on their supply-side history till 2017. Finally, the chapter reviews the impact of these developments on the expected role of 'social' renting as rental housing with affordable costs.

Affordability Outcomes in Germany and the Netherlands

Germany and the Netherlands can be considered opposite cases in the market share of private/-commercial/market renting. However, the rental sector in the Netherlands (over 30%) amounts to about the average share of the 28 member countries of the European Union (EU), measured as share of population. The German (private) rental sector is the largest, even though not all EU member states are shown. Data refer to 11 member countries of the 28 in the EU, those considered comparable with Western advanced economies (Figure 18.1). Both countries are more similar than different when comparing the shares of the at-risk-of-poverty population, those with an equivalized

DOI: 10.4324/9781003172949-18

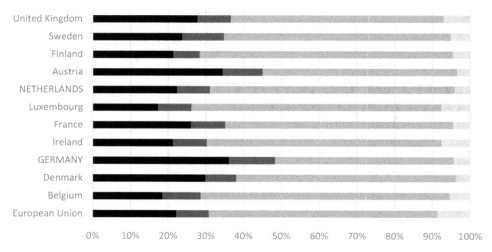

FIGURE 18.1 Tenure Structure Percentage of Population by Income Group[1,2], 2016.

1 As classified according to share of population with an equivalized disposable income lower or higher than 60% of the median national equivalized income after social transfers. Equivalized indicates that income is corrected for household composition (Eurostat, n.d.-a).

2 Data refer to 11 member countries of the 28 in the European Union.

Source: Eurostat (n.d.-b) (EU-SILC 2016 data base): calculation based on groups of ilc_li02 and ilc_lvho02.

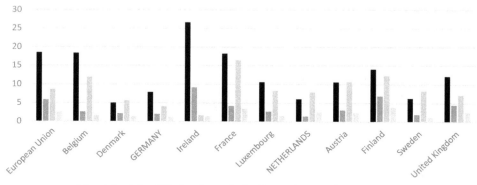

FIGURE 18.2 Share of Population with Arrears on Mortgage Payments/Rents or Utility Bills[1] by Income Group[2], 2016.

1 Eurostat (n.d.-a): "These arrears take into account the amount owed (bills, rent, credit/mortgage repayment…) which is not paid on schedule during the last 12 months for financial reasons".

2 For definition of income group, see note 1, Figure 18.1. Data refer to 11 member countries of the 28 in the European Union.

Source: Eurostat (n.d.-b) EU-SILC 2016 data base: ilc_mdes06 and ilc_mdes07.

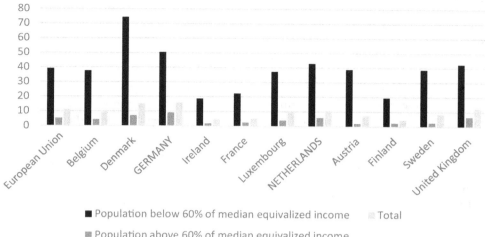

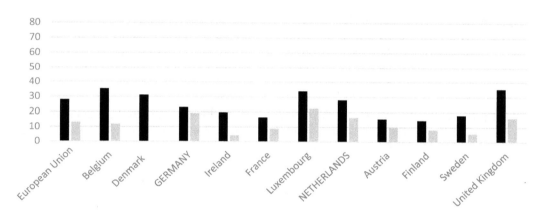

FIGURE 18.3 Housing Cost Overburden Rate[1], 2016: (a) by income group[2] (b) by rental status[3,4].

1 Share of population living in households where the total housing costs ('net' of housing allowances) represent more than 40% of disposable income ('net' of housing allowances) (Eurostat, n.d.-a).

2 For definition of income group, see note 1, Figure 18.1.

3 Tenant rent at market price includes tenants for which the distinction between both categories of renting is unclear (Eurostat, 2017).

4 Low reliability for share of tenants with rent at reduced price or free. Data refer to 11 member countries of the 28 in the European Union.

Source: Eurostat (n.d.-b) EU-SILC 2016 data base: ilc_lvho07a and ilc_lvho07c.

disposable income below 60% of median equivalized income. Together with Austria and Denmark, both countries house the lowest shares of such populations in owner-occupied dwellings.

In the fight against poverty and social exclusion, the 28 member states of the EU have been drawing up *National Action Plans for Social Inclusion* since the Lisbon European Council (European Council, 2000). To monitor progress, the EU set up the EU Statistics of Income and Living Conditions database providing a variety of measures on housing affordability (EU-SILC; European Commission, 2009). Data on subjective measures, such as resident's perceptions of housing costs as a (heavy) financial burden, indicate that 70% of the EU-population is in this category. Using two 'objective' measures as indicators of housing affordability, the two countries perform in a similar way (Eurostat, n.d.-b). With their population in arrears on mortgage/rent payments or on utility bills in the groups below (low income) and above 60% of median equivalized income, Germany and the Netherlands both score below EU-average (Figure 18.2). The shares of their population in arrears are lower or equal. However, in Germany, the lower-income population is more likely to be in arrears when paying energy costs, while in the Netherlands, it is more likely to be in arrears when paying rents.

Figure 18.3 shows the so-called housing cost 'overburden' rate by income group and by rental tenure. It is expressed as share of population living in households where the total housing costs ('net' of housing allowances) represent more than 40% of disposable income ('net' of housing allowances). The costs include energy costs, among others, as well as maintenance costs and rents. The population at risk of poverty is more likely to be housing cost overburdened (Figure 18.3a), as well as the tenants paying market rent (Figure 18.3b).

In relation to the latter group, tenants paying market rent, when housing affordability is at stake, the distinction between reduced rent/free is not clear. Eurostat (2017: 169) explains: "In a situation where there is no clear distinction between a 'prevailing rent' rent sector and a 'reduced rent' sector, all renters would be classified as 'tenant or subtenant paying rent at prevailing or market rate'." This applies to the Netherlands, where most of the existing social rental housing is classified as market rent in this figure, while only 0.7 percentage of the total 31% of the tenant population is classified as paying reduced rent. The shares for Germany are more in line with those given in the literature. The tenant population amounts to 48.6%, while 8.4% is classified as tenants paying reduced rent in 2016.

As last indicator of affordability, Figure 18.4 shows the impact of housing costs on the at-risk-of-poverty rate. Housing costs clearly more than double the share of the population considered to live at risk of poverty in the Scandinavian countries, the United Kingdom, as well as Germany and the Netherlands, more so than the average in the 28 EU-countries. Therefore, housing costs on average push a larger share of population into living at risk of poverty.

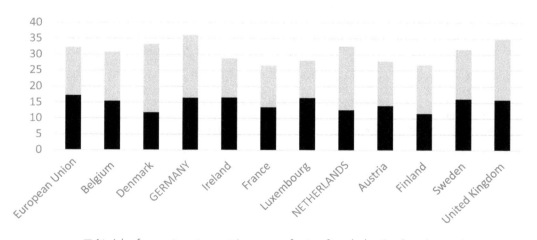

■ At risk of poverty rate ▨ Increase of rate after deducting housing costs

FIGURE 18.4 After-Housing Costs at-Risk-of-Poverty[1] Rate Increase[2], 2016.

1 Population at risk of poverty is defined as population with an equivalized disposable income below 60% of median equivalized income in a country (Eurostat, n.d.-a).

2 Increase of rate after deduction of housing costs from income, calculated per group rather than per person. Data refer to 11 member countries of the 28 in the European Union.

Source: Eurostat (n.d.-b) EU-SILC 2016 data base: calculation based on groups of ilc_li45 and ilc_li02.

In conclusion, this section shows the outcomes for different types of affordability indicators all being based on some relation between housing costs and income, which would be considered a usual definition of affordability (Haffner, 2018b). The indicators show an impact resulting in tenants being deemed to live at risk of poverty, being overburdened with housing costs or being in housing arrears. The latter two come with a standard definion of housing costs being deemed 'too high', and therefore being unaffordable. While a discussion about standards of unaffordability is possible, arrears definitely expose an affordabilty problem. On arrears, Germany and the Netherlands score better than the EU-average, while on both of the other indicators, they score worse. As 'reduced-rent', often called social rent, is associated with housing being more affordable based on a public task definition and supply-side subsidies, the remainder of the chapter focuses on its development and impact in the two countries under review.

Origins of 'Social' Rental Housing in Both Countries

Even if affordability outcomes are similar today, Germany and the Netherlands made different choices after the Second World War (Boelhouwer and Van der Heijden, 1992; Haffner et al., 2009; Whitehead et al., 2016; Elsinga and Haffner, 2020). The Netherlands made the more usual choice in Western countries at that time entailing the designation of certain non-profit housing associations (and local authorities) for operating a social rental sector. More unusual was the choice to put these organizations at arm's length and designate them as non-profit rather than public.

Germany did not set about to create a social rental sector linked to the ownership of the dwelling. Germany designed a supply-side subsidy system with the aim to temporarily subsidize any interested investor (public, private, commercial or non-profit) for providing subsidized housing limited to the subsidy period. Therefore, Germany does not operatie a formal social (rental) sector, but a private rental sector, next to (private) homeownership. Within these private markets, the country follows its social aims by temporarily subsidizing dwellings which are to be offered to the policy target group. Subsidized dwellings would be realized with lower-than-market price, depending on relationship between building costs and market price in a location.

In both countries, 'market', private or no longer subsidized rental dwellings, however, operate with the support by rent allowance (demand support) and rent price regulation. Private renting, as well as 'social' renting, is regulated in terms of 'indefinite' tenant security. This would entail indefinite rental contracts linked to a limited number of eviction reasons identified in the relevant legal framework (Haffner et al., 2008, 2009).

Germany

Important for the housing policy design in West Germany was the social market economy philosophy (Boelhouwer and Van der Heijden, 1992; Haffner et al., 2009; Elsinga and Haffner, 2020). After the Second World War, Germany put into practice that social welfare is best served by bringing about economic progress, while government intervention is designed to support the market (Busch-Geertsema, 2000, 2004). Implementation entailed (1) temporary government intervention in the market and (2) tenure neutral housing policy design in order to prevent favourable treatment of one tenure above another. Housing allowances are available, irrespective of the status of the occupier, being tenant or owner (Elsinga and Haffner, 2020). Bricks-and-mortar or supply-side subsidies for housing also fulfilled the criterion of tenure neutrality (Leutner, 1990; Haffner et al., 2009; Oxley et al., 2010). Furthermore, they were also designed as temporary support with a limitation of the subsidy period. The period lasted up to five decades in the early days of subsidization, while it was reduced to ten to 15 years more recently (Cornelius and Rzeznik, 2014; Kofner, 2017).

The *Housing Law of 2001* overhauled the law of 1956, but kept the supply-side subsidy mechanisms intact (Busch-Geertsema, 2000; Bundesministerium für Verkehr, Bau- und Wohnungswesen 2001; Haffner et al., 2009; Haffner, 2011; Oxley et al., 2015; Elsinga and Haffner, 2020). In the case of rental housing, the investor in rental housing could receive either a low-cost loan or an interest subsidy and agreed in exchange to limitation of initial rent levels and on rent increases in combination with dwelling allocation rules to facilitate access for the policy target group. Such system of bricks-and-mortar subsidies operates as a concession model. It ring-fences temporarily subsidized dwellings from the rest of the housing market under a special regime. Once the subsidy period ends, the dwelling becomes an unsubsidized rental dwelling.

The *Housing Law of 2001* also brought some changes. First, the subsidy started targeting low-income and other vulnerable groups rather than the population more broadly; second, it shifted towards buying rights of access to existing private rental stock (strengthening neighbourhoods) rather than being applicable to newly built stock only (Bundesregierung, 2006; Brech, 2014; Kofner, 2017). The supply-side subsidy system required all levels of government in the German federal country to cooperate: the national/federal government, the governments of the 16 federal states and the local governments (Haffner et al., 2009). The local governments negotiate subsidized housing with the local potential investors. In the past, the national government formulated the legal framework for the system (Bundesregierung, 2009; Haffner, 2011; Elsinga and Haffner, 2020).

This changed in 2006 when the national government transferred its powers for subsidization, including the regulation of prices/rents and allocation, to the 16 federal state governments. This transfer was to allow federal states to design their own 'social' housing investment policies within urban and spatial policies in response to differentiated population development. The shift in responsibility from national government to federal state governments was accompanied by a financial compensation paid annually by the federal government until the end of 2013, which was later extended until to the end of 2019 (Bundesregierung, 2009; Oxley et al., 2010, 2015; Haffner, 2011; Bundesgesetzblatt, 2013; Kholodilin, 2017; Kofner 2017; Elsinga and Haffner, 2020).

Potential investors in subsidized rental housing used to be commercial investors/developers/-landlords. More recently, the so-called housing companies became dominant as a seven-city case study by Bundesinstitut für Bau-, Stadt- und Raumforschung indicates (2012: 4). The shares of the housing companies are in the hands of local authorities, so this shift explains the lack of interest from other investors due to the low returns from subsidized rental dwellings (Oxley et al., 2010, 2015). The outcome is related to the fact that (personal and corporate) income tax depreciation deductions that compensate for lower negotiated returns from renting have become less attractive than they were in the past. Furthermore, Kofner (2017) observes that in the past, most subsidized projects were large-scale, located outside of city centres. The smaller and scattered projects of this century do not allow for such economies of scale and the advantages associated with it. The system of supply-side subsidies is designed as a concession model and the dwellings become part of the unsubsidized rental sector when the subsidy period terminates. As the subsidy periods have shortened in time, as well as the funds provided have decreased, the supply of subsidized rental housing has fallen. Cornelius and Rzeznik (2014) estimate the share of 'social'/subsidized rental stock at 4% in 2011, and Kofner (2017: 62) at 3.3% (see also Bundesamt für Bauwesen und Raumordnung, 2007; Kofner, 2014).

The Netherlands

In contrast to the developments in Germany, the Netherlands had established a social rental sector with the *1901 Housing Act*. It enabled social landlords to become active: housing associations are registered (licenced, accredited) private non-profit housing providers or organizations (Boelhouwer and Van der Heijden, 1992; Haffner, 2002; Elsinga et al., 2005, 2008; Elsinga and Haffner, 2020). They were to obtain supply-side subsides from the national government, particularly after the Second World War. The choice for non-profit organizations rather than public organizations fitted well with the liberal spirit at that time (Van der Schaar, 1986).

After the Second World War, the reduction of the enormous housing shortage dominated the housing policies (Van der Schaar, 1987; see also Elsinga and Haffner, 2020). Among other measures, supply-side subsidies were introduced to increase rental housing production. The subsidy system was designed as annual revenue or management subsidies, which the national government paid for 50 years to the social landlord from the moment a dwelling was constructed. This subsidy closed the financial gap between rent level and norms for costs, both set by the government. As the national government determined the locations of newly built stock and the eligibility conditions, housing associations in fact turned into implementation organizations rather than independently operating entrepreneurs.

In the decades that followed, housing remained a subsidized service in the social rental sector. Homeowners also benefit from tax breaks (Boelhouwer and Van der Heijden, 1992; Haffner, 2002; Elsinga et al., 2005; Elsinga and Haffner, 2020). Tenure neutrality was implemented in the rental sector, where the same policies applied to private and social landlords with respect to rent setting, rent adjustment, indefinite rent contract and the number of eviction reasons (Haffner, 2018a). Furthermore, the supply-side subsides that were available for the housing associations were also available to private landlords. As the take-up required some administrative capacity, only private organization landlords/investors (insurance companies and pension funds) took advantage of them. Although financial support for social rental housing changed over the years, the supply-side subsidy regime remained intact for decades. The social rental stock increased from 12% in 1947 to its highest market share of around 40% in the late 1980s, contributing to affordable stock for lower- as well as middle- and higher-income households.

The model that had been in place since the Second World War came to an end by the mid-1990s due to privatization notions permeating government policies. The subsidy obligations for 50 years for each newly built rental dwelling conflicted with EU financial requirements concerning national government budgets in preparation for the introduction of the common currency (Elsinga et al., 2005; Haffner et al., 2009, 2014; Elsinga and Haffner, 2020). Therefore, in the 1990s, all future subsidy obligations were paid in lump sum to the social and private landlords. This was called 'grossing and balancing', as the national government traded in its outstanding government loans that it had provided to the landlords to finance their investments in social rental housing. This operation cut the financing and subsidy link between the government and the social/private landlords. Social landlords were to operate as social entrepreneurs, acting in a commercial way, without supply-side subsidies for new construction, but fulfilling their public task of providing affordable housing for those in need. Financially, they were to operate as a revolving fund, earning revenues and using those revenues for improving the quality and quantity of their stock (Elsinga et al., 2005; Elsinga and Lind, 2013; Haffner et al., 2009, 2014; Elsinga and Haffner, 2020).

To facilitate and safeguard financial independence, two organizations were created. The Central Public Housing Fund, as safety net, was to step in when housing associations risked bankruptcy. Second, the Guarantee Fund for Social Housing Construction backed by government was to provide a guarantee to banks for loans taken out by housing associations; therefore, this constituted a new subsidy instrument. Furthermore, local authorities often lowered the price of land for the new construction of social rental housing.

After a period of 'experimentation' with the new system, in which the local authority and social landlord worked together to realize social rental housing, the conservative-liberal national government set the aim to balance the housing market. This entailed a move towards market activities and away from social renting. The aim was to stimulate more private-commercial rental supply to help solve shortages in rental housing in the medium-price segment in the urban markets (Elsinga et al., 2008; Haffner et al., 2009, 2014). Different measures followed, such as an income limit for the allocation of social rental dwellings, which was introduced in 2011; it entailed explicit targeting to lower-income groups for the first time (Elsinga et al., 2005; Elsinga and Lind, 2013; Elsinga and Haffner, 2020). Meanwhile, these income limits have been lowered in the allocation of social rental dwellings to improve the fit between income and rent level (Haffner et al., 2014; Priemus and Haffner, 2017; Haffner, 2018a). Furthermore, social landlords no longer retained their exemption for corporate income tax, while a new 'property' tax was introduced in 2013 for dwellings with a low rent level. Particularly, the latter levy lowers social landlords' investment capacity. Another measure was making rent price regulation for social landlords stricter than for private landlords (Haffner, 2018a).

These measures contributed to the slow but steady decline of the share of the social rental sector reaching 30% in 2015, down from 42% in 1985 (Ministerie van Binnenlandse Zaken en Koninkrijksrelaties, 2016), while the private rental sector continued its decrease to 8% of dwelling stock in 2009 (Haffner, 2018a). These market share losses were compensated by the growth of homeownership starting from around 40% of stock at the end of the 1970s (Van der Heijden et al., 2002; Haffner et al., 2014).

Impact on Affordability of Rental Housing

The description of the models of affordable rental housing in Germany and the Netherlands, with their focus on supply-side subsidizaton, shows that different policies and tools have been implemented. However, both countries are coping with similar trends: decrease in subsidization, (relative) decrease in affordable rental housing and its targeting to lower-income households resulting in increasing maginalization of the subsidized/social rental sector (Bundesregierung, 2009; Oxley et al., 2015; Kholodilin, 2017, Kofner, 2017; Elsinga and Haffner, 2020; Hochstenbach and Ronald, 2020).

The Netherlands is facilitating such developments with its policies of giving more room to market actors. Measures such as limiting rent control increasingly to the cheaper rental stock and setting a lower-income limit in the social rental housing allocation system help to restrict the role of social renting, while the measures potentially open up opportunities for investment in the middle- and higher-priced segment of the private rental market (Oxley et al., 2015; Haffner, 2018a). Municipalities in unaffordable urban areas may aim to counteract such national measures (Hochstenbach and Ronald, 2020). Extra supply of private renting may increase much less slowly than expected, thereby further limiting options for social tenants to move on. Potential newcomers are thus waiting longer for the allocation of a social rental dwelling (Kromhout and Wittkämper, 2019).

Germany has lost subsidized stock, because of the conversion of subsidized rental housing into unsubsidized rental units after the end of the subsidy term of the respective dwelling(s). This causes households with a low income to be housed in the private rental sector with some form of demand-based subsidy and rent regulation to soften the move in the shorter term (Haffner et al., 2008; Haffner, 2011; Haffner et al., 2018). The loss of stock also causes Germany to have one of the smallest shares of subsidized/ 'social' rental housing on offer in the EU (Haffner et al., 2009; Oxley et al., 2010, 2015; Whitehead et al., 2016), as the stable rent levels did not require much new subsidized supply. For example, Berlin had stopped providing subsidies to 'social' housing in 2010 (Kofner, 2014).

Similar to Amsterdam, German cities have been discovering that the market share of subsidized rental housing may be too small to cope with the more recent growth of rent levels in a number of cities, signalling an increase in demand (Cornelius and Rzeznik, 2014; Kofner, 2017). Cities reacted by developing their own models of affordable housing provision. For example, Munich has developed a model of affordable housing, which is not aimed at the most needy, but is affordable to lower- to middle-income households. Other cities followed the lead (Cornelius and Rzeznik, 2014). In such models, planning gains need to be partially used for realizing affordable housing, similarly to the British Section 106 model. A big diversity in uses and schemes exist, while evaluations about effectiveness and efficiency are scarce (Cornelius and Rzeznik, 2014; Kofner, 2014). In both countries, the role of cities has increased and a variety of models and startegies has evolved to provide affordable housing to lower- to middle-income groups in growing metropolitan areas (Kholodilin, 2017; Hochstenbach and Ronald, 2020).

Conclusions

The country descriptions highlight how the supply-side subsidy models of affordable rental housing provision in Germany and the Netherlands have been implemented. The evolution since the Second World War has not changed their core characteristics and mechanisms for a large part of the 20th century. They can be described as path-dependent systems with mostly incremental changes, particularly the German system, which was/is steered by the market in combination with the societal/politically identified social needs and funding. The Dutch system has survived for a long time due to political agreement in Dutch society, which subsidized most housing from a paternalistic point of view. In the new century, the agreement has disappeared. The supply-side subsidy models of affordable rental housing provision in the Netherlands and in Germany were and still remain different in an important way. The Dutch model entails ownership of social rental housing by non-profit housing associations, creating a more permanent social rental stock. In contrast, the German system produces a temporarily subsidized rental stock, depending on the length of the subsidy periods and the continued subsidization of new housing to ensure replacement of housing units and growth of the stock.

Regardless of the type of social/subsidized rental model, both countries have been coping with similar developments recently: decrease in funds for subsidized/social renting, a decline in the stock of affordable rental housing, as well as the increased focus of allocation to lower-income households. In Germany, these results are due to the temporary system, term-limited subsidization that is not set up as a revolving fund. In the Netherlands, the focus of the government has been on moving towards a more market driven provision. Social/subsidized rental housing therefore is becoming a scarce service, particularly in large growing metropolitan areas where city governments are stepping up their efforts to build more.

Both countries are expected to increasingly house the needy in the private rental sector, where investments are largely driven by commercial motives. Germany has come further along this trajectory than the Netherlands, which more recently started betting on the market. The balance between regulation to protect the tenant and non-regulation to 'protect' commercial investors in rental housing turns out to be delicate, as the Dutch case illustrates in its enormous reduction of market share of private renting up to this century. German developments show that such 'tit for tat' influence quickly affected the supply side when tax breaks became less attractive for investors, higher returns were to be earned elsewhere (in non-subsidized residential real estate) and commercial investors were no longer investing in subsidized rental housing.

This task was left to the housing companies whose stock is owned by local authorities. A system like the German one will work, as long as it can truly be flexible and build up quickly where needed.

A more 'permanent' stock of social dwellings provided and managed by social landlords within an institutional framework that makes the provision of affordable housing a public task as in the Dutch case, will allow for strong protection of the tenant. It also benefits the insider—existing tenants—when the right to the rental contract is not means-tested, except at the entry point of dwelling allocation. Such lock-in prevents tenant mobility, also constraining tenants in need from accessing social renting.

Both the Dutch and German system allowed for some extent of freedom of operation. In the Dutch case, social landlords experiment with social entrepreneurship within the limits of the public task regulation, combining the commercial and social dimensions of residential real estate management with negotiation with the local authorities. The German supply-side system is based on negotiations taking place between investors and the subsidy providing local authority about the conditions under which subsidized housing will be realized. Cooperation is a must to realize affordable housing in urban areas.

Acknowledgement

An earlier version of this research was presented at an International Conference at the University of Calgary in 2018. I am grateful for Dr Tsenkova's invitation to participate in this exciting exhange of best practices for affordable housing and for her assistance in the development of this chapter.

References

Boelhouwer, P.; Van der Heijden, H. (1992) *Housing systems in Europe*. Delft: Delft University Press.

Brech, J. (2004) "Germany." In Gruis, V. and Nieboer, N. (eds). *Asset Management in the Social Rented Sector. Policy and Practice in Europe and Australia*. Dordrecht: Kluwer Academic Publishers, 141–160.

Bundesamt für Bauwesen und Raumordnung (2007) *Wohnungs- und Immobilienmärkte in Deutschland 2006*. Bonn: Bundesamt für Bauwesen und Raumordnung.

Bundesgesetzblatt (2013) *Gesetz zur Errichtung eines Sondervermögens "Aufbauhilfe" und zur Änderung weiterer Gesetze (Aufbauhilfegesetz)*. Berlin: Bundestag, Part 1, No 38, 18 July.

Bundesinstitut für Bau-, Stadt- und Raumforschung (2012) *Kommunale Strategien für die Versorgung einkommensschwächerer und sozial benachteiligter Haushalte*. Bonn: Bundesamt für Bauwesen und Raumordnung.

Bundesministerium für Verkehr, Bau- und Wohnungswesen (2001) *Der soziale Wohnungsbau wird reformiert*. Bonn: Bundesministerium für Verkehr, Bau- und Wohnungswesen, No 49/1, 14 March.

Bundesregierung (2006) *Wohngeld- und Mietenbericht 2006*. Berlin: Bundesministerium für Verkehr, Bauund Wohnungswesen.

Bundesregierung (2009) *Bericht über die Wohnungs- und Immobilienwirtschaft in Deutschland*. Berlin: Bundesregierung, 3 June.

Busch-Geertsema, V. (2000) *Housing Policy in Germany*. Bremen: EUROHOME- IMPACT project working paper.

Busch-Geertsema, V. (2004) The Changing Role of the State in German Housing and Social Policy. *European Journal of Housing Policy*, 4(3): 303–321.

Cornelius, J.; Rzeznik, J. (2014) *National Report for Germany*. Bremen: Tenancy Law and Housing Policy in Multi-level Europe, Grant Agreement No. 290694.

Elsinga, M.; Haffner, M. (2020) "How the European Commission Affected Social Rental Housing in the Netherlands and Germany." In Anacker, K. B., Nguyen, M. T., and Varady, D. P. (eds). *The Routledge Handbook of Housing Policy and Planning*. New York: Routledge, 220–227.

Elsinga, M.; Haffner, M.; Van der Heijden, H. (2005) *A Unitary Rental Market in the Netherlands? Theoretical Exploration and Empirical Evidence.* Paper presented at the ENHR-conference "Housing in Europe: New Challenges & Innovations in Tomorrow's Cities", Reykjavik, Iceland, 29 June–3 July.

Elsinga, M.; Haffner, M.; Van der Heijden, H. (2008) Threats to the Dutch Unitary Rental Market. *European Journal of Housing Policy*, 8(1): 21–37.

Elsinga, M.; Lind, H. (2013) The Effect of EU-Legislation on Rental Systems in Sweden and the Netherlands. *Housing Studies*, 28(7): 960–971.

European Commission (2009) *Portfolio of Indicators for the Monitoring of the European Strategy for Social Protection and Social Inclusion – 2009 Update, September 2009 Update.* Brussels: European Commission.

European Council (2000) *Lisbon European Council. 23 and 24 March 2000. Presidency Conclusions.* Lisbon: European Council. www.europarl.europa.eu/summits/lis1_en.htm. Accessed July 19, 2018.

Eurostat (n.d.-a) Statistics Explained: Category: Living Conditions Glossary. http://ec.europa.eu/eurostat/-statistics-explained/index.php/Category:Living_conditions_glossary. Accessed June, 12, 2018.

Eurostat (n.d.-b) Statistics on Income and Living Conditions (EU-SILC) to Monitor Poverty and Social Exclusion in the European Union (EU). http://ec.europa.eu/eurostat/web/microdata/european-union-statistics-onincome-and-living-conditions. Accessed June, 12, 2018.

Eurostat (2017) *Methodological Guidelines and Description of EU-SILC Target Variables, Directorate F: Social Statistics, Unit F-4: Quality of Life.* August. http://ec.europa.eu/eurostat/documents/1012329/-8658951/Household+data+-+housing.pdf/6c5216f2-b40b-49d6-a0aa-9c2c4bb32348. Accessed December 31, 2020.

Haffner, M. (2002) *Dutch Social Rental Housing: the Vote for Housing Associations.* Plenary paper presented at 9th European Real Estate Society Conference, Glasgow, UK, 4–9 June.

Haffner, M. E. A. (2011) *Secure Occupancy in Rental Housing: A Comparative Analysis. Country Case Study: Germany.* Delft: Delft University of Technology, http://repository.tudelft.nl/search/ir/?q=haffner andfaculty=anddepartment=andtype=andyear=.

Haffner, M. (2018a) "The Role of Private Renting in France and the Netherlands." In Schmid, C.U. (ed.) *Tenancy Law and Housing Policy in Europe.* Cheltenham: Edward Elgar Publishing, 19–38.

Haffner, M. E. A. (2018b) Housing Affordability in the European Union. *IzR Informationen zur Raumentwicklung.* No 4: pp. 22–33. www.bbsr.bund.de/BBSR/DE/Veroeffentlichungen/IzR/2018/-4/Inhalt/inhalt.html?nn=422250. Accessed July 19, 2018.

Haffner, M.; Elsinga, M.; Hoekstra, J. (2008) Rent Regulation: The Balance between Private Landlords and Tenants in Six European Countries. *European Journal of Housing Policy*, 8(2): 217–233.

Haffner, M.; Hegedüs, J.; Knorr-Siedow, T. (2018) "The Private Rental Sector in Western Europe." In József, H., Martin, L., and Vera, H. (eds), *Private Rental Housing in Transition Counties. An Alternative to Owner Occupation?* London: Macmillan Publishers Ltd., 3–40.

Haffner, M.; Hoekstra, J.; Oxley, M.; Van der Heijden, H. (2009) *Bridging the Gap between Market and Social Rented Housing in Six European Countries.* Amsterdam: IOS Press BV. http://repository.tudelft.nl/view/ir/uuid: d35c0ed4-7874-4413-8b90-25352ec8c980/. Accessed July 19, 2018.

Haffner, M.; Van der Veen, M.; Bounjouh, H. (2014) National Report for the Netherlands. Delft: Delft University of Technology, Tenancy Law and Housing Policy in Multi-level Europe, Grant Agreement No. 290694.

Hochstenbach, C.; Ronald, R. (2020). The Unlikely Revival of Private Renting in Amsterdam: Re-Regulating a Regulated Housing Market. *Environment and Planning A: Economy and Space*, 52(8): 1622–1642.

Hoekstra, J.; Haffner M.; Van der Heijden H.; Oxley M. (2012) "Private Rental Landlords in Europe." In Smith, S. J., Elsinga, M., Fox O'Mahony, L., Seow Eng, O., Wachter, S., and Tsenkova, S. (eds). *International Encyclopedia of Housing and Home*, Vol. 5. Oxford: Elsevier, 387–392.

Kholodilin, K. A. (2017) Quantifying a Century of State Intervention in Rental Housing Germany. *Urban Research & Practice*, 10(3): 267–328.

Kofner, S. (2014) *The Private Rental Sector in Germany, OECD Research on Private Rental Sector. Consultancy Report: Germany.* No place of publication: Stefan Kofner.

Kofner, S. (2017) Social Housing Germany: An Inevitably Shrinking Sector? *Critical Housing Analysis*, 4(1): 61–71.

Kromhout, S.; Wittkämper, L. (2019) *Stand van de woonruimteverdeling. Wachttijden en verdeling in de tijd.* Amsterdam: RIGO Research en Advies.

Leutner, B. (1990) *Wohnungspolitik nach dem 2. Weltkrieg.* Bonn-Bad Godesberg: Bundesministerium für Raumordnung, Bauwesen und Städtebau.

Ministerie van Binnenlandse Zaken en Koninkrijksrelaties (2016) *Cijfers over Wonen en Bouwen 2016.* The Hague: Ministerie van Binnenlandse Zaken en Koninkrijksrelaties.

Oxley, M.; Lishman, R.; Brown, T.; Haffner, M.; Hoekstra, J. (2010) *Promoting Investment in Private Rented Housing Supply. International Policy Comparison.* London: Department for Communities and Local Government, Crown Copyright, Queen's Printer and Controller of Her Majesty's Stationery Office. https://assets.publishing.service.gov.uk/government/uploads/system/uploads/attachment_data/file/-6359/1759530.pdf. Accessed July 19, 2018.

Oxley, M.; Tang, C.; Lizieri, C.; Mansley, N.; Makic, D.; Haffner, M.; Hoekstra, J. (2015) *Prospects for Institutional Investment in Social Housing.* London: IPF.

Priemus H.; Haffner, M. (2017) How to Redesign a Rent Rebate System? *Experience in the Netherlands, Housing Studies*, 32(2): 121–139.

Van der Heijden, H. M. H.; Haffner, M. E. A.; Reitsma. A. A. (2002) *Ontwikkeling van de woonuitgaven in zes Westeuropese landen.* Delft: Delft University Press.

Van der Schaar, J. (1986) *De non-profit huursektor: woningbeheer en −exploitatie.* Delft: Delft University Press.

Van der Schaar, J. (1987) *Groei en bloei van het Nederlandse volkshuisvestingsbeleid.* Delft: Delft University Press.

Whitehead, C.; Scanlon, K.; Monk, S.; Tang, C.; with Haffner, M.; Lunde, J.; Lund Andersen, M.; Voigtländer, M. (2016). *Understanding the Role of Private Renting − A Four-Country Case Study.* Cambridge & Copenhagen: University of Cambridge & Boligokonomisk Videncenter.

19

SOCIAL SUSTAINABILITY IN SOCIAL AND AFFORDABLE HOUSING

Meryn Severson and Esther de Vos

Introduction

Sustainability is generally understood as meeting the needs of current generations without compromising the ability of future generations to meet their own needs (Brundtland, 1987), or, as Dujon and colleagues (2013) write, sustainability is simply "a fulfilling present and a renewable and regenerative future" (p. 2). Within this understanding of sustainability, the three dimensions or pillars – environmental, economic and social – have been well established in research and theory (Colantonio & Dixon, 2011; Dillard et al., 2009). However, in spite of the recognition of all three dimensions, there has been less emphasis on developing the social dimension, with no agreed-upon definition or form of measurement (Shirazi & Keivani, 2019).

At the same time, there is growing recognition that the current model for social and affordable housing[1] in Canada is unsustainable. However, this dialogue tends to focus more so on the financial or environmental dimensions. While these dimensions are important, we argue that conceptualizing social sustainability in the context of social and affordable housing is no less important, and that in order to operationalize social sustainability in the sector, it must also be measurable. With federal, provincial and municipal governments all increasingly recognizing the value of social sustainability (Government of Alberta, 2017; Government of Canada, 2017; City of Edmonton, 2010), the development of Capital Region Housing's measurement framework is timely and will contribute to the literature on evaluating social sustainability.

Capital Region Housing is one of the largest social and affordable housing providers in Canada, managing over 4,500 social housing units, 700 affordable (near market units) and 130 mixed-income units. Capital Region Housing is actively working to improve the sustainability of the affordable housing sector and support the well-being of tenants. Sustainability is a guiding principle at Capital Region Housing, and, consequently, Capital Region Housing has invested in developing an understanding of social sustainability that is specific to the context of social and affordable housing.

We have taken steps to conceptualize social sustainability for a social and affordable housing provider in Edmonton, Alberta (de Vos & Severson, 2018). This conceptualization takes into account the literature on social sustainability and includes sustainable community considerations as well as individual and community resilience. This chapter builds on the previous work designed to develop an understanding of social sustainability in the context of social and affordable housing in Canada to measuring social sustainability in this context. In this chapter, we will first

DOI: 10.4324/9781003172949-19

provide a brief overview of this conceptualization before turning to a review of other social sustainability frameworks and their measures. We then outline the measurement framework we have developed based on the best practices from the literature and our conceptualization of social sustainability drawn from the literature and our context as a social and affordable housing provider.

Conceptualizing Social Sustainability in Social and Affordable Housing

There has been an increased focus over the last number of years on social sustainability, predominantly from urban researchers, but also from the work of municipal governments, such as the City of Vancouver and the City of Edmonton amongst Canadian municipalities. However, current conceptualizations are often pragmatic and limited by available data (Littig & Griessler, 2005; Boström, 2012). Thus, some argue that social sustainability is best understood as a framework rather than a definition, which must be developed and clarified to be used as a tool to communicate, make decisions and measure development (Boström, 2012).

The literature predominantly recognizes two models of sustainability: the concentric model which predicates the social and financial dimensions on the environmental dimension, and the Venn diagram model where all dimensions are equal to each other (McKenzie, 2004; Manzi et al., 2010). These two models have informed the way in which social sustainability has been approached. We have adopted the anthropocentric approach, which draws from the Venn diagram model and emphasizes human relationships and livability (Littig & Griessler, 2005; Colantonio, 2009; Vallance et al., 2011; Manzi et al., 2010). Based on the literature on sustainable cities and communities as well as individual and community resilience, we believe that both aspects are important when conceptualizing social sustainability in the context of social and affordable housing.

In developing our conceptualization of social sustainability for social and affordable housing, we recognize that housing plays multiple roles in our lives, including both as a physical built environment and as a home where people live with associated pyschosocial impacts. This conceptualization draws from Ancell and Thompson-Fawcett's (2008) model of the social sustainability of medium-density housing which recognizes the multiple roles played by housing. We also draw from the City of Vancouver's (2005) definition of social sustainability which includes basic needs (labelled primary needs in Ancell and Thompson-Fawcett's model) and individual and community capacity building (labelled higher-order needs or ultimate needs in Ancell and Thompson-Fawcett's model) that contribute to improved quality of life in both the built environment and human environment.

We understand social sustainability as meeting both primary and basic needs, such as access to affordable nutritious food and safe and affordable housing, and higher-order needs, such as capacity and well-being, to improve quality of life for current generations without compromising the ability of future generations to meet these needs. For an affordable housing provider, the key methods to improve quality of life is through the housing we provide, but we also recognize that housing provides opportunities to meet non-housing needs and higher-order needs. This conceptualization not only recognizes that social sustainability is ultimately grounded in improving quality of life and liveability but also housing's unique role in meeting basic needs and facilitating higher-order needs, and specifically focuses on both housing and tenants.

We also recognize four principles that must guide the actions taken to meet these basic and higher-order needs. These four principles are:

1. equity – understanding that some individuals and groups require differing levels of support in order to flourish;
2. inclusion – both the right and the opportunity to participate in and enjoy all aspects of community life;

3.   resiliency – the ability to adapt to change; and
4.   security – both economic and physical security and stability.

Further, the actions we take to meet these needs must align with intergenerational equity (reducing inequality for this generation) and intragenerational equity (ensuring that the actions taken today do not negatively impact future generations and instead act to improve equity in the future). Building from this conceptualization of social sustainability, we have worked to develop a measurement framework based on the literature, which we outline next.

Measuring Social Sustainability: A Review of the Literature

While there is no agreed-upon conceptualization and measurement framework for social sustainability, there are a number of frameworks that have been developed for both social sustainability and other similar concepts such as social value that are geared towards the measurement of social outcomes and impacts. For example, social value has a well-developed measurement framework and is generally understood as the benefits created by social programs and activities (such as affordable housing) and experienced by people and communities that are not captured by the market, and as such it is easier to miss (CIH UK, 2015). It includes consideration for the well-being of individuals and communities as well as of the environment. It is often measured through the social return on investment (SROI) ratio, which is the social, economic and environmental value of an activity's impact relative to the investments and costs to operate the activity (CIH UK, 2015). Social impact assessments, on the other hand, try to assess the possible social, cultural and economic impacts of a proposed project or change on individuals or communities (Colantonio, 2009; Vanclay, 2003). While these frameworks have been increasingly adopted and share some similarities with sustainability, their applicability to social sustainability remains contested (Colantonio, 2009). Particularly, these measures miss the focus on current and future generations that is key to a sustainability approach (Dujon, Dillard & Brennan, 2013). Further, in contrast to social value/SROI or social impact assessments frameworks, a single summarized measure for social sustainability is not possible due to the multidimensional nature of social sustainability that includes both tangible and intangible factors (Colantonio et al., 2009; Colantonio & Dixon, 2011; Bacon, Cochrane & Woodcroft, 2012).

Instead, most social sustainability measurement frameworks do not try to establish a single aggregated outcome, instead tending towards data visualization methods that allow the different dimensions of social sustainability to be compared without being aggregated (Colantonio et al., 2009; Bacon, Cochrane & Woodcroft, 2012). These frameworks are also often focused on a specific scale, as social sustainability is considered to be multi-scalar but most practically applied and experienced at the neighbourhood or community scale (Magis, 2010; Shirazi & Keivani, 2019). Combined with the focus on urban places and cities within the social sustainability field, much of the work on measuring social sustainability to date has focused on policy development at the regional and municipal level, developing frameworks that can guide political decision-making and policy development (Davidson, 2012). As a result, these frameworks often focus more on the assessment of policy than on tangible social conditions (Colantonio, 2009; Murphy, 2012) and function more as guidelines for decision-making than as formal assessment tools. These policy frameworks are useful in conceptualizing the larger system in which actions to improve social sustainability are situated and accounting for factors such as cultural change and the need to actively design policies that benefit the poorest and most marginalized citizens (Polèse & Stren, 2000).

Further, with the increasing role of municipalities in supporting social development and responding to social issues, it is often their responsibility to create conditions for reducing exclusion and to develop "bridges" to link disparate parts of the community together, another key aspect of social sustainability (Stren & Polèse, 2000; Davidson, 2010; Magis, 2010; Polèse & Stren, 2000; Colantonio & Dixon, 2011; Dempsey et al., 2011). As such, measures for social sustainability adopted by municipalities are often measured at a collective level. For the City of Edmonton, reflective of their approach to social sustainability at a policy and program role, the City has developed a corporate measure for sustainability as a whole, measured as the percentage of Edmontonians who live in "complete communities". Similarly, the City of Vancouver's indicators for social sustainability are drawn from the Federation of Canadian Municipalities Quality of Life Indicators (City of Vancouver, 2006), again recognizing the role of municipalities in social sustainability and improving quality of life.

Within these policy frameworks for social sustainability, housing is a recurring theme, recognizing that factors like spatial segregation, affordability, zoning practices, and the physical quality of housing can have major impacts on individual and community well-being (Polèse & Stren, 2000; Polèse, 2000; Colantonio et al., 2009; Carlson & Everett, 2013). However, there are few frameworks for analyzing social sustainability in the context of housing presently available. Those that do exist (Dixon & Woodcraft, November 2013; Bacon, Cochrane, & Woodcraft, 2012; Ancell & Thompson-Fawcett, 2008; and to some extent Pullen et al., 2010) tend to select measurement indicators situated at higher levels of needs, such as the dimensions "Social and cultural life" and "Voice and influence" in Dixon and Woodcraft's framework or relationships in the community and neighbourhood quality in Ancell & Thompson-Fawcett's framework (2008).

Looking at these frameworks in more detail highlights that these frameworks are still mostly focused on housing in the context of neighbourhoods. For example, In the UK, where national planning priorities have incentivized housing developers to consider the social implications of their development strategies, the Berkeley Group commissioned researchers (Bacon, Cochrane & Woodcroft, 2012; Dixon & Woodcroft, 2013) to develop a social sustainability framework for their role as private housing developer. Their conceptualization of social sustainability is strongly rooted in the neighbourhood and built environment, reflective of their role as a developer and builder (Bacon, Cochrane & Woodcraft, 2012). Their measurement framework consists of three dimensions of social sustainability – "infrastructure and social amenities", "voice and influence" and "social and cultural life" – which are measured using 13 different indicators drawn from a survey conducted in each neighbourhood, as well as publicly accessible data from national surveys. These indicators predominantly focus on the neighbourhood, such as "accessible street layout" and "physical space on development that is adaptable in the future". Although social equity, justice, access to education and employment are common themes in social sustainability frameworks more generally, the authors chose to exclude them from the housing framework, arguing that they fall beyond the scope of a housing developer (Dixon & Woodcraft, 2013). The dimensions and indicators in their measurement framework are summarized in Table 19.1.

While Bacon and colleague's framework for the Berkeley Group focuses on the role of the private developer and measuring and supporting social sustainability in new and revitalized neighbourhoods, Shirazi and Keivani's (2019) framework focuses on measuring social sustainability in urban neighbourhoods more broadly. Similar to Bacon and colleagues, Shirazi and Keivani include three dimensions of social sustainability, which they call the "triad of social sustainability in urban neighbourhoods" and which all include the concept of "neighbour" in different ways. "Neighbouring" focuses on soft infrastructure or non-physical

TABLE 19.1 Summary of Key Social Sustainability Measurement Frameworks Reviewed

Source	Focus	Dimensions	Indicators
Bacon, Cochrane & Woodcraft (2012)	New and revitalized neighbourhoods	Amenities and infrastructure	Provision of community space
			Transport links
			Place with distinctive character
			Integration with wider neighbourhood
			Accessible street layout
			Physical space on development that is adaptable in future
			Positive local identity
		Social and cultural life	Relationships with neighbours
			Well-being
			Feelings of safety
		Voice and influence	Perceptions of ability to influence local area
			Willingness to act to improve area
Shirazi & Keivani (2018)	Urban neighbourhoods	Neighbour (population profile)	Social mix
		Neighbouring (soft infrastructure)	Social networking and interaction
			Safety and security
			Sense of attachment
			Participation
			Quality of neighbourhood
			Quality of home
		Neighbourhood (hard infrastructure)	Density
			Mixed land use
			Urban pattern and connectivity
			Building typology
			Quality of centre
			Access to facilities
Ancell & Thompson-Fawcett (2008)	Medium-density housing	Fundamental needs	Affordability
			Housing quality
		Intermediate needs	Transport
			Facilities
		Ultimate needs	Neighbourhood quality
			Relationships in the community

Source: Summarized from Bacon, Cochrane & Woodcraft (2012); Shirazi & Keivani (2018); and Ancell & Thompson-Fawcett (2008).

factors, "neighbourhood" focuses on hard infrastructure or physical factors and "neighbour" highlights the population profile or social mix of the neighbourhood. From this conceptualization, they selected 13 indicators from the literature that are associated with social sustainability and well-being, such as sense of attachment, participation, density, mixed land use and social mix of the population. Shirazi and Keivani's (2019) framework is unique in that it is an operational, integrative framework that moves from conceptualization all the way to measurement. It is also unique in that it is broad enough to be used across all neighbourhoods, without reflecting a specific role within that neighbourhood. The indicators in this framework are summarized in Table 19.1.

While higher-order needs are thoroughly explored in almost all social sustainability frameworks reviewed (see Bramley et al., 2009; Chiu, 2003), basic needs seem to be implicitly assumed as a foundation for community well-being but are not specifically addressed (Magis & Shinn, 2009), except for the City of Vancouver (2005) and Ancell and Thompson-Fawcett's model (2008). Their model of social sustainability in medium-density housing (2008) explicitly recognizes needs, based on Maslow's hierarchy of need. In this model, they emphasize that basic needs must be met before higher-order needs can be the focus of social sustainability work. They include affordability and quality as fundamental needs in their conceptual evaluation model, but do not include non-shelter basic needs. However, their model is still unique in that it explicitly recognizes primary or basic needs as well as higher-order needs and focuses on housing, specifically medium-density housing. This model is also summarized in Table 19.1.

There are some key caveats that recur throughout the literature on measuring social sustainability that should be considered when designing and interpreting frameworks for social sustainability. Colantonio and colleagues (2009) contend that social sustainability is better understood as a socio-historical process than as an end state; the target for social sustainability is constantly moving, and a final state of "ultimate" social sustainability will never be achieved. This differs from environmental sustainability which might be oriented towards a hard target (such as carbon neutrality), which could eventually be attained. Conversely, McKenzie suggests that social sustainability is often described as a "condition" which can exist at a given point in time (2004), but more recent work has tended in the direction of a process-oriented view of social sustainability. This temporality has been reflected in many definitions of social sustainability, which identify the well-being of future generations as present goals that must be planned and accounted for.

While some consensus is beginning to emerge in measuring social sustainability, particularly in policy frameworks and frameworks at the neighbourhood scale, frameworks for measuring social sustainability in the context of social and affordable housing providers remain limited. In general, the literature seems to agree on the importance of developing frameworks based around indicators that:

- are community-oriented rather than individually oriented,
- can be benchmarked to standardized data sources such as censuses and other national surveys,
- are concerned with a range of aspects of social sustainability and
- can be compared across time to evaluate progress in promoting social sustainability and guide actions to support social sustainability.

Drawing from this review of social sustainability frameworks and from our conceptualization drawn from the social sustainability literature and housing literature, we now turn to our measurement framework developed for the context of social and affordable housing.

Creating a Measurement Framework for Social and Affordable Housing

Based on our conceptual model for social sustainability, we have developed the following measurement framework illustrated in Figure 19.1. We identify four key dimensions for social sustainability within the context of social and affordable housing:

1. housing standards,
2. non-housing needs,
3. community integration and social inclusion and
4. capacity building and resiliency.

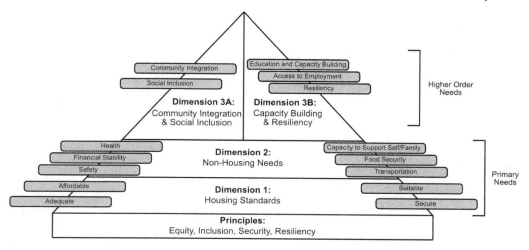

FIGURE 19.1 Conceptual Model for Measuring Social Sustainability in Social and Affordable Housing.

Source: Capital Region Housing.

Each of these dimensions has a series of indicators drawn from the literature which can be measured both quantitatively and qualitatively. Recognizing that all areas of the framework are necessary to support social sustainability, none of the indicators are weighted. However, a larger number of indicators are included for the basic needs-levels of the framework, both because these areas have more tangible and measurable factors and recognizing the importance of satisfying basic needs before higher-order needs can be addressed (City of Vancouver, 2005; Ancell & Thompson-Fawcett, 2008; Magis & Shinn, 2009).

Like the other measurement frameworks reviewed, this framework includes a mix of survey collected measures, administrative data and external measures. Most of these measures are collected through Capital Region Housing's biennial Tenant Wellbeing Survey which is based on best practices in the well-being literature and uses standardized questions from Statistics Canada as much as possible (see Capital Region Housing, 2018). External measures such as neighbourhood crime statistics and the CMHC/Statistics Canada's social inclusion and proximity measures (CMHC, 2020; Statistics Canada, 2020) are also included. In total, our measurement framework for social sustainability includes 49 different measures for 15 different indicators along the four different dimensions. Each of these dimensions and their indicators and measures will be outlined below.

Dimension 1: Housing Standards

Housing retains a unique place within the framework of social sustainability as it is both a basic need and fundamental to survival, but also contributes psychosocial benefits (Carter & Polevychok, 2004; CMHC, 2004; Dunn et al., 2006). However, these benefits of housing are conditional on housing being affordable, adequate, suitable and secure. If these conditions are not met, housing cannot contribute to higher-order needs (Ancell & Thompson-Fawcett, 2008). Thus, our framework recognizes that the first set of needs we must work to meet are centred on providing housing and ensuring it is affordable, adequate, secure and suitable.

This necessarily determines our indicators for this dimension of social sustainability. These indicators are already defined by Statistics Canada and CMHC (Statistics Canada 2017). Housing

TABLE 19.2 Indicators and Measures for Dimension 1: Housing Standards

Indicator	Measure	Data Source	Target
Affordable	Number of new units under construction	Administrative data	Increase
	Percentage of portfolio in mixed-income developments	Administrative data	Increase
	Percentage of priority (wait) list allocated housing	Administrative data	Increase
	Difference between household net income and annual living wage amount	Administrative data	Decrease
Adequate	Years since construction or last renovation	Administrative data	Decrease
	Facility condition index	Administrative data	Decrease
Suitable	Accessibility	Administrative data	Increase
	Number of people per bedroom	Administrative data	Decrease
Secure	Number of months in housing	Administrative data	Increase
	Feeling of safety in home	Well-being survey	Increase
	Number of evictions	Administrative data	Decrease
	Vacancy rate	Administrative data	Decrease

Source: Capital Region Housing.

is considered affordable when it costs 30% or less of a household's before-tax income. Adequacy is defined as housing that does not need major repairs, and suitability is defined as housing with enough bedrooms for the household based on the National Occupancy Standards (Statistics Canada, 2017). Security is also considered a component of the right to housing (CESCR, 1991), and so we have included it as an indicator of these housing standards.

However, while indicators are necessarily determined for this dimension, the measures are not. Statistics Canada and the CMHC measure these housing standards as the percentage of the population who report falling below one or more of these housing standards (except for security). This does not make sense though for a housing provider whose mandate is to provide safe, secure and affordable housing and who uses these standards in our operations. This includes using the suitability standard when allocating housing to new tenants and using the affordability standard to set monthly rent amounts. Rather than assessing the households who live in our housing as measured by Statistics Canada, we want to assess the housing we are providing and ensure that we are providing housing that meets these standards. These measures are outlined in Table 19.2.

Dimension 2: Non-Housing Needs

As an affordable housing provider that is specifically concerned with support for pathways out of poverty, Capital Region Housing has adopted a more holistic model of social sustainability, with indicators that fall outside the mandate of a typical landlord or housing developer (-see Dixon & Woodcraft, 2013, for an alternate perspective). Tenants have other, non-housing needs, especially food security (Kirkpatrick & Tarasuk, 2007). Living in affordable, safe and secure housing provides an opportunity to facilitate meeting other non-housing basic needs (Dunn et al., 2006; CMHC, 2004), which, in turn, support social sustainability. Thus, the second set of primary needs focuses on our tenants and facilitating meeting other, non-shelter needs that they have, including food security, transportation access and health. The indicators and measures we have chosen for this dimension are primarily measured at the household level and are drawn from the City of Vancouver's social sustainability framework (2005). These measures are outlined in Table 19.3.

TABLE 19.3 Indicators and Measures for Dimension 2: Non-Housing Needs

Indicator	Measure	Data Source	Target
Capacity to support self/family	Change in ability to support self/family	Well-being survey	Increase
Food security	Access to good food (quality)	Well-being survey	Increase
	Healthy eating habits	Well-being survey	Increase
	Frequency of food bank use	Well-being survey	Decrease
	Ability to afford food	Well-being survey	Increase
Transportation	Proximity Measures	CMHC/Statistics Canada	Increase
	Percentage of tenants who are satisfied with access to transit	Well-being survey	Increase
	Number of tenants accessing Ride Transit Program	Partner agencies	Increase
Health	Mental health – feelings of stress	Well-being survey	Decrease
	Physical health – satisfaction with access to medical care	Well-being survey	Increase
	Physical health – satisfaction with access to dental care	Well-being survey	Increase
	Satisfaction with overall personal health	Well-being survey	Increase
Financial stability	Percentage of tenants with stable (non-temporary) income sources	Administrative data	Increase
	Percentage of tenants who indicate that income meets their needs	Well-being survey	Increase
	Percentage of tenants who struggle to pay bills	Well-being survey	Decrease
Safety	Percentage of tenants who feel safe in community	Well-being survey	Increase
	Neighbourhood crime rates	Edmonton police service	Decrease
	Percentage of tenants who feel safe with family	Well-being survey	Increase

Source: Capital Region Housing.

Dimension 3A: Community Integration and Social Inclusion

It is crucial to recognize that housing – the places we live in and make our home – is the primary built form impacting the social sustainability of the city and largely mediates our experiences of social sustainability at the individual level. Housing occupies a unique role, spatially situating its occupants within a neighbourhood and city, but also socially impacting its occupants (Dunn et al., 2006).

Further, urban social sustainability research typically emphasizes the role of the urban built environment on social sustainability and, more specifically, explores the impact of housing types and characteristics on social sustainability, such as higher density, mixed use and location to amenities and green space (Bramley et al., 2006; 2009; Ancell & Thompson-Fawcett, 2008; Dempsey et al., 2011). By focusing on the built environment, the neighbourhood and the city, and their relationship with social sustainability, the concept takes on a specific spatial dimension (Polèse & Stren, 2000; Dempsey et al., 2011).

As a housing provider, then, we need to consider this socio-spatial role of housing and work to ensure our housing is integrated into the community and reduces socio-spatial exclusion, as identified by Polèse and Stren (2000), and has good access to supportive urban factors, as

TABLE 19.4 Indicators and Measures for Dimension 3A: Community Integration and Social Inclusion

Indicator	Measure	Data Source	Target
Community integration	Percentage of all tenants involved in tenant advisory activities	Administrative data	Increase
	Volunteer engagement in community organizations	Well-being survey	Increase
	Political engagement (advocacy efforts, volunteer for political candidates or parties, voting)	Well-being survey	Increase
	Engagement in a religious or spiritual community	Well-being survey	Increase
	Ability to influence community	Well-being survey	Increase
Social inclusion	Access to social services	Well-being survey	Increase
	Supportive networks	Well-being survey	Increase
	Feeling of belonging	Well-being survey	Increase
	Feeling of fair treatment (inclusion)	Well-being survey	Increase
	Social inclusion index	CMHC/Statistics Canada	Increase

Source: Capital Region Housing.

highlighted by Dempsey and colleagues (2011). This set of indicators and measures reflect the socio-spatial role of housing, with measures for community integration focusing on capacity, participation and engagement (City of Vancouver, 2005), and measures for social inclusion focusing on geography and the built environment (Ancell & Thompson-Fawcett, 2008; Bacon, Cochrane & Woodcroft, 2012). These measures are outlined in Table 19.4.

Dimension 3B: Capacity Building and Resiliency

Equally though, as a housing provider, we must consider the people who live in our housing and their higher-order needs. Reflecting this importance and recognizing that the people that live in our housing are reciprocally impacted by the socio-spatial aspect of housing (Dimension 3A), these two dimensions are placed at an equal level in the framework. As identified in the City of Vancouver's (2005) social sustainability definition, supporting higher-order needs in the context of social sustainability is particularly centred around working to build individual capacity and resiliency.

Reflecting on resiliency in more detail, individual resilience should not be seen as an individual trait, although it remains coupled with individual capacities, relationships and availability of community resources (Liebenberg & Moore, 2018). As with community resilience, defining individual resilience involves disruption, or adversity followed by adaptation and growth (Liebenberg & Moore, 2018). However, it can be difficult to identify causal influences (Rutter, 2012) as well as measuring adaptation and growth (Liebenberg & Moore, 2018). What is clear is that individual resilience is influenced by the social and physical environment as well as more individual factors/capabilities (Liebenberg & Moore, 2018; Rutter, 2012). As it relates to what level of individual capabilities people must have, Doorn, Gardoni and Murphy (2018) suggest that from a social justice perspective, determining an acceptable level of individual factors requires that all people are able to be placed above the threshold level and that an average level is insufficient.

In recent decades, models for understanding resilience in children and adults have moved away from a biomedical view, which located the source of illness in an individual, towards an ecological systems approach that views the individual as situated in their family and community

TABLE 19.5 Indicators and Measures for Dimension 3B: Capacity Building and Resiliency

Indicator	Measure	Data Source	Target
Education and capacity building	Satisfaction with access to personal development opportunities	Well-being survey	Increase
	Satisfaction with access to libraries	Well-being survey	Increase
	Satisfaction with access to recreation	Well-being survey	Increase
	Number of tenants accessing Leisure Access Pass	Administrative data/partner agencies	Increase
	Number of partnerships or MOUs between CRH and community partner agencies	Administrative data/partner agencies	Increase
Access to employment	Percentage of tenants who change status from student to employed	Administrative data	Increase
	Percentage of tenants with full-time employment	Administrative data	Increase
	Percentage of tenants in mixed-income developments who increase their income over the Household income limits due to employment income	Administrative data	Increase
Resiliency	Statistics Canada resiliency measures	Well-being survey	Increase

Source: Capital Region Housing.

relational networks (O'Dougherty Wright, Masten, & Narayan, 2013). This perspective on resilience recognizes the role that environmental and social factors can have in developing resiliency in individuals. Many of the identified "protective factors" that provide some form of shielding from the negative effects of risk or adversity are also factors that reoccur in social sustainability frameworks, such as levels of community violence, access to affordable housing and good public health care (see City of Vancouver, 2005; Colantonio et al., 2009; Dempsey et al., 2011).

Resiliency, like social sustainability, has many different measures. We focus on the measures for resiliency as developed by Statistics Canada (2019) for their Canadians at Work and Home survey, which allows us to compare our results to national data and ensures that these measures are valid and reliable. We also include measures for education and capacity building and access to employment, again drawing from the City of Vancouver's (2005) framework. These measures are outlined in Table 19.5.

Key Measures of Social Sustainability

Because of the multidimensional and multi-scalar nature of social sustainability and recognizing that these measures are a mix of quantitative and qualitative data, these measures cannot be summed or aggregated into a single total measure of social sustainability. Rather, we have

TABLE 19.6 Key Measures in Capital Region Housing Social Sustainability Framework

Dimension	Indicator	Key Measure
1: Housing standards	Affordable	Percentage of priority (wait) list allocated housing
2: Non-housing needs	Capacity to support self/family	Change in ability to support self/family
3A: Community integration and social inclusion	Social inclusion	Feeling of belonging
3B: Capacity building and resiliency	Education and capacity building	Number of partnerships or MOUs between CRH and community partner agencies

Source: Capital Region Housing.

chosen four key measures for each dimension of social sustainability. These key measures are not intended to reflect the full breadth and depth of each set of measures for each dimension. However, we argue that they do capture the goal of each dimension and serve as a snapshot of the social sustainability of social and affordable housing and the people who call our housing home. These key measures are summarized in Table 19.6.

In order to visualize our progress along these indicators, we suggest using a red-amber-green (RAG) or traffic light rating system, similar to the Berkley Group (Bacon, Cochrane & Woodcraft, 2012). This system requires first setting a baseline for each measure, and then setting target increases or decreases in this measure. In this visualization, green indicates a positive result where we meet or exceed the target; yellow is near the target or static; and red is below the target. Through this visualization system, we will be able to visually assess how our actions have contributed to social sustainability and quickly see indicators where more action is needed.

Conclusions

In this chapter, we have developed a framework for measuring social sustainability that is specific to the context of social and affordable housing and to our role as an affordable housing provider. It clarifies housing's role within the social sustainability paradigm, recognizing that because of housing's role in meeting basic and higher-order needs, and its socio-spatial role in the city and people's lives, housing provides a key entry point to improving and mediating people's experiences of social sustainability. This provides social and affordable housing providers with a specific point for operationalizing social sustainability within their work, as Capital Region Housing has done by focusing on both our housing and our tenants. This framework is also scalable and can be measured at the level of individual buildings, neighbourhoods or across the Capital Region Housing portfolio of over 5,000 homes. This framework is also specific to the Alberta context for social and affordable housing, and includes some measures specific to the Alberta regulatory framework, such as the percentages of tenants in mixed-income developments who increase their income over the income thresholds.

Our framework includes "inter and intragenerational equity" as a key feature, and grounds social sustainability in the project of *improving* quality of life, not simply measuring it. Therefore, while it is important to view any measure of social sustainability as a snapshot of the community's strength and quality of life at a single point in time (Bacon, Cochrane, & Woodcraft, 2012), it is *between* these snapshots that the work of social sustainability occurs, with indicators and measuring guiding future actions to support social sustainability. We plan to measure social sustainability biennially, so that we can compare our progress across time. The framework, based on Maslow's hierarchy of needs, also prioritizes action, focusing on meeting basic needs first.

Our framework also specifically recognizes the important role our partners play in supporting social sustainability. Some of the measures included here go beyond those generally indicated as the responsibilities of housing providers in the literature (Dixon & Woodcraft, 2013), such as supporting tenants in meeting basic needs such as food security. Capital Region Housing, as an affordable housing provider with a commitment to a holistic understanding of social sustainability, recognizes that meeting basic needs may be a persistent problem for tenants – who have low income and struggle with poverty. The organization has chosen to expand its framework to include indicators that can be improved through partnerships with community and non-profit organizations, municipal services and various levels of government.

Further, it is essential that indicators of social sustainability be viewed holistically in relation to one another, as social sustainability is multidimensional. Dillard and colleagues (2009) caution that there are interactive relationships between social and environmental sustainability, and the two do not always align in the same direction. The conceptualization of social sustainability developed by Capital Region Housing considers it as distinct from, but connected to, environmental and financial sustainability. None of the social sustainability frameworks reviewed in this chapter tried to capture all three forms of sustainability in one measurement system, and indeed this type of evaluation would likely be too unwieldy to be useful. However, future work in this area should focus on developing methods for putting the measurement frameworks for each form of sustainability in conversation with one another to gain a picture of the relationship between the three interrelated forms of sustainability.

Overall, this is the first iteration of the development of a social sustainability measurement framework in the context of social and affordable housing in Alberta. We are in the process of testing these measures and setting goals, and we anticipate that this framework will continue to evolve in future iterations, as the field of social sustainability continues to expand and there is increased research in the social and affordable housing sector.

Acknowledgement

We gratefully acknowledge the work done by Kenzie Gordon through the University of Alberta's Sustainability Scholars programme that assisted with the development of this measurement framework.

Note

1   We differentiate social and affordable housing whereby social housing uses a rent geared-to-income approach to setting rent, and affordable housing have rents that are approximately 10–20% lower than market rent housing.

References

Ancell, S.; and Thompson-Fawcett, M. (2008). The social sustainability of medium density housing: A conceptual model and Christchurch case study. *Housing Studies*, 23(3): 423–442.

Bacon, N.; Cochrane, D.; and Woodcraft, D. (2012). *Creating strong communities: How to measure the social sustainability of new housing developments.* Cobham: Berkeley Group.

Boström, M. (2012). A missing pillar? Challenges in theorizing and practicing social sustainability: Introduction to the special issue. *Sustainability: Science, Practice and Policy*, 8(1): 3–14.

Bramley, G.; Dempsey, N.; Power, S.; and Brown, C. (2006). *What is "social sustainability", and how do our existing urban forms perform in nurturing it.* Sustainable Communities and Green Futures' Planning Research Conference. Bartlett School of Planning, University College London, London.

Bramley, G.; Dempsey, N.; Power, S.; Brown, C.; and Watkins, D. (2009). Social sustainability and urban form: Evidence from five British cities. *Environment and Planning A*, 41(9): 2125–2142.

Brundtland, G. (1987). *Our common future: Report of the 1987 World Commission on Environment and Development*. New York: United Nations.

Capital Region Housing. (2018). *Tenant Wellbeing Community Report 2018*. www.crhc.ca/reports-and-publications, accessed December 22, 2020.

Carlson, M. J.; and Everett, M. (2013). "Social sustainability and the social determinants of health." In Dujon, V.; Dillard, J.; and Brennan, E. M. (eds). *Social sustainability: A multilevel approach to social inclusion* (pp. 103–125). New York: Routledge.

Carter, T.; and Polevychok, C. (2004). *Housing is good social policy*. Ottawa: Canadian Policy Research Networks.

Chiu, R. L. (2003). "Social sustainability, sustainable development and housing development: The experience of Hong Kong." In Forrest, R.; and Lee, J. (eds) *Housing and social change: East-west perspectives* (pp. 221–239). London: Routledge.

CIH UK. (2015). *New Approaches to delivering social value*. Coventry: Chartered Institute of Housing.

City of Edmonton. (2010). *The way we live: Edmonton's people plan*. Edmonton: City of Edmonton.

City of Edmonton. (2012). *The way we live implementation plan*. Edmonton: City of Edmonton.

City of Vancouver. (2005). *Definition of social sustainability. Policy report, social development*. Vancouver: City of Vancouver.

City of Vancouver. (2006). *City of Vancouver social development plan update*. Vancouver: City of Vancouver.

CMHC-SCHL. (2004). Housing and population health – research framework. *Research Highlight, Socioeconomic Series 04-016*. Ottawa: CMHC-SCHL.

CMHC-SCHL. (2020). *NHS housing needs data*. www.cmhc-schl.gc.ca/en/nhs/housing-needs-data, accessed December 22, 2020.

Colantonio, A. (2009). "Social sustainability: A review and critique of traditional versus emerging themes and assessment methods." In Horner, M.; Price, A.; Bebbington, J.; and Emmanuel, R. (eds). *SUE-MOT. Conference 2009: Second international conference on whole life urban sustainability and its assessment: Conference proceedings* (pp. 865–885). Loughborough: Loughborough University.

Colantonio, A.; and Dixon, T. (eds). (2011). *Urban regeneration and social sustainability: Best practice from European cities*. West Sussex: Wiley-Blackwell.

Colantonio, A.; Dixon, T.; Ganser, R.; Carpenter, J.; and Ngombe, A. (2009). *Measuring socially sustainable urban regeneration in Europe*. Oxford: Oxford Institute for Sustainable Development.

Committee on Economic, Social and Cultural Rights. (1991). *General comment no. 4: The right to adequate housing*. New York: United Nations.

Davidson, M. (2010). Social sustainability and the city. *Geography Compass*, 4(7): 872–880.

Dempsey, N.; Bramley, G.; Power, S.; and Brown, C. (2011). The social dimension of sustainable development: Defining urban social sustainability. *Sustainable Development*, 19: 289–300.

de Vos, E.; and Severson, M. (2018). *Conceptualizing social sustainability in the canadian social and affordable housing sector*. Paper presented at the XIX ISA World Congress of Sociology. Toronto, July.

Dillard, J.; Dujon, V.; and King, M. C. (eds) (2009). "Introduction." In *Understanding the social dimension of sustainability* (pp. 1–12). New York: Routledge.

Dixon, T.; and Woodcraft, S. (2013). Creating strong communities: Measuring social sustainability in new housing development. *Town and Country Planning*: 473–480.

Doorn, N.; Gardoni, P.; and Murphy, C. (2019). A multidisciplinary definition and evaluation of resilience: The role of social justice in defining resilience. *Sustainable and Resilient Infrastructure*, 4(3): 112–123.

Dujon, V.; Dillard, J.; and Brennan, E. M. (eds). (2013). *Social sustainability: A multilevel approach to social inclusion*. New York: Routledge.

Dunn, J. R.; Hayes, M. V.; Hulchanski, J. D.; Hwang, S. W.; and Potvin, L. (2006). Housing as a socioeconomic determinant of health: Findings of a national needs, gaps and opportunities assessment. *Canadian Journal of Public Health/Revue Canadienne de Santé Publique*, 97(3): S11–S15.

Government of Alberta. (2017). *Provincial affordable housing strategy*. https://open.alberta.ca/publications/9781460134160, accessed December 22, 2020.

Government of Canada. (2017). *National housing strategy: A place to call home.* https://assets.cmhc-schl.gc.ca/sf/project/placetocallhome/pdfs/canada-national-housing-strategy.pdf?rev=97491935-2a97-405f-bd38-decf72266ee9, accessed December 22, 2020.

Kirkpatrick, S. I.; and Tarasuk, V. (2007). Adequacy of food spending is related to housing expenditures among lower-income Canadian households. *Public Health Nutrition,* 10(12): 1464–1473.

Liebenberg, L.; and Moore, J. C. (2018). A social ecological measure of resilience for adults: The RRC-ARM. *Social Indicators Research,* 136(1): 1–19.

Littig, B.; and Griessler, E. (2005). Social sustainability: A catchword between political pragmatism and social theory. *International Journal of Sustainable Development,* 8(1–2): 65–79.

Magis, K. (2010). Community resilience: An indicator of social sustainability. *Society & Natural Resources,* 23(5): 401–416.

Magis, K.; and Shinn, C. (2009). "Emergent principles of social sustainability." In Dillard, J.; Dujon, V.; and King, M.C. (eds). *Understanding the social dimension of sustainability* (pp. 15–44). New York: Routledge.

Manzi, T.; Lucas, K.; Lloyd Jones, T.; and Allen, J. (2010). "Understanding social sustainability: Key concepts and developments in theory and practice." In Manzi, T.; Lucas, K.; Lloyd Jones, T.; and Allen, J. (eds). *Social sustainability in urban areas: Communities, connectivity, and the urban fabric* (pp. 1–28). London: Earthscan.

McKenzie, S. (2004). *Social sustainability: Towards some definitions.* Magill: Hawke Research Institute, University of South Australia.

Murphy, K. (2012). The social pillar of sustainable development: A literature review and framework for policy analysis. *Sustainability: Science, Practice and Policy,* 8(1): 15–29.

O'Dougherty Wright, M.; Masten, A. S.; and Narayan, A. J. (2013). "Resilience processes in development: Four waves of research on positive adaptation in the context of adversity." In Goldstein, S.; and Brooks, R. (eds). *Handbook of resilience in children* (pp. 15–37). New York: Springer.

Polèse, M. (2000). "Learning from each other: Policy choices and the social sustainability of cities." In Polèse, M.; & Stren, R. (eds) *The social sustainability of cities: Diversity and the management of change* (pp. 308–334). Toronto: University of Toronto Press.

Polèse, M.; and Stren, R. (eds). (2000). *The social sustainability of cities: Diversity and the management of change.* Toronto: University of Toronto Press.

Pullen, S.; Arman, M.; Zillante, G.; Zuo, J.; Chileshe, N.; and Wilson, L. (2010). Developing an assessment framework for affordable and sustainable housing. *The Australasian Journal of Construction Economics and Building,* 10(1/2): 60–76.

Richardson, J. (2010). *Housing and the customer: Understanding needs and delivering service.* Coventry: Chartered Institute of Housing.

Rutter, M. (2012) Resilience as a dynamic concept. *Development and Psychopathy,* 24: 335–344.

Shirazi, M. R.; and Keivani, R. (2019). The triad of social sustainability: Defining and measuring social sustainability of urban neighbourhoods. *Urban Research & Practice,* 12(4): 448–471.

Statistics Canada. (2017). 2016 census of population: Housing. *Release and Concepts Overview.* www12.statcan.gc.ca/census-recensement/2016/ref/98-501/98-501-x2016007-eng.cfm, accessed December 22, 2020.

Statistics Canada. (2019). *General social survey: An overview, 2019.* Ottawa: Statistics Canada.

Statistics Canada. (2020). *Proximity measures data viewer.* www150.statcan.gc.ca/n1/pub/71-607-x/71-607-x2020011-eng.htm, accessed December 22, 2020.

Stren, R.; and Polèse, M. (2000). "Understanding the new sociocultural dynamics of cities: Comparative urban policy in a global context." In Polèse, M.; & Stren, R. (eds) *The social sustainability of cities: Diversity and the management of change* (pp. 3–38). Toronto: University of Toronto Press.

Vallance, S.; Perkins, H. C.; and Dixon, J. E. (2011). What is social sustainability? A clarification of concepts. *Geoforum,* 42(3): 342–348.

Vanclay, F. (2003). International principles for social impact assessment. *Impact Assessment and Project Appraisal,* 21(1): 5–12.

Woodcraft, S. (2012). Social sustainability and new communities: Moving from concept to practice in the UK. *Procedia-Social and Behavioral Sciences,* 68: 29–42.

20

PRIVATE RENTAL HOUSING IN CANADA'S FOUR LARGEST METROPOLITAN AREAS

Trends and Prospects

J. David Hulchanski

Introduction

Canada is a nation of homeowners. About 68% of households are owners and 28% are tenants in the PRS. In Canada, 96% of households either buy or rent in the housing market. Canada has one of the smallest non-market social housing sectors among comparator Western nations, at about 4% of the nation's housing stock compared to 10% to 30% in much of western and northern Europe (Crook & Kemp 2014; Housing Europe 2019; van der Heijden 2013). The PRS is a significant segment of Canada's housing market and housing system (Gibb et al., 2019).

The housing system here refers to the "full range of inter-relationships between all of the actors (individual and corporate), and institutions involved in the production, consumption and regulation of housing" (Bourne 1981:12). Slightly more than a quarter of Canada's households depend on the PRS for the provision and maintenance of their housing. The PRS plays an important role by providing an option for households unable or unwilling to become homeowners or for households unable to access social housing due to ineligibility or long waiting lists (August & Walks 2018; Bourne 1986; Crook 1998; Hulchanski 1988; Hulchanski & Shapcott 2004; Miron 1995; Steele 1993; Suttor 2009; Tsenkova & Witwer 2011; Wolfe 1998).

Yet since the mid-1980s in Canada, the supply of new and the rehabilitation of ageing PRS housing have been largely ignored by federal and most provincial governments (Bacher 1993; Chisholm & Hulchanski 2019; Crook 1998; Pomeroy & Falvo 2013; Suttor 2009, 2016). There is no explicit public policy about the role of the PRS, and there is very little public funding for new supply, especially in comparison to subsidies provided to homeownership. As a result, Canada has an ageing stock of rental housing and a growing share of units in need of rehabilitation. Households living in rental housing affected by disrepair due to ageing and neglect are disproportionately from lower-income disadvantaged population groups, including racialized minorities, Indigenous people, female-led single-parent families, the elderly, and people with disabilities (Bunting, Walks & Filion, 2004).

Canada's PRS has not been ignored by Canadian and global speculators and investors (August & Walks 2018; Kalman-Lamb 2017; Ley 2015; Walks 2014a, 2014b; Walks & Clifford, 2015). Since the 1990s, there is a new reality for housing systems in many nations, the hyper-commodification of housing (Aalbers, 2016). A transnational class of super-rich housing investors is disrupting our understanding of local housing markets. Residential land and

DOI: 10.4324/9781003172949-20

housing were always commodities, but mainly as a very localized commodity in a market focused on meeting the actual residential accommodation needs of households in a particular geography. The change in the macro context in which the housing system operates, producing the hyper-commodification, are powerful financial and political forces and dynamics we have come to generally refer to as deregulation, financialization, and globalization (Madden & Marcuse, 2016:52–62).

Deregulation, which mainly means *different* regulations over housing and not necessarily fewer regulations, removes, changes, and/or introduces regulations that do not impede the commodity aspect of real estate (Boudreau et al., 2009; Hackworth & Moriah, 2006). The financialization of housing has converted, with the help of the changed regulations, housing into large-scale globally traded financialized instruments ("products") to be bought, sold, and speculated with, including use for money laundering and tax evasion. The global financialization of housing refers to the easy flow of wealth networks that seek quality real estate assets in prosperous localities in safe countries (Ley, 2015; Madden & Marcuse, 2016; Rogers & Koh, 2017; Walks, 2014b).

Housing, particularly in the larger metropolitan areas, is no longer just housing – a physical structure where people in a particular locale live. There is now more housing that is used for purposes other than as a main residence, something Doling and Ronald (2019) term as "not for housing" housing (NFHH). There are four types of NFHH that are now very common: second homes, foreign buying of investment properties, houses as hotels, and houses as offices (Doling & Ronald, 2019:24–25; Grisdale 2019). These subcategories of NFHH are not based on the housing needs of the local housing market or even local or national economic conditions. Canada's real estate is particularly attractive to global investors and speculators. There are few regulations on ownership and very weak disclosure requirements about who the beneficial owners are or where the money came from. In addition, real estate investment and speculation benefits from the fact that the 2008–2009 global financial crisis had limited impact on Canada's housing system, enhancing the sense of investment safety and stability (Walks, 2014a).

This chapter focuses on macro-social and economic issues and trends affecting three facets of the PRS: the existing supply and potential new supply, the quality of the existing rental stock, and the socio-economic status of tenants in the PRS. The focus is on the four largest census metropolitan areas (CMAs): Montréal, Toronto, Calgary, and Vancouver. These have a population of 14 million people, 40% of Canada's population, housing 44% of Canada's renter households (2016 Census). Montréal and Toronto alone house one-third of Canada's renters.

Definition: What Is the Private Rented Sector?

When the term "private rented sector" (PRS) is used it might be easy to assume there is general agreement on what this part of a nation's housing system actually is, that is, what are the boundaries between private for-profit and social (public and non-profit) rental. Housing tenure, the terms and conditions (rights and responsibilities), legal and cultural, by which housing is owned, occupied, and maintained, is very different between nations and even somewhat different between provinces and territories in Canada. The PRS can be defined based on key attributes such as the forms of subsidization, differences in ownership, the method by which rents are determined, and/or the bundle of property rights. The definition used here, however, is that provided in Haffner et al.: "rented housing that is not allocated according to socially determined need" (Haffner et al., 2010; Granath Hansson & Lundgren, 2019). This provides a common basic fact about the PRS separating it from public and non-profit non-market rental housing. PRS units may or may not be subsidized and may or may not have some restrictions on initial rent levels for some percentage of the units, as is often the case for new construction that receives some form of subsidy. It is "private" in the sense that it is owned on an entrepreneurial basis as a market commodity that can be freely transferred (sold, traded) to others, locally or globally.

The housing units within the PRS comprises primary and secondary forms of rental housing. The primary rental sector consists of purpose-built rental housing, that is, residential construction developed for the rental housing market, including, but not limited to, multi-unit rental apartment buildings (Canada Mortgage and Housing Corporation, 2016). The secondary rental sector consists of housing that was not originally intended as rental but is made available as rental. This includes detached and semi-detached houses, freehold row/town houses, accessory apartments as separate dwelling units within another structure, and investor-owned units in condominiums which are offered for rent. This distinction is necessary because different laws and policies, from building codes to landlord-tenant regulations, apply to the different types of rental housing (Harris & Kinsella, 2017; Suttor, 2017).

Trends in the Supply of Private Rental Housing

A majority of Canada's rental housing is in the larger metropolitan areas. About 40% of all rentals are in the four largest CMAs of Montréal, Toronto, Calgary, and Vancouver (Figure 20.1). But the concentration is even greater than that given the large population of the Montréal and Toronto metropolitan areas. These two CMAs have one-third of Canada's rental housing. Significant additions to the purpose-built rental stock took place from the 1950s to the 1980s, then levelled off, with some additions in the recent decade. The rental stock data in Figure 20.1 are from the census. It thus captures all types of rental, primary and secondary. Some of the

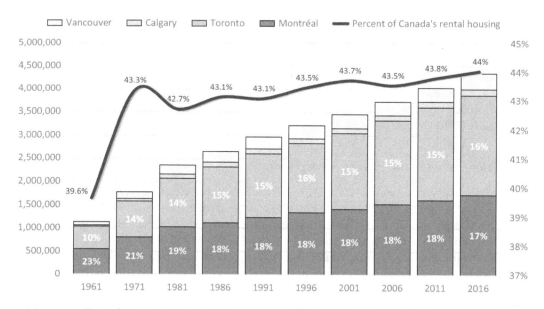

FIGURE 20.1 Rental Housing Total and Percentage of Canada's Rental Housing, 1961–2016.
Source: Statistics Canada, Census 1961–2016 and National Household Survey, 2011.

increase in rentals are apartments in houses, many in basements. Many of these are poor quality (Patterson & Harris, 2017).

As the rate of homeownership increased after the 1960s, and as the number of households in metropolitan areas increased, the percentage of renters in the four largest metropolitan areas decreased (see Figure 20.2). This is not a decrease in the number of renters, rather a decrease in the share of renters relative to owners. More rental housing was still required given the continuing increase in the population, the decrease in average house sizes, and the need to replace aging housing.

Canada is an exception in terms of the growth in the share of households in the PRS in Anglophone homeownership societies (Chisholm & Hulchanski, 2019; Maclennan et al., 2019). There has been a decrease in homeownership in the UK, Ireland, the USA, Australia, and New Zealand. The housing markets in these countries were more seriously impacted by the global financial crisis than Canada. Though the trend to an increased share of private renting predates the GFC, it has become more rapid since 2008 (Hulse et al., 2019; Pawson et al., 2017).

As more of the land around the cities in the post-war era was serviced (physical and social infrastructure), most of the land was zoned for low-density homeownership. The combination of more housing supply intended for homeownership and the end of significant PRS supply subsidies by the 1980s, the start of fiscal austerity, represents an explicit public policy abandonment of low- and moderate-income renters. Direct budgetary subsidies and indirect tax system subsidies for the PRS were provided from the mid-1940s to the mid-1980s (Clayton, 2010; Clayton Research Associates, 1998; Department of Finance, 2019; Dowler,

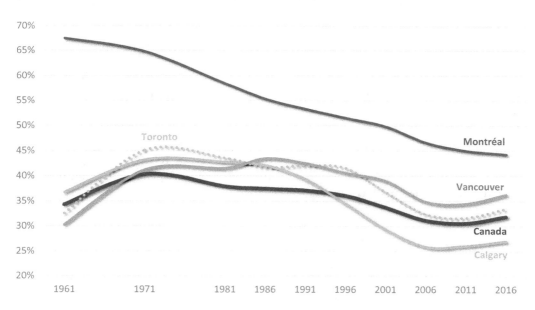

FIGURE 20.2 Rental Housing Percentage, 1961–2016.

Source: Statistics Canada, Census 1961–2016 and National Household Survey, 2011.

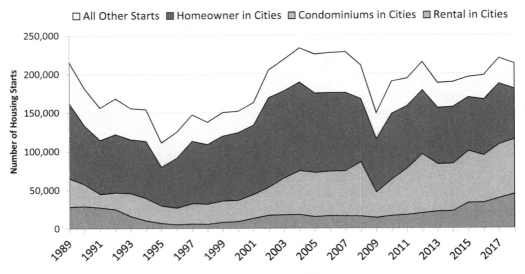

FIGURE 20.3 Housing Starts by Intended Market, 1989–2018.

Note: Canada, cities over 50,000 population, and total. CMHC Starts & Completions Survey data. Rental refers to dwellings constructed for rental purposes, regardless of who finances the structure (for-profit; non-profit). Some condominium units are investor owned and offered for rent. Ownership here refers to detached and semi-detached houses, and row townhouses.

Source: Statistics Canada, Table: 34-10-0148-01 and CMHC Housing Market Portal.

1983; Hulchanski, 2004). Canada entered the contemporary era of neoliberal public policies about a decade after the US Reagan and the UK Thatcher administrations. The major income support and social housing expenditure cutbacks by the federal and provincial governments came in the 1990s. Subsidies for homeownership were maintained and new ones added. This was not the case for rental housing, whether for the private sector or for the social housing sector.

Over recent decades, housing supply, the construction of new housing nationally, has proceeded at record levels, with only a relatively slight fall due to the GFC. Most of the housing built, however, are intended for the ownership market. As Figure 20.3 indicates, there has been a slight increase in purpose-built rental housing in recent years. Some condominiums are investor-owned and contribute to the PRS stock of housing, at least until they are sold to an owner occupier or converted to short-term tourist rentals (e.g., Airbnb rentals). That is, rentals in condominiums, unlike purpose-built rentals, may not necessarily be rental over the long term.

Condition of Housing in the PRS

In Canada, about 60% of rental housing were built prior to the 1980s (Figure 20.4). About 50% were built during a 50-year period (mid-1940s to mid-1990s) when the federal and some provincial governments were subsidizing both private rental (generally 1945 to 1984) and social rental (mainly 1965–1995). The post-1980 rental housing stock consists of some social housing (until 1995), an increasing number of condominiums for rent, and many informal sector rentals (e.g., secondary suites).

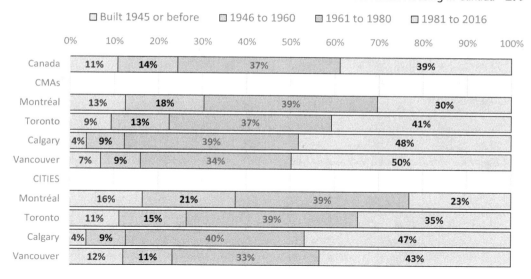

FIGURE 20.4   Age of Rental Housing Stock, 2016.

Note: Period of construction for rented dwellings occupied by usual residents.

Source: Statistics Canada, Census 2016 Data Table 98-400-X2016221 and Custom Tabulation EO2986.

Canada had a modest program for rehabilitation of ageing housing. The Residential Rehabilitation Assistance Program (RRAP) was initiated by the Government of Canada in 1973. It replaced urban renewal, which focused on demolishing existing neighbourhoods in favour of neighbourhood and housing preservation (Falkenhagen, 2001). In the 1970s and 1980s, RRAP funded rehabilitation of about 10,000 units annually. After 1994, more modest funding was provided for about 2,000 units annually (Sutter, 2016).

The Rental Housing Disadvantage Index

The Rental Housing Disadvantage Index (RHDI) was developed by the Neighbourhood Change Research Partnership to identify specific locations of inadequate rental housing and housing-related distress among tenants in Canada's metropolitan areas (Maaranen, 2019). The RHDI identifies geographic areas with concentrations of low-income renters living in inadequate housing for purposes of further research and potential policy and program intervention.

The RHDI has both similarities and differences with Canada Mortgage and Housing Corporation's measurement of core housing need (CHN) (Pomeroy et al., 2004). CMHC's CHN is based on three housing indicators from the census: adequacy, affordability, and suitability. The RHDI uses these same three measures but adds low-income renters. In addition, the RHDI has a geographic focus, at the census tract level, so as to identify and map the location of the concentrations of rental housing disadvantage by level of severity.

The RHDI is calculated as the average of four location quotient indicators that measure the concentration of disadvantage at the census tract (CT) level in comparison to the CMA average. Only census tracts with 25% or more rental housing are included.

The four indicators are:

- *Inadequate housing* defined as the percentage of rented occupied dwellings requiring major repairs.
- *Unaffordable housing* defined as the percentage of renter households paying 50% or more of income on rent.
- *Unsuitable housing* is defined as the percentage of renter households with a bedroom shortfall based on the number of bedrooms, number of household members, and household composition (gender, age).
- *Low-income status* is defined as the percentage of renter households with before-tax total income that is below half (50%) of the CMA median household income (all households, owners, and renters).

The RHDI is a measure of the spatial concentration of housing-related disadvantage experienced by people who rent. It reveals where inadequate, unaffordable, unsuitable rental housing and income deficiencies coexist in significant proportions in particular neighbourhoods. Figure 20.5 provides a summary of the percentage of CT (as a proxy for neighbourhoods) that have high and low rental housing disadvantage. The City of Toronto has the highest share of census tracts with high RHDI (50%).

The chart needs to be understood in conjunction with the size of the rental stock in each CMA and in the context of the relative size of the central city within each CMA. Renters in each of these four CMAs comprise the following share of households:

- Montréal CMA: 765,000 renters, 44% of CMA households, 64% of these renters live in the City, 63% of City households are renters.
- Toronto CMA: 715,000 renters, 33% of CMA households, 74% live in the City, 47% of City households are renters.

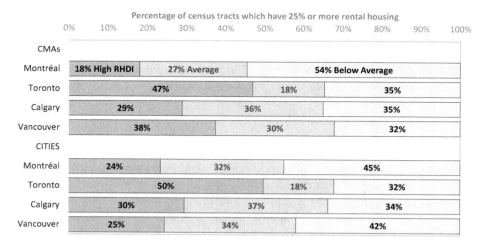

FIGURE 20.5 Rental Housing Disadvantage Index Distribution, 2016.

Note: Disadvantage Index (RHDI) is the average of four location quotient indicators which measure the concentration of disadvantage at the census tract level in comparision to the census metropolitan area (CMA) average: adequacy, affordability, suitability and low-income intensity. Below average disadvantage refers to RHDI < 1.0; average disadvantage refers to RHDI 1.0 to 1.19, high disadvantage refers to RHDI 1.2 or more. Figures exclude CTs with less than 25% rental housing in 2016.

Source: Statistics Canada, Custom Tabulation EO2986, Census 2016.

- Calgary CMA: 140,000 renters, 27% of CMA households, 95% live in the City, 29% of City households are renters.
- Vancouver CMA: 151,000 renters, 36% of CMA households, 43% live in the City, 49% of City households are renters (2016 Census).

Housing Tenure Income Inequality

The income gap between renters and owners was about 20% in the 1960s (Hulchanski, 1988). It has increased to about 90% nationally, with some variation among the larger metropolitan areas (Figure 20.6). The housing tenure income gap has paralleled the growth in income inequality. For the PRS, this has great significance. The private rented sector never could house low-income households, other than in substandard housing (down filtering of the aging rentals). Gentrification and ever rising market values of land and housing in successful metropolitan areas have led to filtering and rising rents for even poor-quality rentals. The end of federal PRS supply subsidy programs in the early 1980s coincided with the rise in income inequality and neoliberal fiscal austerity affecting programs that once provided better income support and services to lower-income, mainly renter, households. Markets respond to effective market demand (people with money), not to social need. The growing gap in incomes between owners and renters has been an inducement for more "apartment buildings" to be condominiums, intended for the ownership market, rather than rental. The fact that some condominium units are investor owner and rented is positive but further harms the prospects for investment in new purpose-built rentals. Rents in new rental buildings are higher than existing average rents. Condominium units for rent satisfy some or most of the market demand for new and more expensive rentals.

Another implication of growing income inequality is the increasing age of homeowners compared to renters. Though Canada's homeownership rate has been relatively stable, owners are increasing from an aging demographic. The rental sector is housing younger households

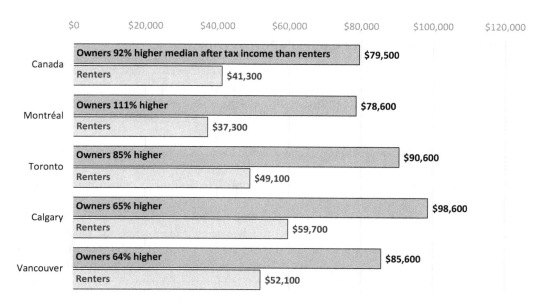

FIGURE 20.6 Owner/Renter Household Income Gap, 2017.
Source: CMHC, Real Median Aer Tax Income of Owners and Renter Households, 2006–2017 Data Tables. www.cmhc-schl.gc.ca/en/data-and-research/data-tables/household-characteristics..

TABLE 20.1 Housing Tenure in Canada by Age Group, 1981–2016

Homeownership Rate					Difference	Difference
Age Group	1981 (%)	1991 (%)	2006 (%)	2016 (%)	1981–2016 (%)	2006–2016 (%)
15–34	43.9	41.9	44.4	43.1	−0.7	−1.3
35–44	72.2	68.9	68.1	66.3	−5.9	−1.8
45–54	76.2	75.3	74.1	73.3	−3	−0.9
55–64	73.7	76.1	76.6	76.3	2.5	−0.3
65–74	66.1	71	76	76.3	10.1	0.2
75 and over	57.4	59.3	67.7	72.3	14.8	4.6
Age 15 and over	62.3	63.3	67.4	67.8	5.5	0.4
Rental Housing Rate					Difference	Difference
Age Group	1981 (%)	1991 (%)	2006 (%)	2016 (%)	1981–2016 (%)	2006–2016 (%)
15–34	56.1	58.1	55.6	56.3	0.2	0.8
35–44	27.8	31.1	31.9	33.2	5.4	1.3
45–54	23.8	24.7	25.9	26.3	2.5	0.4
55–64	26.3	23.9	23.4	23.4	−2.9	0
65–74	33.9	29	24	23.5	−10.4	−0.5
75 and over	42.6	40.7	32.3	27.6	−15	−4.7
Age 15 and over	37.7	36.7	32.6	31.8	−5.9	−0.8

Note: The probability of each age group living in home ownership or rental tenure. Primary household maintainers age 15 and over only.
Source: Statistics Canada, Census Public Use Microdata 1981, 1991, 2006. Census 2016 Data Table 98-400-X2016226

than in the past (see Table 20.1). This does not add to the prospects for significant private sector investment in purpose-built rental.

Key Policy Characteristics of Canada's Post-WWII PRS

Canada's PRS has the following four key characteristics that shape, mainly constrain, the supply and demand mechanism in what ought to be a functioning market.

(1) New PRS supply subsidies: Very limited since 1984

Most of the post-WWII supply of new purpose-built rental housing was subsidized until 1984 and had favourable tax treatment until early 1970s.

In 2001, the federal government announced an Affordable Housing Framework in collaboration with provinces and territories, cost shared on a 50/50 basis, to re-engage in providing some housing assistance. The federal funds, compared to levels prior to the mid-1990s, were very modest. Funding could be used for new rental supply, assisted homeownership, rehabilitation, and rent allowances. Subsidies for rental housing supply were in the form of one-time capital grants. In contrast to the approximately 20,000 social housing units that were funded annually from the mid-1960s to the mid-1990s, the Affordable Housing Framework subsidies resulted in 4,000–6,000 market rental or social rental units per year. In 2011, the new Investment in Affordable Housing (IAH), 2011–2018, provided a very modest $3.7 billion over ten years for construction, renovation, and affordability assistance. Funding ended in 2018–2019, with only $0.3 billion in 2019–2020 (Canada, Parliamentary Budget Officer, 2019:14).

In 2017, the federal government released a document outlining a number of new housing programs scheduled to begin in 2019–2020 (Canada Mortgage and Housing Corporation, 2017). Details of the proposed spending on the various promised programs over the ten-year housing strategy have been provided by the independent Parliamentary Budget Officer in a 2019 report, *Federal Program Spending on Housing Affordability*. Loans and some modest subsidies to encourage construction of purpose-built rental are significant for the housing strategy.

(2) Housing tenure neutrality: Only homeownership matters

Canada does not have a tenure-neutral housing subsidy system. Homeownership is consistently favoured and promoted by Canadian governments (Hulchanski, 2004). As in other Western nations, there has been a shift away from direct subsidies for addressing social needs typical of the post-war welfare state to an asset-based approach promoting social well-being through wealth accumulation (Doling & Ronald, 2010; Housing Europe, 2019; Ronald, 2008). Home-ownership provides the opportunity for asset-based welfare serving as yet another rationale for homeownership as the focus of Canada's national housing policy (Walks, 2016).

Federal annual subsidies for homeownership equal to about $7 billion; social non-market rental housing has a stream of subsidies that in recent decades reached $2.5 billion (inflation adjusted), and is now decreasing to about $0.5 billion over the coming ten years because few new social housing units are being funded. Tenants in the PRS receive little or nothing in financial terms from the federal government. The lack of a tenure-neutral housing subsidy system, one favouring ownership, means that higher-income renters are encouraged to become owners. While it may be beneficial at an individual household level, it means that for the PRS, new rental buildings, which have higher rents than older existing rentals, have a smaller pool of renters able to pay the higher rents. Homeownership in Canada receives the following subsidies:

- Non-taxation of capital gains on principal residence, since 1972 = $6 billion in 2018
- First-Time Home Buyers Tax Credit, since 1991 = $110 million in 2018
- GST Rebate for New Housing, since 1991 = $550 million in 2018
- Home Buyers Plan (use of $35,000 of RRSP for down payment) = $15 million per year admin cost
- First-Time Home Buyer Incentive, Budget 2019 = $40 million per year admin cost
- Shared Equity Mortgage Provider Fund, Budget 2019 = $20 million per year.
  (Source: Canada, Finance Department, 2019; Parliamentary Budget Officer, 2019)

(3) Housing inequality by housing tenure

The income gap between renters and owners is now about 100%. Renters in all parts of Canada have about half the income of homeowners (Figure 20.6). There is some variation among metropolitan areas, but not very much. The small percentage of high-income renters, who can afford rent levels that new rental buildings require, are either on their way to homeownership saving for a down payment, or are having most of their demand for higher-quality rental apartments being met by the investor-owned rental condominium units. In Toronto, about 40% of condominium units are rentals, equalling about 20% of the city's rental stock (CMHC, 2018). While there are many impediments to new private sector rental supply, the fact is that most renters constitute a *social need* for adequate rentals they can afford, rather than generating *effective market demand* that encourages new market rental supply.

(4) Rental only municipal zoning

Canadian municipalities have engaged in residential density regulations (via zoning bylaws) since the 1920s. Canada had rental only zoning until the late 1960s when legislation allowing condominium ownership was introduced (Hulchanski, 1988; Steele, 1993). Condominium legislation allowed apartment buildings to be built as either registered condominiums intended for the ownership market (though investor-owned units within some condominiums are rentals), or as conventional purpose-built rental buildings.

Given the gap in incomes of renters and owners, condominium developers can outbid rental developers for building sites, and in doing so raise property values in general. Market rents thus need to be even higher in new rental buildings if they are to be financially viable. This helps explain why so few primary (purpose-built) private sector rental housing have been built since the end of significant PRS supply tax subsidies in the 1970s and the last supply subsidy program, the Canada Rental Supply Plan, was terminated in 1984. The income gap between owners and renters was smaller in the three decades following the Second World War, there were no condominiums to compete for the higher-density residentially zoned building sites, and there were significant direct and indirect (tax system) subsidies for private rental supply. Those conditions no longer exist.

Conclusion

What is next for the private rented sector in the medium and long term? There are plenty of interrelated issues and complicated relationships: market demand, social need, supply, subsidies, location, quality, choice, distribution, regulations, discrimination, affordability, investors, owners, management, and the PRS's institutional role within the housing system and the related social welfare system in general. The PRS should not continue to be treated as a low priority part of Canada's housing system.

There are plenty of actors – politicians, policy-makers, civil society actors, real estate investors, engaged citizens – who need to better understand and rethink the nature and role of the PRS within Canada's housing system. Can we make progress on building a more inclusive housing system if we do not make the system more tenure-neutral in terms of the policies and subsidies benefitting homeownership versus renting? Canada's housing system needs to (1) stimulate adequate rental housing production; (2) help produce a mix of rental housing choice (location, size, quality); and (3) assist those who cannot afford adequate, appropriate rental housing. How likely is it that Canada's housing policy will change significantly over the coming decade?

A reason for being pessimistic about PRS progress is that housing is such a major and profitable, wealth-enhancing part of so many key societal institutions that change, while not impossible, will meet with strong resistance from those who benefit most from the current, almost-purely, market-based housing system. The broad institutional context in which the housing system operates is relatively stable. For several decades there has been little change in the size, functions, and relationships between housing tenures in Canada. Change is not impossible, but it will meet with strong resistance by those who have been able to define the rules of the housing game in their favour and have the financial and political resources to continue doing so.

Unless there is significant change in Canadian housing policy, which is mainly up to the federal and provincial cabinets, that is, those who actually have the power to change the rules of the game, existing negative trends in the PRS will not only continue but be intensified. Among the trends, fewer renters will become owners as ownership becomes more difficult; there will be increased overcrowding in existing ageing rentals as individuals and households double-up; landlord/tenant relations will become more difficult consuming more legal resources of all parties and society; the political debate over stricter rent regulations will be even more turbulent; there will be continuing deterioration in the quality of and need for rehabilitation of an aging stock of rental housing; there will continue to be inadequate levels of new purpose-built (primary vs secondary) rental housing; and more renters will find themselves in unsafe, unregulated, illegal, and exploitative forms of residential rental situations. This will further residualize rental housing. Residualization here refers to an ongoing process and a policy direction that leads to rental housing, and tenants in general, in a high homeownership and highly unequal (income and wealth) nation like Canada, becoming an increasingly low status, stigmatized, and undesirable part of the housing system, subject to financially exploitation and displacement by local and global financial forces.

What policy options should be considered for the PRS? The following are within provincial and federal jurisdiction (there is, in addition, much for municipalities to do in planning and zoning).

- Significant incentives (subsidies) for new supply in the PRS as well as for new social housing supply.
- Attract large institutional investors to the PRS with targeted tax incentives.
- Provide significant rehabilitation subsidies for the existing rental stock.
- Regulate rent increases and end vacancy decontrol given the decades-long market failure in the PRS (failure of affordable market supply).
- Provide and enforce better security of tenure to tenants in all forms of rental housing.
- Seriously address and punish housing discrimination.
- Educate landlords and tenants about their rights and responsibilities.
- Require full disclosure of the beneficial owners of real estate and the source of investment funds.

Though these may seem reasonable to many, Canada's housing system is built on five main principles. These benefit the minority who profit from the system as it is, and each is an impediment to a just and inclusive housing system: (1) rely almost exclusively on the market mechanism; (2) privilege homeownership and generally ignore private and social renting; (3) avoid investment in non-market forms of housing; (4) allow continued financialization of, and speculation with, Canada's stock of housing and real estate in general; and (5) deny that Canadians have the *justiciable* human right to adequate housing. This set of principles leads to a housing system that is an effective mechanism for increasing wealth for some, providing overly expensive and often inadequate housing for others, institutionalizing mass homelessness, and increasing economic inequality. Canada has the resources and the knowledge to do better.

Acknowledgements

This research was supported by the Neighbourhood Change Research Partnership, funded by a partnership grant from the Social Sciences and Humanities Research Council of Canada. Data analysis and preparation of the charts were by Richard Maaranen, Data Analyst Research Associate, Neighbourhood Change Research Partnership, Factor-Inwentash Faculty of Social Work, University of Toronto.

References

Aalbers, M.B. (2016). *The financialization of housing: A political economy approach*. Abingdon: Routledge.

August, M., & Walks, A. (2018). Gentrification, suburban decline, and the financialization of multi-family rental housing: The case of Toronto. *Geoforum, 89*, 124–136.

Bacher, J.C. (1993). *Keeping to the marketplace: The evolution of Canadian housing policy*. Montréal: McGill-Queen's University Press.

Boudreau, J.A., Keil, R., & Young, D. (2009). *Changing Toronto: Governing urban neoliberalism*. Toronto: University of Toronto Press.

Bourne, L.S. (1981). *The geography of housing*. London: Arnold.

Bourne, L.S. (1986). Recent housing policy issues in Canada: A retreat from social housing? *Housing Studies, 1*(2), 122–128.

Bunting, T., Walks, A.R., & Filion, P. (2004). The uneven geography of housing affordability stress in Canadian metropolitan areas. *Housing Studies, 19*(3), 361–393.

Canada, Department of Finance (2019). Report on federal tax expenditures: Concepts, estimates and evaluations. Ottawa: Government of Canada.

Canada Mortgage and Housing Corporation (2001). *Understanding private rental housing investment in Canada*. Ottawa: CMHC, Research Highlight, Socio-economic Series 42.

Canada Mortgage and Housing Corporation (2016). *A profile of purpose-built rental housing in Canada*. Ottawa: Government of Canada.

Canada Mortgage and Housing Corporation (2017). *Canada's national housing strategy: A place to call home*. Ottawa: Government of Canada.

Canada, Parliamentary Budget Officer (2019). *Federal program spending on housing affordability*. Ottawa.

Chisholm, S., & Hulchanski, J.D. (2019) Canada's housing story. In Maclennan, D., Pawson, H., Gibb, K., Chisholm, S., & Hulchanski, J.D., editors. *Shaping futures: Changing the housing story, Australia, Britain, Canada*. Glasgow: Policy Scotland, University of Glasgow, 21–28.

Clayton, F. A. (2010). *Government subsidies to homeowners versus renters in Ontario and Canada*. Toronto: Federation of Rental-Housing Providers of Ontario and Canadian Federation of Apartment Associations.

Clayton Research Associates (1998). *Economic impact of federal tax legislation on the rental housing market in Canada*. Toronto: Canadian Federation of Apartment Associations.

Crook, T. (1998). The supply of private rented housing in Canada. *Netherlands Journal of Housing and the Built Environment, 13*(3), 327–352.

Crook, T., & Kemp, P. A. (Eds). (2014). *Private rental housing: Comparative perspectives*. Cheltenham: Edward Elgar Publishing.

Doling, J., & Ronald, R. (2010). Home ownership and asset-based welfare. *Journal of Housing and the Built Environment, 25*(2), 165–173.

Doling, J., & Richard, R. (2019). "Not for housing" housing: Widening the scope of housing studies. *Critical Housing Analysis, 6*(1), 22.

Dowler, R. G. (1983). *Housing-related tax expenditures: An overview and evaluation*. Toronto: University of Toronto, Centre for Urban and Community Studies.

Falkenhagen, D. (2001). *The history of Canada's residential rehabilitation assistance program (RRAP)*. Ottawa: Canada Mortgage and Housing Corporation.

Gibb, K., Pawson, H., & Hulchanski, J.D. (2019). Private renting. In Maclennan, D., Pawson, H., Gibb, K., Chisholm, S., & Hulchanski, J.D., editors. *Shaping futures: Changing the housing story, Australia, Britain, Canada*. Glasgow: Policy Scotland, University of Glasgow, 55–68.

Granath Hansson, A., & Lundgren, B. (2019). Defining social housing: A discussion on the suitable criteria. *Housing, Theory and Society, 36*(2), 149–166.

Grisdale, S. (2019). Displacement by disruption: Short-term rentals and the political economy of "belonging anywhere" in Toronto. *Urban Geography*, 1–27. www.tandfonline.com/doi/full/10.1080/02723638.2019.1642714

Hackworth, J., & Moriah, A. (2006). Neoliberalism, contingency and urban policy: The case of social housing in Ontario. *International Journal of Urban and Regional Research, 30*(3), 510–527.

Haffner, M., et al. (2010) Universalistic, particularistic and middle way approaches to comparing the private rental sector. *International Journal of Housing Policy, 10*(4), 357–377.

Harris, R., & Kinsella, K. (2017). Secondary suites: A survey of evidence and municipal policy. *The Canadian Geographer/Le Géographe Canadien, 61*(4), 493–509.

Housing Europe (2019). *The state of housing in the EU 2019.* Brussels: The European Federation of Cooperative and Social Housing.

Hulchanski, J.D. (1988). The evolution of property rights and housing tenure in post-war Canada: Implications for housing policy. *Urban Law and Policy, 9*(2), 135–156.

Hulchanski, J.D. (2004). What factors shape Canadian housing policy? The intergovernmental role in Canada's housing system. In Young, R., & Leuprecht, C., editors. *Municipal-federal-provincial relations in Canada.* Montréal: McGill-Queens University Press, 221–250.

Hulchanski, J.D., & Shapcott, M. (2004). *Finding room: Policy options for a Canadian rental housing strategy.* Toronto: University of Toronto, Centre for Urban and Community Studies.

Hulse, K., Morris, A., & Pawson, H. (2019). Private renting in a home-owning society: Disaster, diversity or deviance? *Housing, Theory and Society, 36*(2), 167–188.

Kalman-Lamb, G. (2017). The financialization of housing in Canada: Intensifying contradictions of neoliberal accumulation. *Studies in Political Economy, 98*(3), 298–323.

Ley, D. (2015). Global China and the making of Vancouver's residential property market. *International Journal of Housing Policy, 17*(1), 15–34.

Maaranen, R. (2019). *The NCRP Rental Housing Disadvantage Index (RHDI): What it is and how it is calculated, 2016 census update.* Toronto: University of Toronto, Neighbourhood Change Research Partnership.

Macdonald, D. (2019). *Unaccommodating: Rental housing wage in Canada.* Ottawa: Canadian Centre for Policy Alternatives.

Maclennan, D., Pawson, H., Gibb, K., Chisholm, S., & Hulchanski, D. (2019). *Shaping futures: Changing the housing story, Australia, Britain, Canada.* Glasgow: Policy Scotland, University of Glasgow.

Madden, D., & Marcuse, P. (2016). *In defense of housing.* New York: Verso.

Miron, J.R. (1995). Private rental housing: the Canadian experience. *Urban Studies, 32*(3), 579–604.

Oxley, M., & Smith, J. (2012). *Housing policy and rented housing in Europe.* Abingdon: Routledge.

Pomeroy, S., Dalton, T., Stegman, M. A., & Wilcox, S. (2004). *An international comparison of housing need indicators.* Ottawa: Canada Mortgage and Housing Corporation.

Pomeroy, S., & Falvo, N. (2013). Pragmatism and political expediency: Housing policy in Canada under the Harper regime. In Doern, G. B., & Stoney, C., editors. *How Ottawa spends, 2012–2013: The Harper majority, budget cuts, and the new opposition.* Montréal: McGill-Queen's University Press, 184–195.

Patterson, A., & Harris, R. (2017). Landlords, tenants, and the legal status of secondary suites in Hamilton, Ontario. *The Canadian Geographer/Le Géographe Canadien, 61*(4), 540–549.

Pawson, H., Hulse, K., & Morris, A. (2017). Interpreting the rise of long-term private renting in a liberal welfare regime context. *Housing Studies, 32*(8), 1062–1084.

Rogers, D., & Koh, S. Y. (2017). The globalisation of real estate: The politics and practice of foreign real estate investment. *International Journal of Housing Policy, 17*(1), 1–14.

Ronald, R. (2008). *The ideology of home ownership: Homeowner societies and the role of housing.* Basingstoke: Palgrave Macmillan.

Steele, M. (1993). Conversions, condominiums and capital gains: The transformation of the Ontario rental housing market. *Urban Studies, 30*(1), 103–126.

Suttor, G. (2016). *Still renovating: A history of Canadian social housing policy.* Montréal: McGill-Queens University Press.

Suttor, G. (2017). Basement suites: Demand, supply, space, and technology. *The Canadian Geographer/Le Géographe Canadien, 61*(4), 483–492.

Suttor, G.F. (2009). *Rental paths from postwar to present: Canada compared.* Toronto: University of Toronto, Cities Centre.

Tsenkova, S., & Witwer, M. (2011). Bridging the gap: Policy instruments to encourage private sector provision of affordable rental housing in Alberta. *Canadian Journal of Urban Research, 20*(1), 52–80.

van der Heijden, H. (2013). *West European housing systems in a comparative perspective.* Amsterdam: IOS Press.

Walks, A. (2014a). Canada's housing bubble story: Mortgage securitization, the state, and the global financial crisis. *International Journal of Urban and Regional Research, 38*(1), 256–284.

Walks, A. (2014b). From financialization to sociospatial polarization of the city? Evidence from Canada. *Economic Geography, 90*(1), 33–66.

Walks, A. (2016). Homeownership, asset-based welfare and the neighbourhood segregation of wealth. *Housing Studies, 31*(7), 755–784.

Walks, A., & Clifford, B. (2015). The political economy of mortgage securitization and the neoliberalization of housing policy in Canada. *Environment and Planning A: Economy and Space, 47*(8), 1624–1642.

Wolfe, J.M. (1998). Canadian housing policy in the nineties. *Housing Studies, 13*(1), 121–134.

INDEX

Note: **Bold** page numbers refer to tables; *italic* page numbers refer to figures; page numbers followed by "n" denote endnotes.

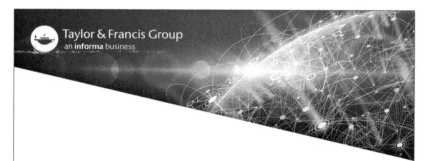